Written out of History

Memoirs of Ordinary Activists

Bette Steinmuller
Nancy Teel
Beatrice Nava
Linda Stern
Steven Norris
Kendall Hale

Introduction
by
Richard Levy

Cover and book design by Marc Alonso/Leap Year Press

For more information about this project, visit
http://writtenoutofhistory.com

Abby —
 I'm so glad That you've
been like a daughter long after
you stopped being my daughter —
in-law.
         Love,
            Bebe
November 2011

Contents

❧

Acknowledgements

The authors would like to thank the following people for their support, encouragement and help along the way:

Bianca Abramoski, Jean Alonso, Marc Alonso, Dan Alvarez, Michael Carman, Nancy Chase, Connie Egan, L. Roberto Fernández "Lúminito", Veronica Golos, Terry Haywoode, Josh Hulbert, Justin Hulbert, Judy Kaplan, Benjamin Lambert, Gwen Lambert, Nancy Love, June Makela, Georgia Mattison, Janet Melvin, Judith Rosenberg, Laurie Scher, Amy Stern Stoffelmayr, Maureen Sweeney, Peter Teel, Toby Teel, Rene Theberge, Susan Koff Theberge, Gloria Withim.

Collectively, we thank: Paul Atwood, Lady Borton, Demetria Martínez, "The Divers", the William Joiner Center at the University of Massachusetts Boston, Roxbury Community College, Common Ground and all who attended our readings.

Finally, many thanks to our co-author Kendall Hale for publishing her book *Radical Passions: A Memoir of Revolution and Healing* (2008). When *Written Out of History* was complete and posted on the Web, Kendall pursued her dream and continued writing to share her inspiring journey from youth to maturity. Two chapters from *Radical Passions*, "On The Barricades in Madison" and "New Harmony Sisterhood Band," are included here with her permission. The two books are complementary, and we hope you read both.

Foreword

As devastating wars in the Middle East unleash the current upsurge of antiwar activism, focus on the collective movement eclipses the individual lives that create it. *Written out of History* contains memoirs of six activists from the 1960s onward that show how ordinary people became involved in the movements for peace and justice, in the US and Latin America. It describes demonstrations, political groups, arrests, hands-on work, and cultural expression and honors the pain, excitement and personal changes the authors experienced. The sacrifices and rewards remain with them as they pursue their lives as citizens, parents, grandparents, and professionals. Wiser and more reflective, they continue as committed activists today.

Although all the events described are real, in some instances names have been changed.

To see the book online, go to http://writtenoutofhistory.com. Reach us via email at contactwooh@yahoo.com. If you do use any portion of the book in an educational setting, we would like your feedback.

Introduction

As I TEACH my courses at Salem State College on the Vietnam conflict and the Sixties and their respective legacies, it becomes clear that most students know the period in the simplistic stereotypes of sex, drugs and rock 'n' roll, with little if any element of politics. They are not, of course, to blame for this lack of awareness because it comes from that period being some forty years ago. More importantly, as the web site is titled, those years have been Written Out Of History despite the incredible, yet in some ways limited effects they have had for society today.

The list of movements described in these memoirs is long: Students for a Democratic Society (S.D.S.); community organizing; the tragically but necessary continuing anti-war movements (responding to so many US wars); the different elements of the feminist and anti-racist movements; the largely but not exclusively Marxist-Leninist-led movements to go into the workplaces to organize, and the many international solidarity movements. They have all left an indelible mark on the people who have shared their experiences. Many others, some activists and some not, were touched by these writers and the movements of which they were a part. Moreover, they continue to affect the political currents of today, as reflected in the various elements of support and criticism of the policies of the Obama Administration.

What these stories, memories and legacies bring is the reality, the complicated, reinforcing, and contradictory nature of the various movements that made up the Sixties and Seventies and Eighties and beyond. They reveal the incredible excitement, commitment, idealism and accomplishments of numerous movements as well as the elements that were naïve, self-deceptive and, in many ways, disenchanting. The commitment to building a better, more egalitarian and more human society had an underlying inspiration and commitment. But, it was also frequently inspired by and then increasingly disillusioned by models from China and Cuba.

As these activists tell their stories, we see the effects of the Vietnam and Latin American conflicts, the writers' political commitment and growth , and we read about their personal lives, a factor frequently left out of what does make it into history.

The ongoing outrage that led these people to join in and continue to be part of these movements is apparent in *"Shut it Down: Students against the War"* when Nancy Teel writes of the village San Carlos in Colombia in 1966:

> Ragged children sit on doorsteps covered with the same gray film. There are no open spaces for play...No trees grow on the streets... The adults walk alone and do not speak" (Senior Report in College)

She continues:

> In contrast, in the *barrio* Juan XCCIII...people live in shacks made of scavenged materials that clung to hillsides so steep that even college students like myself had difficult climbing them. There were no roads, no sewers, no water, just paths and shelters made of trash...We had a revealing meeting...with a representative from USAID...who...admitted that most of the aid money went to pay for interest on loans from American banks and contracted goods and services from American companies. One small fraction went to develop housing and provide...powdered milk.

Years later, Steve Norris discussed the possibility that the community center he has volunteered to help construct in Nicaragua could become a target of US supported (if not created) *contra* terrorism. This reminded me of my own brief time in Nicaragua as a volunteer picking coffee on a state farm near the Honduran border. On the first night, I saw a young Nicaraguan wearing a ripped coffee bag as protection against the wind. He was taking apart his AK-47 rifle and explaining he was going to be on guard all night in a foxhole protecting us and the Nicaraguans picking coffee from the *contras*. These were the very *contras* who our tax dollars were supporting in their efforts to kill people just like him.

And we see the legacies of all of this. For many activists, as Linda Stern describes it in *"Looking for Answers: From Marxism-Leninism to the Suburbs"*:

> Forever changed by our work, most of us took a break, then became reengaged in other political activity which in most cases con-

tinues to this day in one form or another…The networks of people that formed around this time are still in existence"

And we see as well how these experiences still influence the jobs, child rearing, and a myriad of experiences in the lives of others today, many of whom are no longer, either by choice or not, a direct part of a mainstream machine that in many ways dominates society. There were also other activists who did burn out and/or reject the very values to which they had dedicated themselves.

On a broader level, the narratives expose how profoundly these individuals and movements have contributed to today's society. Without them, there would be less likelihood that so many women are in higher education and have such a wide range of occupations, or that gay marriage would be on the table. There would be far fewer social justice campaigns that develop so quickly and continue in their myriad forms—with the aid of the technology of today and some of the lessons of the Sixties. The anti-war movements and the fact that younger people are so much less racist than the adults of the sixties—all of the above would be far less. Simultaneously, while these narratives show the continuation of activism through decades, it is unclear how the legacies of these movements can carry over today in a world with far greater and more coordinated corporate-dominated globalization. Add to that mix the possibility of instant worldwide communication among activists—as well as corporate and government organizations. How this will play out as the present economic and fiscal crisis develops worldwide is yet to be seen.

There have been voices and actions Written Out of History apart from the individuals whose experiences are included here, and many more have been influenced by these activists directly and indirectly. I expect all of them will be part of the movements to restructure and reorganize the world politically, socially, and economically, as the present crisis further exposes the faults and contradiction of the system that they have been fighting against for so long.

Richard Levy

Boston, 2009
Professor of Political Science
Salem State College, Salem, MA
richardlevyus@yahoo.com

Activists for Peace

Written Out of History
Memoirs of Ordinary Activists

Synopsis of Four Parts

PART I: ACTIVISTS FOR PEACE (4 chapters) Illustrating the effects of the Cuban Missile Crisis and the Vietnam War, Linda Stern, Nancy Teel, and Kendall Hale relive their student years, as race, gender, and class contradictions turn university campuses upside down; Beatrice Nava, a generation older, shows how the tumult reached suburbia.

PART II: RECREATING COMMUNITY (5 chapters) Radical social experimentation engages the authors. Steve Norris abandons academia and becomes a community leader in Boston's working class neighborhood, Mission Hill. Linda Stern teaches elementary-school children in Roxbury who already show "signs of damage." She wishes the resources fueling the Vietnam War could be poured into "urban neighborhoods." Beatrice Nava contrasts the worlds of her grown children with that of the impoverished youngsters she cares for in Mexico. As student and peace activist, Nancy Teel seeks wisdom in communes from Ithaca to Boston. For Kendall Hale, "music *was* the revolution" in the New Harmony Sisterhood Band.

PART III: FROM THEORY TO PRACTICE (3 chapters) Nancy Teel, Linda Stern and Bette Steinmuller recall their flirtations with Marxism-Leninism, the first two in blue-collar jobs in Boston, where they try to organize workers into labor unions. Bette was convinced she had "visited paradise" when she toured Cuba in 1979, but her lens widens when she lives and works there from 1989 to 1994.

PART IV: NICARAGUAN SOLIDARITY (3 chapters) Bette Steinmuller, Steve Norris and Beatrice Nava describe working in Nicaragua during the Sandinista years, and look back to explain what drew them there. Bette lives and works as an educator for three years in Estelí, the spirited revolutionary stronghold. Steve leads a brigade of US Americans to construct a much-needed health clinic there. Beatrice works in the Nicaraguan Foreign Ministry, in Managua, during the last two years of the Sandinista administration.

Cuban Missiles and Vietnam Advisers

Linda Stern

A SMALL SAILBOAT sits out on the promontory in the harbor, the Boston skyline in the distance. A friend and I are at The John F. Kennedy Library and Museum. The sailboat is on display as one of the artifacts belonging to JFK. We pass by various exhibits, everything from his desk to an exhibit of his support of the space program to a display of places and buildings all over the world named after him in the aftermath of his assassination. And then we come upon the Cuban Missile Crisis exhibit, the one we've come to see: it showcases some photographs, maps, and a documentary film. As we sit in the partially lighted theater waiting for the next showing of the film, I think back and remember...

Overflowing ashtrays and abandoned half-emptied coffee cups littered the living room. By the front door, unopened mail was piling up on the table. Two typewriters clattered in the office and the phone kept jangling. I heard the sounds of pots and pans clanking from the kitchen; someone remembered to start dinner.

My job was to answer the phone.

It was October 1962 and I was one of the staff members at the Student Peace Union (SPU) national office, housed on the ground floor of a brownstone just across the Midway from the University of Chicago. Cold War tensions had just boiled over in Cuba and we were about to go through one of the most frightening times of the Cold War.

Just two days before, on Monday, October 22, in a televised address, President Kennedy showed photos and announced that the Soviet Union was installing missile bases in Cuba. He called for a major arms blockade of the island. His sober countenance and tone of voice spoke to the seriousness of the situation. There was deep concern all over the country, and organizations involved with peace and disarmament issues wasted no time in reacting.

"Student Peace Union, national office," I kept repeating. There were calls from the AFSC, the Committee for a Sane Nuclear Policy, the Committee for Non-Violent Action, and other peace groups.

Calls came from Antioch and Oberlin, from the University of Minnesota, from Austin and Houston, from Chapel Hill, Detroit, Columbus and Cleveland, Seattle, Berkeley, Miami, Bloomington, Indiana, and even from Hawaii, all the places we had chapters. Our 15,000 members were mainly students on college campuses.

"We'll get back to you later," I kept repeating. "The steering committee will be meeting in a few minutes."

Then: "Gail, you'd better take this call right now—it's *The New York Times*." Gail Paradise was the national secretary of SPU and its official spokesperson; hair askew and looking frazzled, she grabbed the phone from me.

The steering committee members met at 8:00 that evening. They were the more experienced and political people. Somewhat in awe of them, I was content to work in the office with a couple of other ex-students like myself. It was almost 11 when the steering committee came out of their meeting and started to return calls on our two phone lines.

They told us that they'd hammered out an official position. The Student Peace Union was officially opposed to the US blockade of Cuba as a threat to peace. While alarmed by Soviet missiles in Cuba, we saw that U.S. military bases in Turkey and Greece were no less a threat to the Soviet Union. We called for UN negotiations. Our organization, however, did not support Fidel Castro and his government, as did the Fair Play for Cuba Committee, among others. A major protest was planned for Washington, D.C. with sympathy demonstrations all over the country.

What I remember most about this time is the fear. After a day busy with typing and making phone calls, we gathered in one of the upstairs bedrooms. Listening to Miles Davis's *Sketches of Spain* and drinking cherry kijafa wine in a room barely lit by a single red light bulb, we were glad just to be together.

We knew we couldn't sleep, so a friend and I took a long walk around the Point along the shore of Lake Michigan. Listening to the waves break, we jumped from rock to rock, making our way out to the end of the promontory where a radar station of some kind was perched; I wondered if it had any military significance. We could see the sparkling lights of the downtown skyline mirrored in the lake. In hushed voices, we tried to talk of normal things but our thoughts kept slipping back to the fear.

"What time do you have to go to work tomorrow?" I asked my friend.

"At 7:00, as usual," he answered.

But in the back of our minds we wondered: what was "as usual" now and would there be a tomorrow? Would our government really risk nuclear war? I felt that familiar dread from the nightmare of nuclear war that I'd grown up with.

During the following days we kept close to the radio, listening to regular news reports and bulletins and reading several daily newspapers. Sections of *The New York Times, Chicago Tribune, The Washington Post* were scattered all over the house. We were glad to have something important to do—maybe we would even have some impact on the government, and it helped to keep the anxiety away.

There were negotiations; angry statements; high-level government meetings; official communiqués to the Soviet government; involvement by U Thant and the UN; an American U-2 plane shot down over Cuba, its pilot killed.

Finally, after several tense days, the Soviets agreed to remove the missile bases under U.N. supervision; in return, the U.S. pledged not to invade Cuba. Fidel Castro, Cuba's leader, clearly subservient to the Soviet Union, learned of the settlement on the radio.[1]

I relived some of the anxiety of this time as I watched the documentary film. The East Coast was in a high state of alert. The army positioned rocket launchers on Key West beaches. Groups of men in dark suits sat around tables endlessly in discussion. The Strategic Air Command called a "Defense Condition Two," the last step before war. Panicked people emptied grocery shelves. On TV, Walter Cronkite said that we were almost at the point of saying "there goes the whole ball game."

Yes, I thought to myself after we came out of the theater into the daylight, we were close to nuclear war in those tense days in 1962. Were we that expendable to our government? Are we still?

In writing this, I did some research to try to understand more of this crisis. It was quiet in the library on the reference desk where I spend my days and I decided to check out *The New York Times* for those days in October. I pulled down the *Times* Index for 1962 and had no trouble locating the vast coverage of the paper during that time.

The week's banner headlines in *The New York Times* read:

U.S. IMPOSES ARMS BLOCKADE ON CUBA ON FINDING OFFENSIVE-MISSILE SITES; KENNEDY READY FOR SOVIET SHOWDOWN

(Tuesday, Oct. 23,1962, the night after Kennedy's speech)

SOVIET CHALLENGES U.S. RIGHT TO BLOCKADE; INTERCEPTION OF 25 RUSSIAN SHIPS ORDERED; CUBA QUARANTINE BACKED BY UNITED O.A.S.

(Wed., Oct. 24, 1962)

SOME SOVIET SHIPS SAID TO VEER FROM CUBA; KHRUSHCHEV SUGGESTS A SUMMIT MEETING; THANT BIDS U.S. AND RUSSIA DESIST 2 WEEKS

(Thurs., Oct. 25, 1962)

KENNEDY AGREES TO TALKS ON THANT PLAN, KHRUSHCHEV ACCEPTS IT; BLOCKADE GOES ON; RUSSIAN TANKER INTERCEPTED AND CLEARED

(Friday, Oct. 26, 1962)

U.S. FINDS CUBA SPEEDING BUILD-UP OF BASES, WARNS OF FURTHER ACTION; U.N. TALKS OPEN; SOVIET AGREES TO SHUN BLOCKADE ZONE NOW

(Sat., Oct. 27, 1962)

U.S. GETS SOVIET OFFER TO END CUBA BASES, REJECTS BID TO LINK IT TO THOSE IN TURKEY; U-2 LOST ON PATROL, OTHER CRAFT FIRED ON

(Sun., Oct. 28, 1962)

U.S. AND SOVIET REACH ACCORD ON CUBA; KENNEDY ACCEPTS KHRUSHCHEV PLEDGE TO REMOVE MISSILES UNDER U.N. WATCH

(Monday, Oct. 29, 1962)

And much to my surprise, I found the news story that was written the day after Gail was interviewed on the phone! It appeared on Thursday, October 25, right on the front page under the headline!

Then I went to our online catalog to see what we had in our own collection. I pulled down a couple interesting-looking books from the shelf, brought them home, and stayed up half the night reading them.

At the time of the Missile Crisis, we could not have known, of course, what was going on behind the scenes. But with the collapse of the Soviet Union, the ending of the Cold War, and the release of classified information on all sides, much more information became available. Three conferences were held in the late 1980s that included U.S. and Soviet policy makers, and the last, belatedly, included Cuban officials, too. Notes were compared and information from all sides and all points of view was shared.

The negotiated settlement that ended the Cuban Missile Crisis centered on a secret agreement whereby the U.S. did, in fact, abandon its bases in Turkey in return for the Soviet Union's dismantling of its bases in Cuba. According to James Blight and David Welch in the book, *On the Brink: Americans and Soviets Reexamine the Cuban Missile Crisis*, this was kept top secret, not only from the American people, but also from all but a tiny handful of presidential advisers. Not even the two men who followed Kennedy in the Presidency, Johnson and Nixon, knew of the trade. It was kept secret until the late 1980s.[2]

I realized, then, that our fears from that long-ago night on Lake Michigan were quite justified.

Could this have been the reason that foreign policy during the Johnson and Nixon administrations was marked by confrontation, obstinacy, and inflexibility, particularly in Southeast Asia? And wasn't that in keeping with the mistaken perception of the effectiveness of standing firm, as the world thought the U.S. had done during the Cuban Missile Crisis, with no apparent compromise?

The other book that absorbed me was the recently released *Kennedy Tapes: Inside The White House During the Cuban Missile Crisis*. The tapes reveal that Kennedy stood up firmly, and nearly alone, to his own civilian and military advisers. The Joint Chiefs of Staff called for an immediate air strike. But Kennedy prevailed, insisting on negotiation and a political settlement rather than a military confrontation. His toughness may have averted World War III.

The year before the Cuban Missile Crisis, I was a junior at Carleton College, in Northfield, Minnesota. Aware of the ongoing arms race, atmospheric testing of weapons, and contamination of cow's milk by strontium 90, I was scared. I remembered "ducking and covering" in elementary school, as well as the Civil Defense drills my mother, a Civil Defense nurse, had taken my siblings and me to, made up as bandaged "victims" no less. I wrote a letter to President Kennedy, the new young president in the White House, protesting atmospheric nuclear testing. After I mailed it, I felt my action was almost totally futile. I'd begun to feel at the mercy of a political process that was neither visible nor accountable.

But what a relief it was to find that other people on campus were talking about these very issues! The college counselor was a Quaker, who presented a pacifist position, and there was a small chapter of the Young Socialist Alliance that held study groups. Some of us were beginning to question almost everything!

In the fall of 1961, students from two other mid-western colleges went in sequence to Washington to picket, to talk to government officials and the press, and to fast. Sixteen of us decided to go, too, making Carleton the third college to join in. It was mid-November, right before Thanksgiving break, and the student handbook clearly stated that students would be penalized a quarter of a credit for each missed class if they left early for vacation. But the penalty only made us more determined so we went anyway, and the rule was changed later that year.

Our group piled into two cars and a panel truck and drove straight through the night, traveling almost thirty hours from Northfield, Minnesota, to Washington, D.C., non-stop. Washington was a blur of activity: picket lines at the White House, a three day fast, press conferences, and a meeting with Senator Eugene McCarthy of Minnesota. We were even invited into the White House. Although McGeorge Bundy, Kennedy's special assistant for national security affairs, refused to meet with us, one of Bundy's assistants did. Our picket signs politely read: "We Ask You to Reevaluate US Nuclear Policy" and "Minnesota Students Fast for Test Ban." We kept up a 24-hour picket line in front of the White House. It was not easy being on the 2:00 to 4:00 a.m. shift one very early morning, putting one foot in front of the other on a lonely and freezing Washington night, while two D.C. policemen made sure we kept moving. *The Washington Post* interviewed a few of us from Carleton and an article with photographs appeared in the paper. I still have the yellowed newsprint of that article.

Fasting over Thanksgiving made our sacrifice more symbolic. Even breaking the fast on the fourth day was a powerful learning experience for our privileged group who certainly had not experienced real hunger in our personal lives. Back on campus, debate continued. Some students had fasted in solidarity with us, but the Carleton Student Association Senate wrote letters to the press and White House criticizing our methods. The college itself continued to make plans to use the tunnels connecting campus buildings as fallout shelters.

Energized by our activity and by our contacts with other students, we soon got in touch with the Student Peace Union which we knew had chapters on college campuses all over the country. Loosely associated with the Fellowship of Reconciliation, its national office was in Chicago. We traveled to Chicago to attend meetings; they sent their organizer to our campus. We traveled to Minneapolis and St. Paul to picket a local Woolworth's in support of the civil rights struggle. We soon formed our own chapter of the Student Peace Union on campus. A fellow activist, Jim Hellmuth, and I were elected co-chairpersons for the coming year; then we all dispersed for the summer.

I headed for the Bay Area. While I worked as a camp counselor by day, I hung out with fellow peaceniks in Berkeley on the weekends. I attended a demonstration to mark of the bombing of Hiroshima and Nagasaki, not really so far back in history in 1962.

I couldn't of course have foreseen the tragedy that would take Jim's life over that summer; he was killed in an accident on a bike trip. This was my first experience of losing a friend to death. Suddenly life seemed very tenuous and college life largely irrelevant. I knew I wanted to do something meaningful with my life. And I was impatient; I did not want to wait a whole year when I would graduate from college. So I dropped out of school after my junior year and went to Chicago to work in the national office of the Student Peace Union. My parents, never ones to actually stand in my way, acquiesced to my plans. I was twenty years old and determined to seek my own way.

As staff members at the national office, we were busy seven days a week: we updated membership lists, kept in touch with chapter reps, mailed educational literature to campuses, researched and wrote articles, ran messy mimeograph and addressograph machines, and sat in endless meetings. We sent out fact sheets about the arms race, the SPU statement of purpose, as well as copies of the 1962 Port Huron Statement, the document that established Students for a Democratic Society (S.D.S.).

We published a regular newsletter. One of us tediously "justified" the margins on each line with options of half spaces We also shopped, cooked, and kept the house in some degree of cleanliness. Once a month we put in an all-nighter, stuffing envelopes with the Student Peace Union Bulletin, and then, bleary-eyed the next morning, lugged canvas bags full of the newsletters down to the post office. The Bulletin included articles on nuclear testing, the sit-ins in the South, progress toward a test ban treaty, ROTC, Vietnam, Laos, and other foreign policy issues.

The official statement of purpose of the S.P.U. held both the US and the USSR responsible for the arms race; it read:

> "Because both East and West have pursued foreign policies which are not in the interests of their own people or the people of the world and because both bear major responsibility for the cold war, the Student Peace Union believes that the peace movement must act independently of both East and West, must apply the same standard of criticism to both, and must seek new and creative means of achieving a free and peaceful society."

Our Bulletin reported on the increasing numbers of advisers and arms being sent to Vietnam. It had been a French colony and in 1954 French troops, defeated at Dien Bien Phu, pulled out. The US took sides, even then, by substantially aiding the French in this doomed effort--financing up to 80% of their costs.

The newsletter reported that the Geneva Peace Agreement in 1954 between the French and the Vietminh provided for free elections within two years to reunify Vietnam. The US, while pledging not to interfere with the elections, did not actually endorse the elections. Instead, our government moved to set up Ngo Dinh Diem, a strongman who had resided for several years in the US, as head of South Vietnam. He proceeded to brutally suppress Buddhist opposition to his regime and he blocked the promised elections. They raided pagodas, attacked demonstrations, jailed and executed Buddhists. The US gave him money, weaponry, and more advisers. By the end of Eisenhower's presidency in 1961, the U.S. maintained a force of 700 military advisers to support Diem. Just two years later, under Kennedy's presidency, advisers numbered 16,000.

Mme. Ngo Dinh Nhu was the sister-in-law of Diem; her husband served in the government as head of the secret police. Nicknamed the Dragon Lady, Mme. Nhu traveled widely, acting as spokesperson for the regime. When several Buddhists set themselves on fire in protest against Diem, she went on record stating that she would "clap hands at seeing another monk barbeque show."[3]

She came to New York in October 1963 to begin a 20-day, 12-city tour. The SPU and other peace groups tracked her trip across the country. She planned to visit Chicago so the SPU called on local activists as well as University of Chicago students to protest her visit.

She came to Chicago, staying at a hotel in the downtown Loop, and we planned to greet her. Some of us from the office drove down to the Loop in the van with our hastily made picket signs. We were a noisy and informal group as we carried signs and chanted, circling the sidewalk in front of the hotel.

Buildings towered around us, cabs screeched to a halt in front of the hotel, exhaust filled the air. Horns blared and the doorman looked decidedly nervous. A couple of police cars were parked down the block and a local TV station had set up shop near the hotel.

"Look," I said, as her limousine slid to a stop in front of the hotel, "the *Times* said she wears mink." A tiny, five-foot tall Asian woman stepped out of the limo, wearing an *Oa Dai,* the side-split Vietnamese garment.

"Stop the war in Vietnam! Stop the war in Vietnam!" we chanted.

Suddenly we were aware of another group of students who had quietly begun their own picket line alongside ours. Vietnamese students, clothed in the colorful jackets and pants native to their country, were marching with us. Gathering from several mid-western states to protest the Diem government, they quietly circled in front of the hotel. How could these gentle people be our enemy?

One afternoon about two months after this protest, I was running late for my history class. I had returned to college at Roosevelt University in Chicago. As I slid into an empty seat in the front, the class was discussing what kind of president Lyndon Johnson would make. Confused, I turned to the student sitting next to me. She said, "Kennedy's been shot."

The entire country was about to embark on a whole new chapter of the Vietnam War, a major escalation under President Lyndon Johnson.

Notes

1. James G. Blight and David A. Welch, On the Brink: Americans and Soviets Reexamine the Cuban Missile Crisis, 2nd ed. (NY: Noonday Press, 1990) p. 344.

2. James G. Blight and David A. Welch, On the Brink: Americans and Soviets Reexamine the Cuban Missile Crisis, 2nd ed. (NY: Noonday Press, 1990).

3. "Tiny Saigon Warrior: Mrs. Ngo Dinh Nhu", *The New York Times*, August 22, 1963, p.3.

Shut It Down: Students Against the War

Nancy Teel

I TURNED 21 in Bogotá, Colombia in 1966. As a Catholic exchange student on a social mission, I had a Colombian family and close American friends with whom to celebrate. I remember a magical night: a family fiesta at home, a late dinner at a dressed-up downtown restaurant, and a passionate good night kiss from a young man I admired.

Above 8000 feet on the Colombian plateau, that August evening was so cool that I wore a wool jacket over my dress. I remember talking earnestly with my friends, trying to make sense of cultural and linguistic chasms. We struggled to comprehend how poverty and economic backwardness contrasted with the warmth and consciousness of the people we encountered. On our way home, we heard gunshots in the distance, a nightly occurrence in Bogotá. Colombia was just then emerging from a period called *la violencia*, which it would sadly reenter and where it remains today. That night began my dizzying journey into the heart of the 1960s and a process of change that still continues.

Many hours in the library, weekend mixers, Notre Dame football games and boyfriends marked my college years. The spiritual atmosphere of Saint Mary's College went beyond conventional religion, and an air of quiet reflection infused the campus. We were searching for truth, for beauty, for the sparkling structures of nature. I took the required courses, worked on my academic skills, plunged into reading English literature. I found I was looking for meaning beyond traditional academic study and dating. It surprises me still that I did not find it in my religion.

In the fall of my junior year, I met students in the organization called CILA, Council for the International Lay Apostolate. These Notre Dame students organized work/study projects in Latin America, through personal contacts with missionaries and others connected to the University. Nineteen sixty-six was the third year of the project and the first year that Saint Mary's women joined. Our ethic was to serve others, in order to learn and grow ourselves. It worked. CILA mounted international projects with dozens of students each year. All the student participants were deeply moved by the experience, and perhaps some helpful work was accomplished in host countries in Latin America as well.

I went to Bogotá for three months in the summer of 1966, having prepared for most of the previous academic year. I lived with the Gomez family, all nine children at home, and studied Spanish daily at the Javeriana University for the first month. After class I would travel by city bus to one of two *barrios* or neighborhoods, San Carlos or Juan XXIII, to do our project work. In San Carlos we assisted at a parish school, visiting classes, painting classrooms, and handing out cheap ruled notebooks, emblazoned with the American eagle and "USAID". We learned that there were no public schools. Families had to buy uniforms and books for their children to be allowed to attend the parochial school, and many could not afford to go. There was much talk about Ciudad Kennedy, a high-rise public housing project funded by American dollars. Once we were asked to mix powdered milk (from big packages with those eagle logos) with water from the school tap and serve it to the children. I gave one little boy a cup of milk. He drank it straight down and promptly threw up. I panicked about the water. We didn't drink it. Why were we being directed to give it to the children?

I wrote this in my report when I returned to Saint Mary's for my senior year:

CILA: Bogotá, Colombia Report: Summer 1966.

Every day a haze hangs over San Carlos. The barrio sprawls on low flat land at the base of the hill that marks the southern edge of Bogotá. Beyond San Carlos begins the campo. But within the barrio the freshness of the country is not felt. The haze is dust rising from unpaved streets, open sewers, useless piles of dirt. The murky air blends with the aspect of a typical street. The houses and stores are all low, oblong buildings that crowd against one another and the street. The brick is yellow-brown or dusty red—the weather-stained doors are always closed. Ragged children sit on doorsteps covered with the same gray film. There are no open spaces for play. No color is clear. No trees grow along the streets. Stale smells fill the already heavy air, smells

Nancy Teel with neighborhood children in Bogotá, 1966

of food in stores or on corner grills, of animals and people, of sewage and dung. On a weekday, few people are on the streets, except children in varicolored uniforms chattering home at the noon break. The adults walk alone and do not speak.

Nancy, age 21

San Carlos had poor houses on regular blocks of unpaved streets. The streets were dusty, the houses unpainted and poorly furnished, but they were houses nonetheless. Every so often a corner store broke the monotony. In contrast, in the barrio Juan XXIII, there was none of the above. People lived in shacks made of scavenged materials that clung to hillsides so steep that even college students like myself had difficulty climbing them. There were no roads, no sewers, no water, just paths and shelters made of trash. The only intact structure was a tiny whitewashed clinic, the project of the local priest, a missionary from Argentina, who no doubt consoled himself that something, anything was being done to alleviate the catastrophic condition of these new migrants to the city. But the clinic was virtually unstaffed by medical personnel, so it was only a cement dream. Besides cleaning the clinic and helping to build a small recreation center, all we

CILA students could do was visit people and admire their children. I think we did cheer up the priest a bit as well. He was a lonely man, with a huge faith that somehow he was making a difference.

During that summer the enormity of poverty in Colombia slowly struck me. I remember being shocked by homeless people in doorways begging for money and food. My Colombian "sister," Leonor, pulled me away from them and instructed me to ignore them. Little did I know that thirty years later I would see similar people in Harvard Square. I knew enough about Latin America to perceive that this kind of poverty must be the case for most countries, and I saw the paltry nature of American foreign aid. We had a revealing meeting at a fancy Bogota hotel with a representative from USAID, a smooth young bureaucrat who answered our questions rather frankly. He admitted that most of the aid money went to pay for interest on loans from American banks and contracted goods and services from American companies. Only a small fraction went to develop housing and provide that powdered milk. No doubt this was the case in other poor countries as well, I concluded. AID was really a subsidy and insurance policy for American businesses trading in Colombia and other developing countries.

That summer, newspapers were filled with news about the war in Vietnam. Escalation was in full swing. My Colombian family and friends wondered loudly, why? What had the Vietnamese done to merit this violent inter-vention? They told and retold the story of the Panama Canal: the land of Panama had originally belonged to Colombia until it was determined to have value as a canal site. At that point American interests fomented a re-volt and the province broke away from Colombia, only to quickly sign over the Canal rights to the US. The parallel to Vietnam was clear to them; co-ercion by the giant power was a grave threat to national sovereignty and re-sistance was right and proper. I had never heard this argument before. Up to that summer I had mildly opposed the war on humanitarian grounds. Now I began to see a different side. By living in Bogotá, not as a tourist but in the fold of a middle-class Colombian family, I could begin to participate in their world view. Why indeed? I asked myself. What was at stake in Vietnam? My search for answers to that question would shape my life in ways I never could have imagined on my twenty-first birthday.[1]

During my senior year at Saint Mary's I prepared for another summer project with CILA, this time in Mexico. We left just after graduation, a small caravan of two cars and a Ford van, all donated by auto dealers in South Bend. We drove straight through to Austin, Texas, where we crashed in a dorm at the University for a night. The next day we crossed the border at Nuevo Laredo and pushed on to Saltillo. I saw the desert for the first time. In one straight stretch of a full hundred miles the highway was lined with flowers germinated by the recent spring rains. I have a faded picture of myself standing next to a blue Ford, looking past a border of yellow daisies, across a sandy plain at distant purple mountains. The next day we made it to Guanajuato, the old university town, with its beautiful cathedral. I was amazed by the ancient stones, the testimony of faith built by people so long ago, and continued in sacred use. I had not yet seen the cathedrals of Notre Dame or Chartres, but today they evoke in me the same sense of continuity of faith, my own faith, searching for answers. Then we drove west into Michoacan, higher and higher into the mountains, past mythical Lake Pátzcuaro, gray and cold, down to the small Spanish town of Tacámbaro.

CILA Project Report: Tacámbaro, 1967

...Perhaps the worst conditions we saw were in a house on the outskirts of Tacámbaro. It is built over a sewer-like drainage ditch along the side of a road leading off into the fields. The walls were mud, the roof thatched, the floor dirt. Pigs and chickens moved in and out freely, along with dogs, bugs and, of course, the children. We found only four of the large family at home. The oldest girl of fifteen was taking care of a tiny baby and two little girls. The mother was working and the nurse was unable to find out the whereabouts of the father and the other children. All of the children had fevers, and the little girls were covered with infected sores. We had met these same conditions many times before, caused by the exceptionally bad water during the summer rainy season and also by dirt and malnutrition. I think the impression of this particular episode is so vivid to me even now, because in some way I was able to identify with the oldest girl. The nurse asked why she was not in school. Her reply: "There is no one else to help my mother." I can only wonder what possible future she has—almost certainly no better than the life she shares with her mother and family now. An early marriage, perhaps motivated by a desire to get away from her family conditions, children, a disappearing husband or one who works very hard for ten pesos a day will mean the same conditions in the end, made worse in comparison with the slow but perceptible progress taking place in Tacambaro. I was left with questions. Why? What future for these people? Is that girl doomed to a less than human environment for life, at an age when the world should just be opening up for her? There are no answers. I find though that in my personal life I have to come to terms with questions like these. My life touched hers for a

moment—I scratched her arm with a needle and smallpox vaccine. Is that enough? Somehow I have to remain aware of her and others who are now a part of me.

Several current myths were exploded for me forever during the summer. One was the fable that people are really happier in poverty (lacking all of the psychological pressures that the affluent person has, etc.) People are neither free nor happy when they live in filth and are continually sick and have insufficient food and clothing and housing. I saw continual evidence. Another insidious and widespread myth says that people live this way because they are lazy; they simply don't have the Yanqui spirit to work. On the contrary, they work harder and in primitive conditions and get nowhere; without water or soap or, most important of all, without basic education. Ignorance was the worst barrier that I encountered. Understanding concepts such as "bacteria", "germs", "infection" is absolutely basic. Without it, illness is surrounded by superstition; no connection is made between polluted water and disease, between boiling water and milk and good health. I remember explaining to one sick family repeatedly in my poor Spanish how important it was to boil the water and to keep the chickens and dogs out of the house and the pigs away from the children, that this was why they had fever and dysentery. Each time I came back, the conditions were the same. The antibiotics we brought them finally ran out. A massive and highly organized education effort is needed. A few conversations with a foreign girl like me did not touch the problem. The terrible irony is that particular family lives in a solid cement house with running water and an indoor bathroom. It was built four years ago by CILA.

Nancy, age 22

As I read this report thirty-odd years later, I see the truth in it. Our actions had no lasting effect on the condition of the people we visited, with the possible exception of the immunization against smallpox. The lasting effect of our work was on ourselves, our young psyches, our values, our questioning of the verities of the world. Why indeed should some people be so poor and others so rich? The question has only become more poignant since I walked the trails around Tacambaro.

With each trip to Latin America my spiritual life widened. My world became much larger and conversely, distances between places and people became much smaller. Suddenly it mattered what happened to a little girl named Juana in an orphanage in rural Michoacán. And it mattered what happened to people in Vietnam. I knew for certain that they were human beings like me.

I had been raised as a Catholic amid traditional forms of worship and extreme gender differentiation. Different did not mean unimportant or less lovable to God, we were told in words and writing, but actions spoke differently and much louder. Men were in the lead in every sphere of church life and women were relegated to helping roles. Only the teaching nuns like the Sisters of the Holy Cross at Saint Mary's were an exception to the message that the physical aspect of being a woman was primary and should determine her life.[2] She should begin by making herself attractive, find a suitable mate, raise children and devote herself principally to the reproduction of the species, in a broad sense. Any personal, intellectual or spiritual development should be secondary. This was, of course, a convenient male perspective that women internalized, seeing themselves as reproductive animals and service providers while fighting inner battles to push aside their other needs and talents. This often led to depression, as I had already experienced up close in my mother, who suffered from it all her life. The message from the nuns was different: they maintained that our spiritual and intellectual development was extremely important, fudging the question of whether it was more or less important than our role in reproduction.

My family's ideas, particularly my father's, were more progressive. He believed that women were as capable as men, if given education and offered challenges. He taught me that I had to choose to accept the education and accept the challenge. He pointed to many examples of achieving women in Erie, teachers and administrators. Most of them were single and some, I realized many years later, were lesbians. He explained that any woman could be left without a husband, widowed or divorced, there were many examples, and I must be prepared to have a career if I should want or need it. As radical as he was, he couldn't directly challenge the prevailing view that women must be housewives first. He alternately cajoled and demanded that I take on risks and challenges, and I did. We had a stormy relationship, but with deep love and affection underneath.

As my life unfolded in the mid-1960s, the assumptions I was raised with were shaken and toppled one after another. Each year in college rules were looser and parietal hours were later. In my classes and in late night bull sessions moral and philosophical issues were paramount. No one could explain exactly why birth control was wrong, including my Moral Theology instructor. Suddenly it seemed as if there were no rational justifications for any of "the rules." Experimentation was wild. One close friend got pregnant and married in a matter of months. Six Notre Dame students and one professor took way too much LSD and had to be hospitalized. The professor was fired, and the students lost a whole semester as they slowly recovered. One later became a good friend. Notre Dame SDS was born, and there were groups of radical charismatics who were said to "speak in tongues." Even though it was rumored that the ecstatic mumblers were saying the Lord's Prayer in Greek, I came away from one of their services repelled. I felt they had left reason behind and given themselves over to passions whose source was less than heavenly. And through all my college years, like a hard driving backbeat, the killing continued in Vietnam.

I entered college just before President Kennedy was assassinated and I graduated in 1967, the Summer of Love. There was turmoil everywhere. The assassinations of Robert Kennedy and of Martin Luther King, Jr. in 1968 ripped the seams of my world. It was like an old stuffed animal that I took to college, finally coming apart.

Transformation by Fire

Ithaca, New York, is a beautiful college town with a friendly business district, its few square blocks dominated by Ithaca College on the south hill and Cornell University sprawling on the glacial ridge to the east. Lake Cayuga, a deep remainder of the last ice age, spreads north for 20 miles. In the late 1960s and early 1970s when I was in graduate school at Cornell, the town's population of 31,000 contained an uneasy mix of factory and service workers, middle-class academics, a rainbow of college students and a significant number of hippies, drop-outs and wannabes. Communes sprouted in the countryside where students and hippies tried subsistence farming and organic gardening, getting high on nature and other drugs.

During the five years I spent in Ithaca the alternative culture grew. It drew its politics and style from the national counter-culture, but with significant differences. In politics, the bent in Ithaca was decidedly toward non-violence and connecting with ordinary folks. The influence of Dr. Martin Luther King and Mahatma Gandhi was felt and actively preached by religious antiwar activists, most notably Father Dan Berrigan, a visiting professor from 1967 to 1969. Annabel Taylor Hall, an interfaith center, was also a center of antiwar organizing and agonizing. I spent many hours in the coffee house there in those last years of the 1960s.

SDS was a pivotal organization in the New Left nationally and Ithaca was no exception. Open meetings at Cornell drew huge crowds of students, hippies and curious academics. Scruffy young men, vibrant with the political and sexual energy of the times, would talk, joke and harangue the crowd about the war, planning yet another "action:" another picket at the draft board, demonstration on the Arts Quad, or leaflet distribution downtown. As each academic year progressed, meetings would grow in attendance and "actions" would become more frequent until they reached a veritable frenzy in the spring, coinciding with the enormous leap of joy and hormones as the snow finally melted and gentle green colored the hills. Protest was almost normal, an expected and accepted part of the academic calendar.

Once, on an airplane, a well-dressed middle-aged woman in the seat next to me struck up a conversation.

"Have you ever heard of this SDS group?" She asked.

"Yes, " I replied, realizing that my appearance gave me away as a likely antiwar student.

"Do you go to school?

"I'm a grad student at Cornell."

"Then you must have some idea—why are people attracted to, uh, an organization like that." She asked.

I noted her delicate avoidance of the word "communist" and I surprised myself with the enthusiasm of my answer.

"Because they're against the war," I said. "And because they act on their beliefs. And they're actually the most democratic organization I've ever seen."

She bit her lip, but her eyes betrayed her surprise and disapproval. She proceeded to tell me about her married daughters and how happy they were. As our plane landed I was feeling the distance between us, between my generation and hers, between what she wanted for her daughters and wherever life might take me.

In November 1967, I joined a crowd sending off buses of students going to march on Washington against the war. It was early evening, the air was cold, and twilight was giving way to starlight. The buses would drive all night. My boyfriend urged me to go and we almost jumped on the bus at the last moment, but I was still recovering from a bout of mononucleosis, contracted in Mexico the previous summer. It was my first semester in graduate school, and I was behind in my work because I had been ill for several weeks. The memory of the non-stop three-week headache was still fresh in my temples and every time I swallowed, I could feel the remains of a vicious sore throat. Afraid to risk a relapse, I finally declined to go. I still regret it, although I probably made the right decision.

At home I had grown up with an easy patriotism, the lingering grateful-ness of immigrant grandparents who were welcomed to Ellis Island by the Statue of Liberty. My father displayed the flag proudly from sunrise to sun-set on Flag Day and the Fourth of July. Without warning, at age twenty-two, my deepest personal experiences in Colombia and Mexico led me to oppose the actions and explanations of the US government. I read the New York Times every day and watched the nightly news in the student center. Peace talks in Paris were stalled. The bombing continued. American casu-alties soared as the North Vietnamese and Viet Cong counterattacked dur-ing Tet. In the vicious winter of 1968, we marched to the Ithaca draft board one day. I was thinking hard about my reasons for standing as a witness to a young man burning his draft card. Onlookers jeered and screamed obscenities at us, even spit in our faces. What did it mean to defy the gov-ernment in this way? If I had had a draft card, would I have done the same?

When President Johnson announced on television that he would not run for reelection, I was visiting a friend's family in Syracuse, New York. My friend and I and his sister cheered while his parents scowled and scolded us for disrespecting the President. I went home to Erie and immediately volunteered to work for Senator Eugene McCarthy, whose near-win of the New Hampshire Democratic primary had prompted Johnson's decision. I spent a few days giving out buttons and flyers and then returned to Cornell, unconvinced. Beyond ending the war, McCarthy didn't have much of a plan. I already understood that the war was part of a bigger picture of economic relations. Moreover, the electoral process seemed like an ancient beast, unable and unwilling to move, but capable of eating you alive. Many of my friends went "clean for Gene," shaving beards and cutting hair to be presentable. It's hard to believe now, but in 1968 you could guess someone's politics by the length of his hair and beard if a man, and by the style of her clothes and lack of make-up if a woman.

Although I voted for Eugene McCarthy in the Pennsylvania primary that spring, I was not actively involved in the campaign for the next couple of months. Martin Luther King's assassination in April left me stunned. How could they do this to him, a man who stood for non-violence? In June, when Bobby Kennedy was shot, I was overwhelmed. What little remaining faith I had in the American system to right itself by an election died that morning. I remember sitting in the little den in my parent's home, listening to the radio, holding my knees tightly in a kind of fetal position. I felt shocked, then sad, then very afraid. At that moment, it seemed that there was no possible future; there was only action and feeling in the present tense. As my mind began to work, I told myself that the world I knew, the one I had grown up in, had just broken like a raw egg on the floor. Something new would have to take its place.

I did vote in the presidential election in November 1968, but not for Hubert Humphrey, whom I viewed as responsible for the Chicago police attack on antiwar demonstrators at the Democratic National Convention that summer. Rather, I voted for the Peace and Freedom Party. After that, I didn't vote again until 1984.

Three days after Bobby Kennedy's death, I left for Cuernavaca, Mexico, on a Cornell-sponsored study. I was to find no respite there; huge demonstrations were already in progress, particularly in Mexico City. I spent two months at the *Centro Intercultural de Documentacion* (CIDOC), the radical language school and think-tank led by Ivan Illych. Since I already spoke Spanish well, the daily classes were easy and helped me to achieve real fluency in the language and culture. Every day intellectuals from various disciplines and countries lectured on their views of radical change in the "Third World." CIDOC was a melting pot, cooking on a hot stove.

Earthquakes were common between the twin volcanoes in the Mexico City area, but they were nothing compared to the social shocks that revolutionary students were administering to the Mexican bureaucracy. For weeks police roadblocks cut off the capitol from the rest of the country. When we heard the road was open again, my friend and I flagged down a bus on the outskirts of Cuernavaca and disembarked in the Zócalo, in the old heart of Mexico City, just after dark. As we walked across the huge open square, debating about which direction to look for a restaurant, we heard the close and unmistakable crack crack crack of gunfire. Terrified, we started to run and ducked into a narrow side street. Caught in the trap of confused identity, we did not know who was shooting nor if we would be seen through their sights as student comrades or damned Yankees. We kept running until we saw a modern hotel dead ahead. In the door we scrambled and, breathless, asked for a room. The man at the desk was polite, but eyed us suspiciously, carefully reviewing our identification and signatures in the hotel guest book, as we conferred over the price and determined we had just enough money. We collapsed in the room for a while, then sneaked out to a nearby restaurant for a late supper; keeping the revolution going still required plenty of calories. Though it was confusing and frightening, it seemed that revolution was happening everywhere in the summer of '68, in Mexico and in France, as well as in Vietnam and China. It seemed inevitable.

In the spring of 1969 Cornell was torn apart by an escalating series of events with epic overtones. Black students, by then numbering about 250 in a university of 13,000, were pressing demands for an independent Black Studies program. Rhetoric and tactics intensified. Someone burned a cross in front of the black women's residential co-op. We were all (selfishly) afraid. What if hippie communes were next? In response to the cross-burning and the refusal of the faculty to endorse the independence of the Black Studies Program, one hundred and twenty black students occupied the student center, Willard Straight Hall, on Parents' Weekend. Everyone was forced to take a stand.

The phone rang at 6:00 AM. Someone from SDS was telling us about the building takeover and asking us to join a picket line in support of the black students. My roommate Carol ran out right away and I followed after a couple of cups of coffee. Our commune sat just below the Cornell campus, near a number of fraternities. Spectacular natural beauty is commonplace at Cornell, and that day pale spring greens were just beginning to emerge and the lake in the distance was a peaceful gray-blue. It was hard to believe that anything could be wrong. As I started the climb up "libe" slope to join the picket line, I saw a middle-aged African-American couple slowly walking up the sidewalk toward the campus. Their heads were bowed and they seemed to be carrying a great weight on their shoulders. I knew instinctively that they had a child involved in the protest. My heart went out to them; I remembered how important Parents' Weekend had been to me and to my parents when I was an undergraduate. I wanted to say something, but no words came. They didn't seem to notice me as I passed behind them and cut uphill on the steep, wet grass to join the picket line in front of the Straight.

The April sky alternately doused us with big wet snowflakes and freezing drizzle. We walked in a broad circle meant to show our support for the black students inside the occupied building; many of my friends were marching with me, and news was shared quickly. We learned that fraternity brothers from Delta Upsilon, our neighbors, had tried to break into the occupied building; an ensuing fist fight had slightly injured several black and white students. Rumors spread about guns. They were believable because as we SDS supporters marched, we could see sharpshooters from the New York State Police take positions above us on the roofs of the libraries to the north. That night the black students brought guns and ammunition into the student center.

The crisis intensified. On the picket circle, rumors flew that white students from fraternities were armed and ready to storm the student center. We could almost believe it. Then we heard that two hundred upstate New York farmers, armed, angry, and inspired by racism, were assembled in a shopping center parking lot downtown and hastily deputized, ready to be called to the campus. Two hundred students in the rain, in the sharpshooters' sights, walking in a ragged circle could not have been such a threat. To me it seemed like a very small group. It was the race of the students holding the building hostage that drew the police firepower. Marching in that line was one of the scarier moments of my life. I remember thinking that if I were shot, at least it would be for a good cause.

Negotiations and picketing continued. President Perkins, a Quaker and the force behind the recruitment of black students to the university in the first place, negotiated a settlement that included amnesty for the protesters. The students emerged carrying their guns, seemingly victorious, and the pictures flashed around the world.[3] But the next day, Monday, the Cornell faculty refused to accept the administration's resolution, creating a greater crisis of university governance. Ten thousand students had heard the news of the faculty's decision in the field house, Barton Hall, and screamed their disbelief.

Still, I kept working. Syntax 306 was such a tough course that I was taking handwritten notes in class and typing them at home to organize the complex material. As I sat in class on Tuesday after the faculty vote, I was paying close attention to the lecture.

Three students burst into the room.

"Stop the class! Stop the class!"

The professor paused.

"Come to the field house. SDS demands a new vote!"

"On strike! Shut it down!" They chanted as they rushed out to another classroom.

I remember holding my pen in mid-air, deciding after a long moment to close my notebook and walk out of the classroom. Behind me, I heard the rest of the students and the professor following me toward Barton Hall.

Six thousand students packed the field house that afternoon. The faculty, under great pressure, changed its vote. The students were not punished and the Black Studies program demands were met in part. But there was a huge cost. The faculty was split and bitter, and student life, always on the edge of disorganization, was fractured. In the end it was the academic year that was shot.

Many of the Black undergraduates who were recruited to Cornell were not fully prepared for the academic demands of the university, nor were they prepared for the isolation they would face. Just in my own experience in five years at Cornell, I never had a Black student in any of my classes, nor ever encountered a Black teacher. Top students in their own high schools in New York, they were hurt and shocked by the gap between their education and that of their white suburban classmates. Today there is at least an ac- knowledgment that students receive unequal education in high school, and tutoring programs, writing centers and other academic support services are available in most colleges and universities. But there were few support services in 1968; everyone was expected to know how to write and use the library. To its credit, Cornell did establish a tutoring program for the Black students, and I volunteered to be tutor and mentor to one of the freshmen. Dan was serious, smart, and grateful for the opportunity to study. He had had very little experience writing in high school and needed to learn a lot fast. We met twice a week to work on writing, but many times we would just talk. I concluded that he needed an older friend as much or more than he needed a tutor. White Cornell, with its highly competitive atmosphere and parallel student cultures of fraternities and hippies, was a cold place indeed for a couple of hundred young Black students from the inner city.

During the crisis I ran into Dan on the Arts Quad. I asked him the ques- tion I hadn't asked my friends on the picket line. Why? Why had it been necessary to go to such an extreme length to make the point about Black Studies? Couldn't rational argument have carried the day? We squatted on the grass, to keep our conversation just between the two of us, as other students passed by. We both knew that black and white students were not talking to each other. He said simply that it had to be done. The university was not going to recognize the real needs of the Black students. He said that I wouldn't be able to understand but all the Black students knew it was the truth. He got up and walked on and I was left sitting now on the wet grass, wondering about the vast gulf that had opened between us.

Today, I admire the restraint and good sense of the Cornell adminis- trators who negotiated a peaceful settlement to the crisis and even tried to turn it into an educational opportunity. And indeed it was. No one remained the same. The sight of the sharpshooters on the library roof remains burned in my memory. I learned that while white SDS members might meet hostility and derision, the full power of the state would come down immediately on black students, and some people seemed willing to shoot them down with overwhelming force. It was a chilling lesson on the different worlds inhabited by black and white Americans. The fragility of the peaceful, tolerant university environment was betrayed. The black students, bright, strong, and isolated in an almost entirely white world of power and privilege, used disruptive tactics to create a space for growth, a new place for themselves and those to come after. And time has shown that they were successful. The liberalism of the faculty was revealed as a kind of noblesse oblige that turned ugly when challenged.[4]

While supporting the black students' demands for greater support from the university, I didn't hesitate to take advantage of the opportunities that Cornell afforded to me. During the summer of 1969, I studied German at the Goethe Institut in (West) Germany and spent time hitchhiking with my partner Mark in Bayern, Austria and northern Italy. From a crowded sidewalk in Munich I watched Armstrong step out on the moon, and in the *International Herald* I read about Woodstock. What a party I missed! Still, it was a good summer. The solidity and confidence of European culture helped me to feel sane and normal again. And the European students I met were as strongly opposed to the war in Vietnam as I was. In fact, opposition to the war was mainstream sentiment in Europe, not a counter cultural fringe view. I returned to Cornell feeling stronger, and knowing enough German to pass the third and final language exam required for my doctorate.

In November 1969, I answered the national call for a strike against the war and went to Washington to demonstrate. Then I took several months break from politics to study non-stop for my written doctoral exams. I passed in the spring, in March, 1970. Just as I began to relax a bit (I was taking a full load of classes and working as a teaching assistant as well), events way beyond my control took hold of my life. I felt like I was riding in a small boat amid huge waves, any one of which could send me to the bottom of the sea.

Although I faced the grave issues of the day, the war in Southeast Asia, the violence at home, the ongoing struggles for civil rights and economic

justice, I didn't think much about myself or about where waves of demonstrations were taking me. I simply studied and acted on the issues.
Eventually, after three years of increasing activism, I began to look at my
own role as a woman. Partly I was forced to, as capitalism in the guise
of Playboy Inc. pounced on the questioning of morals and declared that
sex should be free and unfettered by commitment. Hippies experimenting
with drugs and new lifestyles fed into the same river of change. All people
were challenged, but while young men were faced with going to war, young
women had to make hard personal choices. The male political leaders made
it clear that they thought that women should service them in all areas of
life, work and play. Stokely Carmichael responded to a question about a
woman's place in the movement: "On her back", he said. He spoke the
truth, as seen by most of the male leaders of the day.

By 1969, women were fed up. While SDS was preoccupied nationally
with the political splits caused by the Weathermen, a quieter but ultimately more important schism took place. The women simply walked out. I
remember a meeting at the student center where we were sitting on the
carpeted floor in a circle, in a place where so many times we studied to
classical music. This time about twelve of us, all student leaders, were in
earnest conversation. With tears and laughter, we explained our grievances:
men didn't listen to us, didn't take us seriously, didn't follow our leadership.
The next level went deeper: men expected women to do all the "shitwork,"
like typing, phoning, cleaning up after meetings, while they attended to
important conversations with each other. And deeper still: in the spirit of
liberation of the times, women were expected to be sexually available and
not get "hung up" or possessive of men. The male leaders at the meeting,
all of twenty-one or twenty-two years old, listened with sympathy and concern. It didn't matter; once spoken, the words could not be taken back and
we women withdrew to form our own collectives and study groups. Within
weeks there was a meeting of the National Organization for Women on
campus and consciousness-raising groups were forming everywhere, from
freshman students to faculty wives.

Women faced enormous obstacles in those days, many of them internal,
but others clearly external, like the limits on percentages of women admitted to Cornell. We learned that only thirty percent of us were allowed as
undergraduates. Almost as soon as the quota became known, it was done
away with. I still remember a NOW forum at Cornell in which male professors directly challenged women's ability to overcome their "hormonal tides"
and think rationally. They believed in the biological inferiority of women
and said so. The women on the panel struggled to overcome their anger as

they attempted to rebut the argument with limited success. History took the side of the women, however, as barriers came down in the ensuing years. But the argument of biological inferiority is still with us. Today, it takes the form that women do not have the moral ability to make judgments about their own bodies and reproductive capacity or that women do not have the biological capability to do certain (powerful and well-paying) jobs. The glacial pace of inclusion of women in decision-making bodies such as Congress, legislatures, and corporate boards of directors testifies to the strength and depth of these beliefs.

The natural strategy of the early women's movement was to withdraw into women-only groups and refuse support to the men. There was carnage in relationships and organizations, but the hostility evoked in men and in the media only made the women more resolute. I remember my own conflicting feelings. As the only child of a powerful and doting father, I had been raised with high expectations of myself. As a graduate of a women's college, I had a reasonable measure of self-confidence and a positive attitude toward other women. But the world I grew up in had few women role models who could show me a life-path. I had only one woman teacher in five years at Cornell, and she was an older, single woman with an arcane academic specialty. My mother was not a role model for reasons that would soon become starkly clear to me. What path to a meaningful life could be found for a young well-educated woman? I liked men and enjoyed having them as friends. And I was definitely heterosexual. This put me immediately at odds with women-identified-women, who, whether lesbian or not, wanted to banish all men from their own and their sisters' lives. I was constantly criticized for wearing dresses, and (the original) mini-skirts. Somehow I managed a compromise position, absorbing the feminist energy, without changing my identity.

I remember an afternoon of inner crisis, walking the Arts Quad by myself, unable to sit in Olin Library, restless, angry, on the verge of tears, thinking about the vision I had finally seen: how men saw me. It was devastating. I had denied it for so long. Sitting in my favorite room in the Straight, that one where classical music always played, I finally reached a point of acceptance. I knew I had to take some action to get rid of my own inner reflection of that male view. Eventually I knew what to do. I went to the newsstand and bought a pack of cigarettes and a copy of Playboy. I was a light smoker in those days, but I smoked several buts, then carried the magazine outside and burned it to a crisp on the grass. I left the little pile of ashes on the lawn as memorial to that old piece of myself.

The most difficult time in my years in Ithaca was the spring of 1970. My mother had a "nervous breakdown," as it was called in those days. This was her first since my elementary school days, and it was a terrible worry for my father and her sisters. They feared she was so depressed she would overdose. I was called home to help watch over her and, indeed, she was visibly happy to see me. A couple of weeks went by; and the pressure built, subtle but clear. I should leave graduate school and come home to take care of my mother. I was torn and terrified. I did not want to be with my mother. I could not get over feelings that she abandoned me as a child when she went into a deep post-partum depression following a miscarriage when I was about eight years old. She barely spoke to me for two years, instead spending her time lying on the living room sofa staring at the ceiling. My father was my source of life, affection, and guidance during those dark days. I looked to my aunts for solace and was lucky to be part of an extended family. I survived, but I disliked my mother's continuing manipulation of me through her condition. When she wanted me to be closer to her, she would develop symptoms, headaches, dizziness, or palpitations. She would refuse offers to call the doctor. She wanted us to sit with her and hold her hand for days on end; what satisfied her most was for one of us to stroke her arm or hand as though she were a kitten. It took years to understand it but when I did, I was angry on some level and kept a safe, albeit small distance between us. My mother wanted merger; I wanted space. I took what I needed.

When she fell into depression again in February of 1970, this time with no clear physical cause, there was lots of room for speculation and lots of need to assign blame. My aunts blamed my father who, as Assistant Superintendent of Schools, was in the middle of highly public and controversial negotiations with the teachers union and with community groups demanding the hiring of more black teachers. Always sharp tongued, undoubtedly he took out some of his frustration at home. This was a lifelong pattern, exacerbated by my mother's refusal to talk back to him or to do any activities that did not involve him. She preferred to claim that he prevented her from visiting her family. In fact, he never stopped her; he did not want to go himself but even encouraged her. She did not cross town without him.

The other direction that blame was directed was toward me. I was twenty-four years old, unmarried, and looked like a perpetual student. I had been financially independent since I graduated from Saint Mary's but not many in the family believed that. Besides, I was against the Vietnam War and had some kind of radical politics. This aberration in someone who used to be a good Catholic girl bothered people. That level of independence in a young woman was intolerable to many, both men and women. I was seen as someone who was dangerously talented, too smart for her own good, or for the good of the family.

Nor was I was willing to blame my father for my mother's depression. I studied as much psychology as I could, and I knew that my mother's problems predated her relationship with him. I fought hard with my father over political issues, but supported him in his decisions about my mother.

I was reminded that women were supposed to marry and have children and devote themselves to family. My family had supported me during the earlier crises with my mother and now it was time for me to pay it back. And of course I had internalized the patriarchal, Catholic, American view of myself as a second-class being. I was fighting it, but that part of myself was painful. I was attractive in those days, in a dangerous kind of way, a nice girl with a hippie edge, long hair below my waist, an athletic body, no bras, but wearing feminine clothes and manners when the spirit moved me. I was arrogant, too, my wits sharpened in constant study and debate in graduate school. I'm sure that lots of people wanted to tame me.

I felt trapped in Erie, and I wanted desperately to escape to California with my boyfriend. Feeling desperate, I went to see my mother's psychiatrist. Dr. Parsons was the father of one of my best friends and had known me since I was a little girl. I asked him directly if my staying with my mother would make her well. If so, I was prepared to withdraw from school and remain in Erie to help her. His answer changed the course of my life.

"You did not cause your mother to become ill, and you can't make her well. You should go on with your own life and do what you need to do for yourself," he said.

Relief washed over me. I had known in my gut I wasn't to blame, but to hear it from a learned, trusted authority meant so much to me. I traveled to California; then returned to Ithaca to write my dissertation. Although I visited Erie often after that, I never lived at home again.

In late April, I returned to see my mother. Driving west on the New York Thruway my non-stop-rock station blared the news of the US invasion of Cambodia and Laos. I knew enough about Southeast Asia to know that this massive attack would devastate huge civilian populations and create thousands more American casualties. Holding that awful knowledge, I spent several days with my mother, who was unwilling to get out of bed, hardly spoke, and cried constantly. She was worse than before. Driving back to Ithaca, I heard on the radio that the National Guard had shot dead four college students at Kent State University for no apparent reason. I remember my hands shaking as I held the steering wheel, struggling to keep the car on the road.

I arrived at Cornell to find a silent, empty campus. The whole university was in the field house, thousands strong, protesting the widening of the war and the killings at Kent State. For years, the antiwar movement had made the connection between violence in Southeast Asia and violence at home. That link was now brutally visible and the majority of students mobilized and declared a strike.

Many faculty members appeared at Barton Hall to join the protests. Of all the distinguished professors at Cornell, the most exciting was Father Dan Berrigan, SJ. Dan was a teaching chaplain for my first two years at Cornell, and I was deeply influenced by his faith and strength of character. At the moment of his appearance at Barton Hall, however, he was on the run from the FBI. He had been convicted of destroying draft records with blood and fire in Catonsville, Maryland. Instead of going to prison, he had fled and was living underground. During the tumultuous protests against the widening of the war and the killings at Kent State, he reappeared. He hadn't been far away anyway. In his autobiography he tells us:

"Out of my rural solitude, on a faultless spring night, I duly made a sudden descent at Cornell, into the lights and noise and electric air of Barton Hall...I arrived on campus with an apocalyptic roar, a dazed passenger on a gargantuan, smoky motorbike. I was disguised, head to toe...in the helmet, goggles, and coverall of a cyclist fresh from the open road.[5]"

Two memories stand out. Dan looked like a hardened member of Hell's Angels when he walked on-stage. When he took off his helmet, there were swells of laughter and shrieks of joy, multiplied by the thousands. He spoke briefly and it was wonderful to hear his voice. When he disappeared underground again in another costume, a wave of thankfulness washed over me. He was a light in a dark time. I did not want to see him in the hands of the FBI men who were waiting for him. At great personal cost, he never backed down and never disappointed the young people who looked to him for guidance. I think it's important to say that he was a mentor, a moral and spiritual teacher, not a political leader. I never saw him take part in the ongoing debates of tactics and strategy that kept lights burning 'till dawn in movement houses. In fact, one of the major reasons that the antiwar movement in Ithaca remained non-violent had to do with the model that he and other antiwar faculty provided. They were few in number, but had a huge influence on the young, desperate movement.[6]

My own story continued. I plunged into daily antiwar demonstrations and meetings. Two more students were killed at Jackson State. The academic year disintegrated. There were no final exams as students and professors alternated between despair and anger at the disruption of Cornell's peaceful idyll. The war was ripping apart the spiritual network of the university. Hundreds of militant antiwar activists and thousands of sympathetic followers protested every day. Everyone was on strike. Barton Hall was filled every night. Finally, most students went home for the summer, and I went to Olin Library to begin work on my dissertation.

Except for the commune where I lived and my new Ph.D. candidate status, my world fell apart that spring. My mother's depression worsened, and she was under constant suicide watch. My relationship with my boyfriend broke apart as the campus was riven by protest and counter-protest. Classes were not held; the professor I was assisting went back to the University of Texas, leaving me alone to answer his students' questions. No grades were given in many courses because the university stopped functioning. Dan Berrigan was still underground, out of touch. Walking toward the library, I had to step around a barricade of burning logs on the bridge over the Cascadilla Creek gorge, the beautiful south entrance to Cornell. Lost and depressed, I had no idea what to do.

I'm not sure what kept me working on my dissertation, except stubbornness perhaps, and the careful habits of an only child. My original project had been to do field work and ethnographic study on Quechua, the language spoken by the descendants of the Inca in the *altiplano* of Bolivia, Peru and Ecuador. My program required study of a non Indo-European language so I had spent intensive classroom time learning the basics of the language. Cornell had an ongoing project in Peru with a *simpatico* director. I had a minor in Latin American studies so Quechua study was a natural choice. However, the summer of 1970 revealed a disturbing rupture in the collegial fabric of the university. An adjunct professor in the Southeast Asian Studies Program was accused of being a CIA agent, sent to spy on all of us antiwar academics.[7] He denied the accusations and remained at the university, but the episode caused me to rethink my whole dissertation project. I realized that anything I wrote, any data I collected, would be available to the Department of Defense for counter-insurgency. In 1965 Che Guevara had gone to the Andes, to the region where I was planning to do my study. He planned to ignite revolution by forming a guerrilla army. He died in 1968, killed by Peruvian officers overseen by the CIA, leaving the guerrilla movement in shambles. His defeat had created an artificial peace, but I knew that the conditions of the poor subsistence farmers of the region would lead to continued revolt.

I thought about the people in Peru with whom I would be living and working for a year or more. They would give me the data I needed to get my degree. Then I would go back to Cornell and a secure future. They in turn would be at the mercy of both sides in the conflict. By revolutionaries, they would be seen as collaborators with the *yanquis*. And on the other side, the data they provided to me could be used to perfect US counterinsurgency techniques, which had already demonstrated their brutality in both Southeast Asia and Latin America. I decided I couldn't do it. It was a clear ethical decision and I felt good about it. I switched my topic to a study of the new genre of Latin American literature, now called "magical realism", and explored for two years in Olin Library the connections between linguistic theory and literary structure. In the academic year 1971-1972 I struggled to write. I had been devastated by earlier criticisms of my ideas from sympathetic professors. My dissertation committee was tolerant but not especially helpful. I kept writing anyway, creating a mental structure that was finally deemed worthy of a Ph.D. in a June, 1972 oral defense. I spent another few weeks editing the final draft and overseeing the typing. Finally it was bound and finished. I felt light, unconnected, as alive in the present moment as I ever have been.

One reason I stayed to finish that dissertation was that it provided continuity and stability in an upside-down world. I had graduated from Saint Mary's five years before. I was twenty-six years old. In those five years I had gone from a well-dressed, well-educated, well-mannered Catholic girl to an independent hippie woman completing a doctorate in a man's world. I had attended antiwar demonstrations monthly, weekly, sometimes daily for my entire adult life. I had participated in demonstrations supporting civil rights and had been working in the alternative media producing a radio show called "The Rest of the News." I was part of a women's collective that was setting up a free health clinic. And, along with two other graduate students, I was an unofficial foster parent of a runaway teenager. I had experimented with drugs as well, although I was too levelheaded to get dangerously involved. I was living in my fifth commune and had had various up and down relationships with men, leading to both heartbreaks and highs. It was too much change. I needed to settle down, but that was not to be.

The Vietnam War forced me and the movement, boomers all, to grow up. We had been spoiled by the good times we had grown up in. We had come to the university with a sense of entitlement, to become leaders in our fields and in our communities, solid citizens, destined to gain the appropriate personal rewards that status carried with it. In working against the war, we expected that if we really wanted peace badly enough and worked hard enough, it would come. But as years of protest dragged on, these childish illusions were exposed. Some acted like spoiled children and began throwing rocks and bottles. A few turned to serious violence or serious drugs. Many dropped out. Just about everyone lost faith in the American political system. We appealed to unenlightened national leaders who just didn't get it. Gradually we had to admit they knew what they were doing; however, only many years later was the extent of their knowledge and cynicism revealed, for example in Robert MacNamara's 1995 book, *In Retrospect*. In 1971, we in the antiwar movement still mostly believed in non-violence and democratic process. These beliefs were to be tested again and again.

Mayday

By the spring of 1971, America and I had witnessed nearly a decade of marches, vigils, and national demonstrations against the war in Vietnam. Still, peace was not at hand. Lobbying by citizens' groups continued non-stop in Congress. In April, 200,000 people attended a peaceful antiwar rally in Washington, and Vietnam Veterans lobbied, demonstrated and returned the medals they had won with so many sacrifices.

Over the years that I had been a part of it, the antiwar movement in Ithaca had hardened. Despite our best efforts, despite the mass outpourings of sentiment against the war, the government and military were fixed on "winning," whatever the cost. That year, a different kind of Mayday rally sprouted in the garden of civil disobedience. For six cold months, the People's Coalition For Peace and Justice organized across the country. This demonstration was to be different; the goal was to stop the city that was running the war, to actually shut down Washington, DC just for a day. The idea was to stop blood from flowing to the heart of the monster, the war machine, by stopping traffic into the city. The metaphors were mixed, but the plan was clever. While local groups agreed to abide by a non-violent philosophy and to follow the general strategy, they were autonomous. Representatives from around the country met once in DC and targets were assigned. Each regional group was to break into small affinity groups of six to ten people. Each affinity group was to look out for each other and to attempt to block a major road or bridge. We were to sit down in a circle blocking traffic and wait to be arrested. When one affinity group was taken away, a new one was to sit in and take its place, all day long. We were to do this in such numbers that arresting us would be Washington's business of the day instead of running the war. It made perfect sense in a crazy sort of way. Of course I would go!

Ithaca's target was the Key Bridge connecting Georgetown to Arlington, VA. My affinity group was made up of Cornell graduate students, with one visitor from Harvard and the teenage runaway who was staying in my room. It was a distinguished group although we didn't know it at the time; one member later received a MacArther "genius" award as a professor at the University of California. We met for a weekend rock concert and pre-demonstration rally in West Potomac Park. Everyone camped in the park on Saturday night in cool drizzle. There were 50,000 of us by official count, and probably many more in actual numbers. The music had a hard edge. There were too many people looking like police agents in the crowd and some of them were peddling LSD and other drugs. I confronted one man, telling him to stop, reminding him that we were there for a political purpose. He looked away and quickly offered LSD to some passing high school kids. I felt disgusted and then uneasy. The medics were busy with lots of bad trips in very young people. We older folks (still under thirty!) shunned drugs and tried to get some sleep in our tents and cars.

At 6:00 AM I was awakened by a noise like the end of the world. I struggled out of my sleeping bag and out of the tent. Huge helicopters hovered about twenty feet over the heads of the lately sleeping rock fans. It was very foggy and the noise frightened me. After several minutes the helicopters rose into the cloud and I could hear a police bullhorn telling us to clear the park, our permit was revoked. Minutes later, a line of police in white helmeted riot gear appeared, moving toward us out of the mist. For a moment we panicked, memories of the Chicago police riot in 1968 never far away. I actually considered swimming across the Potomac to get away from them. Then we heard the loud speaker say we had until noon to clear the park. After a moment of relief, we began to pack up and regroup. The breakfast crew served oatmeal.

Life magazine carried an article written by its Washington Bureau chief who accompanied the Chief of DC Police throughout the weeks before and after Mayday.[8] From a safe distance of twenty-seven years, I enjoyed reading how the police saw the protest. They planned their actions at the park carefully, down to the distribution of LSD and downers I'm sure, although that part isn't mentioned in *Life*, only the presence of many plain-clothes men. They wanted to scare away the hangers-on and isolate the "hard core radicals." They reasoned that the disruption of plans and the lack of contact with leaders of the protest would make it fizzle. They were pleased to be able to clear the park with no resistance, but they were surprised the next day. While some kids who just came for the music left, the antiwar protesters stayed. We hadn't come to listen to music or party in the park; it was just a place to camp. Our goal was still to shut down the war machine. The decentralized organizational strategy worked. We didn't need instructions from the stage or any more contact with the leaders of the Mayday Tribe. We knew what to do.

When we drove out of the park, affinity groups scattered. While many moved into the dorms at George Washington and Georgetown Universities, my group made a slightly plusher arrangement. We stayed the night of April 30th at the home of one member's brother, a nice apartment in Georgetown. We ate pizza at midnight, then tried to catch a few hours of rest in our sleeping bags on the floor. By the time one woman called home late in the evening, it was clear that the phone was bugged. By 5:00 AM a plainclothes policeman was stationed on the front lawn. We recognized him because he stood at attention in the middle of the small yard and carried a walkie-talkie. We were surprised and scared, but happy at all the attention. Publicity was important. After all, our leaders had announced that we would shut down the city. The police were actually taking us seriously, more seriously than we had taken ourselves until that moment. The situation only grew more serious as the day unfolded.

When we caught sight of our objective at 6:00 AM, the Key Bridge was already occupied by soldiers with rifles and fixed bayonets; they were standing about six feet apart all across the bridge.[9] I read later in *Newsweek* that they were three hundred soldiers from 91st Engineer Battalion. Clearly, we wouldn't be doing a sit-down there. We decided that there was more than one way to stop traffic. We lined up three cars and drove side by side down the three lanes of the expressway, at three miles per hour. Others followed our lead and the morning commute stood still. Meanwhile, another Ithaca affinity group had realized earlier that we would be met with overwhelming force, so just before dawn they rolled a junked garbage truck off a steep hill, crashing it in a pile of scrap metal on the freeway on the opposite side of the river. The soldiers kept the Key Bridge open, but no one could get to it. Our part of the plan worked.

Later, as government workers were told not to report to work and traffic was impossible, we parked our cars and handed out leaflets in Georgetown, with only the text of a poem about seizing the time. Gradually the smell of tear-gas grew stronger and we realized that the police were sweeping the streets and arresting everyone in sight. We had to get inside. We ran into Georgetown University and looked for shelter. Many doors were locked but we made it into the student center, removed our bandannas from our faces, ran to the restrooms to wash and comb, then dispersed and took our places lounging among the Georgetown students, reading magazines. When the police looked into the room, we didn't stand out as demonstrators and they passed us by. On television we saw the helicopters, tanks and clouds of tear gas at Dupont Circle where battles with rock-throwing affinity groups from New York City had taken place all day. The discipline of non-violent civil disobedience was gone.[10] We laughed and applauded when Attorney General John Mitchell actually announced on the news that demonstrators had not "taken" Washington. I remember being amazed that they had thought we had a chance! In our minds it had been a symbolic taking, like a giant guerrilla theater production with a cast of thousands. But the powers in Washington showed they were willing to be in a real war with their own citizens. We learned on TV that thousands had been arrested, including many government workers and ordinary folks. The war had come home again.

When it seemed safe to walk the streets in the late afternoon of Mayday, I returned to our meeting place, a church in Georgetown where volunteers were distributing food and first-aid. Many people had minor injuries from police clubs, teeth knocked out, gashes about the head, and cuts and sprains from running and falling. Many were sick to their stomachs from the gas. I remember being unable to eat although I had had nothing since our midnight supper the night before. Members of my affinity group were together and uninjured. Many people went home that night, but our group decided to stay. I was asked to keep the list of persons from Ithaca, and make sure they were all safe. I kept the crumpled paper with about 75 names in my jeans pocket through many subsequent adventures; it took the rest of the week before all were released from jail and accounted for.

The next day, Tuesday, May 2, 1971, the leaders of the Mayday Tribe asked everyone still in Washington and not in jail to join a march led by the Southern Christian Leadership Conference to the Justice Department. The march was for civil rights and against the war. Our affinity group joined, and I felt safer and more clear-headed under the experienced and disciplined leadership of the SCLC ministers. We sat in at the Justice Department building, filling the space between it and the next building with thousands of bodies. It felt good to march and sit-in with a large group of both black and white people. I remember that at one point, the Attorney General put his head out a window to get a look and we all shouted. It was sweet revenge when Mitchell ended up in jail for corruption a few years later. After an hour or two of the sit-in, the police began closing in. They announced that we were all under arrest; we responded by boarding the police buses with our hands behind our heads, like prisoners of war. The action was symbolic, as so much of our thinking had been.

The police bus took us to the Washington Coliseum. The DC jails were overflowing with the thousands arrested the day before in the enormous street sweeps, and we joined some thousands already in the Coliseum. We were placed into the stands, with young National Guardsmen posted every few rows. The people arrested on Monday were on the main floor already settled in, singing along with guitars, chanting, sleeping, even doing guerrilla theater. In fact, the scene in front of us looked like a movie or a rock concert; for a moment it was hard to believe we were in jail. This episode replayed in my mind with terrible irony when, two years later, thousands of Chileans were tortured and murdered in a similar coliseum during the coup that ousted Salvador Allende, including the wonderful singer and songwriter, Victor Jara.

I remember sitting down on the bench and suddenly feeling tired. I had had only a few hours of sleep in three days, and the only place to lie down was the dirty cement floor between the rows. I wondered how long we would be there. We even had to be escorted to the bathroom by a guardsman. I went with one young man who was about my height, and he actually seemed intimidated. Odd, I thought, I wonder why he would be afraid of me; he's the one with the gun. In the bathroom I looked at myself in the mirror. I was wearing dirty jeans with leather work boots and a wide leather belt. A nondescript T-shirt, a red nylon jacket, long hair reaching below my waist and a red cowboy bandanna around my neck completed the outfit. I did look tough, I decided smugly, and gloried briefly in my newfound image.

It was a long night in the Coliseum. Shortly after we arrived, the Guardsmen began removing the people from the main floor area, those who had been arrested the day before. I felt an undercurrent of fear. We didn't know where they were being taken but hoped for the best, that they would be released and would help get us out. As the sun set, some people from the Red Cross brought sandwiches, bologna and cheese on white, and began tossing them into the crowd. I managed to eat a half sandwich that someone shared with me. We were without water for a long time but eventually some was passed around.

We slept between the bleachers or sitting up. Early in the morning men and women were led into separate buses. Rumor had it that we were going to the courthouse. Our driver drove for a while, then parked our prison bus in the sun and left us for a couple of hours, packed like sardines in one side of the bus, standing room only, while he disappeared into the court house. Two women fainted so we began to scream and pound on the walls of the bus. Luckily for us, we were parked on the street where a crowd of well-dressed Washingtonians, probably all lawyers on their way to work, gathered around the bus and complained loudly about our condition. Our driver and his jailer friends returned and opened the doors in the middle of the van, allowing us to spread out and those who felt worst to sit down. I think they gave us water as well. We began to sing protest songs in two and three part harmony: *Ain't Gonna Study War No More, Solidarity Forever, Bandera Rossa, Guantanamera* and many more. We were in the van for four hours; then we were finally taken to a holding cell in the basement of the court house. There we met a movement lawyer who asked how we were, and what conditions we were held in. He told us to pay the fine and plead *nolo contendere*; they had made a deal and we would protest later. We were fingerprinted and each had a brief moment in court. Then we paid $20 and were free to go. It was the only time I was ever arrested, and I felt proud for having done it.

After our release, I went back to the church headquarters and began to look for people on the Ithaca list. By that time, those who had eluded arrest on Monday and Tuesday were mostly in jail because, while we were tying up the court, the entire crowd at a huge demonstration on the Capitol steps was arrested, including Congressmen who were speaking! I knew I had to wait until they were all released.

The Mayday demonstration had drawn 50,000 participants from around the United States. Some had been frightened away by the police tactics of revoking the camping permit and showing military force in the fog at West Potomac Park. But tens of thousands had remained in spite of their fear and participated in civil disobedience and other acts of protest to "shut down the war machine." Thirteen thousand four hundred were arrested over the course of four days, the largest mass arrests in US history. Arrayed against us were 5,100 DC Police, 1,400 DC National Guard and 10,000 Army and Marine troops from nearby bases.[11] It's a tribute to all that no one was killed or seriously wounded. And while we didn't stop the war, we certainly made citizen protest the business of the week.

Adrenaline and coffee, brewed by the gallon in the church hall, kept me going. We slept on hard floors with much commotion, only a few hours a

Protesting the war, ca. 1970s

night. Meetings and rallies continued. By Friday the last member of the Ithaca contingent was safely out of jail and had a ride, so I packed my sleeping bag into my '67 Mustang and made the seven hour drive home.

Back in Ithaca, Mayday caused an immediate change in the movement, as political study groups started spontaneously. Survivors of an historic confrontation between the citizenry and the state, we had to try to understand what had happened and why. We were still focused sharply on ending the war, but the experience of standing face-to-face with the hostile power of the government caused us to rethink the foundations of our actions. Everyone began to take the Marxists seriously. As we kept talking, I knew my life was going to change drastically. I still had one year of graduate work to do, and I had already altered my plans for political and moral reasons. Now I began to question whether I wanted to teach and do research in the university at all. The repercussions of that first week in May still echo in my life.

Notes

1. The best brief explanation I have ever found for US involvement in Vietnam was given by Noam Chomsky:

In the 1950s, US planners were deeply concerned over the possibility of successful social and economic development in North Vietnam and China, and in South Vietnam under the NLF if the "internal aggression" should succeed. This might lead to efforts to emulate their achievements elsewhere, so that Southeast Asia would no longer "fulfill its function" as a dependency of Japan and the West, serving their needs rather than its own. It was feared that ultimately Japan, an industrial power dependent on foreign markets and resources would "accommodate" to a new emerging system in Asia, becoming the industrial heartland of a region to which the US would not have privileged access. The US had fought Would War II in the Pacific to prevent Japan from creating a "co-prosperity sphere" of this sort, and was not inclined to lose World War II in the early postwar period. US policy makers were therefore committed to ensure that the rot would not spread. In this context, Vietnam attained significance far beyond its own meager importance in the world system. (*On Power and Ideology: The Managua Lectures*. Boston: South End Press, 1987, p. 15).

2. The women's movement called this view "biology is destiny."

3. President Perkins died in August, 1998 and in his obituary it is reported that Thomas Jones, the black student whose picture was identified with the takeover, is now a Cornell trustee and has established a scholarship in Perkins name. Another circle closed.

4. Dan Berrigan wrote a detailed account of the takeover of the Straight from his perspective as a faculty member. See *No Bars to Manhood* (New York: Bantam, 1971).

5. Daniel Berrigan, *To Dwell In Peace* (San Francisco: Harper and Row, 1987), 243-244.

6. Berrigan's letter to the Weather Underground probably helped persuade them to give up on terrorism. See *America is Hard to Find* (New York: Doubleday, 1972) p. 95 ff.

7. This was not a paranoid fantasy. A recent *Boston Globe* article cites CIA training of Tibetans at Cornell in the mid-sixties. See also *Rads* by Tom Bates on the large extent of FBI surveillance in Madison, WI.

8. *Life* (May 14, 1971) 30-38.

9. *Newsweek* said they were 300 soldiers from 91st Engineer Battalion of the Marines. See "The Biggest Bust," *Newsweek* (May 17, 1971) 25.

10. According to *Newsweek*, a battalion of the Tenth Marine Regiment "held" Dupont Circle. See "The Biggest Bust," *Newsweek* (May 17, 1971) 25.

11. See "The Biggest Bust," *Newsweek* (May 17, 1971) 24.

On the Barricades in Madison

Kendall Hale

1989 Madison Reunion

"WOULD YOU BELIEVE my little sister and my Mormon grandmother were both visited by the FBI looking for me after the bomb blast?" I said as I laughed with the other grownup radicals sitting around our table in the reception hall. I felt triumphant with two hundred leaders of the sixties liberation struggles at our 20-years-later college/movement reunion organized by a core of activists from the Days of Rage at the University of Wisconsin. "Frieda," I said to my former college roommate, "we are true survivors of the youth movement." My eyes roamed the room searching the faces of the 60's street fighters. Two tables away sat Helen, once a hippie-freak without a bra and tie dyed bell bottoms, now a lawyer with the American Civil Liberties Union. Next to her sat Gail, a peacenik physician with a familiar-looking, hand carved wooden peace symbol around her neck. There was crazy Peter, a long hair who carried the anarchist flag, now an environmental science teacher.

But then I thought of Robert Fasssnacht. Several hundred people fell quiet as all eyes riveted on Karl Armstrong walking to the podium. Before his wild brown hair reached his shoulders, now his balding head marked the passage of time. The weekend had been confirmation of all that was right about our battle. Everyone here had work or a lifestyle related to values expressed in our college years. But now the ex-prisoner, ex-bomber whose truck of dynamite had killed Robert Fassnacht spoke.

"I want to apologize for what I did. It was wrong."

No one moved. No one spoke. Then, a ripple of clapping grew thunderous.

August 23, 1970

What was that? It was 3a.m. on Sunday, August 23, 1970, and I sat up in bed, dazed, blinking at the glass fragments piercing the sheet. Had there been an explosion? Then I felt air flowing over my head and shoulders. There was a star shaped hole in the window over my head.

Alone, I sat there and wondered if Madison had been attacked by nuclear weapons. I was reminded of all the childhood drills in my elementary school, when we marched into the school halls and crouched, covering our heads with our hands, or hid under our desks. The inch-thick wooden desktops would protect us from radiant holocaust. Our teachers seemed to think so.

"Help me," I croaked, running outside onto Bassett Street. Dozens of other people who lived in the student ghetto were also out in the dark, walking toward the university. A girl I didn't know turned to me in the crowd. "It's got to be Sterling." We soon knew the blast had come from Sterling Hall, the building that housed the Army Math Research Center (AMRC), the focal point of the campus antiwar movement.

Sterling, bombed? All right! But I felt a mixture of horror and glee from the pit of my stomach as we approached the police cars and barricades. Lights whirred over emergency vehicles, blue white blue white blue white, and I smelled acrid smoke. I stood there in the crowd for an hour, watching, then shuffled home, hoping to find a friend.

The following day I learned that Robert Fassnacht, a physicist, had been killed in the blast. Poor guy, I thought. But everyone knew the research in those labs was funded by the military. Why was he experimenting at 3 a.m. on a Sunday night?

Getting Radical

"We walked up the rise behind the Washington Monument to the sight of thousands of people already gathered. It was at that moment the sense that this was to be a remarkable, historic event claimed us. The remainder of the day was marked by exquisite courtesy and kindness. It was like the millennial dream of peace and brotherhood which later in the day was perfectly enunciated by M.L. King's 'I have a dream' speech."

Alys Miles Hale, my mother
Columbus, Ohio (August 28, 1963)

Author Harriet Beecher Stowe and abolitionist Harriet Tubman were two of my mother's heroines, so it seemed natural that Mom and Dad would go with other civil rights activists to hear Dr Martin Luther King speak at the March on Washington. It was August, 1963. I was thirteen and thrilled to hear the details.

It was a twelve hour ride from Columbus, Ohio on the little bus with straight hard seats and folding chairs in the aisles for overflow passengers. My parents were the only white people on board. Mom had worked with a civil rights group to get a fair housing bill passed by the Ohio State Legislature. The bill made it illegal to keep blacks from buying or renting housing in white neighborhoods. Through the NAACP, they made a reservation on the Reverend Fred Shuttleworth's bus. "We must help the Negroes get jobs and better housing," Mom explained to my sisters and me: "We'll go on a school bus with food and two canteens of water."

Forty years later, in 2002, the local newspaper in West Lafayette, Indiana interviewed my parents. "It was the high point of my life. My children are sick of hearing about it. I don't cry much, but it was unbelievable," Mom told the reporter. " I don't want to say it was a religious experience, but it was so quiet as we all listened to this man. He moved everyone." Dad recounted, "When he started and said 'I have a dream,' and talked about what he hoped would happen, his dreams for America, it was moving, believe me. After serving in World War II, I'm not easily moved by events, but this was moving. You could have heard a pin drop."

Heady, inspiring stuff for a thirteen-year-old. As the child of these two, how could I not be an activist?

Four years after the March on Washington, I was watching the 6:00 news. My mother was cooking dinner while as usual, my father and I sat in front of the television, following world events and preparing to discuss them over the evening meal. On our little boxy, black and white TV, there was a big antiwar demonstration with students carrying crosses. I said to Dad "That's where I want to go to school. Look at that! All those people are against the war in Vietnam!" "Is the University of Wisconsin a good school, Dad?"

Mom and Dad wanted me to go a good college but didn't pressure me much about it. We spent a lot of time sorting through The College Handbook: " Too far away. Too expensive. Not good enough."

In the late 1960s, high school in Columbus was one grayish grind, day after day of increasing alienation and growing anticipation of leaving home for a more political, sophisticated world where I would find my place. But

I was nonetheless a teenage girl, too. Longing to be popular, I ached for the fashionable prep school clothes my classmates wore, a new matching skirt and sweater for each day of the week, and hated my liberal academic parents for denying me what I wanted. Because my father was a political science professor at Ohio State University, I begged to attend the private university high school offered to professors' children for a minimal fee. There, it was cool to express discontent by wearing protest buttons and Joan Baez-style sandals. I despaired at my parent's constant answer,

"We don't have enough money."

Feeling hollow and defeated, I stopped talking at school. Playing the violin became my sole emotional outlet, but even the music could not calm all my anger. So I routinely hit my stand with my bow, shedding horsehair all over the rug. I clung to the belief that nothing could be worse, so life would likely get better.

I sought meaning in the works of Jean-Paul Sartre. Being and nothingness and existentialism—red meat for a discontented teenager. My father gave me mind-boggling and confusing books, too. *The Communist Manifesto* and *Quotations from Chairman Mao* (although years later he argued that I gave Mao's Red Book to him).

What planet had these two parents of mine come from? After the Second World War, six months after my birth in Salt Lake City, Utah in 1950, they left Zion, their pioneer Mormon community, so Dad could attend graduate school at Columbia University where he studied political theory. It was in Shanks Village, a large housing facility of converted army barracks (sprayed pink, green or yellow) for World War II veterans attending universities in Rockland County, New York, where the seeds of my life long quest for communal living took root.

Shanks was remarkable not only for the community-run carpool, food co-op, nursery school, newspaper and theater, but for being a fully integrated community where families of all races and backgrounds lived, worked and played together. I was never surprised as a young girl when I saw people with different color skins. But Shanks life also had its pioneer hardships—the barracks weren't insulated, had no storm windows, ice had to be brought in to keep the leaky refrigerators cold, and electric fuses often blew when too many appliances were used. All laundry was hung out to dry. (Now, of course, with climate change, it's politically correct to sundry laundry.) I can vividly remember the monstrous brown space heater that had to be filled several times a day from an outdoor oil tank.

The government paid a married student ninety dollars a month, and thirty dollars for each child. No one had much, which helped foster a strong resourceful network of friends and neighbors. With money from the GI Bill, (Mom and Dad were both veterans) my mother found cheap, used furniture and household goods, and Dad used scrap boards and bricks to make bookshelves and empty orange crates from the market for end-tables by the couch and beds. An old army barrack was a great place for a kid to be—Dad drilled holes in the ceiling for a swing above my bed and Mom taught me to draw and paint on the walls. My younger sister and I took baths in the kitchen sink since there wasn't a tub and my father used a three by three by six foot closet for a study. The PhD closet. I can still hear the sound of the black typewriter keys clacking away night after night as Mom put me to bed.

When it rained, I raced outside in my underwear to splash with all the Shanks kids, or jumped into a plastic pool with ten other children in the common yard. Mom showed colored slides of this community to us until the day I came home with modern children who demanded television and video.

People tell me my Dad was the resident expert on politics and government. In 1952, when Eisenhower beat Adlai Stevenson for president, Dad said the country had survived a lot of bad and mediocre presidents and would continue to do so as long as the balance of power established by our Constitution was maintained. By the time George Bush was elected in 2000, Dad was too old to understand that we almost lost it. The balance, that is.

In 1956, Mom cried when we drove away from her beloved Shanks Village to my Dad's new university job in Austin, Texas, home state of the future burning bush.

Late Sixties

My mother was the one who bore the brunt of my restless longings and daily, violent outbursts fueled by my isolation from my peers. I knew from an early age that being a professor's wife did not fulfill her intelligence. She made it crystal clear. From the kitchen stove, jabbing a pan of sauce with a spoon, she complained to me: "I should have finished my graduate degree. If only I had become an anthropologist or historian." The sad refrain's lost career would change from year to year. But the if-only longing and bitterness remained constant.

I was so full of youthful, anxious pain, I hated seeing hers. Mom had watched her own mother experience the Mormon Church's enforcement of female inferiority and discrimination. My college educated grandmother who wrote, acted and taught school, struggled with Mormon dogma—church law made her quit teaching as soon as she married my grandpa She eventually left the Latter Day Saints, but lost her mind to depression in a culture that treated gifted women like mental patients. In the end, it was easier just to forget, and float around her neighborhood of thirty years in her lacy white nightgown like a lost dandelion puff. I know it wasn't Alzheimer's disease. It was grief, plain and simple. And the teenage me sure didn't want to end up like Mom or grandma.

As it turned out, a few Mormons, Mom and I included, needed and wanted change. But she looked stuck and I was shedding my skin. The protesters I saw on TV presented me with what felt like my very last chance: college and rebellion.

The greatest psychic in the world could not have seen how great my mother's suffering would become as America went to war with itself.

By the end of my senior year in high school, I was sure that more time in this part of the Midwest would kill me or drive me to suicide. My alienation was so intense that I refused to apply to Ohio State University, but was rejected by all the private eastern schools I longed to attend, despite a 3.7 average. Hope began when I opened the acceptance letter from the University of Wisconsin: I was in!

My excitement temporarily deflated when Dad was hired at Purdue University, which meant uprooting and re-adjusting for three months in West Lafayette, Indiana, before the fall semester of college. "God, why wasn't it somewhere in the East or at least Chicago," I muttered everyday all summer long, dreaming of the Madison campus.

After our family's move to Indiana, I met Frank, a long, lanky perennially stoned Purdue freshman who was transferring to Wisconsin for his sophomore year. He introduced me to acid rock, marijuana, and rebellion. I no longer wanted to be a virgin, so one evening sitting in the haze of pot smoke and candles at his student apartment I made a feeble attempt to seduce him by putting my head in his lap. But Frank continued to talk excitedly about the upcoming Democratic Convention in Chicago, his eyes widening at the thought of the planned protest demonstration through the streets and into the hall.

"All the big, important radicals will be there, Kendall. Everyone who's down on the system, SDS—you know, Students for A Democratic Society."

"Hey, maybe I'll go too," I exclaimed. "I wonder if my parents would let me?" Obedient Kendall, virginity intact, contemplated asking parental permission to overturn the American political system.

He laughed. "Don't ask. Just go. Come with me." I made a face, and sighed, "I've never done anything they didn't know about." "What do you mean? They don't know you are here with me, do they?" He turned over the Jimi Hendrix record.

He had a point. But it looked like Frank didn't want to sleep with me, so I left, pondering protest instead of sex, I saw myself participating in the biggest organized confrontation I could imagine. I had been on picket lines with my parents to protest segregated housing in Columbus, and the March on Washington was family legend. I thought about Chicago for days, but my father wasn't too excited about my attending and I wasn't ready to plot against him. Instead, Dad and I watched the 1968 Convention on TV. Lines of cops in black jackets and white helmets advanced in unison toward the protestors, then charged, batons battering anyone they could reach. Nightsticks swung randomly, rhythmically onto skulls, and I could lip-read their curses. Four uniforms threw a woman bodily through the air into the back of a paddy wagon. The cameras closed in as people held their hands to faces streaming with blood and tears. I screamed, "Look at those cops, Dad. Look!"

My body was shaking as I paced back and forth. "They're clubbing those people! That could be Frank! And the Students for a Democratic Society. My God, I don't believe it. Why? Why?" Angrily I asked, "This is a democracy isn't it? Why can't they protest?" I knew we had a right to voice opinion without being brutalized.

My stunned father was speechless. Walter Cronkite's urgent voice sounded as if he believed we were living in a police state.

Even though I knew next to nothing about SDS, I knew a lot about Vietnam, and the history of US involvement, and had been persuaded by my father that the war was unjust because the US had blatantly violated formal agreements. Now in Chicago, two hours away from my bedroom, young people just like myself, angry at makers of US foreign policy and the inequality in American society, were being beaten, their skulls cracked by a bunch of cops following the mayor's orders. I was furious. That night I closed my eyes but still heard and saw the sounds and images of bodies being dragged through the streets, of tear gas and screams. And a neighbor's bumper sticker, "America, Love It or Leave It".

Madison, 1968

I had not died, I had not committed suicide, and I was finally escaping to college. As my Dad and I drove into the Gary, Indiana, smog towards Madison, I was rattled by my mother's last frightened, sad expression. There were no words of support, encouragement, or even good luck, just simply her deep sorrow and lingering words:

"Once they leave, they never come back."

And she was right. I never did come back; not because I didn't want to, but because the movement, the energies of change that were shaking America, propelled me into a new world she did not, could not, and would not understand. This same movement engulfed my total being and turned me inside out, rendering me unrecognizable. It was transformation by fire.

My mother and I lost each other in America's second civil war, connected only by the go between efforts of my father, who suffered silently between us. I had no compassion for my frightened, anxious mother who directed blame at me instead of Richard Nixon for the darkness in America. Trapped in suburban despair, she criticized almost every action and decision I was to make for the next fifteen years. Consciously or unconsciously, she saw her lost opportunities embodied in me, and I had walked out the door into the larger world. I was physically free, but I was carrying some big, heavy suitcases of guilt and resentment when I arrived on campus in Madison.

Naomi. My brilliant, crazy, wild new friend. Naomi drew me out of a long, deep, depression into joy and freedom. In Madison, she drew me from our dorm room into as many parties as we could find. She wore old blue jeans and moccasins, and her thick, stringy hair hung down like a curtain as she fired up the next joint, which was frequently. Fearless, she led me in and out of the student union, up and down streets in student neighborhoods, stoned with pleasure, frolicking, laughing, dancing, rolling on floors. The University of Wisconsin was far from the cozy, cloistered college campuses back east that I thought I wanted. On the Madison campus there were two choices: You either drank beer with the fraternities and sororities or smoked dope with hippies and radicals. The healing water of beautiful Lake Mendota gave all 40,000 students our common bond: we swam, canoed, sailed, and skated. In the winter, some of us demonstrators even escaped from tear gas onto the frozen lake.

My new life was joyful, but first semester classes were a terrible disappointment, dull repetitions of high school memorization and regurgitation. Where were the encounters with authentic political and social movements, the changes that were roiling America? So I found intellectual stimulation from meeting people at parties and demonstrations. I threw myself into what I thought of as a movement that would force us to re-examine everything we had ever been taught.

One of the first pamphlets I read was *Student as Nigger*, an angry, bitter attack on the students' powerless position in the university. This was just the beginning of an onslaught of flyers, pamphlets, speakers, rallies, student union debates, and sidewalk preachers that stimulated me to insomnia night after night. After tossing for hours, I would calm myself by taking a plastic flute, a cup of warm milk, and a stack of reading material to the laundry room floor. Here I pondered these wondrous concepts until I got sleepy at sunrise. "This is the dawning of the Age of Aquarius" the lyrics sang to me with joy and hope. The new astrology promised that now was the last of the dark ages, the end of a Pisces-cycle era of war, divisions, and patriarchy. And the birth of a new era. My era.

Second semester. The University of Wisconsin teaching assistants were striking for better working conditions, smaller classes, and higher salaries. I joined the picket line, of course, proudly wearing my red and black RESIST button. This strike took me into the next one, led by black students demanding a Black Studies program. In the bitter cold February of 1969, with a copy of Eldridge Cleaver's Soul On Ice under my jean jacket, I closely watched the protesters wearing berets and leather jackets and realized that they wanted nothing to do with white people. As I watched them marching in rhythm, chanting "Black Power!" and terrifying most of the white students, I knew they were right. After all, these were real Black Panthers from Chicago. Malcolm X had come alive! Slogans about guns and armed struggle, echoed through library mall and appeared scrawled on campus buildings, sidewalks, and bathrooms. "Seize the Time!"

"On Strike, Shut It Down, On Strike, Shut It Down!" Our voices reverberated off Bascom Hill, the center of campus. Within days University President Fred Harrington called the governor, who brought in two thousand National Guardsmen armed with machine guns, automatic weapons and grenade launchers.

In response to Harrington's move, 10,000 students rallied, waving signs and chanting.

"Pick up the Gun! Seize the Time! Off the Pig! Off the Pig!",.

"All they want is black teachers and counselors and scholarships!" I yelled furiously at an armed guardsman standing in front of me. His frozen white face didn't get it.

"Power to the People! Right On!"

So new! So exhilarating! I thought everyone was saying "Right Arm!" So I punched my right fist into the air. If only the people I knew at high school could see me now, I thought, surrounded by hundreds of people like me, expressing our rage! Demanding justice! I felt a rush of high-octane energy surge through my body. I was no longer scurrying through locker-filled high school hallways, mouse-like and isolated, wearing my protest buttons that no one cared about: "Black = White," "Eugene McCarthy for President," " US Out of Vietnam," "Don't Trust Anyone Over Thirty," buttons that no one noticed. I was in my true element, with my people.

I threw my fist into the air again, "Power to the People, Right Arm!"

Apparently, the days of begging for an equal piece of the pie had ended. Nonviolence seemed impotent in the face of armed police and war. As the university and the government escalated tactics, students did too. The Black Panther Party meant business! To them political power came out of the barrel of a gun!

"Pick up the gun!"

Was that really me saying those words, a white middle class girl from Columbus? I was frightened and intrigued. Fred Hampton, a militant Black Panther, preached revolution and drew thousands when he spoke at the Memorial Student Union. At twenty-one he was a charismatic leader and an orator, so powerful the auditorium pulsated as he described how the rich and powerful at the top of the hill would be brought down by the poor at the bottom. All chairs emptied for a standing ovation that shook the hall. The same moment that thrilled us rattled the FBI. Hampton was winning allies for the Panthers' political platform among the white middle class students who responded with anger and rage at his description of racism and class exploitation. A year later, in the winter of 1969, the Chicago police riddled his apartment with 100 bullets. Fred Hampton was murdered in his sleep.

Overnight after the murder, all the young white men who considered themselves revolutionaries began wearing black leather jackets and berets. A week later as I sat in an anthropology lecture hall, one of the white SDS leaders and two black militants ran down the aisles, jumped up on the stage, knocked over the professor's desk and smashed the glass cover to a fire extinguisher. "Avenge Fred Hampton! Black Studies now!" Throwing chairs around, they disappeared as fast as they had come. I pitied the professor as he vanished backstage. Quaking and confused, I sat holding onto the arms of my chair. Those of us sympathetic to the rebellion saw looks of contempt and fear on most people's faces as they filed out into the sunlight. But that didn't stop me.

"Avenge Fred Hampton!" I screamed at a girl scurrying by.

From then on, boycotting classes became the norm. I stopped opening my textbooks to embrace the movement, but never questioned its logic. I realized that our educational system was racist and each of us was being confronted personally and challenged to take responsibility to change the university. Black people had a right to learn their own history and heritage. Acts of violence in and of themselves were meaningless, but I began to believe that violence was necessary when connected to a political or social cause.

I felt connected to the rest of the country and the world when The San Francisco Mime Troupe, the Weather Underground's Bernadine Dohrn, and a multitude of other famous radicals visited the Madison campus. I can still see the red and white face paint smeared on Abby Hoffman and Jerry Rubin, two of the seven Chicago Conspiracy defendants, as they waved to throngs of students crowded onto Library Mall. Leaders of the International Youth Party, better known as Yippies, Abbey and Jerry described Judge Julius Hoffman's courtroom and the three-ring circus confrontation that exposed the judge's "fascist soul."

"Our strategy was to give Judge Hoffman a heart attack. We gave the court system a heart attack, which was even better," Jerry grinned.

The Yippie leaders laughed at sick Amerika (with a 'k', not a 'c', Nixon's country being a fascist county) and cheered on revolution, talking to the thousands listening about their own feelings of emptiness, pain, anger, and their contempt for a corrupted political system with no answers to their questions about Vietnam or social injustice. It was thrilling.

The antiwar agitation mounted and focused on the Army Math Research Center working under a contract that the University of Wisconsin had won from the Defense Department in competition with many other universities. Army Math was suspected of research and development of chemical warfare being used in Vietnam. Our campus could be housing the same people who produced the napalm that descended on thousands of innocent villagers, burning and maiming in a fiery horror. Student groups picketed, leafleted, and performed guerrilla theater day after day to raise consciousness about the university's contract with the military. I was a dedicated protester by this time, becoming more and more horrified at the atrocities being committed against the Vietnamese, especially the use of napalm. The meaningless death of the US soldiers whom I considered both victims and agents of imperialism haunted me day and night. Thinking that this might be the direct result of a University of Wisconsin physicist's collaboration with the US Army tormented me even more.

By the end of the second semester my life had become one continuous protest from dawn till dusk, marching behind Vietnamese flags, anarchist red and black banners, and a multitude of organizational signs. "Ho, Ho, Ho Chi Minh, The NLF is Gonna Win," we cried. Many demonstrated stoned, but I got high on my friends, my own convictions and adrenaline. Night after night I fell asleep exhausted from running from Bascom Hill or Library Mall down State Street to the capitol building, choking from tear gas the cops used to break up the crowds of thousands. Pandemonium followed each police attack, making it necessary to function in affinity groups of four to five people for personal safety and to avoid being arrested by plainclothes cops.

Covering our faces with bandannas, we escaped wherever we could from the toxic gas, into bars or sliding onto icy Lake Mendota, all the while chanting, singing, stomping, clapping. Groups with names like "The Motherfuckers" and "The Stone Throwers" dodged police on their way to attack ROTC, the Land Tenure Center, AMRC and other scientific/military targets identified in leaflets distributed by organizers. As the demonstrations grew larger and larger, and the US government continued the bombings and raids in Vietnam, our tactics became more violent. The inhumanity of the death and destruction in Vietnam so gripped me that watching my fellow students smash windows on and off campus didn't bother me. What was a window? I had come to believe that this war had to be stopped at all costs including the demolition of public and private property. Nothing else mattered. I had become a student of the revolution.

There was a sexual element to the ferment too. The male heavies in SDS appeared almost like angry gods, frightening but attractive, and the women close to them intimidating. At SDS meetings, I was almost awestruck by how articulate and intelligent each speaker sounded, but never ventured a word myself. Meetings were run by men, and only the most aggressive women or those sleeping with the most powerful men were permitted control. So I settled for Jerry, a poetic, Jewish leftist with black curly hair, who sympathized but kept his distance from the heated core. A friend introduced us and immediately I wanted his calm protection. His off-campus apartment and gentle love gave me my first caring relationship with a man. Not to mention, losing my virginity on his living room floor— a huge bonus.

Being a hippie and being a radical held no contradictions for me. A wild acid-taking, music-loving, group of political young men who lived communally on one whole floor of a dormitory became my closest friends. I moved across campus to be roommates with some women who were friendly with these men. Through them, we had access to all the experimental drugs circulating on campus, and soon I had to decide whether to try LSD.

Scary LSD stories frightened me, but when my roommate, Regina, a good student whom I respected "dropped" and lived, I did too. Turning on, yes, tuning in, yes, but dropping out for me meant becoming an active revolutionary. Mind expansion and politics went together. In order to believe we could confront the power structure we needed to suspend our own limiting beliefs. Taking pure psychedelics forced me to reach deeper into my imagination and to create a reality worth living for. High, I watched the Madison state capitol dome vibrate in the heavens, trees oscillate over sidewalks, age lines on the stump of a tree squiggle and breathe, sticks turn into snakes, all of life reveal itself down to its component parts under the giant microscope of LSD.

Though I'd thrown myself into the movement with the fervor of a new initiate ("Right Arm!"), I'd gathered some perspective on what I was doing. Here is a letter I wrote to a childhood friend after my freshman year:

August 1969

Dear David:

…My first year at the University of Wisconsin was really a mind-blowing experience. I really fell for the radical rhetoric and felt at times that life wasn't worth living unless I was involved with the movement. I didn't miss one SDS meeting, and attended every rally…

I figured out that many radicals are really disturbed idealists seeking refuge from reality on college campuses. They spend all their time writing ON STRIKE SHUT IT DOWN on cement walls or throwing bricks and smashing windows. A martyr complex wanting to get busted. I know how fucked up things are, but parading around forever on a campus won't change much. Maybe we should work within the system, just a tiny bit. Maybe? ......
I'd been smoking grass all year then graduated to acid, mescaline etc. Drugs are so big in Madison, but I guess now there isn't a college anywhere that is completely straight. Just wish freaks would use them a little more cautiously. Popping any capsule for kicks is insane! My acid trip was unbelievable... It was another dimension, another reality. Thoughts rushed through my brain…truly mind expanding…although I think they weren't as profound as I imagined at the time…

Well, I'm living on Bassett perpendicular to Mifflin. The newspapers call it the "hippie ghetto." Yeah it's communal living, but at times feels like a permanent sex orgy. It's all right to sleep around if that's what you want, but all it takes is one kid with VD and wow... bad scene.

Sometimes, David, I really want to believe in the revolution and I do, but at other times I laugh at myself for being so naive. Then again, which revolution? Black, radical, drug, gay? Tell me David!

Love, Kendall

In my sophomore year my interests in history and sociology converged as I sought out leftist professors and sat with hundreds of other students absorbing the lessons of prior revolutions and radical social theory. Harvey Goldberg was the best. A strange, brilliant, almost deranged looking man with messy hair, blinking eyes, and a hooked nose, Goldberg was also a story teller and dramatist who could keep a lecture hall of almost 1,000 students perfectly quiet. Professor Goldberg collapsed time, catapulting our minds back to the lives of Rosa Luxembourg, Kropotkin and Bakunin, Lenin, Trotsky, anarchists, socialists, communists, and social democrats, then fast-forwarding us into the cyclone of the current American drama playing on the campus and streets of Madison. It was like being sucked through a worm hole into another time-space dimension, a dimension in which we were present on the battlefields of Cuba and Che Guevara, Latin America and Regis Debray, Southeast Asia and Ho Chi Minh, China and Mao Zedong. American blacks, women, workers, homosexuals linked America to the world and its oppressed peoples.

"Revolution is the way to lasting peace," I recall Goldberg saying, one hand on his forehead, the other waving his thick black glasses over our heads at the end of the lecture.

My fellow students and I considered Communism. Were they achieving that dream in Russia? Where was utopia? Certainly not here in Amerika. Not in Europe, based on what I knew about European protest movements and the eight million worker-student uprising in Paris against the system, led by French university leader "Danny the Red." Thus continued my endless search for truth, among Marxist study groups, guerrilla theater troops, student co-ops, women's consciousness raising groups, weekend rock festivals, and spontaneous travels to the West coast.

Anyone who did not believe that violent revolution and bloodshed were better than living under a corrupt social system was an idiot. Becoming a revolutionary was my only goal; the idea of becoming a professor or violinist laughable. I saw myself armed in the jungle, fighting or perhaps dying in the mountains of South America before adulthood. Money was a bourgeois evil, so even my parents were part of the enemy, and might have to die in the class struggle on behalf of the proletariat.

By now, my gentle Jewish poet had transferred to a more subdued atmosphere at Reed College and I was dating Alan, a twenty-six-year old graduate student who took me to Chicago the same October weekend the Weathermen crazies attacked downtown. The Weathermen were a group of students driven by magical fury who had given up on the white working class as an agent of revolution. They were going to do it themselves. Driving around in his VW bug we, viewed the aftermath of the Four Days of Rage. Two or three hundred students and ex-students equipped with chains, pipes and clubs had trashed cars and windows, and smashed into police lines.

The broken glass, boarded up windows and property damage reminded me of the newspaper photographs of the 1965 Watts race riots. Shaken by the destruction, I asked, "Do they use clubs and shields to fight the pigs like the Japanese students do?"

"Yeah, man," Alan grinned. "Three hundred of them did this shit. And they have guns and explosives too." His black eyes darkened. "And fuckin Mayor Daley said, shoot the looters to kill." I nodded quietly, alarmed by the rampage.

Back in Madison, I attended a meeting with a Weatherman boyfriend. Though I professed a belief in violence, the pillage of downtown Chicago was all too real. Off the pigs? No. I was not prepared to use the weapons or tactics of violent revolutionaries. The broken windows of Chicago had made it real. Too real.

The War Comes Home

In my sophomore year, I moved off campus to live with some women friends on Basset Street near the heart of the counterculture-student-hippie ghetto on Mifflin Street, better known as Miffland. Our area's city council representative was a declared socialist, and Tom Hayden also proclaimed Miffland one of America's seven liberated zones, a region of freedom. The revolution had its own cuisine; we shopped at the new Food Co-op, where I bought brown rice and ate delicious oatmeal-raisin "guerrilla cookies."

Free love bloomed, and everyone could share a bed with a different person every night. Since crabs and VD (still curable with a shot of penicillin) were the worst consequences of this pre-AIDS lifestyle, non-monogamy became an attractive option, a way for me to avoid a committed relationship and eventually experiment with bisexuality.

In the spring of 1969, Miffland was denied a block party permit by the conservative mayor, William Dyke, or Bull Dyke, as the male movement heavies called him. Block parties were held every spring in different neighborhoods, but the mayor refused to grant us a permit . Defiant and angry, we held the Miffland block party anyway. Anticipating a confrontation of some kind, organizers plastered posters all over Madison, bands were brought in, and we all prepared to "Bring the War Home," literally a block from my doorstep.

On a brilliant green, spring day, hundreds gathered on the corner of Mifflin and Basset Streets to celebrate youth and flower power, an affirmation of our own culture of peace, music, and dance. All was well for the first few hours, and then the police marched in with a pepper fogger. This new piece of equipment was capable of shooting tear gas the distance of a city block. The city fathers were out to crush and destroy all that we stood for, whether in Vietnam, the black ghettos, or on Mifflin Street, so I began dancing to the Rolling Stones "Street Fighting Man" blasting from a porch stereo. In front of me, a pink and white paper-mache pig's head waving wildly on a stick. Whomp! When the tear gas exploded, my eyes burned red, first with blood, then with tears. Nearby friends vanished into the thick smog now enveloping our neighborhood. Screaming and choking, I lowered myself to street level coming face to face with a young man bleeding from his head. He was being attacked by a policeman.

"Oh my God, it's the Gestapo! They're killing us," I screamed and reached to help him. But I slipped sideways into the gutter as the cop's club swung up and down. "Run," the boy grunted, "before they get you too." So I ran in the direction of the university.

By the end of the afternoon, a new battle line had been drawn, and Amerika was no longer my country. I'd sneaked home from campus. Back on my front porch, I saw flames in front of the food coop and heard Jimi Hendrix's anguished version of the "Star Spangled Banner" playing sadly over the trees in blossom. Huddled together, my friends and I cried. We cried at the hatred and horror that we had thought our flower power would heal. The Age of Aquarius was really a bad moon rising, as the

Credence Clearwater Revival band had predicted. A little later I wrote an anti-anthem:

> Amerika, Amerika where are your specious skies?
>
> But clouded with pollution, tarnished black with lies
>
> Purple majesty and amber grain waves
>
> Created by workers, created by slaves
>
> Broad stripes and bright stars fly low on the mast...

Kendall 1969, 19 years old

In Miffland, the war came home more than once. This was about force and economics. A second near-blood-bath was the battle between the C.C. Riders biker gang and rent strikers who were protesting substandard housing. Recruited by a slumlord, the motorcycle thugs confronted young students who called themselves the Madison Tenants Union and had occupied several houses on one block of Mifflin Street. I did not know that a group of Mifflander men had stockpiled guns in preparation. Early one morning, the C.C. Riders showed up in the neighborhood and were met by hundreds of young people waving North Vietnamese flags, shotguns, and garden tools. I heard the shouting and ran joyfully to join the throng, completely unaware that my comrades in the houses were prepared to shoot if necessary. The bikers stared in disbelief, then sped away to the sound of our cheers.

In the fall of 1969, I went to Washington, DC. Thousands of antiwar protesters assembled with bandannas over our faces, while huge helicopters swept over our heads. Gradually the smell of tear-gas filled the air, and the police began sweeping the streets arresting everyone in sight. An army tank rolled toward the intersection. Pop! Pop! Canisters blew up in circles in front of the Justice Department. I knew that hundreds of students and leftists had already been arrested, and thousands had camped out at the Washington Monument, in the largest national mobilization then seen against the war. My anger at the US government was at an all-time high, my studies at an all time low.

Antiwar violence was now an everyday occurrence in Madison. In May 1970, Nixon invaded Cambodia, resuming the bombing of North Vietnam. In response, students all over the country ransacked and burned ROTC buildings and stepped up a wave of demonstrations, boycotts, and strikes.

When I learned that the National Guard had killed four students at Kent State and two at Jackson State I became convinced that it was time to "smash Army Math" at any cost. One afternoon, 2,800 of us battled 250 local and county Madison police knowing we might be shot or killed. I imagined my body returning to my mother and father wrapped in a Viet Cong flag. Part of me envied the dead as I hurled myself onto the barricades.

As Amerika deteriorated, I hoped my Garden of Eden might exist in Cuba. The Venceremos Brigade in Madison had started recruiting and sending students sympathetic to the Cuban revolution to cut sugar cane and see socialism first hand. I began reading about the history of pre-Revolutionary Cuba, a country strangling under US economic control. Filled with facts and images of poverty, crime, and illiteracy, I eagerly listened to details about the current conditions from wide-eyed, young North American brigadistas with enthusiastic stories of the Cubans' support for their new government.

Once a vacation land for tourists, gamblers, and prostitutes, it now sounded like the vanguard of world revolution, with free medical care, free universities, no starvation, no commercial billboards, and the highest literacy rate in Latin America. Batista was the evil dictator, not Fidel Castro. This hairy, cigar-smoking man had been portrayed as our dreaded enemy by both the government and the media, but Castro became a hero of third world liberation. Che Guevara's image now hung on every radical's wall, looking bold and handsome, a symbol of freedom for our sisters and brothers suffering under US imperialism. When I attended the International Youth Festival in Cuba nine years later, in 1978, social conditions appeared so superior, I became convinced that the government had created a new society and a new socialist human being. The artistic billboards promoted public health, and the people I saw and spoke with looked healthy and happy. Almost twenty years later, Che became my son's middle name. Thirty years later, the CIA confessed to having murdered and buried our hero under an airport runway in Bolivia.

Love is a Gun

By the end of my sophomore year in 1970, I saw no point in the university as an institution, with its thousands of students and distant, all male teaching hierarchy. My only goal was to organize "The People" to overthrow capitalism. Confusion about myself as a woman emerged and deepened as I participated in women's meetings, analyzing sexism and its pervasive and insidious role in society, the university, and the movement. As an activist I had to look at my own oppression, a long, painful process that lasted well into my forties. Relationships with men and lovers got angrier and more distant as I found myself deeper in the women's movement. I gravitated toward socialist-feminist theory and a collective of women, most of whom were graduating and looking for a way to help liberate women from chauvinist husbands and boyfriends. It was imperative we participate as equals in the future party and new society. Romantic love was now impossible. All women were members of a "Fourth World" that limited their personal and economic freedom. Robin Morgan's book, Sisterhood Is Powerful, and our battle cry "Free Our Sisters, Free Ourselves" united young women around the country.

Once, during a rare moment while I was cleaning my apartment, my then-boyfriend Alan walked in with a smile on his face. "Hi, Kendall," he grinned cheerfully. Without looking up, I furiously yanked the vacuum cleaner across the tattered rug rattling dust in his face.

"Men are the enemy, Alan! Women have been exploited for centuries by you guys," I roared at him over the noisy machine.

"Uhh, would you like to go for a walk or for a sandwich?" he calmly asked.

"No, Alan. You exploited me! You're no better than the rest! It's over!" I continued without looking up, concentrating on the floor.

"You mean that's it?" He seemed shaken.

"Yes. I don't want to see you anymore. Go struggle with your sexism." I shot visual darts at him over the vacuum handle.

"OK, Kendall." He turned slowly and closed the front door. I never saw him again. He had once told me he'd never touched anyone as beautiful as me. But at that moment, being a sister in the struggle was all that mattered.

A splinter group from the Weathermen was recruiting members from Madison to form political collectives in Milwaukee and Racine to work in factories with the industrial proletariat, as defined in Marxist-Leninist theory. I remember visiting the homes of these young radicals, now working as members of trade unions, and publishing radical grassroots newspapers. Many were red diaper babies, children of American Communist party members (CPUSA), who believed they were picking up where the party had failed after the Stalin era and its descent into revisionism.

Awestruck by their courage and integrity, I told myself "This is the next step, Kendall." But I noticed that the women were, again, in fairly serious monogamous relationships. Part of me was jealous and wanted to be comfortable and cozy with a man and a political party that had the right answers, but I also questioned their labeling of feminism and homosexuality as "bourgeois decadency." I had plenty of anger to go around, as I wrote to my parents in 1970:

Dear Mom and Dad: I have become one of the people you warned me about. The military industrial complex – the Bank of America, Standard Oil, IBM, Mobil now hold 95% of the world's wealth and profit from the rape of the Third World by Nixon and the warmongers. Here in Wisconsin, monkeys in the zoo are allotted 58 cents per meal and welfare mothers are expected to live on 16 cents per meal!!!! The only solution is revolution. Armed revolution. Unfortunately, since you are members of the middle class and the silent majority, our People's Army will have to fight any-one who stands in our way. This means I could be face to face with you and have no choice but to shoot. I will not be coming home this summer. Kendall, DARE TO STRUGGLE, DARE TO WIN!

It was unthinkable to go home in the summer of 1970 to bourgeois mid-dle-class Indiana, so I stayed in Madison. And that summer, my political awareness found a comfortable alignment with my personal beliefs as an emergent feminist. Living in Miffland, I joined a political guerrilla the-ater troop of about ten students that performed for people in Madison and nearby towns. Our bold, adventurous surprise appearances in shop-ping malls, parks and beaches attracted crowds with drums and music. With simple props and ten minute skits we stimulated heated conversa-tions about racism, sexism, and imperialism. Our women's liberation skit featured a female character who became a wind-up mechanical puppet controlled by her boyfriend. The anti-imperialist skit featured Uncle Sam as an evil character who propped up dictatorships in South America.

We drove all over in a bumpy VW van with no air conditioning, and for three months I felt calm, focused, creative, and relaxed with my family of political friends. In this setting, women were not only respected, but were in the leadership. Men were sensitive and occasional lovers.

Enchanted by the success of our collective creativity, by midsummer I had decided to drop out of college, leave Madison with a women's collec-tive, and stop shaving my legs, a radical act in 1970. I was most comfortable expressing myself in an all-female setting, where I felt valued for who I was, not overrun, dominated, or awed by arrogant male political heavies. They no longer dazzled me and their sexism pushed me to a political belief that women needed to live and work separately from men. I believed I had no positive female role models. The only women I admired or respected were revolutionaries. Who could I turn to other than my sisters in struggle? My parents were relieved to hear I was doing theatre, but dropping out was the end of the world. Worse than wearing the same old blue jeans for four years.

Six of us, all under the age of 24, decided to form a collective to organize working class women to take control of their lives. A clear, easy goal. Four had graduated from the university and two of us were dropping out. We divided into three groups, each picking a different part of the United States to visit and observe the political /social scene. We agreed to return to Madison later in the fall with a report from each group, and determine where to sink new roots and build a working class women's movement. I grabbed Miriam, a tough minded, spunky graduate , and we decided to go West.

To celebrate my decision I went to a local Woodstock. A county farmer sympathetic to the student movement offered his land for a rock festival that drew hundreds of young people, and our guerrilla theater troupe intended to perform. But huge amounts of LSD were dumped into a bottle of wine circulating through the crowd, creating one collective acid trip that included the police. Rows of people stood facing the music while I danced ecstatically, weaving in and out, inviting them to follow.

It was here that I freaked out and charged past the security guards to the stage. I sat on a piano bench transfixed by the musician's long black fingers, then jumped to the ground and ran into the woods, screaming, sliding down slope into a streambed. Floating away, I felt joyous at leaving this world. Covered in soft, oozing mud becoming weaker and weaker I almost lost consciousness—until I got hungry. Thank God for survival instincts! I needed food. You can't live on your own in the woods a voice told me. I screamed.

"Help, won't somebody help me?" And the tribe heard. A few tripped out kids carried me up the slope to a police car. Can you believe they put me in the enemy's hands. The pigs! Or as the Beatles called them, the blue meanies. Especially when I was out of body!

"Take her to a hospital," some mature, hairy, naked freak yelled. But the cop was so stoned, he drove his squad car off the road into the forest.

At this point, my consciousness quit hovering and reentered my body, and I jumped out of the car. As I ran through trees toward the sound of the music, I stopped to lean on a tree trunk. Spontaneously the sound OM welled up in my throat and out of my mouth. I had never heard or read about this word, about its use as a meditative chant by wisdom traditions that believe it to be the sound of the primordial universe. But I uttered it, mystically and magically, once, twice, and again. OM, OM, OM.

Then I turned to look behind me, and there stood a boy with a copy of *The Little Prince* by Antoine de Saint-Exupery. He looked into my eyes, handed me the book, and while wrapping a blanket over my shivering body said, "You are my little prince." Momentarily I felt protected, back on earth, ready to re-enter, leaving the mystical search for my lost vision for another time. Like until I was fifty.

"Thank you," I whispered, grateful for his tender contact. Moments later he disappeared.

It had been the happiest summer of my life. Then on August 24, 1970 and anonymous phone call came in the middle of the night to Madison police headquarters.

Listen Pigs, and listen good. There is a bomb that is going off in Army Math in five minutes. Clear the building. Warn the hospital. This is no bullshit man.

And then the bomb blast shattered the window over my head.

The bombing of the Army Math Research Center split my memory of college into before and after, forever. Before the explosion of 1,700 pounds of nitrogen fertilizer soaked with about 100 gallons of fuel oil, and after. It reverberated around the country, giving Nixon's White House, J. Edgar Hoover's FBI, and John Mitchell's Justice Department the excuse to wage all-out war against the Left. An innocent physicist had been killed.

A week later our guerrilla theater troop spoke on the student union terrace. Our topic was the bombing and Robert Fassnacht's death.

"No, he didn't deserve to die. There was a phone call to the cops. It was their fault for not evacuating him," my friends and I told stone-faced physicists sitting on the union terrace. "It was an accident," we pleaded, passing around a leaflet explaining that Army Math had been an antiwar target for several years.

"SssssssssSSSSSSSSSSSSSS."

The hisses rose, as we quietly retreated. For the first time in my life I felt myself the object of complete contempt. Radicals were now completely ostracized. My summer was transformed into another tortuous debate within myself about violence, war, and death, one that drove me west, looking for meaning, hope and the path to my dream of peace.

Search for the Working Class

My women's collective sister, Miriam, and I hitchhiked across the country with strangers, mostly men who were fascinated to meet real live hippie chicks and to listen in what must have been fascination and disbelief as we talked to them with the revolutionary fever of the guerrilla theater troop.

Each driver who motioned us into the car became a potential convert to our cause, a prisoner trapped in his own vehicle with two socialist women. Some might have been thinking about free love, but Miriam and I were all politics. We left Madison in the fall, where it was still warm enough to stand on the corner with our thumbs out, and headed straight into the freezing winter of South Dakota. To this day I am thankful for those honest, hardworking truck drivers who sheltered us from the cold, dangerous highways, driving us hundreds of miles, letting us sleep in and under their trucks, sometimes buying us food and listening to our story. Rarely did they proposition us; they never harmed us but simply wanted company on their lonely long distance drives. We didn't think that two young women on the road needed protection. We believed we were invincible because we were revolutionary and righteous.

As we approached Berkeley, my heart thumped wildly. I knew California was a landscape for seekers, a mixture of head shops, crash pads, be-ins, demonstrations, concerts, free clinics, and street theater, a refuge for alienated hippies, Yippies, radicals, draft dodgers, anyone wanting to break with tradition or live on the fringes. My kind of town. We spent the next few weeks immersed in the counterculture, enjoying each other's company and reveling in a new world of bizarre freaks from all over the country. I had a little money from my parents and from a job in the student union cafeteria, but counted primarily on free rides, free shelter in churches, parks or communes, and free food wherever I could find it. This 24-hour-a day street festival was home to the Diggers, Mario Savio and the Free Speech Movement, Huey Newton and the Black Panthers, Joan Baez, The San Francisco Mime Troupe, flower children, and Route 1, overlooking the most spectacular ocean cliffs in America. Particularly spectacular if the viewer was stoned. San Francisco won my heart, but Miriam felt overwhelmed.

Our next destinations were Eugene and Portland, Oregon, where we visited various political collectives. Since Portland had not yet been infiltrated by radical fringe groups, Miriam argued it would be an easier city to organize without the competition, so we persuaded the other collective members to move there.

In the midst of waterfalls, ocean, and mountains, the six of us hung out with each other and other local activists, traveled around Oregon, and participated in a May Day antiwar demonstration in solidarity with student protestors who shut down Washington DC for a whole day. I joined a rock band, began playing electric violin and composing music. I met a lesbian couple who lived in the same house with a heterosexual couple and learned they were just as normal.

Each day I woke up wondering how all the theory we learned in Madison applied to the real world. Slowly I experienced the sufferings of real life. I worked briefly in a nursing home, but was fired for handing out the local radical newspaper and inciting the patients. Then, Tracy, a sixteen-year-old runaway from California, moved into our living room. Next, our house was broken into and my violin was stolen. And then I was raped.

Three black men had picked me up hitchhiking to a bookstore. Completely naïve and flattered by their offer to smoke a little weed, I naively believed they were fellow militants. Before I realized what was happening, we arrived at a middle-class house in the Portland suburbs, with photographs of smiling white people on the mantle. After a few puffs on a joint, I expected a discussion to follow, as often happened with university men. Stunned when they asked me to remove my clothes and dance on the coffee table for them, my instinct told me to get out quick. For the last two years on campus, I had partied with men and never been treated like a sex object. I didn't even know sex was all they had in mind.

"I didn't come here to parade around in front of you," I said fiercely folding my hands. " I believed exactly what you said. I came here to smoke and rap "

One of the men sitting close to me on the couch raised his eyebrows. "Well now, let's rap for awhile. What's your trip, baby? Alcohol, drugs, the revolution? Now, me, I'm an athlete. Football is my game."

"What do you think of the Black Panthers," I butted in.

"Well," he rolled his eyes. " I can dig them. Huey and Eldridge, they're doing a fine job with their breakfast program and all. What do you think?" He swung his right leg over my right thigh. I quickly lifted it back over his left leg. "I have some friends in Wisconsin who have a breakfast program like the Panthers. They've also started a bookstore and a newspaper."

The man leaned over and shoved his hand down the front of my tee shirt, squeezing my breast and pulling at my nipple.

"Stop it!" I felt like striking him hard and fast and bolting outside. Instead, stood up, side stepped the man on the couch and calmly walked to the front door. A man in dark glasses clapped his hands. "Let's get this show on the road." Quickly I was overpowered and dragged upstairs. My heartbeat tripled. I knew they were going to kill me. I was raped three times, one after the other. Breathing rapidly, each man promised, "I'll give you the best you ever had it, baby," fantasizing a scream of ecstasy or at least a moan of pleasure from my lips. Realizing it was futile to resist, I prayed silently that passivity would save me from physical violence, but expected a punch, a knife, then, the trickle of blood over my rib cage. I felt like Mia Farrow in the Exorcist, clawed by the devil.

"Stop, stop, stop, it hurts," but the third man continued his harsh grind, pinning my head to the floor crushing my spine. Dazed, I dressed quickly as the three rapists joked, drank another beer and drove me back to town. In the middle of Portland I got out of the car, numb, feeling lucky to be alive, not knowing in what direction to run.

I didn't report the rapes because, illogically, I was afraid the rapists would retaliate. Passivity had saved my life once and maybe it would again. When I told the women I lived with and shared my story with a larger community of women, no one had clear advice. Since this was before rape crisis centers and counseling existed, it felt easier to try to forget it happened than to ask the male authorities for help. When men became the enemy, I'd thrown my birth control pills out with my razor blades. Pills had dangerous side effects anyway. Me pregnant? No way.

In 1971, violence against women was blamed on women's bad behavior. On the phone from Indiana, my mother expressed anger at me for getting into a car with strange men.

"Let me talk to Dad—Dad….Dad, I've been raped." No comment…. Silence.

"Dad, are you there?" I heard a muffled cough.

I knew rape was a criminal offense, but our feminist communities' confusion coupled with my parents' lack of empathy or assistance left me unable to act. My hatred of these men did not translate to all men or all blacks, though for weeks I crossed the street every time I saw someone of the male gender approaching.

Twenty years later, I finally asked a therapist why I still feared being alone in empty houses and jumped when a cat walked behind my chair. "Were you ever sexually abused? She watched my face closely. "No, not that I remember…well, there was that assault in Portland, but that's all," I shrugged, twirling my glasses, tapping my finger.

Shortly after my rape, I met with a contingent of Vietnamese women representatives from the National Liberation Front in Vancouver, Canada. I touched their hands and gave them flowers, trying to comprehend how these tiny, delicate people were considered our government's enemy. I had seen pictures of women guerrillas armed in the rice fields defending their children and homes. Knowing how much these women had suffered, made the violence of my rape seemed small in comparison. As tears streamed down my face, all I could feel was a tremendous sense of shame for Amerika.

I could hardly believe their warmth and acceptance of us, as human beings first, and Americans second. When I later visited Cuba and Nicaragua, I experienced first hand how many people still reached out to embrace the people who came from a country considered an enemy.

Our Portland collective fell apart and with it our dream of organizing women to take control of their lives. Our experiment crashed the limits of theory and the generation gap finally caught up with us. Floundering and confused, we were all suffering from different versions of post-traumatic stress syndrome. Big ideas need money, a mission statement, structure, and the women leaders over thirty, red baited out of history during the McCarthy era. We needed Mother Jones, (a celebrated agitator and organizer) but she died in 1930. I watched my sisters whom I looked to for strength fall into depression and despair, leaving us with no focus, organization, or sense of direction.

My father had been sending me money, but I knew I had to make an individual decision. One of us went to nursing school and one went back to New York where she had grown up. Returning to the university looked like the only option for me. It felt like a major defeat. Was there no place in the world for me, or my beliefs? From the west coast, Madison looked like home in my frenzy to ground into some kind of reality that I knew and understood.

Once I decided to leave for Madison, I met Sarah, one of our collective members in San Francisco, who was planning a visit back home to Milwaukee. Much of our common philosophy had stemmed from the Yippies, who advocated ripping off the system whenever possible. In the Bay area, Sarah had managed to buy some stolen plane tickets for $10 a piece. It took no convincing to get me to travel by air rather than by thumb. We took on false names, feeling exhilarated as we boarded a plane for the Midwest. But we were discovered before takeoff. Perhaps we looked like victims – young, innocent, middle class girls – because our story of how we bought tickets from a stranger in Berkeley, got us off the hook with no charges. We were only disappointed that we had to hitchhike. Abby Hoffman's Steal This Book convinced us we deserved life for free. After all, the system was corrupt and we were working for the good of humanity.

Sarah went back to Portland. A week later I left with runaway Tracy, her German shepherd, and Ryan, my newest love, an irresistible college dropout mechanic. He wanted to visit family and friends in New York. The three of us decided to pass through Salt Lake City, my Mormon birthplace. Granny Otelia Hale was taken by surprise when I called asking for shelter on my way back to Wisconsin. I don't think I had seen or spoken with her for years, but she didn't hesitate. Orphaned at twelve and raised by relatives, she had run away from Kansas to Oakley, Idaho, where she joined the Mormon Church. My adventure must have resonated with her spirit of escape.

"Of course you can stay here, Kendall," Granny said sweetly from her old black dial phone. "But tell me one thing. Why is the FBI looking for you?"

After we arrived, she was relieved to know that Ryan was a doctor's son. That seemed to make everything all right, despite the FBI telling her I was an Army Math bombing suspect. Other relatives, including my younger sister, received visits by agents. I found this humorous, (my uncle worked for the FBI) exhilarating (Wow, Kendall Hale, wanted by the FBI) and a teeny bit frightening, knowing that I was innocent of any connection to the bombing, but incredulous that the government had these resources and would waste them on a "little" person like myself. I didn't make the connection that my sudden disappearance from Madison might have looked suspicious.

"Granny", I said, "I didn't do it. Honest. But I was a protester."

She sat quietly, her sharp blue eyes focused on her arthritic gnarled hands quilting tiny stitches on an orange and green flower. She had sewn hundreds of quilts for all her children and grandchildren.

"Granny, do you remember when you told me all Hales are related? Granny Otelia and the Mormons loved genealogy.

"Yes, I do."

"Well then, I am a descendant of Nathan Hale, famous American revolutionary. The one who said, "I only regret I have but one life to give to my country."

Her thick, curly, white, head of hair lifted for one second. "Well then." Pause. "I believe you."

The next morning, Granny called one of her sons, who politely took us out to the highway with only one question.

"Are you sure this is what you want to do?" my uncle asked as we stuck out our thumbs like old pros. Nodding yes, we faced the Midwest, riding with the lonely or curious, never doubting our security. When Ryan decided to take a shorter route to New York, I choked back my fear and sorrow. I had hoped he had fallen in love with me. I needed to be strong for runaway Tracy now that I was the older responsible party. Waving good-by to Ryan as he split to the east, with a piece of my heart, I knew he was gone forever. But rides got easier without him though maybe a little riskier and much sadder.

Arriving safely in Madison, after nine months of searching for the working class, I failed to see that I had been in their care all along. At least the male half. Decades later I realized that while our society fought wars abroad, American truckers held us together delivering capitalist goods and sheltering young radicals who dreamed of leading them, the vanguard of the revolution, into a future insurrection. At this time of my life, irony escaped me.

From 1971-1973 the war and the movement were winding down. I spent my last two years of college recovering from the journey of the previous three years. So many of my friends had left or dropped out or transferred away that I returned to a void. I studied for the first time since high school, but it all felt empty. I am still amazed at how little was required of me as a history major, in terms of writing or analysis. Studying the past helped ground me, but offered no answers or methodology to evaluate the turmoil of the student uprising or the critical observations and questions confronting me. The most relevant study group was led by a graduate student who was reading all three volumes of Marx's *Das Kapital*. Once my father's most respected political philosopher and now one of mine, Marx gave me answers I had not found in Portland. The Army Math bombing had eliminated and obliterated everything: the movement, my friends, actions in the streets. My new and closest companion, Frieda, became my roommate at Nottingham Co-op, an old fraternity converted into cooperative student housing where everyone shared cooking and cleaning jobs, and a spirit of togetherness. I continued to have affairs with various men, and finally one with a woman, which seemed perfectly natural after living in a lesbian-feminist community in Portland. But Frieda. Well, I needed Frieda's sharpness and her bag of tricks—astrology, tarot, yoga—sprinkled lightly with political theory because my life was as frayed as the end of my blue jeans. Marx or no Marx.

The most radical personal action I took during those two years was choosing to spend two nights in jail rather than pay a $25 fine when my puppy escaped from the coop and trespassed in a park. Ironically, it was the only jail sentence I ever received. I marched in with a copy of *Das Kapital* and read for two days, occasionally exchanging conversation with a local hooker.

My next intellectual marriage was to Chairman Mao. In 1973, graduate students returning from China confirmed the new truth I had found reading William Hinton's *Fanshen*. I wrote a term paper about how Communism and the collective agricultural communes in the new China had liberated women, puzzled over Mao's quotations, and longed to join

Protesting the war, ca. 1970s

the Red Guard. To Serve the People. I can still see the poster of the rosy cheeked shipyard worker feeding my dreams of an egalitarian worker-run state. At that time no one knew about the brutality of the Cultural Revolution, about the thousands of intellectuals in forced labor and artists imprisoned and humiliated.

My graduation with a degree in history was anti-climatic. I was completely unprepared for a career and at sea about my future. With faith in the dialectical thinking of the Chinese, I threw coins with the *I Ching* (an ancient divination system) and decided to follow Frieda to New York City, hoping for friendship, support, and direction from her.

On the way East, I visited Indiana, much to my mother's relief. She called me her prodigal daughter, returning from sin and misguidance. I welcomed her love and appreciation, but knew that the barriers had not been overcome. We quickly fell into our old fights and patterns of blame and disrespect.

"But what will you do in New York City? And who is Frieda? Shouldn't you think about graduate school?" She looked despairingly at my five year old jeans. My only pair.

"I'll probably work for Liberation News Service, Mom. Don't worry, Frieda's a New Yorker. She has an apartment for us and everything."

"Well, it looks like everything and nothing to me, Kendall."

I grabbed an old photograph off the mantle, one that had intrigued me only because Mom treasured it so. It was my great grandmother Hannah Hall Jacobsen, with her three children, one of them my mother's mother, Eunice, standing in their 19th century clothing each holding a musical instrument.

"Mom, Hannah didn't listen to her mother. No, she ran away from Sweden— from wealth and status to follow her dream across the ocean. To be a Mormon!" I placed the black and white picture before her on the table. "God, Mom. And what about Annie Smith Miles? The grandmother who lived through the last Indian war in Utah. You're so proud of them!

Before she could answer, I raced to the back bedroom, changed outfits and sprinted angrily out the front door in shorts and jogging shoes.

Mom was still looking for a daughter who wanted marriage and a safe, respectable, professional career. I was still looking for the next radical step. Without a guerilla war to fight for, living my life for the revolution was, well, to be blunt, mind boggling. The war in Vietnam was over, yet I burned with the fever of an anti-war protester without a cause. Who was my enemy now?

A few days later I hitchhiked to New York City with a couple of young guys from Purdue University. The rides went smoothly until just outside Manhattan when the driver suddenly pulled a gun on Mike, with whom he was engaged in friendly conversation.

"I know you're going to rob me. Get out," he ordered waving a pistol at him. From the back, I could see the weapon through the bucket seats. So he is the new enemy? What a ridiculous way to die, I thought, moments before he dumped the three of us on the side of the highway.

Voluntary Exile

Beatrice Nava

I STEPPED ONTO the tarmac at Mexico City's Benito Juárez International Airport, walked past four rifle-bearing soldiers, gritted my teeth, and stifled the irony. It was early evening of January 4, 1970, and I was running away from my own military. Later I rationalized that these men in uniform didn't bear my country's insignia; did their dirty work on their own soil, and weren't breathing down my sons' necks. But at that moment, I was concentrating on how to get myself to Cuernavaca. By long distance phone I'd signed up for a series of seminars beginning there the next morning. I was looking for like-minded dissidents. I had no idea that my projected four months in the City of Eternal Spring would extend to 14 years "under the volcano."

I was a sixties mother, of two sons and two daughters. They were now all in college or recently graduated. We all opposed the Vietnam War, and occasionally were on protest lines together. Their father and I were recently divorced; after 20 some years, I was on my own. To a large extent, so were the children. After Margaret, the youngest, graduated from Baldwin, a girls' preparatory school on Philadelphia's Main Line, where I taught history, I left that "safe" position and went to York, Pennsylvania, to become a reporter and editor for *The Gazette and Daily*. *The Gazette* was then the only daily paper in the United States opposed to the Vietnam War. I was the staffer who pulled from the Associated Press wires the results of the first draft lottery, on December 1, 1969. The birthdays of my sons Ed and Jim came up numbers seven and nine.

I knew Ed wouldn't go. He'd taken out Canadian landed immigrant papers just in case. But Jim, three years Ed's junior, and I had been burning the telephone lines trying to think of a legitimate way for him to stay out.

Still an undergraduate at the University of Wisconsin, in Madison, he was giving a passing thought to enlisting for noncombatant service. I couldn't bear the idea that a son of mine might play any part in this war that I considered immoral, unjust, and illegal.

When U.S. escalation began, I was a fairly conventional suburban wife and mother, who'd gone back to school and back to work—teaching this time so I would have a schedule similar to that of my children. Along that path, I got a master's degree in education, as a teacher of social studies, from the University of Pennsylvania, and a master of arts in history from my undergraduate Alma Mater, Bryn Mawr. While researching the congressional career of Francis E. Walter, subject of my history thesis, I attended a meeting on civil rights, of particular interest because above and beyond his political longevity and his stint as chairman of the House Committee on Un-American Activities, Walter had achieved fame—and infamy—in that arena throughout his 29 years in office. At the meeting, a woman sitting across from me asked me: "Where do you stand on Vietnam?"

"I don't know enough to say," I answered.

I could feel myself shrivel when she shot back: "You should."

As a teacher of history at Baldwin, a high-caliber preparatory school adjacent to Bryn Mawr, I had access to excellent libraries. I immediately began reading all I could about the Indochinese quagmire. I read books by international experts: Bernard Fall, Frances Fitzgerald, Wilfred Burchett. I dug into *Ramparts*, *The Nation*, *The Guardian*, *I.F. Stone's Weekly*, *The New Yorker*, eventually *Viet Report*. I found the alternative press far more informative than the presumably more objective, established media, which relied heavily, often exclusively, on government releases. I still credit that immersion with rounding out my academic studies. Indeed, though my post-graduate work concentrated on the history of the United States, I think of Douglas Dowd and comparable iconoclasts writing in *The Nation* as having caused me to realize that the interventionist US policy in Indochina was not an aberration, but, rather, a logical extension of a pattern established early on. (It was much later that I came across Howard Zinn's citation of the State Department's listing, presented to a Senate committee in 1962, of "103 interventions in the affairs of other countries between 1798 and 1945."[1])

I went to countless teach-ins, on the Bryn Mawr and Haverford campuses and at the University of Pennsylvania. I joined the Women's International League for Peace and Freedom and supported Women Strike for Peace. My opposition to US meddling paralleled military escalation (and long preceded my sons' vulnerability to the draft). I felt the US had no right butting into an essentially nationalistic struggle that had turned into a civil war. I was outraged—and ashamed—when I saw the news photo of a Vietnamese mother holding her child, on fire from US-supplied napalm. And I've never forgotten the picture of an officer shooting point blank at a Vietnamese prisoner, or a quotation of the day in *The New York Times,* "It became necessary to destroy the town to save it." It wasn't long before I couldn't understand why everyone wasn't out on the street protesting: Not in my name, not with my tax dollars.

The political began turning personal for me the summer of 1967. Responding to an ad in *The New York Review of Books*, I committed to teach at a "summer enrichment program" at the Booker T. Washington High School (BTW), in Columbia, South Carolina. Ostensibly we summer volunteers were to prepare junior high school youngsters to make the transition to integrated high schools. Margaret, the only one of my children then still home-based, came with me, becoming the "token white" in the oldest group.

Many parents of Margaret's classmates and of my students were regularly employed at nearby Fort Jackson, a send off point for soldiers bound for Vietnam. We were surprised to find that although the kids were quite aware of the well known racism of South Carolina legislators, they fully supported their militarism—and took a dim view of Margaret's and my admiration for Martin Luther King, Jr., and of our outspoken opposition to the war.

Occasionally at night Margaret and I went to a coffee house frequented by young GIs about to be shipped to Vietnam. I was appalled that they knew virtually nothing about the "enemy" they were being trained to battle. They could not differentiate between the guerrilla-type South Vietnamese "Vietcong" and the North Vietnamese soldiers, whose orders came from Hanoi. Nor could they define communism, though they all said "We have to defeat it."

One afternoon Margaret and I drove through Fort Jackson. From the car window we saw a sergeant drilling a group of what looked like a high school team taking a coach's orders. He bellowed: "What's a bayonet for?" "To kill, to kill, to kill," the rosy-cheeked lads called back in unison. I wanted to shout, "That's not what I had sons for."

My summer in Columbia also crystallized my subsurface criticism of schooling. The BTW kids, taken aback by the freewheeling discussions we volunteers tried to evoke, told us their regular teachers would not permit questioning, and that their assignments and tests always called only for single responses: true or false or multiple choice. Back at liberally academic Baldwin, I decided that the difference was one of degree not kind. Members of the various departments always got together to decide the parameters of what would be accepted in response to open-ended essay topics. Interpretations beyond those limits would not be accepted. Furthermore, I'd come to believe that perhaps the unique accomplishment of United States schooling overall was to promote anti-communism and consumerism.

So it was that when I felt I had to get away from my country's militarism and to leave Jim in peace to make his own decisions, I was attracted to an announcement (by chance, again in *The New York Review of Books*, of a series of seminars on Alternatives in Education at the Center of Intercultural Documentation (CIDOC), in Cuernavaca, under the aegis of iconoclastic, defrocked Roman Catholic priest Ivan Illich.

Discussion leaders were to include social critics whose published work I'd been imbibing as part of my sixties' immersion, such as Paul Goodman, Edgar Friedenberg, Jonathan Kozol, and John Holt, whose educational and social analyses and perspectives fortified my own observations and experience. With all my children away from home— and thanks to money I was able to extract from the estate of my recently deceased father—I was soon on my way to Mexico to take part in their seminars.

I knew no Spanish, nor anything of the history or culture of this neighboring country. I carried with me a $1.00 Berlitz mini-book of *Spanish for Travelers*, a copy of *Mexico on Five Dollars a Day*, and, in my head, the name of one person to look up: Carmen Molina, provided by my boss at the *Gazette*, who had boarded in her house during his recent stay in Cuernavaca.

Carmen was the most dynamic person I've ever been close to. She radiated sexuality and intellect, was a magnet to men and women. Her home was a refuge for a young Bolivian student on the fly and a wandering Australian Communist—whom she met during the three years she and her by-then divorced neurologist husband spent in Cuba. It was also a virtual salon for politically oriented intellectuals and visiting luminaries. On an outing she organized, I found myself stuck on the top of a Carnival Ferris wheel with John Holt, author of the educational classics, *How Children Fail* and *How Children Learn*.

Not long removed from life as a suburban wife and mother, small town concerns, and genteel protest, I felt near the thick of the fray when Carmen detailed to me events surrounding the 1968 student uprising during the

Mexican Olympics frenzy, when hundreds of protestors were killed by government forces. She had arranged a temporary hiding place for her friend and political ally Heberto Castillo, who was pursued by the Mexican government for allying himself with the protesting students. A professor of engineering at the Mexican Autonomous University (UNAM), an inventor, columnist, and sometime political prisoner, Castillo later became a Senator, a respected columnist, and until his death in 1997, a pillar of the Democratic Revolutionary Party (PRD).

Carmen's and my conversations were by no means always political. In woman-to-woman talk I told her I was sure I would never again get into a serious relationship with a man because after going out with someone "new," I always felt we "didn't speak the same language"—no matter his native tongue. "You don't want a lover," a man I'd gone out with in the States after my divorce told me; "you want someone to talk to." He wasn't far from the truth. At bottom, it was because we did not connect in our talk that I felt I had to end my marriage to the well-liked businessman, club-addicted father of my children. When I wanted to discuss anything beyond immediate family concerns, he'd say, "I wish I had time to think about such things, but I have to make a living."

The day after Carmen and I had that conversation, I was at her house while she was waiting for her old friend Mario Padilla. She had all but commanded him to be there at 6 p.m. She was counting on him to give the appearance of being "her man" at a dinner party that night, an urgent need because she was having a torrid affair with the evening's host, though her original friend was her lover's wife.

"Oh, my God, I can't take two," Carmen yelled out with uncharacteristic lack of grace when she opened the gate and saw that Mario had come with his friend Oscar. The three had known each other since they were in primary school, though only Mario was close to the other two. He had been just about everything to Carmen: school chum, surrogate brother, lover, legal adviser, political ally.

Carmen cajoled Oscar, who had accompanied Mario only at the latter's insistence and wanted to go right back to Mexico City. "I have a guest who doesn't know Cuernavaca," she told him. "I've just filled up my car with a full tank of gas. Wouldn't you like to show her around?"

Tongues loosened by a half pint of tequila, Oscar and I pieced together bits and pieces of each other's language. He had a big advantage over me, even though he was many years removed from his secondary school days in Mexico City, when, he told me, he'd been "a prize pupil in Miss Davis's English class."

In retrospect, I think our lack of easy language connection may have helped us communicate. Neither of us had the vocabulary for glib talk in the other's language, even had we been so inclined. From the beginning, we talked about issues and ideas. I told him I had come to his country to get away from my country's involvement in Vietnam; and he told me he was in the midst of raising funds for a group of Vietnamese women then in Mexico seeking support. Like Carmen, he was a long-time political associate of Heberto Castillo's, and he himself, with his former wife and their young son, had escaped from the student massacre of 1968—because a soldier had the merciful grace to look the other way. Perhaps, though I don't think we realized it for a while, unconsciously we shared a feeling that in our previous intimate relationships, we had "listened to different drummers" and we hungered for companionable affection. In any case, we were soon a recognized couple, albeit an odd one.

I sometimes try to imagine how we appeared—and appear—to others. Unmistakably Mexican, Oscar's features still resemble the clay Indian-face relic I've treasured ever since workmen unearthed it while digging the foundation of the house Oscar and I planned and lived in together for well over a decade. While I have never come close to fitting the blue-eyed blond gringo stereotype, most Mexicans assumed I was from the United States. On the surface Oscar and I probably had nothing in common but our short stature—and dissatisfaction with the status quo.

From a comfortable background, with 20 years of formal education behind me, I never lacked any creature comforts or modest luxuries. Oscar had dropped out of the University because his attendance imposed too much sacrifice on his family. But notwithstanding my two degrees from Bryn Mawr and one from the University of Pennsylvania, my general knowledge and awareness often paled in contrast to his. He had been bright and fortunate enough to attend Mexico City's selective public secondary school at a time when the country's outstanding poet Carlos Pellicer and physicist Alberto Barájas, who had worked closely with Albert Einstein, taught there, whetting and nourishing Oscar's innate intellectual curiosity. His knowledge of astronomy and geography put mine to shame; at most I was on a par with him in world history and current issues.

As I was growing up, my family praised me; his rebuked him. Proud of his intelligence ever since he began to read as a preschooler, his mother never ceased to anguish because, unlike his Catholic tradition-following brothers, he steadfastly refused to kneel down for her religious blessing—continuing rebellion that he had initiated in childhood. After recovering from a serious illness at the age of 12, he adamantly refused to obey his mother's command to kiss the image of a saint when she took him to church to fulfill her prayerful promise.

His retired, self-educated elderly father shared Oscar's religious incredulity, but nevertheless disparaged Oscar as a "Communist" for his political and social ideas. For many years an electrical engineer for a silver mining company whose US owners never gave him due recompense for his inventions, he fumed when Oscar disdained the turkey the company sent the family at Christmas. Oscar's rejection of what came from "the belly of the beast"—as Cuban nationalist Jose Martí referred to the United States—had made him consciously put behind him the English he'd studied enthusiastically in his secondary school days, though he later regretted the lapse on both political and personal grounds. After I was pretty much acknowledged as part of the family, his father told Oscar I was "God's vengeance" for his prejudice against the United States.

My family looked benevolently on my radical tendencies, even as they sharpened with age. The vague discomfort I felt ever since my first glance inside a ghetto window, from a train window in New York, when I was about eight years old, took on academic substance throughout my adolescence. I quite agreed with the Archbishop of Canterbury's judgment that "our system lacks moral basis." But that didn't keep me from enjoying many class advantages or leading an essentially conventional life until my mid-forties.

The only girl in a motherless family—my mother died when I was seven weeks old, leaving my father also with three boys, then seven, nine, and 13 years old—I had always been the family's shining light, was rarely denied anything I really wanted. I had my own car as soon as I passed the driver's test when I was 16. At 17, I went to one of the country's costliest, most prestigious colleges, living on campus until I graduated four years later. And not long thereafter, towards the end of World War Two, I gave up a promising career-beginning in the journalistic career that I'd coveted in order to embark on a quite conventional marriage—in which I remained until the turbulence of the sixties and Vietnam War fallout fertilized my latent radicalism and set me off in new directions.

I was hardly rich, but I could pretty much do what my modest tastes sought. Oscar had to count pennies before inviting me to even the most modest eatery. He was living by odd jobs. He'd been blacklisted a year or so before we met, after trying to organize a union when a US-based transnational bought the company where he'd worked as an accountant.

The new owners brought in their own mid-level employees, with wages substantially higher than those paid to similarly employed Mexicans, a standard operating practice.

"Don't be dreamers. You're right and you are justified in your fight, but we don't fight Uncle Sam," the Conciliation and Arbitration Board of the State of Mexico told Oscar and his cohorts when they sought protection of their constitutionally-ordained right to form a union. The government officials warned: "You'll never win against such a powerful company. They have $20 million ready to fight you."

A company attorney subsequently summoned Oscar, holding out a check for 50,000 pesos (worth about $4000 at the time). "You'd better accept this," the lawyer counseled. "Forget the struggle, and hold on to your job." When Oscar declined, the attorney admonished: "You've put up a good fight, but now it's time to give up. If you'll give up this fantasy, I can get you a better job with some of my friends. But if you insist, you'll be out of work and you'll be blacklisted in this state and all the surrounding ones."

"It's too common a story," a *New York Daily News* reporter said when I asked if he thought I might be able to write Oscar's story for publication in a liberal magazine in the United States.

Oscar, often with Mario, acquainted me with Mexico and a deeper kind of patriotism than I had ever known. They delighted in showing off their country. They took me to Xochicalco, in the state of Morelos, explaining the "ball games" and the Mesoamerican astronomical conferences held there at summer solstice long before the Spaniards colonized the country; to the presumed resting place of the remains of Cuauhtémoc, the last Aztec emperor, whom Hernan Cortés ordered to be hanged for refusing to reveal where the Aztec fortune was buried; and to the birthplace of Emiliano Zapata, "Land and Liberty" leader of the Mexican Revolution of 1910, a native of the state of Morelos (whose "drummer boy" was the owner-operator of the hardware store I patronized throughout my years in Mexico). Driving through Chilpancingo, in the state of Guerrero, they told me about Genaro Vázquez, whom Mario had represented as defense attorney. Considered a cow hustler by the local elite, Vázquez had been a school teacher who won both fame and infamy as a kind of Robin Hood who robbed from the rich to give to the poor. He'd turned to guerrilla activity after local political powers prevented his taking office when he was elected municipal president of Iguala, one of the most important cities in the state of Guerrero. After the car in which Vázquez was riding was forced

Bette Steinmuller visiting Beatrice and Oscar Nava in New York, 2004

off the road in what turned out to be a fatal "accident," Oscar told me that he had originally been slated to drive him that day.

The first time Oscar and I went out by ourselves, we went to Tepoztlán, described in *Mexico on Five Dollars a Day* as an "unspoiled" Indian village, and subject of various well-known anthropological studies. Here I took Oscar up a steep hill to the home of Marco Polansky, a guru of sorts to young hippies who flocked to CIDOC. The house Marco shared with his North American wife and their three young children overlooked the village and valley, bordered by majestic, craggy, rough hewn mountains on either side. We sat on a low wall as the sun went down (always abruptly and early there) and marveled at the succession of colors reflected on those rocks: red, gold, purple. "Some day I have to live in a place like this," Oscar said, not imagining, I am sure, that soon we would be doing so, together, for 14 years.

Despite initial ambivalence, before long I was saying to a friend, "I'm about as happy as I can imagine being in this crazy world." A visitor from California, complaining of never finding a man who shared her values, said to me, "How lucky can you be!" She and I had met originally at CIDOC, where Oscar occasionally accompanied me—most notably when we attended seminars led by Paolo Freire, whose seminal *Pedagogy of the Oppressed* and discussions thereof expanded my conception of learner-centered education. In this strange, beautiful land of even greater contrasts than those at home, I felt closer to the pulse of life, yet more at ease with myself. I had found what I hadn't known I was looking for.

Notes

1. Howard Zinn, *A People's History of the United States, 1492-Present* (Revised and Updated Edition) New York: Harper Perennial Edition, 1995, pp. 290-291.

Recreating Community

Kendal Hale and Steve Norris building their house in Mission Hill, Boston, MA

Mission Hill

Steven Norris

I N 1974, I moved into the leaky second-floor apartment of a dilapidated three-decker on Boston's besieged Mission Hill. Anne Nugent was already living there with Jim McDonnell and John Leek. Anne and I had lived together for a couple of years in Middletown, Connecticut, when she was a student and I a professor, at Wesleyan University. We'd met while demonstrating against a company that made fuses for bombs being dropped in South East Asia. When Anne left me to go to Boston, I was devastated. I was afraid of my feelings for her—and of the rootlessness and restlessness of my life. I had already resigned from Wesleyan. Young, brash, and self-confident, I had fought to uphold the activist requirement I set for students to enroll in my course, "Strategies for Radical Change." I probably could have weathered the tap-on-the-wrist censure imposed by the faculty Senate, but I was too conscious of the gulf between what was expected of me as a teacher and what I wanted to expect of my students. I'd been forever marked by the comments of a member of a therapy group of working class young people that I'd joined.

"You use all those high-falutin' big words," this young man who hadn't graduated from high school told me. "I don't even think you know what you mean. Speak English, man, speak English."

Too, I felt a vague impulse to experience the energy of an inner city. So I followed Anne to Boston, a move that would take me into community organizing, factories, Marxism-Leninism—and into a new vocation and new marriage and family.

At the age of thirty, I'd already gone through many changes. Betraying the dreams of my Yankee parents, I'd dropped out of West Point, married and, after we had two children, divorced my high school sweetheart. I'd earned a doctorate at Cornell when the campus was a hotbed of radical action, with calls for black power, revolution, and deep social change. When I failed in my marriage, I moved in with a group of laid-back hippies. The grief we shared when our house mate Susie was killed riding on a motorcycle gradually merged into a sense of community and caring that many of us experienced for the first time. I'd headed for my appointment at Wesleyan with optimism, then left it for another new life.

When I moved to Mission Hill, in the spring of 1974, the neighborhood was as racially diverse as could be found anywhere. The Irish flavor still held from its original settlers, but

Latinos, African Americans, Chinese, Poles, and Greeks now outnumbered the Irish. Our landlord was an 80 year-old Scotsman from Cape Breton who had once made violins. The neighborhood itself was under siege by the expansion of Harvard University, which had already laid several city blocks to waste and was in the final stages of evicting tenants from what it labeled a "blighted" area. "Premeditated blight," a local newspaper reporter called the complicity of the State of Massachusetts and Harvard when the University received $250 million in government-assisted loans to build a power plant where there had been houses.

One of the first meetings I attended was a gathering of neighborhood activists and lawyers from Boston Edison, the very powerful local power company. These very different people were trying to find common ground to oppose the Medical Area Total Energy Plant (MATEP), an electricity generating plant whose toxic fumes Harvard admitted would cause deaths by cancer in the neighboring areas. I also attended a formal black tie gathering at Harvard Medical School Library for which an activist had somehow obtained several tickets. As the ceremonies began, one of our number sounded a gong, another read aloud a history of Harvard's rape of the area, and fifty of us walked out, chanting "Harvard out of Mission Hill." Unfortunately, Harvard won the war. While generating electricity and heat for the hospitals, MATEP has turned hospital trash into toxic fumes that spread over surrounding neighborhoods, rich and poor, even as its smokestack despoils the Boston skyline.

Earlier, the community had successfully organized to stop encroachment by Leahy Clinic and Ruggles Street Baptist Church. The two institutions had bought up an eight-block area, evicting tenants from 50 triple-decker buildings—each with three apartments—in order to build a hospital and a church. Nothing was built and the ten acres they'd ravished and abandoned became wild, overgrown land. It seemed pastoral when a neighbor of mine grazed a pony there, but it was also a place for drug deals and illegal dumping. Years later, the bodies of two young Latino men were dumped there when I was starting to build a house for myself a block away.

The neighborhood had been redlined for years: banks would not lend money to residents for mortgages and home repairs. Families who wanted to sell their houses couldn't find buyers because buyers couldn't get loans. Owners often paid artificially high property taxes, exceeding those in much more expensive neighborhoods. By the time I moved there, grass roots community opposition had forced the State and Federal governments to abandon proposals to extend the I-95 Interstate road system through the center of Boston, but the damage in Mission Hill had already left a swath of wasteland.

The Hill was also a prime target of crime coming from the nearby Bromley Heath and Mission housing projects, whose mismanagement by the Boston Housing Authority had led to widespread neglect and abandonment. I never was mugged or had a car stolen while I lived on the Hill, but my living quarters were burglarized on average once a year. The man who managed the corner store on Delle Avenue was murdered while behind the counter. There were random shootings. One night a woman neighbor knocked on our door all bloody, a mugger's victim. My twenty-year-old son was held up at gunpoint in the park behind our house; my roommate was wounded by a random gunshot as he rode his bike past the projects.

Perhaps most terrifying were the fires. In 1976 and 1977 Mission Hill was ablaze, like other parts of Boston, such as the Fenway. The word in the streets was that Mafia and other gangsters bought old buildings, and laundered their money by burning them and collecting the insurance. Sometimes, in order to avoid bankruptcy or finance a move, owners burned their homes because their value fell below what they'd paid and what the buildings were insured for. Kids sometimes burned buildings for fun. There were three or four fires a week in the blocks adjacent to where I was living; huge old brick factory buildings, storefronts, houses, abandoned schools all burned. On four consecutive nights there were four fires in the same building. Later, banks, insurance companies, landlords, and members of the fire department were found to be working together to profit from such fires. Some public officials went to jail. Most of us in the neighborhood sat powerless, hoping the fires wouldn't get any closer to our homes.

26 Delle Avenue Commune

A few months after I'd moved in with them, Anne, John, Jim, and I bought a two-family house a few blocks away. The house had been abandoned for two years. Kids had played in it. Dogs had lived in it. Copper pipes and radiators had been stolen. Windows were broken. But there were several long term residents and activists on the street and the house was potentially livable. We were willing to pay $9,000 when it was put up for auction, on the litter-filled sidewalk in front. But there were no other bidders, so the house was ours for the opening price of $3,000.

On evenings and weekends during the winter of 1974-5, we cleaned the messes left by kids and dogs, steamed soiled wallpaper off the walls, sanded and varnished floors, and painted. We operated under the old Marxist ideal: "From each according to his or her abilities, to each according to her or his needs." In early spring we moved in, forming the 26 Delle Avenue Commune. We organized to share housework, shopping, and cooking. In weekly house meetings we discussed everything: vacuuming the living room carpet, racism, cleaning out the garage, Vietnam, sex, where to put the TV, and our life stories. Sometimes we drove each other crazy with different attitudes toward food and noise, different standards of cleanliness and chaos, or different personalities and ways of dealing with anger or sadness, frustration or fatigue. Sometimes we played music together or went to the beach. During the next year, we recruited two more women. We all wanted to help the immediate neighborhood and to challenge the U.S. role in Vietnam and the U.S. power structures.

We rode bicycles as our primary means of transportation, each averaging about twenty or so city miles a day. Among the six of us, we had two automobiles. Anne shared hers willingly. We bought food at a coop. Our expenses were low: we figured $60 a month each for rent, plus about $50 apiece for food and $10 for transportation. Those of us with a little money (I had $2000) put it toward the purchase and repair of the house, without any formal agreement about when and how it would be repaid or the structure of ownership. We wrote in a notebook whatever we spent for the commune. At the end of each month, we tallied the expenditures and reimbursed everyone from what we put in for rent. By the late seventies when the commune broke up, the house had appreciated about ten or fifteen times. We each made a small profit, and after mostly amicable discussions, we figured a formula for distributing the proceeds of the sale.

The caring, courage, and example of the five people with whom I shared 26 Delle Avenue galvanized my determination to confront the evils of

United States capitalism and foreign policy, and to assist the struggles of people on Mission Hill. We did not break up because we didn't like the commune. I was thinking about having another family and needed more time by myself. I moved into a vacant apartment next door, where I lived alone for the next two years. Then I moved down the block and started living with Kendall Hale, who became my wife and the mother of my two younger children. All of us who were part of the commune have remained friends. Most of us come together periodically, though we live a thousand miles apart.

Marxism-Leninism

Along the way to increasingly intensive community involvement, I took a number of detours. First was a brief flirtation with Marxism-Leninism and workplace organizing. Camping on Cape Bretton Island with Anne in 1975, I read William Hinton's *Fanshen*, which told how the Chinese Communist Party organized peasants in northwestern China during World War II. It made me think that a mass-based revolutionary upheaval was possible in the United States. If Mao and the Chinese Communist Party could do it in China, a country without an educated population and mass communication, or a large urban working class, I reasoned, we who fought for civil rights and against the Vietnam War could do something similar in the United States. I spent the next 15 years or so experimenting with various approaches to this purpose.

I had my doubts about Communism. While a graduate student in 1967, I'd traveled in Poland and the Soviet Union. My impression of the latter was a dark place where people were proud of their history but afraid of their government. Furthermore, I'd watched the New Left splinter in the seventies and a bewildering array of sectarian Marxist-Leninist-Maoist groups emerge. Their differences—centering mostly on whether to follow the Soviet or Chinese line—seemed petty and academic, as if they were more interested in theoretical purity and arguing with one another than in doing the organizing needed to promote revolution.

However, I was impressed by reports of visitors to China and by films and periodicals produced there. Though China was a very poor country, a doctor who produced a slide show said he'd never seen a beggar or poorly fed person there. I didn't learn until a few years later that during the Cultural Revolution instituted by Mao, many people were murdered and intellectuals and other professionals punished simply for their status, and many families uprooted and careers ruined.

A few of us from the commune joined a group of other friends to study Marxist-Leninist classics. We read Marx's *Communist Manifesto and Capital*, Lenin's *Imperialism and State and Revolution*, and a number of works by Mao and Stalin. On my way to a Ph.D. I'd read standard theories of historical change and development, but none had made as much sense to me in explaining history. I felt that the theories of Marx, Lenin, and Mao also provided guidelines to resolve the inequities and injustices I was seeing on the streets of Mission Hill. Globally, many former colonies had become independent, and socialist inspired national liberation movements, had sprung up all over the world, as in Vietnam. Even Cuba, a small island 90 miles from the U.S., had overthrown U.S. control. Nicaragua and El Salvador were in the process of doing so. In South Africa, a popular resistance movement, partially inspired and greatly supported by communists, was gaining momentum.

I had serious doubts about the "Dictatorship of the Proletariat" and "Democratic Centralism," basic organizing principles of the Soviet Communist Party and the Chinese Communist Party. Both resulted in highly centralized power and repressive governments and had been guilty of mass violence. But I realized that the radical changes I wanted probably could not be made with the laissez-faire type democracy practiced in the United States and Europe, where access to media and money usually determined what happened at the ballot box and in the legislature.

In September 1975, I applied for a factory job where some friends of mine, including Nancy Teel and Kendall, were working. Anne was also working in a factory, and of my other Delle Avenue house mates, Jim worked for Vocations for Social Change, John participated in the Cambridge Bicycle Repair Collective, which helped people repair their own bikes; and Dorine and Jan worked with labor unions. In early November I was hired as a clerk in the stock room of the Joseph Pollack Company, which manufactured switches and electric connectors for cars and trucks. It employed a few hundred people, mostly women and many immigrants. I remember crying for more than an hour the night before I started. I'm still not sure why. I'd been eager for the experience. But I knew I would be isolated in some ways. Perhaps I had a premonition that the work would require more sacrifice and discipline than I could sustain for the long haul I suspected revolution would require. Or perhaps it was that I was giving up the privileges of middle class life I'd been born and raised with, or that it reminded me of West Point.

I liked the people I worked with at Pollack. They weren't a lot different from people I'd known growing up, or my neighbors on Mission Hill. But I couldn't tell them much about myself. I'd have been fired if I told them, "I went to West Point once, and then used to teach college, but I quit, and now I've taken this job to try to organize workers here into a labor union." The work itself was easy. My job involved counting small electronic parts for switches and jacks to deliver in baskets to various assemblers in the plant. On the first of each month I'd be given an inventory sheet of parts to count out from the bins in the stock room and deliver within a calendar month. It took me no more than two weeks each month to complete that month's work. For the last two weeks I'd write letters and try to look busy. Sometimes I'd go in the men's room and fall asleep on the pot. Sometimes I wrote poetry—the only time I was ever paid to be a writer. The bosses were mostly aloof, but didn't interfere much with me. There was one guy named George Jenks who would walk by my worktable about the same time every day. He never bothered me, but he always looked gruff and un-approachable. Every day I smiled at him and said: "Hello, Mr. Jenks, How are you today?" But I never succeeded in getting him to smile back.

Periodically I met after work with five Marxist-Leninist women, also Pollack employees, to discuss organizing strategies. We realized we had to be model workers, and to appear to be doing everything right. The prob-lem for me was that my job was often so slow and boring it was difficult to look busy. We needed to identify co-workers who might be interested in supporting a labor union. This was hard for me, since I didn't work closely with anyone. I had most contact with my supervisor, and I had very little to do with him. There I was in the middle of the industrial proletariat with no friends or allies, and little prospect of making any.

By late winter of 1976, I was looking for a way to quit the job honorably. In February I caught a bad case of flu, and was sicker than I've ever been in my adult life. At the same time I read an article in *The Call*, a newspa-per of a small Marxist-Leninist organization which was organizing in the inner city. This time, instead of being inspired, I was disgusted. I remem-ber thinking the article must have been lifted from material Lenin wrote in 1917 to outline organizing strategies for the Russian Revolution. Here I was sacrificing my freedom and health, and the strategy I was offered was 60 years old and had resulted in a country that seemed to me to be incred-ibly repressive. On a lovely day, as crocuses were beginning to bloom, in March 1976—the 200th anniversary of the signing of the Declaration of Independence—I called my supervisor and said I was quitting. I took a long walk in the sun and felt free. I went back to Pollack only to collect my last paycheck, and was shocked when the fellow I knew best asked if I'd quit because of something he had said or done.

Digging Into The Grass Roots

My disillusionment with Marxism-Leninism gave me time and opportunity to throw myself into neighborhood grass roots. Shortly after I left Pollack, a neighbor asked if I'd repair the gutters of her house. After I did the repair, word spread. Another neighbor had some rotten front steps. Then my first "employer" got a substantial loan and called to ask if I'd be interested in a much larger job: plastering ceilings, replacing broken windows, painting, replacing some plumbing fixtures. More or less by accident I was in business, learning as I went along, right in my own neighborhood. Over the next fifteen years I probably worked on fifty or so houses on the Hill, repairing fire-damaged roofs, building additions, demolishing and rebuilding rotten porches and railings, doing minor plaster and sheetrock repairs, and framing one entirely new house on a new foundation. At first I worked mostly on Mission Hill. As time went by, my reputation spread and I did a lot more work elsewhere, sometimes for people I'd first met on Mission Hill who had moved to other parts of the city or suburbs.

I got to know my neighbors well. Mary Edgarton, a 40 year-old black woman with four or five children and grandchildren living with her, taught me to dance on rotted wood and falling plaster. Mary had bought a run-down half-duplex near the Bromley Heath housing project. Half the houses that hadn't been torn down on her street were boarded up or badly vandalized. People sometimes got light-headed or dizzy from fumes from a factory around the corner that relined old asbestos brake pads. After a day painting a house in the neighborhood, my crew complained they weren't feeling well. My complaints to the Environmental Protection Agency and Attorney General's Office were useless.

Mary's house must have been magnificent about 75 years earlier. It had thick curved mahogany door moldings, large double hung windows, a slate mansard roof , and a beautifully crafted stairway and railing to the second floor. A spectacular stone wall, still largely intact, made of rounded and colorful sea stones, separated the yard from the sidewalk. But the house had been abandoned for some time. Debris made approach difficult: the yard was strewn with junk. A telephone wire drooped within a few feet of the front walk. Before Mary moved in, a homeless man had lived in the house, with a pile of dirty blankets for a bed and a bathroom floor in danger of caving in. The leaking roof had caught fire and never been repaired properly. The floors were rotted from rain and age, and the window sashes and frames decayed from neglect. The pocked walls were stained from leaks and careless use. Mahogany moldings, doors, and windows were coated with gobs of peeling paint. The smell of smoke-charred wood seeped from rafters, and the stink of urine rose from the floors.

But to Mary the house was a dream come true. When I'd complain to her about how hard it was to make it look nice, she'd chirp right in: "Look I grow'd up on a hardscrabble farm in Alabama. We didn't never know what new was down there. This place is a palace compared to that. Someday maybe I can make it look like a palace again. For now fix-it and make-do will be great. Those scratches in the paint there. You ain't never gonna get them out of the woodwork. Besides, things like that, and that patched plaster over there, gives the place character, shows the history a bit. Just don't worry so much. I'm lucky to have you here doin' all this dirty stuff."

I didn't yet know how things should be built or repaired. I only knew how to tinker, adjust, and make do. I was working for $5 an hour. The squalor didn't bother me, perhaps because my aging grandfather had lived in a kind of squalor or because my frugal Yankee parents had often made do with homemade clothes and furniture. They always repaired what could be fixed rather than buying something new. So the scene at Mary's house didn't turn me away. It was an opportunity to dig deeper into the neighborhood. For the next ten years or so, until I left Mission Hill, I was Mary's repairman. At times she invited me to stay for lunch. Her teenage daughters baby-sat a few times for my daughter Moriah. I went to her wedding.

Mary's heroic optimism was unusual, but not unique. I spent time in many people's homes, sometimes woke them up in the morning, sometimes had a coffee break with them. I made a mess with plaster dust and lath, and swept up after myself. I shared and contributed to dreams with a skylight here, a new ceiling there, a fresh coat of paint on badly peeling clapboards, a new set of stairs for a front porch. People were as diverse as their cultures and skin-colors—grouchy and quiet, pleasant and accommodating, sleazy, penny-pinching, talkative, shy. But almost everyone I worked for had very little money, which meant they had trouble finding reputable tradespeople and were grateful that I was available.

I also got to know well-meaning members of the business community. Marvin Rosencrantz lived in the suburbs but kept his store on Mission Hill because he loved its people. Fred Ficken, a real estate speculator moved into the neighborhood because he saw an opportunity to make a contribution and a good income (in the latter, I think he was disappointed).

I took part in the neighborhood security patrol. When thousands of people came to the fair the Mission Hill Planning Commission organized each year in the park on top of the hill, we'd patrol in pairs. Once I spotted a middle aged white guy hanging out in front of my house.

"What you doin' here?" I asked, after he'd been there a couple of hours. "We have a lot of crime on this street, and my neighbors and I try to notice when strangers hang around."

"I'm a cop," he said.

Intimidated, I walked away. But then I went back. "Could you show me your badge?"

"No I don't have to do that," he snarled

"Well then I'll just have to call the cops."

He showed me his badge.

No one in the community affected me more than Elena Dodd and her organization, "Streetfeet." Elena lived with her carpenter husband and two kids in one of the three-story attached brick row homes that lined a whole block of Delle Avenue across from the commune. I barely knew Elena when she approached me the first time, saying: "Steve, I need a geographer."

"Don't you mean a carpenter?" I asked.

"No, I mean a geographer. I'm putting together a production of the "The Little Prince," mostly with neighborhood kids. But I need some grownups, especially someone to play the geographer and the snake. Not too many lines, or too much of your time. We'll rehearse in my house, or around the corner in the basement of the public library."

Elena took a ragtag assortment of kids and grownups from Delle Avenue and the projects, of vastly different ages, cultures, and races, and molded us into a cast that performed "The Little Prince" for neighbors. Later she produced "Amahl and the Night Visitors," and the "Wizard of Oz." With bare bones funding from the City of Boston, she organized a summer program for kids. I was just a helper, but I was glad to be part of what must have been one of the most beautiful fabrics ever woven in a poor inner-city neighborhood.

Fisher Avenue

Building my house on Fisher Avenue cemented my love affair with Mission Hill. Building the house was a rite of passage. In my young days in New England, I'd looked at sturdy weather-beaten white farmhouses and wondered what kind of people built them. I wondered if I possessed the creative mettle of my ancestors. Working in other people's houses made me want to do something for myself. I'd been living in rundown 100 year-old houses for years, and I wanted to use my new skills on something of my own.

I had only a couple of thousand dollars in savings. Master Card had once sent me an unsolicited credit card, congratulating me for my appointment as an assistant professor at Wesleyan. After using it for a couple of years, I cut it up as an act of anticapitalist rebellion. I'd also declared a "War Crimes Deduction" on my income taxes in 1972, and been taken to court by the IRS. I argued that the war crimes being committed in Vietnam obliged me to withhold a portion of my taxes. I lost the case, and the IRS claimed I owed several hundred dollars. (After the trial, the young IRS attorney told me he secretly agreed with me, but had a job to do.) I'd also refused to have a bank account. I remember arguing with a house mate who had put forth the eminently sensible idea that "We should keep our house money in a bank account."

"That's just going to support capitalism," I replied. "They'll lend the money to Sikorsky, who will turn around and build more helicopters for the army in Vietnam. Our money will be killing kids in Vietnam. We've got to learn how to live without these evil capitalist institutions."

"But how then can we manage our money, and do any sensible budgeting?"

Angrily, I said: "Budgeting, smudgeting You've got to wake up. This is revolution. Forget about budgeting and get on with organizing."

I finally gave in to my opponent's arguments and felt bad about my self-righteous dogmatism. But I was hardly in much of a position to borrow money to build my dream.

To my knowledge, there hadn't been a modest private house built in Boston in decades, especially on Mission Hill. You probably had to be a little nuts, or simply naïve, to consider it. The market value was so far below construction costs that it was likely that once completed a house would not be worth what it had cost to construct. But those considerations didn't concern me. I went to the Real Property Department at City Hall. "Can you tell me what property the City of Boston owns on Mission Hill?" I asked of the crusty old gentleman behind the counter.

"We don't own any," he said, only half awakening from his daydreams.

"You got to be kidding. There's vacant land everywhere on Mission Hill, and the City owns most of it because nobody wants to pay taxes on it."

"Well I don't know about that."

"Please, can I look at your maps that show who owns what pieces of property? Then I'll check tax records to make sure the maps are okay," I insisted.

As it turned out, the City owned three adjacent pieces of property, totaling about 14,450 square feet, on Fisher Avenue. Not only were the lots buildable, they faced south, had lots of trees, and a beautiful stone wall. From the top, about 30 feet above the street, you could see the ocean to the east and the Blue Hills ten miles to the south.

I petitioned the Real Property Department to hold an auction. On a rainy morning in March 1979, two city officials and I navigated around many years' accumulation of trash and fallen leaves to find a place on the sidewalk across from Resthaven Nursing Home. The City had set a minimum price of $1300 for the three parcels. I was the only bidder. I owned land for a house!

After several months of developing plans, studying principles and practices of solar heating, and finally working out a design I liked, I got cold feet and for a time even gave up the idea. But the dream wouldn't be denied. I applied unsuccessfully for a couple of loans and ultimately filed a complaint of discrimination to the Massachusetts Banking Commission. In the spring of 1980, I was surprised by a call from the Haymarket Cooperative Bank: "We want to loan you money to build your house...." Presumably the bank was responding to pressure to lend money in previously redlined neighborhoods, the basis of my complaint to the Commission. We worked out details on a $30,000 loan, with 14% interest, and on a fall day a few months after the surprise call, Kendall, my mother and father, and I went to the site with a chainsaw and lopping shears. Thus began what the Boston Globe featured in a front-page Metro section story: "Roxbury man Builds His Dream for $35,000. With enormous help from many members of the community and beyond, we'd managed to take a small slice of what looked like a dying city neighborhood and bring it alive again, with an inexpensive but attractive house that had the most ancient and modern heating system—the sun. In March 1980, Kendall became pregnant with our daughter Moriah. Six weeks later we moved in. Within ten days, thieves had broken in twice, stealing bicycles and various valuables. A week later there was another burglary. I was terrified: perhaps, after all, we'd made a terrible mistake. But a neighbor gave us a German shepherd, who, along with an alarm system, solved the problem. In the summer good friends moved into the rental apartment that was part of the house. On a cold, snowy evening in December, Moriah was born, in a home birth assisted by our black Muslim midwife.

The next spring and summer we finished work on the yard. In the process we uncovered stone walls, lilac bushes, roses, and tiger lily patches, all waiting to be cultivated anew. Kendall planted a vegetable garden and lawn. And there, at the greatest party I've ever attended, Kendall and I were married, in a ceremony that included various ancient rituals, as well as elements of a New Age-hippie-flower child wedding. A former female lover of Kendall's made the wedding cake. Our guests included our parents, childhood friends who came from all over the country, and neighborhood friends like Mary Edgarton and Elena Dodd. As he was saying goodbye, the minister of the First Congregational Church I'd grown up in commented: "I've participated in about 500 weddings over the years and this was one of the best."

June Howe And The Ruggles Street Baptist Church Struggle

One cold January afternoon when I was working on the roof of our house before moving in, a gray-haired man in a business suit walked up the fifty concrete steps from Fisher Avenue. After identifying himself as a deacon at Ruggles Street Baptist Church, John Greene said: "Reverend Johnston and the deacons really like what you're doing. As you probably know the Church owns quite a bit of vacant land around here. We'd like to give it to neighborhood residents so they can build houses. Perhaps you can help us."

As I climbed down off my ladder, what little I knew about the history of this part of the neighborhood flashed quickly before my eyes. The ugly foundation hole next to where Mr Greene and I were standing was all that remained of an elegant six family house Ruggles had destroyed fifteen years before. In the sixties, after buying and tearing down most of the 50 or more houses they'd purchased between them, Ruggles and Leahy Clinic had abandoned plans for expansion in the area. Neighbors' attempts to purchase the land had fallen on deaf ears. Now Mr. Greene was offering to give the Church's land to neighbors.

"Well, gee, Mr. Greene, that's quite an offer," was all I could muster at first. "You mean you want to give it away."

"Yes, we've got a few families in the church who might like to build here, and we figure there must be some people like you in the neighborhood who would do it too if they had the land."

I wasn't yet well acquainted with the immediate neighborhood. I suggested that Mr. Greene contact June Howe, who lived across the street: "She's president of the Back of the Hill neighborhood association, which will certainly have to be involved in something like this. You'd be better off talking with her."

"We know about Mrs. Howe. We've heard from people at the New England Baptist Hospital that she can be a little hard to deal with." I detected a slight grimace as Mr. Greene shifted his weight around nervously.

I barely knew June then. But I knew her reputation for getting things done and not being afraid to step on people's toes. I'd been told how she'd taken her young children and some neighbors to Mayor Kevin White's office in City Hall a few years ago, and had a wine and cheese party there all day long, refusing to leave until the Mayor agreed to meet with her.

I told Mr. Greene: "I don't think there's much I can do for you alone, even though your offer is generous. Perhaps I should talk with June myself, and see if we can set up a meeting to discuss this with you and other folks from your church."

After work that day I knocked on the Howes' door. "Can I talk with June?" I asked her husband, Jim, who let me in.

"She's down in the basement storing some stuff. C'mon down."

We walked down the long central hallway. I noticed that the four or five rooms off the hall were so full of furniture and knick-knacks there was little space for living. "June buys and sells antiques sometimes," Jim explained. "Mostly stores them here." On the cluttered kitchen table I noticed a stack of newspapers, and a very official looking book-sized document that read "Preliminary plans for Addition to New England Baptist Hospital."

From the top of the basement stairs off the kitchen Jim yelled down: "June, Steve Norris from across the street is here to see you."

"Send him down. He can help me move these wedding dresses around."

I went down the stairs and saw June holding up a full sized white wedding dress. "You getting married?" I asked.

"No. I just bought out this old bridal shop in Hyde Park that went out of business a year or so ago. They had about twenty-five of these. They're in all these boxes," she said, pointing to the wall of boxes that was crowding machine tools and a table saw. . "I've got to move these out of Jim's workshop and over into that corner where they're less likely to get mildewed before I can resell them. Wanna help?"

June was a short, fifty-year-old woman with a round face, curly reddish brown hair, and intense, sparkling brown eyes. She obviously cared no more about her appearance than she did about the clutter in her house. I started putting the boxes in the area she pointed to, and told her about Mr. Greene's visit.

"Very interesting," she said. "After all these years they must feel guilty about tearing down the neighborhood. Or maybe they just can't afford to manage their land anymore. Not that they've spent much on it over the years. A church doesn't have to pay taxes, and they never even bothered to mow the grass or nothing. Just let the weeds take over. All you've got to do is look around my house and you know what kind of neighbors they are." Her house was surrounded on two sides by overgrown vacant land owned by the church. The side next to her driveway was also a vacant lot, owned by the Boston Redevelopment Authority. The whole area was covered with blackberry bushes, saplings, and random trash, and looked as though no one had paid any attention to it in years, except maybe for some kids who had built a now rotten-looking tree house.

"You can never quite take an offer like this at face value," she said, proceeding to run through the neighborhood's experience with Ruggles and Leahy. "But times have changed and maybe we can work with them. Maybe you should come to the next Back of the Hill board meeting and tell the board about this Mr. Greene and his offer."

June took me up to the second floor of her house. She explained that she and Jim rented their second floor apartment to the Back of the Hill Community Development Association (BOTHCDA). The front two rooms were full of desks and chairs, newspaper clippings, and other office paraphernalia – not unlike the offices of SDS and antiwar organizations in Ithaca fifteen years before. June introduced me to Bill Fried, director of the organization, who gave me a rundown of its history, going back to the sixties. BOTHCDA was learning how to manage the 50-unit, five-story apartment building for disabled and elderly that it had constructed with foundation and government funding obtained after June's sit-in at the Mayor's office. The apartments had opened about the same time that I started building the house on Fisher Avenue. "But," June added, "now we're setting our sights on housing for families in the neighborhood."

New England Baptist Hospital

I'd found Ruggles Street Baptist Church very accommodating and suspected unnecessary polarization between the neighborhood and New England Baptist Hospital. The Hospital's Chief of Security had given me permission to drive across a parking lot of theirs, which gave me otherwise almost impossible access to my building site. So I took it upon myself to write a letter to Ray MacAfoose, President of the Hospital.

"As a newcomer to the neighborhood," I wrote, "I see that there is considerable animosity on the part of people in the community toward the Hospital. It's puzzling to me, and I think it may not be fair to you and your institution. In my short time here I've been impressed by your helpful activities in the neighborhood, and can see that you try hard to be a good neighbor, and to help the community develop and prosper. To that end, I should think that you must be willing to commit yourself to the preservation of the open space and parkland which still exists on Mission Hill, and to avoid purchasing or destroying any more residential property, which has so sorely blighted this area in years past. Perhaps as a newcomer I could help heal some of the old wounds that divide your institution and the community, and help establish a spirit of cooperation and compromise that would be in the interests of both the hospital and the neighborhood."

The response was noncommittal and hedged in bureaucratese, declaring fervent desire to work with the neighborhood, but careful not to commit to anything in regard to land use planning or development. The letter also identified June Howe as "an unreasonable and erratic neighborhood activist who likes nothing better than to stir up dissension and discord in an otherwise cooperative community."

The real answer to my letter came a year or so later when the telephone awakened me at

6:15 a.m. "Steve, they're tearing down the apartments" someone was screaming hysterically in my ear so loudly I could barely understand.

"Is that you, June? What are you talking about? Who's tearing down what?"

"The hospital—they've got bulldozers up there on the hill behind your house. Didn't the noise wake you up? They're knocking down the brick apartments. Jim Coleman who lives across Parker Hill Ave from the hospital just called to tell me. We've been trying to save those apartments so families could live in them, and they're destroying them as we speak. We've got to get up there and stop them. Get out of bed and drive me up there."

I barely understood what she was talking about, but then I remembered she'd been working hard to save single story brick buildings that had been nurses quarters belonging to the Robert Brigham Hospital before New England Baptist bought them. The Baptist Hospital had plans to turn the area into a parking lot.

"Okay, June, I'll pick you up in five minutes." As I hung up the phone I heard the dull-throated moan of heavy equipment operating not too far away.

When we got to the hospital ten minutes later, there were two enormous flat-bladed bulldozers plowing through brick walls, seemingly in a hurry to do as much damage as fast as they could. They'd already laid waste to about a quarter of the 25 or so single story apartments by knocking big holes in the sides of each of them.

"Steve, we got to get in there and stop those 'dozers. Just park here in the road and let's get over there." Hospital security guards blocked our way. I saw their uniforms and badges and felt intimidated. June, in contrast, flew out of my truck in a fury.

"June, you can't go in there. This is hospital property." Dave Walsh, the affable chief of hospital security, said as he tried to block June.

"David, you should be ashamed of yourself. You know as well as I do that those apartments were livable yesterday, and now look at the mess you've made of them. And you don't even have permits to do this, do you?"

"We've got permits."

"You don't have demolition permits, and you don't have authorization to plow the asbestos that's in the basements into the ground. You started early in the morning because you thought we'd still be sleeping and the building inspectors wouldn't be at work yet. You figured you'd have these down before anyone would know about it. Well, I'm going to sit in front of this 'dozer until it stops and the police get here. And then I'm going to tell them and everyone else who will listen how the hospital breaks the law and poisons the neighborhood by plowing up asbestos."

I followed June to the front of the bulldozer, and while she sat down in the muddy grass, I stood uneasily between her and the also uneasy security guards, who looked as though they might try to carry her off. June, never in very good health and dressed in an old coat to ward off the morning chill, looked even more fragile than usual. They probably didn't dare touch her for fear of being bitten or sued if she claimed police brutality or an injury. Dave Walsh called the cops.

Within minutes a squad car came up Parker Hill Avenue, siren blaring and lights flashing. The middle aged cop, who looked as haggard as June, seemed as confused as everyone else to see a frazzled grandmother in house clothes sitting in front of a bulldozer. "You'd better get up ma'am. This is hospital property, " the Captain told June, with just a touch of impatience in his voice.

"Officer, I'm not going to move until the hospital obeys the law. Just yesterday our group met with Mayor Flynn and he said he'd try to help us save these houses from the wrecking ball. Call the damned building inspector. The hospital doesn't have permits to do this. And besides, there's asbestos all over the place now, probably blowing around the neighborhood because they didn't have the good sense and decency to remove it before demolishing these buildings. Steve'll show you."

The Captain ignored Dave Walsh's pleas to arrest June. I took the police into one of the still intact basements of the apartments. Asbestos was still on the pipes. Elsewhere it was simply mixed in with the broken-up brick, crumpled plaster and smashed windows.

Within half an hour, two inspectors from the Building Department appeared and said demolition and construction would have to cease until the matter of permits and asbestos was resolved. Later in the day, after I'd gone to work, Mayor Flynn and his staff showed up to inspect the carnage. And June appeared on the nightly news as a little heroine sitting in a mudhole in front of a huge stalled bulldozer. A young, stylishly dressed hospital spokeswoman then told the hospital's side of the story. "New England Baptist is on a tight construction schedule and has already received authorization from the State of Massachusetts to start spending the $40 million the State has lent us for the construction of the new facilities that will help us better serve our patients. We are only trying to serve the Boston community better. Our contractors assured us that all necessary permits had been granted. We're sorry if they overlooked some technicalities of paperwork. We'll fully cooperate with the City in order to get back to work right away."

They didn't get back to work for months. With its attempted preemptive early morning demolition of the nurses' housing, the Hospital had shot itself in the foot, and almost killed its whole construction project. Our City Counselor, David Scondras, held hearings in Back of the Hill Apartments, covered by the media, in which hospital officials and their builders were subpoenaed and forced to testify why the Hospital had demolished these buildings without proper permits. The Hospital fired its construction supervisor.

A couple of months later, I received a letter from the State of Massachusetts, Health Education Facilities Agency, from which the Hospital had received the $40 million grant. The letter said HEFA had issued a stop-work order. The Hospital couldn't do any more construction or receive any more funding until it negotiated with residents of the neighborhood and came to some agreement about land use, expansion, demolition of housing, and traffic and parking. It was my turn to call June, this time with what we took to be victory. The letter directed New England Baptist Hospital to meet with representatives of the Mission Hill Community and negotiate in good faith. The meetings were to be overseen by professional arbitrators hired by the Hospital, with community approval. If agreement could not be reached, arbitrators were to determine which side was in violation of the good faith standard and report its determination to HEFA.

For the next several months a half dozen of us, including residents from other parts of Mission Hill, met two or three times a week with the Hospital's CEO, a vice-president, two of its lawyers, and its public relations officials. We wanted the Hospital to commit itself to limiting its growth so that no more houses would be destroyed and to develop off-hill parking to relieve traffic congestion on the neighborhood's narrow streets. The hospital's goal was to renew construction, committing to as few limitations as it could. Its representatives argued that without adequate parking for employees, patients, and visitors, people would neither want to work there or to come for care. We argued: "You wouldn't want a hospital tearing down the houses out in the fancy suburbs where you live and putting in parking lots, bringing more cars onto your streets, building ten story buildings. This is a residential neighborhood. We raise families here. We need safe streets and parkland for our children. Besides, no one from Mission Hill can afford this hospital, why should we support your plans to improve and expand your services when this hospital won't even let us in the front door?"

We met for more than a hundred hours, but no agreement was reached. We in the neighborhood were outraged at the hospital's intransigence. The arbitrators, who lived in the posh Beacon Hill section of Boston, said that in their judgment both sides had worked "in good faith," and therefore they could not fault either side. In sum, the hospital had been inconvenienced and delayed, but it was free to pursue its development plans almost as though nothing had happened.

However, after considerable resistance to demonstrations in which we on the Hill blocked traffic, the Hospital abandoned the parking lot on parkland it had occupied for years, and developed off hill parking. So in some ways the hospital became a better neighbor. But the gains were far from our desire for community control over neighborhood development.

While the Baptist Hospital negotiations were taking place, I was also busy organizing the *Vecino* clinic construction project, in which I led a group of Bostonians to aid the Sandinista Revolution. I returned to Boston inspired by the strength and daring of the Nicaraguan revolutionaries and frustrated by the difficulties of our work on Mission Hill. I decided to try some guerrilla tactics. During several months, in 1986, a young woman friend, and I engaged in midnight spray-painting. Mostly it was fun, but we realized we could be in serious legal trouble if we were discovered to be responsible for the billboards that suddenly read: "Stop New England

Baptist Hospital," "Stop Institutional Expansion Now," "U.S. Out of Central America," "Impeach Reagan."

As we gained experience, we got bolder. On the night before a major demonstration for affordable housing, we climbed onto roofs in a commercial area of Jamaica Plain and spray painted billboards: "Affordable Housing Now," "Stop Gentrification," "Housing for People, Not Profit. Once a late night worker emerging from a Dunkin Donuts told us, "Keep up the good work; I'm glad somebody cares," but on the whole we got little feedback and certainly caused no upsurge of activity. I retreated to earlier tactics, though in 1987 I took another detour to Nicaragua, with another building project.

Meanwhile, the City of Boston had been floating proposals for "neighborhood councils" with some appointed and some elected members, who would represent grassroots community, business and institutional interests, giving all parties a voice in neighborhood development. These plans were widely discussed, and enthusiastically supported by groups like ours. But they never got very far. Even Mayor Flynn, who had emerged out of grass roots struggles in South Boston, showed only lukewarm and ambivalent interest in the community councils, and the idea eventually died.

We were more successful, however, in our struggle for affordable housing. The meeting I'd had with John Greene, the deacon from Ruggles Street Baptist Church, led eventually to a series of meetings starting in 1981. The Church and representatives of Back of the Hill hammered out an agreement by which the Church gave free land grants to community residents. These meetings were not easy, as neither the Church nor the residents trusted one another. A group of us from the Hill had at least one demonstration in front of the Church during Sunday services. But the Church needed to be rid of the land, and the Back of the Hill organization was in a position to assume control of it. On some of this land, individuals built their own houses, starting in 1984. On three or four parcels, members of the church built homes and moved in. On most of the remainder, the Back of the Hill organization raised public money and built thirteen attached modular dwellings, which were sold at cost to families who met certain income guidelines.

In the mid-eighties the Massachusetts Bricklayers Union expressed willingness to invest 15 or 20 million dollars of pension funds to construct housing if we could get control of five acres of land Leahy had abandoned and if we'd agree to use brick for the buildings. Within two or three years, 150 brick townhouses, affordable to persons of modest means, were constructed on the former Leahy land. Together with the homes built on the

Ruggles land, this brought fulfillment of June's dream of a multi-ethnic neighborhood to replace what Leahy and Ruggles destroyed twenty years earlier—quite an accomplishment for a small, struggling neighborhood group in the middle of a ghetto.

Victory came at a high price. It cost us our neighborhood group and, for some of us, our sense of community. In both the Leahy and Ruggles projects, powerful actors from outside the community played a huge role in the neighborhood's development and changes. Gradually, those of us who lived there, while realizing pieces of our dreams, were more and more disempowered. We had less and less control over what was going on, and some of us became bitter. Tragically, some of us began to blame one another for our growing powerlessness. Early on, June questioned the design of the housing being built with public money on the Ruggles land. She wanted houses to resemble those already in the neighborhood. The last conversation I ever had with her was about this issue. I telephoned her one night after a Back of the Hill Meeting at which she'd threatened to resign as President if our group didn't hold out for more money and a better design.

"June," I told her. "I think you're being unreasonable. This is the best we can get. If we don't accept this offer, we won't get anything." I knew I was taking a risk in challenging her. But we had worked together for years now. Our families had helped each other a number of times. I'd spent time with her in the hospital when she had breast cancer. I'd been to her son's wedding. I felt we could work this out.

"Steve, you're stabbing me in the back," she screamed at me hysterically. "If you don't support me in this, I don't want to have anything else to do with Back of the Hill or you, and we just don't have any more to say to each other,"

That was it. June was suddenly gone from Back of the Hill, and from my life, leaving a big hole for me personally, and a huge loss of her feisty spirit, indomitable courage, and smart strategizing for the organization.

I didn't understand at first why June felt so strongly or why she let it affect her relationship with me so much. However, as time went on the problem became clearer to me. Within a few months of June's resignation, the Bricklayers Union and the City of Boston had begun to formalize plans for the development of the Leahy land. After some discussions about the overall scope of the project, the Bricklayers' Union hired an architect and contractor, and eventually presented Back of the Hill with its plans. When we questioned some of the decisions, especially regarding the high density of the housing, we were told density was not negotiable. They had to build a lot of houses to keep costs down. We could take their plan or leave it. If we said no, it was probable that the Bricklayers had the power and resources to build the housing without us. In short, the residents of the Back of the Hill were being forced to become rubber stamps for the goals of outsiders. Our dream of community control was seriously compromised.

Many Back of the Hill residents felt that any housing was better than nothing, and that the Bricklayers plans, while not perfect, were a huge step forward. Others, myself included, felt that development without community control was not a step forward. The first group was willing to be a rubber stamp if it meant a safer, more livable community. The rest of us didn't want to have outsiders making the important decisions. The Back of the Hill organization survived, but some of us did not want a part in what felt like a sell-out. My heart was broken.

One of my last public acts as a resident of Back of the Hill was at an impromptu press conference called by Representative Fitzgerald, officials from the Mayor's Office, and the Bricklayers to announce their plans for the building project. It was a small gathering, but there were TV cameras present: Quietly, a group of us protested the loss of neighborhood control. We did not try to disrupt the gathering, but we carried placards reading: "BRICKLAYERS UNION IN CONTROL OF MISSION HILL." I was interviewed by a reporter and appeared on TV that night. At one point I pulled Kevin Fitzgerald aside and said: "Look Kevin, there's one thing I'd like you to do for us."

"Yeah, anything you want," he said.

"I'd like you to make sure that Back of the Hill is treated as an equal partner in this project. We don't want to be just a rubber stamp. We want to have an ongoing voice in these decisions."

"Of course I'll do that for you," he replied without hesitating. But we never spoke again.

Ten years later, I live in the beautiful Smoky Mountains of North Carolina with Kendall, Moriah and Teryn—and an established construction business. There's nary a trace of the grime of Mission Hill, and probably one percent of its crime. But I still long for the sense of community and struggle I lost when I left. So why am I not still living there? One morning in 1988, a distraught tenant started a fire in her apartment that almost burned our house— five days before Kendall gave birth to our son Teryn. This was after a teenager was murdered in the playground of the Trotter School where Moriah was in third grade, and another child was shot across the street in an argument over a hat. Moriah had started crying herself to sleep. One day on the way to school, she asked me what she could do to be less scared. I told her we'd do whatever it took.

Several months later, in the summer of 1990, we moved away from Mission Hill and the house we'd crafted. For months afterward, I literally cried every time I returned. But on a positive note, a week or two before we moved, the New England Baptist Hospital held a public hearing in Mission Church. The Hospital needed more parking space, and was proposing to demolish several houses it owned and pave over a residential area. Several hundred Mission Hill residents attended the meeting, including June Howe, State Representative Fitzgerald and other long time activists. The Hospital trotted out a few of its employees who lived on the Hill to say what a great project this was, and what a great neighbor the Hospital had always been. But despite the defeats we'd endured and the personal acrimony and recriminations we'd laid on one another, the rest of us were unified in our opposition. Even good natured, good liberal Kevin Fitzgerald, who always kept both feet firmly planted in mid-air, was adamant that the parking lot should not and would not be built. It wasn't.

Maybe a small redemption, but a bittersweet ending it was, to my fifteen years on Mission Hill.

POSTCRIPT

At the beginning of the new millennium, there is still some vacant land on the Back of the Hill, empty parcels where stately triple-deckers once stood. However, it's no longer a scary and vacant wasteland. On the side of Fisher Avenue where Kendall and I built our house in 1980, there are six houses built into the side of the hill. Lawn Street, where Back of the Hill built the modular town houses, is a vibrant multiethnic inner-city neighborhood with children playing in the street and small gardens in the back yards. A school that stood abandoned and empty at the end of Fisher Avenue all through the seventies and eighties now has condos in it. Fires are no more common in the neighborhood than anywhere else. Roxbury Community College has built a campus on Columbus Avenue in the abandoned I95 corridor. On Terrace Street, which was a terrifying, potholed, rundown alley where a woman was murdered by her husband in 1988, there's now a restaurant, a building materials coop, and a few other small businesses. Mission Hill survives.

Linda Stern and her second graders.

On the Front Lines in Second Grade

Linda Stern

ONE CRISP FALL day the second grade children I taught tumbled back into the classroom after recess. When I noticed several tearstained cheeks, I asked, "What happened?!" What I finally pieced together from several teary accounts was that the boys had not immediately lined up at the end of recess and that the assistant principal had rattaned six of them as punishment. My stomach lurched as I saw angry red welts on their palms. A set of rules still existed in the Boston Public Schools in the late 1960s allowing corporal punishment: a student could be rattaned, or hit with a bamboo switch, up to three times on the fleshy part of the palm in the presence of a witness; official procedures called for it to be followed up by a written report.[1]

I immediately went to talk to the assistant principal. My eyes filled with angry tears, as I asked him why he hadn't involved me in my students' discipline or even talked to me about the problem. He replied that it had nothing to do with me, that he had jurisdiction over the students during recess. I next spoke to the families of the six boys. The parents were also upset that I as their teacher was not consulted. And, sadly, one mother assumed that if her child was punished he must have deserved it.

Control of the children seemed of prime importance in the school system. As a teacher, I had very little power outside my classroom to have any say at all in school policies. I knew from colleagues that corporal punishment was administered in other parts of Boston, too, meted out in basements and other non-public places. This particular assistant principal was an older white man and the children rattaned were all minority children. In the two years I continued working at this school, after this incident, none of my students was ever subjected to this humiliating punishment again. Long overdue, the law itself was abolished in 1972[2].

Upon my graduation from Roosevelt University in Chicago a couple of years before, I'd spent the summer working as a teacher's aide in a Head Start program located in one of the massive housing projects on Chicago's Southside. 1965 was the first year of Head Start, borne of the just demands by the movements for civil rights and social justice and part of the Johnson administration's anti-poverty initiative.

Then I had moved to Boston to be back East and near friends and I spent a year substitute teaching, waitressing, and temping. I even worked, briefly, as a research assistant handling pigeons; I had to take each bird out of its cage, restrain it enough to stuff it into a cone mounted on a scale, weigh the struggling creature, and then put it into a Skinner box—if it didn't totally escape my grip first and go flying around the room. A few months of job hopping was more than enough to convince me I needed to find a meaningful profession. After spending a year at Boston University getting a master's degree in elementary education, I was hired three scant days before school started to teach second grade at a small elementary school in Roxbury.

The school building itself was dark, dingy, and grimly institutional. The faded paint was peeling so badly that you could barely tell its original color. A circular cutout for a bottle of ink still remained as part of the students' desks. On an overcast day, the lights barely pierced the gloom. Materials were available as if randomly selected and included antiquated

Dick-and-Jane type readers plus a whole closetful of puzzles. However, there was not even a single pencil and I had to buy them all year. Recess, a fifteen minute period for children to run around a paved rectangular yard with minimal playground equipment, was my only break all day from the classroom. During lunchtime, I ate my lunch at my desk in the classroom, while the children ate at their desks.

Jonathan Kozol had been fired from a fourth grade classroom in the Boston schools a couple of years before for including a Langston Hughes poem in his curriculum. He went to school committee meetings with a bundle of rattans under his arm to expose this brutal practice. His powerful book *Death at an Early Age*, which recounted his experiences at the Christopher Gibson School in Dorchester, was published in 1967 and was widely read and discussed, though not at our school. Here it was referred to in hushed tones for, some said, it made the schools look bad.

Children moved through the building in straight, erect, and very quiet lines. The first thing I heard in the morning, as my classroom was near the stairs, was "Straighten your lines." Phonetic rules were shouted down the hall. While order and control were necessary (and my classroom could have used more), it was an oppressive atmosphere for young children.

Though inexperienced and unprepared as a new teacher, I entered the classroom full of energy and optimism. I found the children to be lively, imaginative, and bright. The urban neighborhood along Dudley Street where they lived contained pockets of black, white, Puerto Rican, and Cape Verdean families. Open to new ideas and experiences, the children entered the classroom on their first day of school with enthusiasm to begin reading their new second grade reading books. They eagerly asked to write stories, though some still confused "saw" and "was". Children, ever aware of the status and privileges awarded to those just a little older than themselves, knew that cursive writing was one of the skills they would finally be old enough to learn in second grade.

But the second grade curriculum required that in September the children review their reader from first grade and that printing be reviewed before cursive writing was introduced after November 1st.

"What, Miss Stern, we can't start learning cursive today?"

"I don't wanna use last year's book; it's for babies!"

Their eagerness was dampened and I was not prepared to offer any alternatives to the standard curriculum, such as at least a different first grade reading book.

Most of the children had already experienced failure in the school system. Their reading scores fell below already low city averages. I was astonished to discover that a large majority of my students had already been kept back at least one year. I tabulated the results: out of 23 children, 15 had already repeated kindergarten, first, or second grade. Of the remaining eight, two were doing so poorly that under present school policy, I probably could not promote them.

Reading was considered the most important part of the curriculum, and we were required to spend 585 minutes a week teaching it. A phonetic system of reading was taught almost exclusively, though a few words were taught as sight words. Many children had little difficulty remembering the many rules and were able to learn to read successfully with this method. But some were not. I did experiment with some of the whole language techniques, such as child-dictated stories, which fit nicely into the anti-authoritarian mode of the 60s, as it seemed to me that relying so heavily on phonics left many children behind.[3]

The school district, because of the poverty level of the neighborhood, received special funding through the Office of Economic Opportunity and was entitled to certain compensatory services, including some excellent specialists in music, art, science and a pupil adjustment counselor available at a ratio much more favorable than other schools. We also received some expensive and useful teaching aids such as overhead projectors, tape recorders, and the like. As part of this program, all-school meetings were scheduled after school, presumably to deal with problems of children coming from a poverty environment. At the meetings there was little mention of what these problems might be and there was little sensitivity expressed toward the hardworking and beleaguered parents, who were frequently referred to as "these parents," in a tone that implied little sympathy. Shortly after this, the City of Boston lost $2 million in federal aid because of the questionable quality of this compensatory program.[4]

Nineteen Sixty-Eight was a difficult year for the nation, including my classroom of second graders. In Memphis to support a strike of black sanitation workers, Martin Luther King, Jr. was assassinated in cold blood while standing on a balcony outside his motel room. I was stunned at this violent act against a man of action, non-violence, and principle. The day after the assassination, the children came to school, subdued, and could talk of nothing else. They moved their desks all down toward one end of the classroom, for comfort, hardly a conventional seating arrangement. My supervisor, who made infrequent visits to observe me, chose to come in that day and showed me how to teach the children a nursery rhyme with accompanying finger play, failing to recognize that most of the children had left their childhood behind years before.

Bonnie, a young African-American woman, was one of the third grade teachers. She and I had our classrooms positioned so that we were able to stand in the hall, keep an eye on our students, and exchange a few words. We frequently shared curriculum ideas, both of us were interested in enriching the curriculum with ideas and materials about black history and diversity, and we were pleased to see that a few books were beginning to depict children of various ethnic backgrounds. Many of my former students were in her third grade classroom the following year so we knew some of the same children and shared perceptions of them. One day we talked about how the children, especially the boys, at the ages of seven, eight, and nine already showed signs of damage in terms of self-esteem and assertion.

I was to remember this conversation many years later, when, driving to work and half-listening to the news on the radio, I heard a news bulletin about a man who had gone on a rampage that morning in Boston, attacking several women. Right away, I recognized the name, the same as one of my second graders. As I mentally calculated that they would all be around 32 years old at this point, the announcer described him as a 32 year-old African-American man. Watching the news on TV that night left no doubt that it was my former student. That night I dug through some old files and found the class picture from 1968-1969.

While I was busy teaching second grade, the Vietnam War was expanding exponentially on the other side of the globe. Half a million U.S. troops were fighting an increasingly controversial war in Southeast Asia. Arriving home from school one day, tired from the energy and demands of my young students, I kicked off my high-heeled shoes and rummaged through the day's mail. I put off reading one of my mother's rather predictable letters and settled down to correct papers and make up lesson plans and worksheets for the next day. Later, remembering her unopened letter, I tore it open.

Hans, the boy across the street when I was growing up in Rochester, had been killed in Vietnam. He was piloting a plane and attempting to land on a huge aircraft carrier stationed off the coast. Something went very wrong and his plane plunged into the sea. I sat there numbly trying to understand all the incomprehensible meanings of a young life ended. I remembered... he and his family moved in across the street when I was seven years old. I remembered he and I going to a friend's swimming pool one afternoon playing underwater most of the time, just friends horsing around. In high school I had gone to public school, while he had gone to parochial school.

I'd lost track of him and his family when I'd gone on to college and my parents had moved. I wondered: had he had time to start a family of his own? what were his hopes and dreams? how had he felt about the war?

Several years later my family and I visited the Vietnam Veterans Memorial in Washington, and we found his name on the Wall. Names of casualties appear chronologically by date of death, and a veteran staffing the site helped us find his name. As we looked at the names on the reflective surface of black granite, we saw our own solemn images reflected back to us. On tiptoe I reached up to touch the hard metal edges of the letters forming his name. Then with paper and crayon, I traced his name in blue.

I tried to explain this war to my children, now in their early teenage years. The Vietnam War was wrong, I said. Our government sent a huge military force, half a million soldiers, to fight in a tiny developing country. We teachers, students, working people, even soldiers, people from all parts of society tried to stop the war, and we did. But not before way too many were killed, both American and Vietnamese.

"I see, Mom…But how did people stop the war?…And do you think we can we go for ice cream now?"

At the end of the school year I took a carload of my second grade students to the beach. They played in the sand, dashed into the cold water, jumped over the waves, and had a great time. Just six days later, Prentiss, who was at the beach that day, was struck and killed by a car. The car, stolen by a teenage driver, was fleeing from the police who chased him in hot pursuit. Prentiss, his two year old cousin, and two children from across the street were standing on the sidewalk in front of his house when the stolen car careened out of control and hit the group of children and then a brick wall. Prentiss's parents had, unbelievably, already lost another child, their daughter, ten years before, also struck by a car.

His family invited me to go shopping with them, looking for a suit to bury him in. As we backed out of the driveway, the funeral director, in a late model convertible with the top down, came to a stop in front of the house. Arm across the back of the seat, she was eating an apple as she discussed funeral arrangements with them.

Going to the joint wake for Prentiss and his two year old cousin was one of the hardest things I've ever done. Immobilized by tears, I stared out the door of the funeral home. Jackie, one of the other teachers, came over and put her arm around me.

By the end of my second year teaching in Roxbury, after the families of four or five of my second graders were burned out of their homes in a sudden rash of fires, I came to realize that violence, death, and loss were all too common in poor urban neighborhoods.

Death At An Early Age? Not just a metaphor in this urban neighborhood, what chance would the kids have with the grinding poverty, the decrepit housing, substandard schools, the dangerous streets?

Meanwhile, a war was raging halfway around the world, certainly not in the interests of anyone in *this* neighborhood. What if these resources could be poured into urban neighborhoods all over the country? This poverty was created under capitalism, and significant reforms were not possible. It became clear to me that massive, if not revolutionary changes, were needed.

Notes

1. Jonathan Kozol, *Death at an Early Age* (Boston: Houghton-Mifflin Co., 1967) 6-7.

2. The Massachusetts legislature passed a law, implemented in 1972, called "Corporal Punishment Prohibited." Massachusetts General Law, chapter 71, Section 37G stated that local school committees no longer had "the right to inflict corporal punishment."

3. The whole-language approach teaches word meanings in context while a phonetic approach teaches words by pulling them apart into their component sounds. This debate continues today.

4. Jonathan Kozol, *Death at an Early Age* (Boston: Houghton-Mifflin Co., 1967) 13, 235.

Internado kids and an Antioch colleague volunteer, Colonia Alejandra, late 1970's

The Internado

Beatrice Nava

Winter 1978. A few days ago I was snowbound in Manhattan. Now I'm wiping my brow and swatting away gnats in semi-tropical, low-lying Colonia Alejandra, an isolated spread-out settlement of perhaps a thousand people, in the middle of the state of Morelos, in the middle of Mexico. Beans are perking on the stove. I'm sure to have them ready when the kids get home for lunch. The scent stokes my feeling that I'm where I belong. I've checked that the dorm is in order, the walkways swept, the pigs fed and their stalls scrubbed. I sit down at the table in the little all-purpose house, open my notebook, and start poring out what's been on my mind since my recent visits to my young adult children back in the States and in France. I wonder at the contrasts among our lives and between our lives and those of the dozen girls and boys now under my care at this *internado*, in this remote spot in the state that spawned Emiliano Zapata, Mexico's popular "Land and Liberty" leader of the Revolution of 1910. This bare-necessities home away from home provides room and board to these Mexican 13 to 16 year-olds, giving them an otherwise unavailable opportunity to go to public secondary school.

Suddenly I'm disturbed by oinking outside the open door next to me. I grab the kitchen waste can. This time it's good the kids didn't give the breakfast scraps to the pigs. I use the bait to lure the frisky animals back to their stalls. Mission accomplished, I return to my journal. Gloria walks in from school. "So much writing," she exclaims, "and all in English!"

I murder her language—I knew no Spanish when I arrived in her country a few years back, have picked it up in bits and pieces. But she looks stunned when I say: "English is my language. For me, it's the same as Spanish for you."

Vivacious, curvaceous, hip swinging, sassy, alternately affectionate and rebellious—a consummate teenager in any culture—Gloria personifies the joys and frustrations of life among these adolescents. Their parents have entrusted them to us because it costs too much to keep them at home and send them to school. Many can't come up with the approximately $4 monthly contribution we ask. Furthermore, many live up in the hills of the state of Guerrero, not far from the seductions of Acapulco. The mother of a shapely 13 year-old has told me, "Many girls her age are already prostitutes." Parents of girls and boys alike complain: "They don't go to school; they run off to the beach."

Victor comes in and tells me, "You're not a *gringa* (Mexican slang for a female US citizen)." My immediate reaction is to feel good: he's sparing me the term's implied belittlement. But other kids say he's misinterpreting their teacher, who had pointed out "America" and "Americans" refer to the land and people from Alaska to Tierra del Fuego: it's an offense to other inhabitants of the Americas for United States Americans to arrogate the designation. Inadvertently, Victor contributed to awareness that my husband, Oscar, had sparked, leading me to refer to USAmerica and USAmericans.

At the *internado* we function much like any big family. The youngsters eat, sleep, do or don't do their chores, bring their triumphs and their problems. I'm a temporary surrogate mother, sometimes delegating authority to volunteers, the equivalent of big sisters or brothers. I'm the one to give permission to attend parties, intervene at school if there's a problem, arbitrate disputes, act *in loco parentis* (never, however, fulfilling the authorization of their parents to box ears!). Oscar is the occasional father figure, taking part in weekly meetings but otherwise not around much. Everyone has responsibilities and expectations. Meals are "family style," with everyone seated around the table in the little house three times a day—there's a mid-day break from school, about three kilometers away (traversed by foot or hitchhiked). The youngsters rejoin their families at vacation times, though a few of them take turns staying here in order to care for the pigs and do minimal maintenance. A few have intact families, though most come from struggling, single-mother households—with multiple brothers and sisters. The only single parent with a steady salaried job is a chambermaid in a luxury Acapulco hotel (where a guest did her the favor of impregnating her anew).

What we offer here, about two-thirds of the way between the cities of Yautepec and Jojutla, is extremely modest. The premises have been loaned rent-free to the *internado* by a church group that abandoned a similar project on the site some years ago.

The church had kept up only this little house, formerly home to the property's caretaker and his wife. It is now our center of operations. This is where we prepare our food, eat, meet, and where the volunteers, including me on my frequent stayovers, sleep and share with the girls the only bathroom that has running water (when available from the tank on the roof). Hot water is an unknown luxury; there is no telephone here or nearby, and electricity is always problematic. There is seldom enough power at night for the youngsters to iron the uniforms they wash each day to wear to school the next. They strain their eyes to do their homework. An inveterate reader, I indulge my nightly ritual by the light of a candle at the side of my cot.

In an L-shaped building about twenty feet from the little house, the girls share one of several large rooms, the boys another. Each youngster has a bed, though they often push a couple together. They like to bunch up: they tend to be afraid of the dark, and the surroundings are unfamiliar. "We heard La Llorona," they've told me more than once. Whistling wind or animals moving in the night make them think of that legendary woman whose nightly wailing terrorized Mexicans—in the middle of the sixteenth century! The youngsters keep their clothes and other few belongings in cartons or valises alongside their beds. There is no other furniture. The girls come into the little house to use the bathroom, whereas the boys take water from the *pila* (sink) behind the little house in order to use in the dormitory building's large, multi-stalled bathroom. The *pila* also serves as scrub board for laundry and for showers-by-bucket.

On the other side of the entrance gate, there are rudimentary pig installations with about a half-dozen stalls. They were part of the initial attraction of this site because we hoped a pig-based business might eventually sustain the project. There's space enough for a small vegetable garden, but we haven't been able to protect plantings from four-legged or flying predators. To the kids' delight, there are several fruit trees: papaya, banana, lima (a citrus fruit somewhat sweeter and less juicy than an orange), and *chirimoya*, which my dictionary translates as a custard apple—and which the children love but which is one of the few tropical fruits whose richness escapes me.

How did I get here? I grew up as the more or less pampered only girl in a motherless household, with an adoring father and three much older brothers—though at 14, I had the shattering experience of finding the lifeless body of the youngest of those three, then 21, successful in his second suicide attempt. Later, I lived the role of suburban wife, mother, and eventually teacher for more than 20 years until, probably influenced by the momentum of the sixties, I divorced my children's father and moved in a more unconventional direction. My children grew up in upper middle class comfort. They graduated from "good" schools, and now appear to be making their way up in the world.

I came to Mexico in 1970 in despair over the Vietnam War. I've now been a legal resident for eight years, with a home in Tepoztlán, Morelos, where the climate is temperate and the mountainous views are spectacular. My comfortable adobe house in Tepoztlán lacks such conveniences as washer, dryer, and dishwasher that my children and I formerly took for granted, but also stands in sharp relief from the minimally equipped *internado*. I shuttle back and forth. I am often in Alejandra for days and sometimes weeks at a time. If no one else is available to supervise and work along with the kids, I accept the self-assigned role.

Oscar and I became immersed in the *internado* almost accidentally. On a Sunday afternoon in the early seventies, a college acquaintance—also married to a Mexican— came to visit us at our home, in Tepoztlán. She had with her a Mexican priest and a young man from the United States, who were negotiating for a property about a 15-minute walk from our house. They were intending to establish an *internado* to enable rural kids to go to school and to give them practical agricultural skills to put to use later rather than joining the massive influx of job seekers in Mexico City.

The project had a nostalgic pull on Oscar, who'd been one of the children in the briefly realized *internado* dream of President Lázaro Cárdenas, contemporary of Franklin Delano Roosevelt, who has sometimes been thought of as Mexico's FDR. The idea behind that *internado* was to bring together children from all parts and strata of Mexico to work and study together in a basically socialistic experiment. The youngsters shared day-to-day duties and practiced at least limited self-government, an experience pivotal to Oscar's lifelong credo of social responsibility.

At first, Oscar's anti-religious bent made him wary of the new project because of the involvement of the priest. And I had pretty much had my fill of "liberal do-good" ventures in the United States. However, always eager to be as much a part of the Tepoztlán community as possible, I agreed when those Sunday afternoon visitors asked me to give English classes once the *internado* was established. The idea was to make free English instruction available to the community at large, as a goodwill gesture to offset potential resistance to the "importation" of the impoverished youth from a state many Tepoztecans disdained.

Soon the priest bowed out, followed by his co-founder, who had also served as the first director. When a US friend of ours, Heidi Brandt, reluctantly agreed to take over, Oscar eased some of her apprehension by saying he would attend weekly meetings with the kids in order to lend a male, Mexican, presence. He added he was sure I would also do whatever I could.

I readily agreed to Heidi's first request: to cook a meal once a week. I had heard the kids complain about the food when I went to the *internado* for the community evening classes and when I saw them at the local secondary school, where I was then serving as a substitute teacher of English. Soon they were begging me, "Please come every day," which I did, though I admit it was kind of a shocker when one of them introduced me to his parents as "our cook."

Almost from the start, the kids besieged and beseeched Oscar and me: "You won't let the *internado* close, will you?" They were always aware of its constant and increasing precariousness: the shortage of funds and committed people. I became director—how could I say no?—when Heidi cut back her involvement. Oscar had already become treasurer and chief buyer of provisions.

After a few years in Tepoztlán, the board of directors decided to move the *internado* to Alejandra to take advantage of greater space—and, above all, to eliminate the burdensome monthly rent in Tepoztlán. At a distance of about 40 or so not easily traversed kilometers, the new location meant I could no longer trot back and forth from home. So, since the move, whenever I'm "on," it's 24-hour duty. I see Oscar only when he comes once a week with provisions and to check up on the agricultural end of things and take part in our weekly meetings. After my recent visits to my children in the United States and France, I was home in Tepoztlán only long enough to unpack and take a hot bath. The woman who had agreed to stay at the *internado* in my absence took off as soon as I returned.

I know the kids' euphoria at my return will soon wear off and I'll have to resume a top-sergeant role. But this morning they got up at my first "You got to get up" call at 5 a.m. I didn't even have to go on to the next verse of the reveille song, "Some day I'm going to murder the bugler and spend the rest of my days in bed," or remind anyone about routine duties. In many respects, we probably expect more of them than they're used to. We rotate assignments—never gender specific. Boys and girls cook, clean the premises inside and out, feed and bathe the pigs, clean the stalls, tend the garden.

We try hard to break down gender stereotypes. Sometimes I think our most positive impact may come from chipping away at inbred assumptions, our strikes against machismo, by precept and unconscious example.

Once when we were sitting together waiting for Oscar to arrive at the *internado*, Cipriano looked at me earnestly and said, "He never lets you down, does he?"

When another of the boys came to see us in Tepoztlán and saw Oscar at the kitchen sink, the lad exclaimed: "You mean to tell me don Oscar does the dishes!"

Victor once startled me by asking, "How many times has don Oscar beaten you?"

"Do you think I would live with a man who beat me?" I responded. Later, when I found he had asked Oscar's son if his father beat me, I said:

"You really have that on your mind, don't you?"

"That's the way it is here," his friend Pedro chimed in.

"Well," said I, "if there's one thing that I hope all of you learn at the *internado*...."

Though some original donors were skeptical about a coeducational *internado* for more obvious reasons, our battles of the sexes are mostly in terms of sibling-type rivalry. The boys and girls act like brothers and sisters, often lining up against each other. One day the boys came home for lunch screaming, "Gloria stole hand cream."

After many "he said-she said" allegations, it became clear that the boys were retaliating. Gloria had disparaged the virility of one of them. She had told a friend, "Atanacio tried, but he couldn't make it."

She finally admitted to both charges. She had just wanted to tease shy Atanacio, but she really had lifted a jar of Nivea cream from the back seat of a car when a few of the kids were given a ride home from school. The tempest was over before they all went out to see if they could hitch a ride back for the afternoon school session.

On the other hand, Rosa once ran into the house sobbing, "They say we're not *señoritas*, but we are—and you can take us to a doctor to prove it." (Years later, back in the United States, I find a reverse syndrome: perish the thought that high school girls are virgins!).

Then, more seriously for *internado* decorum, there was Victor's ill-timed transgression: he sneaked into the alcove where Nena sometimes sleeps on a night she had ceded her bed to a visiting father. Victor's usually facile tongue couldn't save him from temporary suspension. Ordinarily, he chatters so incessantly, often squirming out of some task or casting guilt elsewhere, that I once asked his long-time neighbors from Acapulco: "Does he always talk this much?

"No," they said, "at home he's very quiet."

"What's the difference?" I asked Victor.

"At home it's sad."

"And here it's happy?"

"Here I know we're going to eat."

Hunger is no longer an abstract concept to me. Fernando and Atanacio, handsome, green-eyed orphaned brothers, offhandedly mention that at home they often eat only every other day. They live with their aunt, whose maintenance comes from selling her homemade, hand-made tortillas. Little Mauricio shovels food into his mouth as fast as he can. He burst out of his clothes after a couple of weeks at the *internado*. Without thinking I asked, "Do you eat more here than at home?"

"More than twice as much," he answered, his bright brown eyes sparkling. On a day when he ate too much, too fast, I told him to lie down in the little house until his stomach felt better. My son Jim's friend Julie was here at the time. She'd come to stay with me at the *internado* for a few days while she and Jim were visiting in Tepoztlán. She went to the boys' dorm to get Mauricio a blanket from the carton containing his few belongings. Tears were running down her face when she came back from the bare-bones room. "This is enough to make anyone a radical," she sobbed.

We always give top priority to providing a healthful diet, basically vegetarian. We have eggs aplenty—a donation from a hatchery. We get fresh milk from local cows (some of which occasionally wander into our yard, disturbing our nightly peace, devouring growing greens, and once eating a big supply of feed for the pigs). Brown rice and beans are staples; we usually have cheese, and contrary to Mexican custom, fresh fruit and vegetables. We start off the main meal, midday, with a green salad—what the kids call "rabbit food." One weekend afternoon a couple of the boys brought me an iguana they had caught. After they cleaned it, we put it in a big pot with onions, garlic, carrots, and whatever else we could find to add flavor. It tasted rather like chicken, and the only complaint at dinner time was that there wasn't enough.

Once in a rare while we get a few leftover strips of beef, or some traditional Mexican mole, or a meat and vegetable stew-like dish, a bonus along with the day-or-more-old bread that Las Mañanitas, a luxury inn and restaurant in Cuernavaca, customarily gives us whenever someone can stop by for it.

Contrasts are never far off, with the source of those leftovers and with my own straddled life. Shortly after my recent return to the *internado*, I hid a couple of bags of bread from Las Mañanitas to be sure there would be enough to make bread pudding for supper. While checking that we had milk, cinnamon, brown sugar, and raisins to mix in for what would make up our entire meal, my mind conjures echoes from France. "You didn't ask about what I had to eat," my son-in-law had complained to my daughter Joan after he'd dined at a four–star Michelin restaurant, the guest of a museum bigwig. Without waiting to be coaxed, he dramatically narrated his gustatory delight: from snails, delicately prepared with butter, garlic, and parsley, through exquisite sweetbreads served with morels, a superb cheese plate, and an apple tart with caramelized topping, each course served with appropriate vintage wine.

Still, it's a relief to me that as much as most of the kids love meat, they never suggest that we convert our pigs into pork for dinner. Indeed, when one of the sows whelped, Cipriano predicted solvency. "Now we won't need donations," he said, in recognition of the long-range hope of nurturing the animals in order to fund the *internado*.

Impish, short, curly-topped Cipriano probably grasps better than the other kids the dream of a self-sufficient, truly cooperative venture—though he's as full of raging hormones and adolescent deviltry as any of them. He chews over whatever he finds intellectually palatable. When he read about conserving vitamins and minerals, he said: "Ah, *caldo rico*," referring to the "delicious broth" that we make by boiling vegetable scraps, reserving the liquid to cook rice or beans.

When his teacher touched lightly on the subject of socialism, he came home from school, sounded me out, and queried: "You mean they don't put down *campesinos* like they do here?" He likes the slogan, "Who doesn't work, doesn't eat" and thinks we should institute it as policy when kids fail to do their assigned tasks or steal food from the common store. Some of them swipe bananas and oranges, which they hide under their beds, a double offense. Supplies are lessened for everyone else, and the stolen treats lure mice and roaches to the dormitories.

There's no doubt that the kids are work-resistant. When I'm here they're pretty good about the cleanliness and order we try to maintain, but when I'm not, they're much less so.

"We don't mean not to do what we're supposed to do," Paty sometimes says. "We just forget."

"What do you do not to forget, Bebe?" Fernando asks, using an old nickname I've had a hard time trying to shake off.

I just smile and shrug. But whenever I'm ready to leave, they beg me to stay.

"Don't go, Bebe, even if you want to, please don't go," Paty urges when I'm about to say goodbye after a prolonged stay. "Which do you like better, home or here?" Antonio asks. "She misses Chiquita," Cipriano says, referring to my dog.

On a day like that, I went home to Tepoztlán, to my tail-wagging Chiquita, and found a letter from my daughter Margaret, at college then in Saint Louis, Missouri. She was bemoaning the infrequency and difficulty of our contact. I went immediately to the public telephone office—we did not yet have a phone in the house. After an hour, the manager achieved the connection on his old-fashioned crank phone. As soon as he told me, "Your call is ready," I went to the phone booth and uttered a cheery "hi."

Without preamble, Margaret responded: "I still love you, but I went to see a therapist today and I realize I have a lot of hostility toward you. Sometimes when I think about what I want to do with my life, I don't know whether I'm me or you." That, she said, was because I'd always argued that work should be socially useful. Then she complained that she felt uncomfortable because the woman in whose house she was living never stopped shrieking at her kids and "you never got me used to yelling."

I didn't see anything so bad about either of these "faults" of mine, but still I was wrenched inside, just as I was when Ed wrote that he and Abby were splitting up—and that, as he put it, "in typical Freudian fashion," he blamed me for some of his anguish.

Sometimes I think about the contrasting relationships with my own children and my surrogate *internado* kids—and, indeed, how different their relationships are with their biological parents. Not that I would want to inspire either the fear they manifest of their fathers, if they have them in their lives, or the blind adoration they manifest toward their mothers. They may blow off steam at having to leave a party earlier than they'd like, or scream about having some privilege taken away because of failing to clean the bathroom, but they hold no resentment toward me—or toward their parents, who administer far harsher discipline and who do get them used to yelling.

When I make some wry remark about a forgotten or poorly performed chore, Paty says, "Oh, Bebe, you make me laugh—and sometimes you make me cry too."

"And don't you think you kids do the same to me?" I ask.

Plenty of times I almost succumbed to anger, exasperation, or frustration or a combination thereof. More than once I spent a sleepless night battling bedbugs after someone had slept in my bed in my absence. Both Oscar and I exploded when several pigs wandered off permanently when the kids failed to secure the installations properly. And we felt betrayed by the unexplained disappearance of a hammer that belonged to a volunteer, as well as by a few other instances of more or less petty thievery. But somehow the aggravations didn't get personal and psyches didn't get involved. Without my ever trying to articulate it, these kids seemed to realize that no matter what they had or had not done, I still liked them. In various ways they were more reachable than many of the young middle-class, mostly stateside college students who came to work as volunteers.

Slightly younger counterparts of my own children, the volunteers came with great intentions—and little realization of the actual situation, no matter how clearly we tried to prepare them. They probably conceived of their mission in idealistic terms that were quickly lost in the daily grit and grime. Their idea of helping to build a better world hardly encompassed a struggle to get recalcitrant kids to carry out mundane duties. One almost spit out at me when I arrived while she and another volunteer were in charge: "You don't need to tell me the place is a mess. I know it."

One afternoon I found a goodbye note from a volunteer whom I had expected to find awaiting me. "The kids are great," she'd written, "but they're monsters."

Her brief stay overlapped that of a willowy blonde German university student who defied Colonia Alejandra mores by going out with a local married man—and set the whole community talking when she took off her skirt to wrap up tortillas. She had forgotten to take a napkin for that purpose to the *tortilleria* and saw no impropriety in her solution since she was wearing a bikini underneath. "I'm really a city person," she said as she bade us farewell.

Sometimes I had to make the long, hot trek to their school to respond to a summons, as when Luis got into a brawl, or because I had a gripe, as I did after Atanacio's teacher ridiculed him in front of the class because he hadn't brought in anything for a Christmas gift exchange. My protests fell on deaf ears. There was no end to the demands from school for money for whatever—construction paper, projectors, special books, even cleaning equipment—often coupled with threats of a failing grade for non-compliance. One day the kids came back well before lunchtime, explaining: "They sent us home because we didn't sell enough tickets for the Queen of the ETAs (Agricultural Training Schools, one of which they attended).

"It seems as though marks are for sale," Fernando said, which I could easily believe from my own experience. When I was substituting at the secondary school in Tepoztlán —before we moved the *internado* to Colonia Alejandra—I heard a gym teacher tell the office secretary that a student would be coming in with a gift of a volley ball. "When she does," the teacher said, "change her mark to passing."

(From left) Guest, Beatrice Nava and kids exercising at the *Internado*, 1978

We knew that the diploma at the end of the school line was what the kids most coveted, as did their parents for them, blaming their own poverty on lack of schooling. But we had to wonder about the worth of the sacrifice. Probably the only way the *internado* could have worked well would have been with a well-staffed and well-provisioned school of its own—what a dream!

Still, we rejoiced with kids who were with us long enough to get their diplomas. And despite all the frustrations, we were enormously sad when our landlord, the Anglican church, requested return of the property. Sources of support had dried up. There was no way to go on.

For a few months a couple of the youngsters lived with us in Tepoztlán. Paty then went on to normal school to become a primary school teacher. Fernando crossed the border in the trunk of a car and joined a sister in Los Angeles, where I visited him once ("She likes vegetables," he told his sister, as she served me broccoli). Atanacio joined him later, crossing over in similar fashion. At last word he was still there, but Fernando stayed in the United States only until he saved enough to return to the area from which he came, buy a little land, build a little house, and take himself a wife. I don't know if he ever fulfilled his desire to become a teacher of English. Those from around Acapulco returned to the coastal area, where Victor and Nena didn't lose much time before marrying each other. I'm sorry to say I've never heard anything further about Cipriano. At our emotional last goodbye, he nodded knowingly when I said he "could go either way" and that I hoped he would opt for his positive potential.

Oscar, much of whose time is still spent in Tepoztlán, tells me that occasionally he runs across a few of the old timers there, and that they always greet him with affection, ask for me, and speak nostalgically and appreciatively of our shared times. For me, the *internado*—as my whole Mexican experience—was crucial in broadening my understanding of the vast inequalities that separate people, of the enormous differences between the haves and the have-nots, and of deep-rooted cultural idiosyncrasies—but also of bedrock commonalities. And it probably was also responsible for changing my future professional direction and enlarging my pedagogical perspective.

In the mid-eighties I returned to the United States and to teaching, gravitating to what's known as "adult basic education," with so-called minority populations, and English as a Second Language, with immigrants, many from Mexico.

Coming Together

Nancy Teel

PAM AND I were at each other's throats. Her older brother had volunteered for the Marines and was somewhere in Southeast Asia. She heard little news and was sick with worry. She felt that anyone who even questioned US policy was directly contributing to her brother's danger. In our co-op apartment I was quiet about my views, but refused to yield. People who stood for peace were not endangering her brother, I maintained, but rather the government and the military that sent him to Vietnam. We managed an uncomfortable civility for the sake of our studies. Deep in the upstate New York winter, I knew I needed a new living situation. I had heard something about communes and decided to learn more.

The Harrad Experiment was a popular novel my first year at Cornell. Harrad College (a thinly disguised reference to Harvard and Radcliffe) assigned men and women to room together, allowing, even encouraging, a sexual relationship; then, after a prescribed time, the students were required to change roommates. This soft porn text of the sexual revolution featured a thin plot, nude physical education classes and an annotated bibliography. As the school year ended, I met a group of men and women who quietly admitted, after they trusted me, that they had been involved in an experimental commune based on *The Harrad Experiment*, life imitating art. I was mildly shocked and asked again, just to be sure. It was true. Eight students had rented a house and lived in coed pairs in four bedrooms. Every month they switched roommates. The first few switches went smoothly, but the process broke down when one man built himself a room in the basement. Then two roommates fell in love and refused to be separated. The others made makeshift arrangements until the end of the school year. They were all looking for new housemates. Several new communes were forming, with the Harrads acting as seeds.

The Harrad experience forced everyone to think much harder about collective living, the rules, values and expectations. I joined six students to rent a house on Llenroc Court, just west of the campus and below the Arts Quad, one block down the steep hill known as "libe slope." We needed help developing our fledgling commune and called on a professor from the Business School who was an expert in "T Groups," a current buzzword for group therapy designed to force personal change. He agreed to work with us as a favor, and we met once per week during the late summer and early fall. It was a tough group. I'm not a quitter or I would have left after the first few sessions. The process was a constant assault on the ego defenses, to break us down, to force us to accept group authority, to make us absorb the new norms that the group was generating. I started to knit a scarf, the first thing I had ever knit. By the time the meetings ended, my scarf was over twelve feet long. The professor led us to deeper issues and eventually we confronted sexuality, how we viewed each other, what behavior we would expect, what we would tolerate. Because of the Harrad house, no one wanted to discuss sex, and the issue exploded. I remember staying up all night talking to one comrade. Grateful that he would work it through with me, I gave him my scarf and we became close friends. The T-group discussions ended inconclusively, but at least they had the effect of making us take our collective endeavor seriously.

As it turned out, the sexual issues in our new commune were resolved individually. After all our group therapy, there were no rules except respect for each person's privacy and choices. Most of the possible relationships did not happen. I became involved in a relationship that lasted two years, but that was the exception. Mark and I had met at the antiwar coffee house, before the commune was formed. He was a graduate student in economics, and we shared evolving political/religious consciousness. He was a bright, positive, principled man, with the upbeat personality that I craved. We fell in love in the cold Ithaca spring and first kissed in the Cornell rose garden. Our relationship developed at the same time the commune formed and was cemented by the year of living under the same roof, albeit in different rooms. Our monogamy was protective for both of us, as others in the commune respected our relationship.

My description sounds quaint as I write it long after the Sexual Revolution has mainstreamed. But I remember the radical edge even to talking about birth control in 1968. There was no information available on women's health issues: no Internet, no women's health publications; no women doctors.

Drugstores in Ithaca carried foam and condoms, but you had to find them on back shelves and face a smirking clerk to get past the check-out. Or you had to see a male doctor to get the pill. The original edition of *Our Bodies Our Selves* by the Boston Women's Health Collective was printed on newsprint in 1970 and sold out. I owned a dog-eared copy for a decade.

Other communal issues beyond sex were difficult, but easier to talk and yell about. We shared responsibilities for shopping, cooking, and cleaning. There were plenty of expectations that women should cook and clean and men should do "men's work," except that there wasn't much of it to do. The landlord kept up the building and yard, and no one had a car. For men, that left finances, but we had little money. So we all changed. I give the men particular credit because the changes that they had to undergo were immediate and obvious. Those who had never cooked had to learn. For women, the release from stereotyped gender roles was more subtle, and speaking for myself, is taking the rest of my life to complete.

At Llenroc Court we had Jan in our midst, and she challenged us to change. A top student in her class in the Psychology Department, she was a southern belle turned classic hippie with fringe, beads, blonde hair to her waist, long dresses and no shoes, incense and pot smells seeping from her room, along with the Doors playing non-stop. When her boyfriend arrived, I had to hide my surprise. He landed on a huge Harley, wearing black leather and heavy chains. Was he a Hell's Angel or did he just look like one? I didn't dare ask. I was afraid, but the Stones' Altamont concert, where the Hell's Angels killed a fan, didn't happen until later that year, so my fear had not yet hardened into prejudice. He sensed my uneasiness and took time to talk with me, softly and kindly. Although I never got to know him well, he made a positive contribution to the commune for the two months he was there.

Jan made soups with riots of vegetables, fabulous fried chicken, and chocolate chip cookies with oversized hunks of chocolate that she chipped with a knife. Once, she gave a dinner party where all the food was laced with pot. I remember eating a rainbow chicken stew, steamy rice and almonds, and corn bread thick with gold kernels. Dreamy and tired, I went to my room and fell asleep. An hour later, my roommate entered the room, and I woke up, startled. She told me about the pot in the food and the progress of the party, which by then had nearly levitated the house. I splashed water on my face and ran downstairs. I saw food in every room, and people gathered around the bowls of goodies, eating with their fingers and laughing at themselves. The air was smoky from joints, cigarettes and Jan's favorite candles; moreover, she had refitted all the lamps with colored bulbs so that each room had its own hazy tint. Acid rock on full volume made every object and surface vibrate. One group was sitting in a circle on the floor around a bowl, chanting, about to partake in some shrunken old mushrooms. People were dancing here and there, alone or together. We were all too stoned to talk. I remember being sober enough to be slightly alarmed at the candles and full ashtrays. Would we make it through the night without burning down the house? Somehow, we did.

While our commune was buffeted by the sexual revolution and the evangelism of Timothy Leary, urging us to "tune in, turn on, and drop out," the mainstream world was even crazier. In 1968, American bombers dropped untold tons of explosives on North Vietnamese cities, the Vietnamese forces beat back the Americans in the Tet offensive, Martin Luther King, Jr. and Bobby Kennedy, two of the best men in the country, were gunned down in cold blood, and cities across America burned. Strikes and protest spread across the world as students and workers united in France, U.S. athletes gave the black power salute at the Olympics, and hundreds of people were shot dead in the *Plaza de Tlatelolco* in Mexico City. And there were thousands of American casualties in Vietnam. Normal? Safe? What was that? Our commune provided a respite from the cold, killing culture. We cared about each other, helped and supported each other, and worked together against the war.

The next year, some people moved on, and I joined with others to form a larger commune in Collegetown, on the southern edge of the Cornell campus. We were twelve students, seven men and five women, one an undergraduate senior, the rest graduate students. In contrast to previous struggles, everyone easily accepted collective responsibility for chores, sharing possessions like cars and stereos, respect for private time and studies, dinners of rice, beans and veggies, support for political work, pot and parties.

Driving through Ithaca in 1998, I stopped to look at that old house on Dryden Road. Collegetown has a new look, more brick and upscale, but the commune still looks rundown with the same ugly brown asbestos shingles. I didn't see the inside, but when we lived there it was dilapidated. We hardly noticed. Our attention focused on each other, the complex interactions of our community and the larger movement.

From Dryden Road, we answered the call for a strike against the war and demonstrated in Washington in November, 1969. Even so, some were more politically active than others. I took a break from politics for several months to study for my doctoral exams. I passed in the spring, but events way beyond my control took hold of my life. My mother suffered a breakdown at the same time President Nixon widened the war into Cambodia and Laos.

The killings at Kent State and the paralyzing strike at Cornell left me in shock.[1] My world of family, school and commune collapsed as the Cornell year ended in chaos, so I accepted an invitation to go to England with a young man who was pursuing me, and I didn't return until Christmas.

Six months after I ran away, I felt strong enough to face my life again. From England, I wrote to friends at Stuart Little, a graduate-student commune on the steep hill of Stuart Avenue, to see if they had room for me. I had planned to live with them before my spur-of-the-moment trip abroad, so I was welcomed as if there had been no gap. The closeness and openness among the people in that house embraced me and made me begin to feel whole. I knew that I was lucky and in better shape than many students and young people. I wanted to contribute to the community so I joined a work collective, a group of women trying to set up a free clinic. We began as a study group, then started to raise funds. We met in an empty office, which was the donated site of the future clinic. It was there that a collective decision impacted my life for years to come.

"So who is she?" Margo's voice showed her impatience.

"Who knows, just a kid, a runaway." Susan was running the meeting as usual.

"Where is she from?"

"She won't say."

"So when is she going to be here?"

"Tonight, on the bus from New York."

"How'd we get into this?"

"Look, the Women's Center in New York called. She was staying there when she got busted for going through the turnstile in the subway. Somebody covered for her, but they want to get her out of New York. They think she won't be able to stay off the street," Kathy said.

"How old is she?"

"Fourteen"

"Shit! What are we going to do with a fourteen-year old?"

"Somebody has to take her home."

"Well, she can come out to the "Left on Nelson" house. The more the merrier," Jocelyn offered.

"Come on, you're way out in the sticks, she'll have no way to get around. She'll just run again. It has to be some place in town. Some place quiet and stable. She's pretty freaked out, they say. And we don't want the cops to find her."

The words hung in the air. One by one, the women looked at me. Stuart Little was the perfect place for the runaway. It was filled with serious students who did a minimum of drinking and drugs. The house was large and the commune was stable, funded by graduate student fellowships that weren't likely to run out. I felt panic for a moment, but grasped the truth of the situation.

"Alright," I said. "I'll take her home with me tonight. If people at Stuart Little agree, she can stay on."

Over the next year and a half, Kathy sculpted one edge of my life. When she arrived, she had the eyes of a terrified animal. For the first couple of months, she slept in my room, too afraid to sleep by herself in the alcove the commune assigned her. Three of us became her surrogate parents. We kept track of her, gave her books to read, tried to give her advice, occasionally gave her money. We helped her build a set of false identification papers. Whenever we were fed up with her radical lip and dependent behavior, Paula, Ben and I commiserated about teenagers, a state we ourselves had outgrown only a few years before.

When Kathy turned sixteen, one of our friends put her behind the wheel of his VW bug and taught her to drive. Within weeks she had her New York driver's license. It was only a matter of time before she hit the road again. She was strong, not so naive, healthy and confident. We bought her a backpack and hugged her as she left for California, sharing a ride with students for part of the way, planning to hitchhike the rest. I was relieved when she left, but I missed her and wondered if she would make it safely. Two months later, I received a post card from Berkeley. After many side trips, Kathy had reached her goal. We remained in touch for fifteen years until she disappeared again. I still hope she'll come and find me. Kathy Davis, if you read this, call me!

At Farm Street ten women shared a huge two-family house creating a viable women's commune. The larger apartment housed gay women, while the smaller side was home to three straight women including myself. Janis Joplin was music idol for both sides and we mourned together when she died. Living with gay women made me lose whatever uncomfortable feelings I had around gay people, men included, as gay men friends stopped by frequently. I learned slowly of the ways women discover that they are gay. Some had known since childhood; others opened up politically and gay feelings bubbled up after. I looked into myself as deeply as I dared, as deeply as I could, and found only mild curiosity about sex with women. I remained heterosexual, but with a sense of empathy that endures for all gay people. For all its sexual politics, like the other communes, Farm Street provided a safe haven and a place to plan the next big change in my life.

The beautiful spring of 1972 was the worst of times in Vietnam as American soldiers slowly came home, and South Vietnamese troops took over the firepower. American public opinion thought the war was "winding down," but the killing and destruction continued unabated. The movement was tired and frustrated. Our leaders had been jailed and were constantly harassed.[2] Dan Berrigan had been released from jail, but his brother Philip was indicted for conspiracy (to make peace?) and Dan, still on probation, was involved with his defense.[3] All of the legal, non-violent protests seemed to have led to the situation we were in. Tempers were short, and drugs were on the upsurge. If-you-can't-win-you-might-as-well-party became the attitude of the hour, while a steady stream of activists dropped out of the movement to reinvent lives of peace and love in the country. The mood in Ithaca and elsewhere turned ugly as love-fests of music and politics spun out of control. Collegetown rioted in April, 1972. I missed the incident that triggered the standoff, but on my way home from the university I walked into the middle of the riot. I remember running from the police, first just trying to get out of the way, then enjoying the adrenaline as we could clearly outrun them. A few weeks later, the annual spring anti-war rally turned into a rock-throwing spree. Then, as we marched through Collegetown, a local bank building exploded into flames. The movement was at a crossroads, right along with my life.

Normally, a graduate student in my shoes, just finishing a dissertation, could expect guidance from her faculty committee to find employment, or perhaps receive an additional year as a teaching fellow, but I received little help and no offers. These were not "normal" times, and I didn't think to question it; I knew that I was part of the counter-culture. And I was a woman, not considered a serious player in the game of academic politics. In a meeting after the invasion of Cambodia, I had challenged the most illustrious professor in the Linguistics Department to join the strike. Like the country, our department was split between anti-war students and professors and those who supported the status quo. Instead of recognizing me as a woman who could speak up for a cause she believed in, many saw my challenge as a bad move for my future career, even though it was applauded by the anti-war forces. Only the Latin American Studies professor on my committee concerned himself with what might happen to me after I left Cornell. I appreciated his interest, and talked at length about my developing plans to join the movement full-time.

In the cold, early spring four Ithacans convened to discuss what to do after graduation. We understood that the student movement was coming to a dead-end as the soldiers came home. We foresaw that US involvement in developing countries would be covert or indirect as a result of public rejection of the Vietnam War. Lasting change in the culture of war and violence would have to come through other Americans. Our Marxist study pointed to the working class. We decided we wanted to be in the city; not in the ivory tower; and we wanted to join the working class. Indeed, we would have to. We planned to put into concrete practice our principles of love, sisterhood, non-violence, political awareness and community. Soon we made contact with like-minded activists in Boston and New York and agreed to form a new commune in Boston with a political theme.

The academic year and my degree completed, and the women's commune disbanded, I returned to Stuart Little. There was no bedroom available, so I threw my belongings into a friend's and slept on the floor in my sleeping bag or, on clear nights, out on the flat roof beyond his window. It was bittersweet. I felt a sense of closeness to my friends, but it was the end of my era in the ivory tower. In mid-summer I threw my books and clothes into the back of my '67 Mustang and moved again, to Massachusetts. Eleven political activists met in the summer of 1972 to reclaim an old house in Dorchester, a working-class Boston neighborhood. All of the communes that I experienced in Ithaca were a preparation for this serious step into collective living and full-time political work. The Bowdoin Street commune lasted for four years and provided some of the stability and connection I needed so badly. And while we were there, we threw some of the best parties in town.

Whenever I stand at the lookout on Chickatawbut Road in the Blue Hills and look down on the city, I remember the Puritan idea that Boston was to be "a city on a hill." The Puritans who came to New England thought they were going to build a society that embodied the Kingdom of God on earth. They planned to show it off to their European brethren. As the intentional community at Bowdoin Street took shape in 1972, we also had a sense of modeling a new world.

How can I describe Bowdoin Street? The house was built just after the Civil War, part of the development of the "streetcar suburbs." It still stands on the old square at Meetinghouse Hill, just where Adams Street begins. Named after the Presidents, Adams Street runs south to Quincy past the colonial homestead of John and Abigail Adams and the Presidential library. But our end of Adams Street was, and still is, poor. There were drugs, abused children, gangs and desperate people when we moved there in 1972, and it has not changed much since then. Today the neighborhood is more racially diverse and more politically aware and organized; otherwise it looks the same.

Built as one of the first two-family homes, the house had three bedrooms, two living rooms, a kitchen, bath and dining room on each of the first two floors; and three more bedrooms on the third floor, where my room was located, plus another big living room with an alcove. When we moved in, stained wallpaper in Victorian patterns darkened every room, fixtures were filthy and roaches and mice far outnumbered us. Had I not lived in substandard student housing for several years previously, I would have been horrified. Our first communal work was to make ourselves into a clean-up and redecorating crew. We rented a huge steamer and removed the wallpaper. Fortunately, the original plaster beneath was intact. Then each of us painted our own room; I learned about primer, spackle and masking tape in a hurry. Rock music and the excitement of being together made the clean-up like a party much of the time, but the roaches were abominable. We couldn't get rid of them, so we called the landlord. He was delighted with the work we had done to improve his property and sent an exterminator. Roaches departed, but mice kept multiplying until Ginny moved in with her two lean female cats. They had a circus. Every morning Ginny found several dead mice outside her bedroom door. After two months, there were no more. We were able to live in a healthy space from then on.

On March 30, 1973, I wrote to a friend from Cornell:

...Things have changed a great deal since last fall. Kathy moved out shortly after you were here and just about two weeks ago, Jeff also moved out. Sad but true that they were both so involved in figuring out their relationship, what to do with their lives and the structure of their own minds that it was simply not the right time for them to live in a collective. That leaves eight of us in this big house, too few really, and only four of us are committed to staying next year...I guess it's fair to say that we failed to achieve any kind of real unity as a group—which is not surprising when you look at the extreme divergence in our lives—though that wasn't clear last spring or even last fall...I'm concentrating on the people and activities that are important to me...working on radio tapes again and we're putting together a slide show on corporate control of the health care system...Then there is writing and research....

I'm gradually meeting people in Boston...It's exciting...

Love, Nancy (age 27)

Eleven people pioneered the first year at Bowdoin Street. In spite of our success in reclaiming the house from ruin, unity eluded us. By spring, six had decided to move on, four of them victims of romances that failed, leaving the core group from Ithaca plus one New Yorker alone in the huge house. We redeployed ourselves and carried on. New people joined us. Work and meals were shared and there was much conversation late into the night about the meaning of life and the direction of political work. The commune survived.

In 1972, the media depicted a glut of Ph.D.s in the middle of a recession. I interviewed for a few academic jobs but received no offers of full-time work. Meanwhile I was doing political work as a volunteer against the war. Late in the fall Susan and I were offered a small stipend to work with the New England Action Research project at the American Friends Service Committee (AFSC). I began a two-year stint as a movement researcher, one that helped me make what has been the most enduring commitment of my life: to use my intellectual skills for the benefit of working-class people.

My training in research was a critically needed skill. New England Action Research monitored the military-industrial complex in our area and created educational media. I read *Business Week, Aviation Week* and *Space Technology*, the *Congressional Record* and other publications to track the huge flow of defense dollars into New England. We modeled our work on a national AFSC group in Philadelphia, whose NARMIC Slide Show was the most intelligent and influential anti-war media piece of the era. We also made a slide show on the industrial base of the health care system, another important part of the local economy, and wrote about economic conversion to a civilian economy. Developments in New England in the last 25 years have proved that we were right when we said that that military production depressed and restrained the economy and that civilian production would buoy the region. Today, military production is a much smaller part of the local economy. Information technology, biotechnology and Internet companies rule in a prolonged period of prosperity.

I enjoyed my work at AFSC, and tried to understand the Quaker philosophy of non-violence and recognition of the divine light in each person. It was radically different from the Catholicism I had grown up with. The Friends practiced equality and made decisions by consensus, and I came to deeply respect their commitment and faith. Their collective process provided a model for our commune. I was particularly moved by their desire and engagement to stop violence in all its forms; they strove for non-violence in personal relations, as well as in international affairs. While no one I knew was as famous as Dan Berrigan, they were equally principled. I recognized my own weakness and inability to profess a true philosophy of non-violence; for me non-violence remained a strategy of social change, not a religious principle.

At Bowdoin Street, our lives intertwined.

"Hey Kendall, when's band practice?" I called to my new, next-door housemate.

"At about seven."

"Are they going to eat here? I'm cooking tonight...rice and veggies."

"Well, maybe they'll be hungry. I didn't invite them to dinner." Kendall stuck her head out her door and flashed me a smile that could send an ice age into retreat.

"I'm so glad you moved in," I said. "I'll make sure there's plenty..."

On a summer afternoon in 1974, a racially mixed crowd of 200 men, women and children gathered in Dorchester's Codman Square, about a mile south of the Bowdoin Street commune. A few outsiders from Cambridge and Somerville mingled in the crowd, but the majority of us were progressive people living in Dorchester, including many who had lived here all their lives. Three teenagers held a large white banner; someone had sacrificed some old bed sheets and carefully lettered in red paint: Racial Unity Now.[4] A couple of local activists gave pep talks using a crackly bullhorn, yelling over the traffic noise. Then we marched. I remember feeling afraid because we were so few in the vast urban landscape. In recent weeks racially mixed couples and individuals had suffered violent attacks. We could guess what the racist forces would make of this integrated group of 200. We chanted and sang our way down Bowdoin Street. As we reached the triangular park across from our commune, one marcher broke ranks, ran up on the front porch, unlocked the big front door and reappeared with a camera on the second floor deck, to photograph the march from a good vantage point. I recognized Mitchell, one of the men from our first floor apartment, a reporter for the radical newspaper, *The Guardian*. I didn't like him much, his Harvard arrogance offended me, but I felt relieved that it was not a stranger who entered my house. The significance of his photo session didn't dawn on me. We continued the march to the local shopping district receiving polite nods and waves from neighbors. People showed support, but in a careful, restrained way.

The consequences of Mitchell's careless action came the next night. Susan's room overlooked Bowdoin Street, with huge bowed windows facing the park, a wonderful old-fashioned space. She retired early to her mattress on the floor in the middle of the room. She was sound asleep, buried under her quilt, when Rene, her future husband, returned from a late meeting and entered the room. His work boots crunched on the worn oak floorboards. The room was cold. He stopped, spoke softly and turned on the light. Susan sat up and a shower of glass cascaded off her quilt. She was unhurt. The huge rock that had broken the window lay against the back wall, a dent in the plaster showing where it had hit, after sailing over Susan. The next day we tried to gauge the angle and concluded that the assailant had used a slingshot and stood in the park across the street, a little uphill from the house, giving a straight shot to the second floor window. Rene and I and the rest of the commune were angry and upset; only Susan accepted her good luck with grace. Today, when I read about terrorism in various parts of the world, I still feel a chill of recognition.

One night at Bowdoin Street, we met in the third floor living room for one of our irregular discussions called "house meetings." These generated both tension and excitement. Whatever was going on would surely come out in the open, committed as we were to making the commune work. The talk settled on me. I was not being open enough, Rene said and others nodded. I was holding back, I was not letting people into my life. I felt myself harden and withdraw, near to tears. What could they point to that I had done wrong? What could I do differently? But it was how I was, not what I did that mattered at that moment. I had reached that point in an earlier commune and knew that I was confronting one of the limits of the form. There was no resolution. I was defending an inner self that had developed independence both by necessity and training. I valued it as a hard-won asset and could not, would not, let it go. I could not see a third option. I felt if I didn't maintain a distance, I would fall into the merger trap that my mother had first set for me. There was no way I was going there. The meeting was inconclusive, but it left me feeling the boundaries of communal life.

In spite of its limitations, I felt personally calm and settled at Bowdoin Street for the first time since I had left Erie. I belonged finally to a community I believed in, whose values I shared and upheld. We beat back alienation and had a glimpse of the enormous toll in energy and spirit that it takes when it is strong. The torn places in our young ideals healed in a counter-cultural way. I lived at Bowdoin Street until the commune ended in the summer of 1976. I can honestly say I was happy there and I would like to live that way again at another time in my life.

Bowdoin Street Diary

December 1, 1974

It had been a big hard pull but it feels like the house has reached a new level. We are beginning to feel like a family

These old wooden walls have absorbed a lot of pain and struggle over our 2 1/2 years here. In that time we (those of us who stuck it out) have learned to value the pain that brings growth, the struggle that leads to wholeness... — Susan

9 January, 1975

The last quarter of the twentieth century is beginning in...economic and social chaos. By contrast we seem to be a stable and growing little social system/group...

In the last month we've grown closer—more relaxed—more able to touch—to enjoy each other and express our mutual affection and admiration. It feels like a new level—a new high—there's a sense all of a sudden that we've come a long way. — Nancy

No Date

This book is a very nice happy idea. Here is a kiss and hug for everyone:
XXX () () ()

— Kendall

April 30, 1975

Vietnam has won!! A day of celebration and joy throughout the world—

— Dick

Notes

1. See *"Shut It Down: Students Against the War," page 36.*

2. See Linda Stern's chapter on the trial of the Panthers, COINTELPRO etc.

3. See Berrigan's autobiography, *To Dwell in Peace*, (San Francisco: Harper and Row, 1987), p. 266 ff.

4. See Linda Stern's chapter, *"Looking For Answers: Marxism-Leninism To The Suburbs"* in Section III: "From Theory to Practice".

New Harmony Sisterhood

Kendall Hale

What seemed like a little thing to do—play music in a feminist band—now has turned into one of the most exciting phenomena of our lives. We have watched as women's culture has grown from a few attempts to today's present mushrooming of books, songs, movies, and plays. There is real emotional satisfaction in making women's music, but that is not all there is. It is important for me to realize that we are not simply entertainers, but that we are creating the strength for a movement that has the greatest potential for change this country has seen in decades. I am firmly convinced (yes, I have read political and economic theory, Mr. Leftist) that women's culture is revolutionary, and, best of all, it is accessible to large numbers of women.

> Marcia Deihl, New Harmony
> Sisterhood Band *(All Our Lives, A
> Woman's Songbook*, Diana Press, 1976)

For some sixties youth, music itself was the revolution. Others listened to the charged messages of folk-rock singers and then took to the streets in protest. As for me, when I was an infant, my mother sang songs written by Mormon pioneers crossing the plains in covered wagons:

> Put your shoulder to the wheel, push along. Do your duty with
> a heart full of song. We all have work, let no one shirk. Put
> your shoulder to the wheel.

On every family car trip, we harmonized America's favorite folksongs, including many by Pete Seeger and Woodie Guthrie. My childhood connection to music continued with the civil rights struggles of the 1950s and 1960s. In 1962, Mom sang along with Negro spirituals on a record of Civil War songs. At sixteen, I played Bob Dylan and Joan Baez on a guitar, with the only beatnik in town. After the Beatles, music was like food: without it I felt dead.

In the early 1970s, I heard both the Chicago and New Haven Women's Liberation Rock Bands. They blew my mind. I knew then that I wanted to combine feminism with my childhood folk singing and classical violin training. At the time, the three seemed incompatible. But then, I began listening to Holly Near and Chris Williamson, both powerful feminist musician/song writers making the national scene. Then, in 1973 when I was studying left-wing politics at Cambridge-Goddard, an alternative graduate school, I heard women singing Custom Made Woman Blues and Don't Put Her Down, by Hazel Dickens and Alice Gerard, a country/bluegrass duo:

> Well if she acts that way,
> It's 'cause you've had your day,
> Don't put her down,
> You helped put her there.

Immediately I started jamming with these women from school. After practicing a couple of months, we sang for our first audience, at a women's party, and were cheered enthusiastically. We were amateur songwriters and musicians, but our voices matched a call from a growing sisterhood. It was the beginning of connection between the feelings, hopes, and dreams of the women's movement and what became the New Harmony Sisterhood Band.

In our early gigs, five of us fumbled with our instruments and voices, but our lack of technique was overridden by our message. The passionate wild energy between the band and our fans filled me with love for performance, in contrast to the scary violin recitals of my girlhood.

At the time, we could not have imagined how inspirational our performances were or the tremendous support we would receive from hundreds of feminist women and men over the next seven years.

"Men don't have to define their songs as 'men's songs' because almost everything that exists in this culture was created by men," we announced to all our audiences.

After we played and raised funds for women's celebrations, women's centers, and women's studies programs, we were sought by activists from all over Boston. We played free for union drives, striking workers, liberation movements, and early nuclear power protests. In 1976, we recorded with Paredon Records, a record company under the cultural wing of the Marxist-Leninist newspaper, *The Guardian*, and two years later, we traveled south on a tour we created ourselves.

Five of us met weekly for two hours of outrageous, irreverent fun. In an eclectic folk/bluegrass style we sang angrily about being born female. It would go like this:

"It ain't me babe, noo, noo, noo, it ain't me babe," Deborah is imitating Bob Dylan in a nasal drawl, twanging her acoustic guitar.

"Down with cock rock!" pitches Katy, gyrating her hips.

Marcia howls beside her on a mandolin, " And I'm tired of fuckers fucking over me!" She curtseys. "And this ladies and gentlemen is a new musical genre. Live from a real lesbian living room in Boston!"

We all get hysterical as Marcia's mandolin leads us in chorus:

> *When I'm walking down the street and every man I meet says,*
> *'Baby ain't you sweet'*
> *I could scream—.*
> *But although those guys are sick and think only of their prick,*
> *It ain't sweet I feel;*
> *I just feel good and mean—.*
> *They whistle for me like a dog and make noises like a hog.*
> *Heaven knows they sure got problems I agree—.*
> *But their problems I can't solve*
> *'cause my sanity 's involved,*
> *And I'm tired of fuckers fuckin' over me.*
> *Beverly Grant, 1971*

I yell when it's my turn to present a new song, "Attention, attention." Tapping my violin bow on a music stand, I roll up my bare leg and croon into the microphone verses I finished at two that morning:

Went on down to the Two O'Clock Lounge,
looking for a quick day's pay,
From packing meat on the assembly line—
Now it was me who was prey.
Can you dance baby, baby, sweet baby, Can you dance?"

Katy and Pat stare at me in disbelief: "true feminists" do not shave body hair. But I had just been laid off from a local meat packing plant after working only six weeks. My unemployment checks were running out, along with my small savings account. Believing it might be possible to make some easy money until I could refocus my organizing strategy, I'd shaved my legs and blindly walked into a "den of sin," as my grandmother would have described it.

"Did you really go into that sleazy, topless joint in the middle of downtown?" Deborah asked. "And by yourself?"

"Yes and yes," I groaned, "And I stayed just long enough to be shocked at the working conditions those women put up with! Thick smoke under dim lights and creepy, Mafia-looking men scared the shit out of me. After some weirdo guy watched me walk across the stage in a bathing suit, I freaked out and ran!"

Our New Harmony member Deborah Silverstein spoke for all of us in her 1974 copyrighted song, *All Our Lives"*:

> *1. The men listen and then say, I'm sympathetic babe. I know*
> *what you women have been through all your lives. But I'm*
> *not the one to blame, I didn't write the rules to this lousy game.*
> *But you've got nothing for us men already on your side.*
>
> *CHORUS*
>
> *Well you want to see some sweetness, not just streams of angry*
> *words.*
> *You really dig the music but the message is too tough.*
> *It seems we've forgotten about happiness and love.*
> *You think we've said what we have to say but enough's enough.*
>
> *2. Well, I understand their point, they don't think we should*
> *exploit The first chance we've ever had to fight back all our*
> *lives We're told to soften our approach, let some tender feelings*
> *show, And give our sympathizers equal time.*

3. Well, I've only this to say, I look forward to the day When
women won't have to fight for an equal chance all their lives,
And the purpose of our songs is to move this fight along Until
there's room for more than just the struggle to survive.
It's not that we've forgotten about happiness and love But until
the times have changed, it's not enough.

The New Harmony Band became a family for all of us, with caring support, as well as pain, competition, egotism, and disagreement. The product became a unique blend of my classical fiddling, Deborah and Katy's lead and back up guitars, Marcia's mandolin, autoharp, and recorder, and Pat's base. With our music reverberating through our bodies, into the furniture, out the windows across tree limbs skyward over Cambridgeport, we were a true sisterhood, with a song in the heart of the Boston women's movement.

New Harmony was my link to the women's movement, but within the band we also experienced many of the ideological struggles and political line battles playing out in the left. Often we nearly came to blows over absurd shades of difference. Labels were everything. I represented Marxism-Leninism, Deborah became the socialist feminist, Katie Tolles, a libertarian, Marcia a feminist anarchist, and Pat Ouellette a lesbian feminist anarchist.

Squeezed into Marcia's tiny living room, between her piano, gas heater, and TV set, we were surrounded by plastic toy animals, dolls, old high-heeled shoes, bizarre off-color comic strips, and black-humor postcards. This paraphernalia was hanging, sitting, peering, and pasted on the refrigerator, doors, walls, and end table. Together with Marcia's comedian personality and Deborah's horny dog, Timber, it brought relief to our emotional sessions of confessions and personal stories woven around class, race, nuclear power, and third world liberation issues. We debated the lyrics and message of each song.

We had come together to play women's music, but the question became, which women: middle class, working class, African American, Hispanic, gay? And which issues? Was it OK to sing a traditional women's song, or did it need to be feminist?

Before Pat joined, I was the only gay-identified woman to bring lesbian songs to heterosexual women. Ironically, when the band broke up, I was the only straight member. In 1974, we copyrighted "Unfinished Business," by I.M. Reluctant.

CHORUS

I've got some unfinished business, well I just want to say
I've got some unfinished business to take care of today.
Well I know what's on my mind, and I think that it's time
To tend the unfinished business that we left behind.

Well they say that it's not natural.
They try to make you scared
To be a homosexual with feelings to share
With a good friend who it's plain to see
Is of the same sex that you just happen to be.

Oh, it's so easy to run, it's so easy to hide,
It's too easy to find the ways to
Not find the time,
To dig my head out of the sand and
Look for the words
To answer the ones who say
We're out of our minds.....

I was constantly preaching to my band sisters: "We've got to sing about the oppression of poor and minority women too, not just privileged, white feminists like ourselves." I wrote about capitalism and imperialism in songs about my jobs, union organizing, black women's battles, Puerto Rican freedom fighters and other issues new to the white middle class women's movement.

"Yeah, Kendall, but your lyrics sound like a political speech," complained Katy. "Cut the rhetoric!"

"But she's got the right idea. Gay women have been oppressed for centuries," exclaimed Deborah. "No matter what their skin color or social class was!"

Within a couple of years, we created and arranged a song list linking historical figures like labor organizer Elizabeth Gurley Flynn and pilot Amelia Earhart to the most burning social/political issues of our day.

Our Paredon record title "Ain't I A Woman?" was taken from Sojourner Truth's famous speech at a suffrage convention in 1851. New Harmony's mentor from the Cambridge-Goddard program, Lanayre Liggera, put the powerful speech to music and we sang it for years at almost every concert. In their catalog promoting women's music, Paredon said of our record:

From the title statement taken from a speech by Sojourner Truth through songs about the frame up of Ella Ellison, the Joann Little prison rape case, and pioneer woman pilot Amelia Earhart, to songs about women in working class struggles, the strip mining destruction of mountain America, and songs about the painful process of self-discovery and "coming out" for lesbian women, the words give voice to experiences particular to women but of concern and interest to all."

During two years that I worked as a welder in the Quincy shipyard, from 1976 to 1978, I continued to perform with New Harmony Sisterhood. I was living in two separate worlds, one on the performance stage, the other staging construction at General Dynamics. Often my voice was too hoarse from breathing welding fumes to sing, once causing us to postpone a recording session. At times I wondered if throat cancer would be my punishment instead of carpal tunnel syndrome, which plagued some welders. The band members, as well as my family, would have rejoiced at my leaving this "hell hole," but I was in the grip of duty to Marxism-Leninism and the revolution came first.

At one point a Guardian interviewer asked me if I thought think the left had been slow to appreciate cultural workers. I replied:

On the left people don't believe to a large extent that cultural work is political work, and they don't really see it as a priority. Most of the party-building groups do not really appreciate the importance of how people relate to culture. Mass media and the music industry do control and powerfully influence people's emotions and thinking. Also, because our band is all women and sings about women, we have encountered a lot of sexism. Most of these organizations are male-dominated and have a weak position around the woman question as a whole. We've had people really trash us for being bourgeois feminists: Women's music could not be working-class music, because it was feminist.

Feminist was a dirty word then, as it is today. Many people, the left included, believed we were man-hating separatists. But women who loved themselves and their sisters were listening, and by the spring of 1979 our record had reached some feminists in Philadelphia. This led to other invitations to perform further away. We rented a van and headed south to Philadelphia, Richmond and Norfolk, Virginia, Chapel Hill, North

Carolina, and Lexington, Kentucky. On our way to Norfolk we passed through Washington, DC, to join 70,000 demonstrators in front of the Capitol in the wake of the "Three Mile Island" incident. To convey our support for the protest, we sang "No Nukes for Me" at a Norfolk coffee-house the following night.

"We barely survived a melt down," I breathed into the microphone.

"Shut 'em down! Shut 'em down," a voice bellowed from the audience.

I continued, "We sang this song in Plymouth, Massachusetts, at one of the biggest anti-nuke rallies ever held against the Plymouth Nuclear Power Plant! Join us now in the chorus!"

> *"No Nukes for me 'cause I want my world to be,*
> *Free from radiation poison falling down on me,*
> *Those reactors that they're building are a giant hangin' tree,*
> *hangin' tree,*
> *Don't you build your hangin' tree over me."*

After our concert on May 8, 1979, the local *Ledger-Star,* wrote: "There are no leaders in the group. On stage, as they would have it in life, all are equal. They take turns speaking, and Pat Ouellette steps forward to tell names 'so if you have any particular tomatoes to throw, you'll know where to aim them.' The words are angry, yet there's a positive sound in their music, a hopeful note that-very slowly-things are improving."

When New Harmony broke up in 1980, it was a traumatic divorce. At a time when I was most distant from my family of origin, Deborah, Marcia, Katy and Pat had sustained me through a rocky seven years of multiple lovers, communes, jobs, and political organizations. Belonging to a pack of wild women who howled at the moon and everyone else gave me the voice I'd always wanted. Singing from our hearts, we told stories that few people had ever heard. But underground conflicts, combined with different personal agendas, forced us to split up. Marcia wanted to take her music in a new direction. Katy and Deborah were rivals. Pat wanted to move to Western Massachusetts. It was the end, but I didn't want to let go.

The women of New Harmony individually incarnated into many musical expressions lasting well into cronehood. At a summer solstice party in Jamaica Plain in 2004, I backed into one of those sweet old crones, watering a blooming tiger lily with a bit of spilled wine.

"It's Marcia Deihl! I squeal at her through a mouthful of chips and salsa. "You haven't changed at all."

Kendall with New Harmony Sisterhood Band

"No, I'm just twenty pounds lighter with grey hair," She snorts back. " I used to binge after every concert."

Laughing, we embrace harmoniously, take the subway to Harvard Square, and sit down in Club Passim to remember this is where Joan, Bob, and our band sang of civilization and its discontent.

From Theory to Practice

Into the Factories

Nancy Teel

APRIL 30, 1975, 6:00 AM. Dorchester, Massachusetts. I'm sound asleep on my homemade bed, tucked away in the third floor garret of Bowdoin Street. As the first rays of sunlight touch my plants in the dormer, my door slams open and Ricardo leaps into the room yelling: "The war is over! It's finally over!"

The volume of his voice brings me to my feet in a single waking jump.

"What did you hear, where, when…" I stumble.

"Vietnam won! They flat out won. Saigon fell. US forces left. They won! The war is over!"

His bass voice is a trailing crescendo as he runs to wake the rest of the commune. Stunned, I sit on my bed to absorb the news. The South Vietnamese army had been collapsing, and the liberation forces had been advancing, but I hadn't pictured that it would end like this, in military victory. I thought there would be some negotiated settlement at the end. The idea of a clear victory is amazing. Down in the kitchen, I can smell coffee brewing, and hear the radio blaring. I dress and run downstairs to be sure it's really true. Sarah greets me with a golden smile. We have been partners in peacemaking since we met as students more than six years before. Kendall bursts into the kitchen and gathers us all into a huge, collective hug.

Two hours later, as I drive to work (I'm a high school teacher now) in my little Fiat, the radio reports describe the terrible rout in Saigon and the reactions of people around the world. Beyond the radio, I feel a shimmer of joy, a sense of connection to all the people who are celebrating, not the defeat, but the victory. I sense that there is a shout of joy around the world.

By that morning I had been protesting the war for my whole adult life, one third of my years. I remember being euphoric all day and for days to come. It was better than being in love, because lovers have a tiny awareness of how self-absorbed they are. This was an unselfish emotion. We had worked and sacrificed, in whatever small way, to bring about peace. And now we celebrated.

It was also the end of an era. For some people in the peace movement it was the time to stop thinking globally and start paying attention to personal goals like a good job, a family, making money, taking vacations. In less than a decade, my generation would lead the boom of wealth and selfishness of the eighties with its accompanying right-wing political reaction. But for me and for my friends, the Vietnam War and the things we had learned could not be forgotten. Many of our lives were changed irrevocably, including my own. The prospects of careers and marriages that looked attractive and secure as we left high school, no longer held us. The visions of the Third World that I retained in my memory did not let go. I could still see in my mind's eye the orphans in Tacámbaro and the television images of napalmed children amid shattered palm trees in Vietnam. I had no answer to the question asked by my Colombian family a decade earlier: why? Why should some be so rich and so arrogant in their power, and others be so poor and powerless in their suffering? I had learned in a profound way that we are all connected: by humanity, by blood, by emotion, by ideas. How could such poverty exist when such prosperity surrounded us? The deep emotions I felt at the end of the war reflected my sense of empathy with the people who suffered therein. But my intellect had also been active. I studied Latin American politics at Notre Dame and at Cornell, I read the American political scene in the *New York Times*, and I participated in study groups on alternatives to "the system." Since Mayday, five years before, my contemporaries and I turned increasingly toward Marxism.

Marxism attracted me because it explained things so well, the mark of a powerful theory. My first serious reading took place during my first year at Cornell in a study group led by Doug Dowd, Professor of Economics and Rev. Daniel Berrigan, poet, philosopher, and antiwar priest. We read Herbert Marcuse and Franz Fanon and discussed how the rich nations exploited the poor ones. The word "imperialism" entered my vocabulary. Marxism remained an undercurrent in the years that followed, for the main political recipe of the antiwar and women's movements was nonviolence with a twist of civil disobedience (à la Thoreau) mixed with the genuinely American right to protest the overreaching actions of the federal government.

July 4, 1976, the Bicentennial. I spend the day in Saratoga, California helping my cousins prepare for their annual pot-luck barbecue, a tradition started by Al's parents. Once invited you're always welcome, so just bring a dish and come down to the picnic ground at the ranch, a spot on the Calabazas Creek surrounded by ancient bay trees. The scent of their dry leaves is still the scent of California for me. In early July, you can still hear water running in the creek fifteen feet below the rope swing. Kids are a main feature, from babies to college students, and their growth is measured from party to party. There's always a keg and in 1976 we retire behind the trees to smoke pot as well. Later, as the party breaks up and the clean-up continues, I stand by the side of the road looking out at the Santa Clara valley spread below. There must be fireworks in at least a dozen different towns and in various parks in San Jose. It's a spectacularly clear night for California in those days, and the lights of the valley speak of the hope and prosperity to come. This is the life, surrounded by family and friends, with the future a glowing freeway to a secure life. I think about leaving Boston and starting a new life here. The Bowdoin Street commune is breaking up, I'm not in a committed relationship, and my job is dead-end factory work, taken on as a way to join the "working class." Why not just stay in California? I think hard, but return to Boston at the end of the week.

Why not make a move that would be personally rewarding above all? It's a difficult question to answer, one that requires me to go deep inside and look at moral values that I rarely articulate. I was in touch with those values, nevertheless, through the community of politically active people in Boston.

For two years prior to the bicentennial I had met regularly with a group of women who were all activists in the Boston Women's Union, a socialist-feminist organization. The second wave of the women's movement was still young, but we thought we had already seen how its advances would mainly benefit educated, middle-class women like ourselves, and not working-class women. We did not yet see the broad social changes that the women's movement would engender. To pursue our goals, we investigated various types of work where we might organize working women. We settled on a factory, a sweatshop with a large majority of women workers: the Joseph Pollak Company in Dorchester, Massachusetts.

My life took a radical turn: I applied for a job at Pollak and to my amazement, was hired on the spot. In a large second floor workshop we assembled electrical connectors for the auto industry, big ones to plug into trailers of 18-wheelers and little ones used under the hoods of regular cars. Four women from our group were hired with me, including my housemates,

Kendall and Sarah. Steve joined us later, and we set about organizing a union. We had no experience working in factories, no experience organizing workers and none of us had even been a member of a union! Still we had the nerve to interview various unions. The one that we selected was the United Electrical Workers, an old CIO union with a radical past and a present that included active organizing. They assigned a business agent to work with us, an African-American man named Will, who took us very seriously and provided much material help and moral support. And we all had the courage to get up and go to work each day.

The shift at Pollak begins at 8:00 AM. We punch in, take our places at the machines and begin work on the dot. On the first day I arrive not knowing what to expect. An old man named Jerry is on set-up. His face is lined into a worried frown under his white hair and he walks with a permanent stoop. Jerry is kind but in a rush. He sits me down at a plywood bench and shows me how to separate and reassemble a connector. He watches me do it awkwardly. Then he leaves me alone for two hours to redo two large crates of misassembled connectors. Each one takes most of my hand strength to get apart. The pieces are made of metal and plastic and some have rough edges. By the time he returns, my hands are starting to bleed. He looks at me closely:

"Do you want to change jobs?"

"Oh no, I'm just now getting the hang of it," I lie, on a correct hunch that I'm different enough from the other workers already and if I ask for easier work, I'll be out of a job. I last the day, vowing that I will never, ever allow myself to have such soft hands again. (I never have!) The next day I return, pockets stuffed with a supply of Band-Aids of various sizes, and Jerry puts me on a machine.

After trying out on several machines, I get my own regular spot on a drill press. I pass my first test as a working class organizer, an intellectual joining the ranks of the proletariat as the Marxists would explain: I keep that job. But what to me is a painful, difficult experience is everyday life to my co-workers.

There was no explicit formality to the assignment of work at Pollak; yet each worker ended up on a regular machine after a brief period of try-out. The system was piecework. Workers with more seniority or better relations with the foreman got jobs where they could regularly double the rate. The "rate" was the required number of pieces to be made in an hour for the base rate of pay, which was just over the minimum wage. I finally got a machine where I could make 1.5 times the rate if I worked non-stop as fast as I could for eight hours. This gave me just enough money to live, with some dips into my savings. My standard of living was in decline, however. After a year of working at Pollak, I had to decide whether to give up my one-bedroom apartment or my Fiat, because I couldn't afford both.

Besides the low pay, piecework exacted a huge physical price. I was young and in excellent physical shape, having done regular ballet and modern dance for more than half of my life. Still, I had major aches and pains, especially in my neck and back, from the tension of holding a position and working with my arms and hands in motion all day. Pieceworkers knew about repetitive stress injuries and carpal tunnel syndrome long before they were discovered by computer programmers. Older workers at Pollak, not necessarily older in age but with more years on the machines, all had high blood pressure. Many were seriously overweight since eating during breaks was the only pleasure in their work lives. It didn't take long for me to decide that piecework was invented by someone who had made a pact with the devil. It was quite simply an evil system, one that negated the humanity of the worker.

Sitting at my machine, hands following well-worn neural paths, machine humming, my mind is wandering to the music of my little transistor radio. I don't have headphones; this is before Walkman. Suddenly a scream echoes across the aisles of drill presses. Sarah! Her voice in pain...I jump up, turn off the press in one motion and scramble as fast as I can to the other side of the workshop, jumping over crates of electrical parts standing in the aisles. Sarah is slumped at her machine, head bowed, the foreman and set-up man already on either side of her. Blood trickles down the side of her face. I can see a big lock of her long hair in the exposed belt of the drill press. As I approach, Jerry blocks my way.

"It's okay. They're taking her to the hospital. She was lucky, she shut it off when her hair got caught."

"She's my best friend, let me go with her."

"I told you she's okay. The boss'll take her." He catches me by the shoulders and starts to turn me around.

"Go back now, you're gonna lose time."

"But Jerry she's hurt, her eye is all blood..." As I push and argue and he restrains me from going to Sarah, two men in suits come and help the foreman lead Sarah out the front door of the workshop. I stop resisting and Jerry slowly walks me back to my machine, his job done, his arm around my shoulder now in support and solidarity.

After a week's recovery Sarah returned to work on the same machine and continued to work on the union drive. For several months our group lay low. Our first step was to get to know our jobs, the plant, and our coworkers. People were somewhat suspicious; we were different and admitted to having some education to people we trusted. One day, Kendall was fired. Then Steve quit, disgusted by the working conditions. Still, the economy was in recession and jobs were hard to come by. Our explanations were accepted. We began to find some workers who shared our point of view. Will, the UE organizer, gave us much good advice on how to show workers the advantages of being in a union. Over the course of the year we talked to as many people as we could and convinced them to sign cards requesting a union election. Our secrecy was successful, and Pollak only found out when they were notified by the Massachusetts Labor Relations Board that an election would take place. They began a counteroffensive, writing letters threatening people with lay-offs, firing two more people and isolating any they felt were with the union.

Before, during and after the union drive, our women's group met weekly at Doyle's bar in Jamaica Plain where the food and beer were cheap, and the atmosphere was safe and casual. Women could eat, drink and talk there without being harassed. We discussed strategy and tactics and exchanged the usual on-the-job gossip, as well as the highs and lows of our personal lives. Marxism was a part of our discussions, although serious reading was not required. The union organizing group had grown to include Mary, a middle aged African-American mother; Maria, a fiery young Cape Verdean woman, and Don, a young, single Irish-American man, but we did not invite them to join us at Doyle's. Instead, we met with them and the other pro-union workers at various restaurants and homes in Dorchester. In the factory, we operated in a clandestine way, signing union cards on the sly. But we also kept the nature of our group and our backgrounds a secret from the pro-union workers. Our expressed motive was to keep our jobs. The company would certainly have fired us immediately had they known that we had college and graduate degrees. Yet there was something further going on, a sense of conspiracy, a sense that we were agents of a new culture, a new world. What exactly that new world would be was not yet clear, but a form for it would soon take shape.

As our union drive at Pollak progressed, Marxist groups began to court us. We were in touch with a local Dorchester group called the Fightback,

which had ties to a serious Marxist-Leninist organization of older professionals, old lefties, and factory workers. Soon we were being recruited into
a "party-building" effort, a national attempt to form a new (read, not like
the old) communist party, with a pro-China slant. We were not asked to
join the organization but rather to form our own group and participate in
this party-building process as a study group. We joined with a number of
other friends and formed a "unity collective."

Meanwhile at Pollak, we organized feverishly for the union. It was
exhilarating to think that we could just go in and do it. Euphoria was
short-lived, however. We lost the election. I learned that people need their
jobs more than they need a union. There were many other lessons that I
should have learned from that experience, but I did not take time to reflect
or write about it. Nor did our group at Doyle's. In fact, as I became closer
to the Marxists, my ties to the women's group loosened. Not everyone in
our group was attracted by the new party-builders. I think it was my intellectual training that drew me in. That political movement seemed rigorous,
with practice based on theory. Some of our group remained skeptical,
questioning the solidity (what I would later call dogmatism) of the line,
the incredible assurance and clarity about where the movement should go.
I should have questioned this myself. Was Marxism that good that you
could really tell for sure what to do right here in Dorchester? To the point
that you could exclude those who didn't accept that interpretation? This
was the weak point, the sticking point, the dividing point. We stopped
meeting at Doyle's.

Instead my attention had already turned to focus on the long-term task of
organizing working people to win power from the capitalists and bureaucrats and make a wonderful society, with freedom, prosperity, peace, and
equality for all. I think I imagined it would be somewhat like Ithaca. And
the party-building process was well under way. In 1977, my life changed
totally. I moved in with my lover, Miguel, and I became a committed
Marxist-Leninist, or so I thought. In June, the new party was formed and
I got married in July. We lost the election in August and by October I had
quit my job at Pollak and joined a group of young radicals applying for
jobs at American Electronics. I was hired immediately and began another
chapter in my life as a leftist-revolutionary-communist-radical-countercul-
ture worker, but underneath, as I was to discover over the next few years, I
remained a skeptical intellectual.

American: In the Belly of the Beast

The radio announcer says 6:45 AM and all the highways are jammed as I pull into the gravel parking lot, find a spot near the opening in the fence, grab my lunch and run for the plant entrance. The cold chills my bones. I will never get used to going to work this early in this climate. The weather is one more thing to bitch about, one that's allowed. The plant gate is different; I'm brought up short. There are two guards instead of one checking badges, and they're searching bags. What's up? I ask the man ahead of me, but he grimaces and doesn't answer. I'm always asking too many questions, even little ones. We move in single file showing our badges and opening our bags. No one talks. As I walk into the main building and toward my workstation, I see three policemen and two civilians in suits, right at the line where I've been working for the past two months. I try to take in as much as possible; something important has happened. Then another worker breathes the word softly: "Sabotage!"

Oh shit, I think to myself. Am I going to get blamed? A commie working on a line in a defense plant and it blows up. Who else to blame?

I dawdle as much as possible, eyes on the officers, but at one minute to seven I have to report to my station, which happens to be ground zero. I'm expecting someone to put handcuffs on me at any second. Instead, I'm barely noticed. Fred, the foreman of the whole building, sees me and nods. He knows all the younger women by name, but he doesn't speak. One of the suits is talking fast into his ear and Fred looks pained as he absorbs the verbiage. I nod and stand aside, donning my mint green smock and holding my bag containing lunch and personal items, trying to blend into the steel storage shelves behind me. I wish I could run, but there is no place to go. The plant covers acres and is surrounded by high fencing with barbed wire at the top. All the entrances are manned by guards and today, by police as well.

I spot Ian, trying to disappear into a group of workers on the other side of the ruined workstation. We both smile with our eyes. We have spent two good months talking on this assembly line. He is a strong union man, from a family of working class heroes, and he has been busted to labor grade eleven for his attitude, he tells me. At American most men are in the top labor grades of one through seven. I started out at eleven, so working on this line is only a punishment for me because of the grinding nature of the work. I surmise that I have been put here for being too curious, and Ian agrees. We are not allowed to talk, of course, but the foreman is away checking other stations at least three fourths of the time, so Ian and I have shared our life stories to a point. He doesn't exactly tell me who he is close to now. And I don't share my leftist connections either, yet. But he has helped me a great deal, first showing me how to make the copper assembly fast enough and accurately enough to keep up with the line. We have to sit at small presses (newer than those at Pollak, with safety shut-off right at our fingertips.) We face a black rubber conveyer belt that runs just an arm's reach behind our machines. Next to us are stacked shiny copper tubes, about four inches long and two inches in diameter. We have to work with small pieces of very light metal, about the size and weight of the wood letters in Scrabble. They are cut in irregular shapes, trapezoids mostly, and we put them together into an intricate little assembly in the middle of the empty copper tube. The tolerance is close. We have to force them down in at the bottom of the assembly. Sometimes I still get a rheumatic irritation of the joints of my thumb and finger from the pressure I used on that job. Once we finish the assembly, we put the piece on the conveyer belt, and it moves slowly through a squat oven about eight feet long where intense heat melts and fuses the metal. It was on this belt that someone put a small explosive that destroyed the oven last night.

"It could have even been a cherry-bomb." Ian and I are seated at temporary inventory station, counting parts. We can only talk when we agree to mutually break for a moment.

"Could a firecracker do that much damage? The whole thing caved in."

"Sure, it wouldn't take much to screw up that oven, probably cost them a couple a hundred thousand at least."

"When did it go off?"

"Somebody said third shift, toward the end." He looks at me with a twinkle in his eyes. "They can't blame us for this one." He mouths the words without sound.

The next day we report to the same inventory station. Ian tells me he has been called back to labor grade eight at the Lowell plant. We shake hands and I never see him again.

I worked at American from October, 1977 to March, 1980. My first job was in the Power Device division assembling tubes for microwave ovens. The division of the industrial process into many small parts, each unlinked in the worker's mind to the next, was done to perfection in Power Device. I began doing hand assembly of various kinds: putting aluminum foil radiation wrappers on magnets, assembling the copper tube framework, working on the final assembly line, which was actually fun at times because of the volatile mix of young men and women who kept it going. The work was just as boring as at Pollak, but the environment was cleaner and more serious. I was hired into labor grade eleven, the second lowest. I think

I started out at just over seven dollars an hour, more than I could make at Pollak on piece work, beating the rate by 50%. Moreover, at American we also had an excellent health plan, two weeks vacation, long-term disability insurance, holidays and other benefits. Even working many hours of forced overtime, the value of being in a unionized workplace couldn't have been clearer to me.

American's incredible investment in technology astounded me. I had never seen so many complicated machines, most of which I had no understanding of at all. I was wide-eyed and cooperative.

When business slumped in the winter of '78, I was laid off for a few weeks. I collected unemployment, but felt the terrible depression that workers feel when a good job vanishes. We heard that the microwave oven jobs had migrated to Tennessee, to an American subsidiary. Working under so much pressure, and then having nothing to do on lay-off was an extraordinary experience, even for a person like me who had other options. It was before the national lament about the loss of manufacturing jobs, but workers at American knew the value of the jobs they had. During that lay-off, I felt both relieved and bereft. But soon I was called back to another job working on printed circuit boards.

Everyone arrived early in our building except a few young men who came in just before 7 AM. We punched in and waited at our places for the shift to begin. Sometimes there was a night shift just ending. We hit our jobs hard; there was little room for talk or stretching. We got a quarter-hour break in the morning and again in the afternoon, and one half hour for lunch. Lunch was unpaid, so the shift ran from 7:00 AM to 3:30 PM. The work discipline, the tight schedule and the tension meant that it took a long time to get to know people enough to have easy conversation. But when a group of older workers finally accepted me, I was happy to listen to their stories. They remembered with pride working on the Apollo program, building parts for the rocket that took Americans to the moon. They had made every effort to do their jobs perfectly, because they knew men's lives would depend on it. It was the most meaningful thing they had worked on, they said. I listened and learned.

The pace was fast and the discipline was strong, even more so than in Power Device. What was left was military work: better not screw up. We had to get a security clearance; I remember being very nervous at the required interview when I had to provide my passport, which showed a trip to Czechoslovakia in 1969. It was only six years since I had been arrested trying to shut down the government in Washington on Mayday. Not to mention the fact that I now considered myself a communist of a new type and was trying to figure out what that meant in a place like American. In what should certainly be considered proof of the inefficiency of large bureaucracies, I was granted a security clearance and got to work on more sensitive (but not higher paying) jobs in the military electronics business.

As tight as security seemed to be, there was curious leeway granted to some young workers. A whole group of them, mostly men, began to smoke pot each day at the 9:00 AM break. In good weather they went outside, but during the winter I was shocked to see them smoking in a stairwell. I was just over thirty, married, hoping to have children soon, and in a political movement that shunned drugs. Still, it wasn't that many years since my hippie days in Ithaca, and the sweet smell of herb was unmistakable. It wasn't long before I was invited to go out at lunch with a group of young women, all in their early twenties, who smoked dope with their sandwiches and yogurt. I declined, but got sort of stoned anyway from breathing the air in the closed car as we drove around. I was frightened that people worked with dangerous equipment while stoned, and I was amazed that they were never disciplined even though managers must have known. I grew to love and admire this group of young people, all wishing they could be elsewhere, all knowing that this was the best job they could get, smoking on breaks and dreaming as they worked of better times, better choices. On Friday afternoons we used to go the bar across the road to play pinball and have a few beers. I usually had only one beer. I was so tired by the end of the week that if I had more, I had trouble driving home. Most Friday nights, I was asleep by 8 PM. But many people had more than a few and drove home drunk. The lifetime of problems that ensued I can only imagine.

Everyone except me it seemed, played the lottery, and the illegal numbers were available for anyone who wanted to play them as well.

"So Nancy, do you ever gamble? Ever go to Atlantic City or Vegas?"

"No, I've never been."

"What about church bazaars, penny ante poker?"

"Oh sure. My parents love that sort of thing."

"But you don't?"

"Not really, why?"

"Well, I was going to ask you if you wanted to put some money on the number, you know, lots of people do. Odds are a lot better than the lottery."

"But I don't play that either! Thanks for thinking of me anyway."

"Sure. Keep that smile comin'."

Sandy, one of my friends, was twenty-two and beautiful. She had already worked full-time for five years at McDonald's in her home town, one of the constellation of old towns pulled into the economic orbit of Boston by the high tech revolution. For two years she had been manager of the restaurant. She quit and came to American to solder resisters on circuit boards because she could make more money and she needed the benefits. Years later, after my commitment to working in factories ended, I began teaching in a community college, and I have often seen in my students the same pattern of hopes and dreams deferred and later pursued.

American was one of the largest employers in Massachusetts at the time I worked there and for nearly two decades thereafter. My own experience of American's clout goes back to the basics: air and water. One day while working on the etcher, a large machine that etches the copper circuits, I began to feel light-headed. Then I started to laugh and to make goofy jokes, one after another, to the serious, gray-haired man who was my co-worker that day. I was getting sillier by the minute when our foreman, a big avuncular guy, came over and invited—no— escorted me for a walk. We went outside and stood in the lee of our building while he had a cigarette and chatted lightly. It was early spring, bright and cool. I continued laughing and telling jokes, but gradually it began to dawn on me that something was not right. Then we went to the nurse's office. I was examined and told to remain there for an hour, then to go home. I remember looking for something to read, a foreign impulse in our building, but found nothing. I was left to think about what happened. The nurse and the foreman both let me know in a gentle sort of way, not really admitting to anything serious, but yes, I had gotten high from breathing some kind of "bad air".

The next day I returned to work, by then quite sober. Everyone knew what had happened. Several men who didn't work in my area came over to explain; they knew what management wouldn't tell me. They said that it had been fumes from the degreaser that had caused my high. The degreaser was a huge vat of trichloroethylene, heated, I believe, to increase the effectiveness of the solvent. The vat must have been at least 4 feet across. I remember we had to walk up a two-step platform to get to it. It was used for large items only; there were smaller ones for smaller jobs. Every now and then the solvent had to be replaced with clean stuff, so the mechanics would drain it and refill it. On the day I was exposed, the drainpipe wasn't used. The solvent was allowed to run over the subfloor beneath the grate floor where my etchers were located. I had walked the grid all day, over the fumes rising through the open floor. Trichlor has an awful smell, but the smell of ammonia from the etchers was overpowering, so I never noticed the smell of the solvent stream running beneath me.

The men who talked with me included my friend with the numbers for sale and a mechanic who explained that the underground holding tanks were full; therefore, the solvent was being sent out through a regular drain into the Charles River that flows next to American property! I heard that some years later workers filed a complaint with the state environmental agency about similar dumping in the Charles, but it was ultimately squashed because the state bureaucrats did not want to challenge American. Think about this: a military contractor doing government work, creates pollution that is investigated by another government agency and cleaned up by a third. The taxpayers foot the bill for all three, paying for the pollution, the discovery of it and ultimately the clean-up. And everyone on the planet, including future generations, bears the cost of the environmental degradation.

The department where I spent most of my days at American made printed circuit boards for missiles and other classified systems. We only knew this because the managers bragged about it. The process began with sheets of fiberglass material, which were electroplated with copper then etched into circuits. In the lamination room where I worked, we assembled layers of circuits according to blue-prints, placing a layer of fiber glass in between. We put the assembled packages between heavy steel plates and placed those into pressure ovens, where settings of tens of thousands of pounds were standard and temperatures were above 500 degrees. We lifted the packages into the oven by hand then removed them with a big wooden spatula because they were often still hot.

One day in the lamination room, a friendly engineer, always tinkering with better ways to do things, put a stack of steel sandwiches containing his test boards into the oven. When the time came to remove them, he wasn't around, so the job fell to me. The packages were piled high on the top shelf of the oven, about even with the top of my head. Of course I didn't try to take out all three sandwiches at once; I knew that would be way too heavy. I took the top one, using heavy asbestos gloves, but the height and distance from my body put too much of a strain on my lower back. I could feel something give, and a sharp pain shot down my leg. Nevertheless I managed to pull out the boards and put them safely on the bench. I even placed my own package in the oven and set the controls. Then I leaned back against the workbench and confessed to my co-worker, a many-year American veteran, that I had hurt my back and could hardly stand. There were no chairs, since they didn't want us to sit down on the job. She called for the foreman, Alan, who was a genuinely nice man, in my book the only authority figure at American deserving of any trust. Alan sent me home and I remained flat on my back for a month, rising only to use the bathroom. Eating was an impossible chore, reading was difficult and the boredom was deadly. When the doctors said I could finally get up, I was thin and crooked, with one hip noticeably higher than the other, the muscles on that side of my lower back still in spasm. I spent another three weeks at home, walking an increasing number of minutes each day as the cramp slowly loosened its grip. I went back to work around the end of June and that very week found out that I was pregnant. I worked for two weeks on a new job in testing and then the plant shut down for the usual summer break in the last two weeks of July. My husband and I went to California to visit family, and I announced to everyone that I was expecting. When I returned to work, I was over three months pregnant. I have always been grateful for the accident, even though I still must be careful with my lower back many years later. American was filled with toxic chemicals and micro-wave radiation (they tested radar on the roof of our building). I regularly used trichloroethylene and trichloroethane for degreasing. My lucky back injury meant that I was out of that environment for the critically sensitive first trimester of my pregnancy with my firstborn child.

I worked as a printed circuit board inspector until the first of November when, one Sunday afternoon, I went into early labor. I felt the cramps, thinking at first it was just indigestion, a common pregnancy nuisance, but soon it was clear that they were regular and slightly increasing in intensity and frequency. I was just 26 weeks pregnant when I called the doctor and was told to begin drinking wine immediately. I did. I got high, got nearly drunk, but the contractions continued. Both of us terrified, my husband drove me to Beth Israel Hospital. They said that indeed I was in labor and if the baby should be born, he would have a 50/50 chance of survival, much less of a normal life. They asked if I wanted to take terbutaline, a drug not then approved for use in pregnancy in the US, but in current use in Europe to end early labor. I thought about it for only a few seconds and agreed. It worked. After the early labor stopped, I stayed at Beth Israel for three days of observation; then I was sent home to take it very easy. I did. My son's birthday came three months later. I was grateful for long term disability insurance and the excellent health benefits we had. I had never thought I would need either, but I had never been in such a difficult environment.

As I look back on my years at American, I rethink my motives. Why was I working there? My political activity was limited due to the discipline and security of the plant. I could not sell political newspapers or give out information except in strictest confidence with a few trusted friends, away from the plant. Even then, I was inviting them to political activities in Boston, and they lived in distant suburbs. The very left look of our group's newspaper, not to mention the articles, was a put-off for most people; even I was taken aback by it at times. I met once a week with a few political colleagues who also worked at American or had done so in the past. We formed a helpful support group, and spent our time together reading and discussing politics.

I learned some new things, but was this sufficient reason to risk my health and especially that of my child? I saw large-scale high-tech manufacturing. I saw the role of the union as a kind of agent for management, coming down harder on the workers than the bosses ever did. Union officers and stewards were bought off with very small favors, I noted sadly. I got a view of the military-industrial complex that made its power clearer than it had been when I studied and wrote about it for the American Friends Service Committee[1]. I learned more about the conservative consciousness of working people. I still ask myself if it was worth it. Some colleagues remained at the plant, and they have my eternal respect. They stuck it out and changed the union. This same process nationwide has stoked the revival of the labor movement in the new millennium. People with high consciousness and selfless goals can change the world. That is a great thing to know. But I also learned that the risks and sacrifices can be great indeed.

I took advantage of another benefit at American, an extended child-care leave of one year; then, in the winter of 1980 I returned to my job. I left home each day at 6:15 AM hardly seeing my baby or my husband, who took him to daycare; I picked up the baby after work at about 4:30, but it was too long a day for him and for me. Linda, the daycare mom, was becoming his primary caretaker. I wasn't happy; I lasted only about ten weeks before I quit.

Why had I worked at Pollak and American? My answers had everything to do with politics. I had used the bridge of Marxist theory to construct a path from my experiences in Latin America and in the antiwar movement at Cornell to the American working class in factories in Boston. I was against the great power chauvinism and arrogance displayed by the US government in Vietnam and in Latin America, attitudes that are still displayed today. I took seriously what Lenin said: that the state exists to protect the class interests of the people who own the means of production, and it will use force if necessary to maintain its position, even against its own citizens. The COINTELPRO investigations of the 1970s into the destruction of the Black Panther Party and the American Indian Movement seemed proof enough to me. Add to these the killings at Kent State and Jackson State, and it seemed that the government was the enemy and had to be overturned. But by what means?

As far as I could see when I started out, the only successful revolutions were made by revolutionary parties, clandestine organizations organized according to "democratic centralism" with a ruling central committee and branching district structure and local cell groups in workplaces and communities. The groups I worked with sought to emulate this structure and did so successfully. They were so successful that they developed the same bureaucratic top-heaviness that finally hobbled and then toppled the Soviet Union after seventy years. We burned out in only four years. Born in a great burst of enthusiasm in June, 1977, after three years of serious commitment on the part of thousands of activists, our organization began to unravel. Democratic centralism did not work; the most conscious people were not setting policy. The best leaders were not leading. The top leadership was influenced to a compromising degree by free trips to China. The newspaper was not selling; the stand of the organization it represented was far to the left of even the most progressive workers. And some of the positions of the leadership made no sense, like their support for nuclear power because China needed and supported it.

I began to question my commitment. I stayed for a while trying to sort things out, because I worried that it was convenient for me to pull out because I had a baby. I didn't want to base my political decisions on motherhood. After all, mothers can be revolutionaries, can't they? Yes, I realized, but at a price I wasn't willing to pay. I quit. It was partly for my child but more for myself. I could not adapt to an organization that asked me to give up the right to criticize and disagree. I couldn't follow leaders I no longer respected. I remained a skeptical intellectual, hoping for guidance, hoping for an organization to believe in, for something to believe in, but it was not this one. Nor has it been any other in the years since. I felt literally in pain as I was making my decision. I had migraine headaches every week. My best friend cried constantly. Two other close friends left Boston suddenly, leaving the pain behind. Within another year the whole organization was dead.

In the summer of 1982, I attended a reunion in Ithaca, NY. About seventy people came from all over the country. Ten years before, we had taken over the engineering library at Cornell to protest war research and university complicity with the war in Vietnam. It was before e-mail, but other networks existed. In fact, one of the enduring legacies of those radical years has been the networks of friends that continue. Two former activists with a successful software business and a big house in the country opened their home to the reunion. It was wonderful to see everyone again. Some like me came with spouses and small children; others were still or recently single; all still held the same values. It amazed me to talk with one person after another to learn of their commitment. Many had worked in factories, and many were at the end of a commitment to a social change organization. Apologies were offered in some cases where sectarian infighting had been strong and destructive.

The most compelling story I remember from the reunion was told by a friend who had been the top graduate student in East Asian studies at Cornell, an incredibly sharp, well-read academic and antiwar activist. A few years before, he had visited Boston on a speaking tour about the political situation in Cambodia, sponsored by several left-wing groups. At that time grave accusations of genocide carried out by the Khmer Rouge were beginning to surface. Geoff believed that the charges were not supported by the evidence, and he was willing to speak publicly about it. After all, it was typical of the CIA and KGB to spread disinformation; look what they did during the Vietnam war. I stayed up all night with Geoff in Ithaca listening to his story. After the speaking tour he had continued to search the evidence coming out of Cambodia. His best friend, a Cambodian, decided to return to join the revolution in Cambodia. Geoff lost contact and then discovered evidence of his friend's murder. He had been executed within a few months of arriving in "revolutionary Kampuchea." Geoff dug deeper and realized that the disinformation had come from the Khmer Rouge and their supporters. The accusations of atrocities and genocide in the killing fields were true. He was devastated. He stopped his scholarly work, married his sweetheart, a successful businesswoman in California, and was at home raising the children while she ran the business. He thought then that he would never go back to Southeast Asian studies. His was a crushing story, yet through it all he maintained his integrity and honesty.

At the reunion, seventy activists from different parts of the country made the same assessment. Communist parties and organizations were not what they seemed, and did not create a vehicle that would change the US in a direction that any of us wanted to go. The very structure led to authoritarianism, blind faith and tunnel vision. We sat in a huge circle for hours, each one telling his or her history over the past ten years. I wish I had a tape. Sectarianism was dead even though there were a few holdouts. But where could we go next? Like me, many had young families that demanded a primary commitment. Others planned to work on issues of importance; still others remained in the labor movement. In what struck me as a symbol of our re-acceptance into society, Cornell welcomed us as an alumnae group in the old carriage house for a wonderful dinner served by the Moosewood Restaurant. A circle had closed.

Notes

1. See *"Coming Together"* in Section II: Recreating Community.

Looking for Answers:
From Marxism-Leninism to the Suburbs

Linda Stern

IT WAS DUSTY and dark in the attic, and I narrowly missed bumping my head on the rafters. My flashlight played over camping equipment, my children's old art work, rolled up posters, and a box of stuffed animals. I'd come up to look for suitcases to help my son pack for college. Then, I noticed six cardboard boxes, partially closed, in a corner, covered with a fine layer of grit. Kneeling down, I opened one of the boxes: newspapers and articles neatly filed in badly yellowing file folders. So organized? This must have foreshadowed my second career as a librarian. Some fraying copies of *The New York Times* from October 1962 with headlines of the Cuban Missile Crisis emblazoned across the top. A photo cut out of the paper: a group of 7 or 8 white anti-busing protestors brandishing an American flag as weapon, as they attack an African-American lawyer in Boston's Government Center. A red armband reading "Carson Beach," a strike leaflet from Boston City Hospital, a slightly rusty peace button, and some class photographs where I stood at attention in a three-piece suit with my second grade students.

I pulled the first few books out of another carton: *Emancipation of Women*, by V. I. Lenin; *Imperialism, the Highest Stage of Capitalism*, also by Lenin; *Selected Works of Mao Tse -Tung*, all five volumes; *Poems* by Mao. I'd forgotten Mao had written poetry, too. *Blues People* by Amiri Baraka. I saw books on Vietnam, one by Wilfred Burchett.

I piled up a few of the books, took them downstairs, made a cup of tea, and sat down to take a look. I opened the first book, and read.

> *The main strength of the movement lies in the organisation of the work-*
> *ers at the large factories, for the large factories (and mills) contain not*
> *only the predominant part of the working class as regards numbers, but*
> *even more as regards influence, development, and fighting capacity.*
>
> V.I. Lenin in *On Building the Bolshevik Party* [1]

I remembered the optimism I'd felt in the mid-1970s as the Vietnam War finally ended with American troops defeated and Nixon forced to resign. Socialist countries around the world, such as China and Cuba, caught my imagination, and stories of national liberation movements in the Third World inspired me. American leftists found a new focus in workplace organizing in major industry. According to Marxist-Leninist theory, workers were more politically conscious when their working conditions were more social.

I was particularly interested in China. Friends who traveled there brought back reports of the progress made under the Communist leadership of Mao Tse-Tung. He and the Red Army with the support of the vast majority of the population overthrew Chiang Kai-shek and the old feudal order and established a New Society based on a more equal distribution of resources.

At the Old Cambridge Baptist Church in Cambridge, I listened intently to Joshua Horn, an English doctor, who had worked in China over many decades. He spoke about the drastic and effective public health measures taken by the Chinese government. Syphilis had been completely eradicated in a generation; with no new cases, doctors could learn about it only through textbooks. Rampant in the past, it had been wiped out by a combination of antibiotics and political gains in the status of women who were no longer forced into prostitution. "Barefoot doctors" had basic medical training and went out into the countryside to distribute vaccines and other medications and to teach people basic health and sanitation practices.

I respected many of the people around me who had made a commitment to Marxism-Leninism. Some of these activists were teachers, lawyers, doctors, scientists, and others who were involved with workplace organizing. And some were autoworkers, factory workers, and others from the working class and minority communities, who had been recruited into Marxist-Leninist organizations, study groups, and other collectives. They'd been convinced by Karl Marx's ideas that laid out a basic theory of the concentration of power in the hands of the largest corporations and necessity to organize against them.

International Women's Day in New York City, Linda with her cousin, Judith Rosenberg

I knew a few women who had taken jobs in factories, and I too decided to experiment. I worked in a tiny factory in South Boston one summer. We made Christmas tree ornaments, hardly basic industry, but I thought it would give me valuable experience. Huge vats of solvent sat open near our machines. Windows were propped open on hot, humid summer days, to little avail, as there were no fans to bring in fresh air or even circulate the vapor-laden air. My job was to sit at a machine, thrust a plastic ball on a metal spike, then, by pushing a button, start the machine which would wind a glitzy plastic thread around the ball, completely covering it. My shoulders ached, the fumes made me sleepy, and when I didn't insert the plastic ball correctly on the post, it would fly up and hit me in the face.

Breaks were my only time to talk to the mainly immigrant women I worked with. We drank cold sodas and sat on the stairway near an open window. The young men who worked on the loading dock below waved and called to us, the high point of our day.

I was overwhelmed by the physical stress of the job and had a hard time figuring out how to talk to my co-workers. I quit after a summer, thinking maybe I'm not cut out to do work like this. Since I'd been a teacher and I knew some organizing was going on among daycare workers, I started looking for a daycare job. Daycare is a women's issue too, I thought.

I sent my resume to several Dorchester daycare centers, had a couple of interviews, and was hired in 1975 as head teacher at a small daycare center in Uphams Corner, a neighborhood not too far from the meat-packing plants and Boston City Hospital, (now Boston Medical Center). I lived just a few blocks away, and my life felt more integrated, living and working in the same multi-ethnic neighborhood. Located in a church basement, the daycare center was housed in two brightly painted rooms. In the kitchen across the hall, a woman cooked for the daycare program and for the daily lunch program that the church sponsored for some of the elderly poor in the neighborhood. Our group of twenty-five children with five adults towering over them at the beginning, middle, and end of our rambling line took frequent forays into the neighborhood to visit playgrounds and other points of interest. As teachers we were very underpaid, but for the most part, we all got along and enjoyed our work with the children.

One morning, Bunky, a curious three-year-old, arrived at daycare and headed right for the block corner. Suddenly, he exclaimed, "Kitty!" One of the teachers went to investigate and discovered a dead rat. We moved the children to the other room, notified the director, and poked around the basement. We discovered numerous plastic bags of trash, from the various food programs, stored in a corner of the basement, tied up, but not in any kind of protective garbage can. That day after lunch, the center dark and quiet during naptime, I sat among the cots of the kindergarteners and saw six rats jumping in and out of a trash barrel in the kitchen, just two rooms away from the sleeping children.

I called the minister in his upstairs office. He sarcastically called me "honey," and said that he had called about a dumpster but that there wasn't one available. I couldn't believe he would do nothing at all. I talked to several parents when they came to pick up their children, and we called a meeting. We wrote a petition, and one parent volunteered to call about a dumpster, which, it turned out, could have been delivered that day. We took the petition around to other programs based in the church. The minister did finally arrange to have the church exterminated and obvious efforts were made to keep the church and center somewhat cleaner. Though these measures helped, a more sanitary method of trash storage and removal was never instituted. Shortly after this, I was demoted from my position as head teacher and received a pay cut. I could only assume it was in retaliation.

I was friendly with Sam and his wife from various political events; he was an "open" member of one of the leading Marxist-Leninist organizations. His wife worked days, while Sam took care of their two-year-old. I occasionally babysat for them when he had to go to work in the late afternoon and his wife wasn't home yet. He asked me to come early one day and we drove to Castle Island, a South Boston beach near an old fort that still stands guard at the entrance to Boston Harbor. We talked while his daughter played in the sand.

"The Organization would like to recruit you," said Sam.

Stunned, I said, "Well, I'm flattered but I'm a long way from making a commitment like that. That seems like the culmination of a lifetime of political work. I mean, first of all, there's so much theory to learn... "

"But we think the best way for you to study and learn is to be part of The Organization."

"Well, I never thought of it that way. I guess it's something to think about...."

Joining wasn't as hard a decision as I thought it would be. I was living alone in a tiny apartment, and I wasn't in a serious relationship. I'd tried some alternatives, living in a couple of communes that were interesting attempts to relate more equitably but both had had serious problems. I had been involved in the anti-war movement, I'd participated in a women's conscious-raising group and heard speeches by some of the women leading this new movement, and I had worked for school reform in the teacher's union. It seemed like the next step for me politically. I thought Marxism-Leninism might give my life some direction.

We arrived at intervals, 10 minutes apart, at Sam's apartment the evening of my first meeting. He explained that if we were being watched by the police or by inquisitive neighbors, it would be less obvious there was a meeting going on.

The basement apartment was dingy, the shades pulled down tight. We sprawled on a collection of mismatched furniture in the living room. A faint odor of garbage came from the kitchen. I could hear Sam's little girl fussing in a room down the hall.

Our unit leader gave me a folder with my initials lightly penciled on it, containing internal documents. These were recently discussed positions of the Central Committee. "Be sure and keep these locked up," she said. (I went out the next day and bought a locked metal box with a tiny silver key, a lock anyone could have opened with a paper clip.) Our first discussion was planned around the writings of Amiri Baraka, the African-American writer, playwright and activist (who was formerly known as LeRoi Jones.) I was asked to lead the discussion for the next week's meeting and would meet with one of my comrades to plan it. We all lived in Dorchester and would be doing our work in the community.

My sporadic journal speaks of the energy and purpose I felt during this time. "This is more than just my political work; it's a psychology and a philosophy and it ties everything together." Unfortunately, my new activities seemed to keep me very busy, the pace leaving little time for reflection, and my journal stops abruptly a short time later.

The members of my unit became close as we studied theory and political line, discussed issues, and talked about the "advanced workers" we worked with who might be interested in some of our ideas. Also we drove together to various industrial sites as well as area hospitals, to sell our newspaper.

There was a larger community of people that included those who were in The Organization, as well as those who were in agreement with its general principles, those who liked the work it was doing, and contacts. In line with Lenin's idea of secrecy, people didn't disclose where they worked.

"Well, I'm working in a factory. But I don't tell people where."

"Oh, yeah, right. Well, what's, uh, going on there?"

"Well, there are contract talks coming up. What are you doing?"

"Well, I'm working in a hospital; I'm in housekeeping."

"Oh, really? Do you, oh, never mind... So, how're the kids?"

Was this paranoia, was it a romanticized view of how dangerous the government might have considered us, or were these realistic precautions? I'd seen for myself what had happened to the Black Panther Party in the late 1960s and early 1970s. I'd driven down to New Haven to the trial of Black Panthers Bobby Seale and Erika Huggins, who faced unsubstantiated charges of murder and were held in prison for more than 2 years awaiting trial.[2] Only a few years before that, the Black Panthers had been viciously attacked by the police all over the country; Fred Hampton, only 21 years old and a charismatic leader of the Black Panthers, was gunned down in his bed by the Chicago police in 1969.

The FBI, along with local "red squads," kept detailed records on antiwar and civil rights activists; information was gathered through phone taps, surveillance, and infiltration. COINTELPRO[3], the FBI's campaign against these movements, tried to destroy political work by fomenting conflict within organizations, printing bogus leaflets, canceling planned protests and tapping phones of anyone considered opposed to government policies. Martin Luther King Jr.'s phone was tapped as well. This of course became Nixon's downfall when he tapped the phones of the Democratic National Committee at the Watergate. Not only could conversations on the phone be recorded but the receiver itself could pick up conversations in the room even when the phone was not in use.

It was now the mid-70s and in Boston concern grew over the quality of education and the need for integration. The Boston School Committee had, over the years, intentionally drawn and redrawn school district boundaries in order to maintain segregation. A glance at a Boston map showed school districts with strangely-shaped boundaries. A federal court order was handed down in 1974 that required integration through a busing plan. A few years before, I had seen for myself, when I taught second grade in Roxbury, just how poorly equipped and run the Boston Public Schools were and how segregated they were. Separate schools were inherently unequal, as mandated by the Supreme Court in Brown v. Board of Education in 1954.

Local civil rights organizations and other progressive folks in Boston saw busing as a first step towards integrating the schools. While honest arguments were made to keep children close to home in familiar neighborhoods, an anti-busing movement grew, fanned by the racist rhetoric of some community leaders in Boston.

The anti-busing movement was under the control of people like Louise Day Hicks. She was a lawyer and outspoken foe of busing, who appeared at many anti-busing rallies and was frequently on TV. With her large pasty face and mincing voice, she proclaimed she was for neighborhood schools, for the "little people": "you know where I stand." John Kerrigan, another outspoken and arrogant school committee member, was on record mocking a local black TV reporter. Kerrigan stated that "[the reporter is] one generation away from swinging in the trees."[4]

Restore Our Alienated Rights, or ROAR as it was called, capitalizing on insecurities and fears in poorer white neighborhoods, was a militant and well-organized group that led the racist opposition. ROAR was permitted to hold their meetings in City Hall chambers; the windows of Boston City Hall each sported a letter, spelling out "ROAR," to all walking through

Government Center. How could it have been clearer that city leaders were complicit in the violence that tore the city apart.[5]

Several politicians prominent in city politics got their start as leaders of the anti-busing movement. Ray Flynn, then a State Representative, became mayor of Boston for several years. James Kelly, head of the South Boston Information Center in the mid-70s, became Boston City Council president for some years.

Racist incidents were reported all over Boston. Ted Landsmark, the young African-American lawyer in my news clipping, was attacked in Government Center with an American flag as he unwittingly walked into the tail end of an anti-busing demonstration. Widely published, this photograph won a Pulitzer prize.

In another incident, Senator Ted Kennedy went out to address, and to try to pacify, an anti-busing rally. He was booed, jabbed, and pushed. Then people literally turned their backs on him. Shaken, he didn't stay long.

A young friend of ours from Central America was attacked by eight white men with tire irons while passers-by in Fields Corner in Dorchester shamelessly cheered. Hospitalized for several days, he was released with his arm in a sling and badly shaken.

In South Boston, "nigger" was spray painted on school doors; buses filled with children were pelted with cans, bottles, two-by-fours, tomatoes, and rocks; bus windows were broken; students hurt. Mobs filled the streets around South Boston High School and the Tactical Police were called out to protect black children getting off school buses.

I'm glad to say that left political groups took a prominent role in opposing racism in the city. I'm not sure who called the first meeting to take action against this violence in Dorchester, but it took place on a warm summer evening in a church in Uphams Corner. The meeting was late getting started as people nervously straggled in. The leftist folks from various organizations arrived first, some carrying notebooks and newly sharpened pencils. Jean-Claude Martineau, a Haitian activist, arrived next; he knew some of the leftists. Lastly, several white Dorchester activists came noisily into the room; they usually referred to themselves as *lifelong* Dorchester residents to delineate themselves from leftist newcomers. They'd played a vital role in the community, publishing the Dorchester Community News and campaigning against a local judge who consistently charged and jailed white working class defendants. They sat together and looked slightly ill-at-ease.

"So what are we gonna do about these punks that are hassling the blacks," said Donna Finn, a feisty young Irish-American neighborhood activist, her red hair surrounding her face in a halo.

"Let's start a phone chain and get some folks together who could go in to help defend some of these black families," said one of the leftists.

"We'll beat the shit outta those punks," said Ed, a member of the Dorchester group.

"Now, let's just slow down a bit," said Jean-Claude in his mellifluous French-accented English. In addition to being an activist, he was also a poet, playwright, and singer; his songs were hits in Haiti. (He later served as an aide and cultural attache to President Aristide.) "We do not want to be guilty of using the same tactics that the racists are using."

"But isn't there a difference between violent attacks directed against minorities and violence that might have to be used in self-defense," asked another.

"But we believe that not only must we act to defend individuals, we must work to educate those who ally themselves with racists," said Sam.

And from Ed, again: "What, we're gonna try to *educate* these punks, too?!?!"

"I'll pass this pad of paper around. We can start by collecting all our names and addresses, and then we can go back to our groups and get more names."

We named our organization Racial Unity Now, or RUN. Anthony Lukas talks about RUN in his Pulitzer-prize winning *Common Ground*, a book about busing in Boston. We met, argued, and slowly began to build trust and find common ground.

We heard about an interracial couple in Fields Corner who had had several windows broken by flying rocks, some thrown in the middle of the night. Groups of noisy young men, all white, gathered in the front of their house, night after night. Graffiti was spray painted on their fence and an occasional beer bottle was tossed in the street, shattering the tense quiet in the neighborhood. The family called the police who made a report but didn't stay around or provide any protection. The group of rowdy young people kept coming back.

A couple of RUN people went over to talk to this family about how we might be able to help defend their house. We organized a phone tree to alert people night or day and drew up a schedule of shifts to cover weekend nights.

Our first night there one of the Dorchester folks and I spent hours peering out the front windows on the family's third floor, looking up and down the street for anything unusual. Another one of us was stationed in the back of the house, looking out over the backyards down the block. Other RUN folks sat in parked cars down the block with cameras, ready to intervene, to chase perpetrators, take photos. The night was quiet. It was difficult to keep our eyes open, but the tension and fear kept our adrenaline pumping. At any moment the peaceful night might erupt in hate and violence.

Over time we noticed that some of the young people, while gathering, seemed wary of the unaccustomed number of parked cars and people going in and out of the house. They weren't as noisy as usual and they disbanded earlier. The next night a group of them walked noisily by the house, slowing down a bit, then disappearing. They stood around the corner, keeping an eye on the house.

Gradually, things quieted down for this family. Did these kids find something better to do or did they just look for others to harass? Other minority families continued to suffer this kind of violent intimidation. R.U.N. members argued about priorities: do we physically try to defend *every* family under attack or do we need to put our energies into education or community demonstrations? Just a few months after this, several left and community groups led a march through Dorchester.

There were also violent attacks against whites in the minority community at this time, some very serious. But the difference was that in South Boston, it was community leaders that were in the forefront of demonstrations and responsible for the inflammatory rhetoric. Leaders in the African-American community, in contrast, actively planned for the protection of white children being bused into their neighborhoods. They figured out what to do if kids from Southie became sick during the school day. And they called for groups of welcoming adults to meet the South Boston children, who were actually applauded as they got off buses on the first day of school.

Finally, the volatile school year was over and everyone hoped for a respite before Phase Two of the busing plan was to go into effect the following fall. But attacks began again, this time at Carson Beach, which was located between the mainly black Columbia Point housing project and South Boston triple-deckers and housing projects. It was a public beach, which had historically been comfortable for all. But one summer day a group of visiting black salesmen was harassed at the beach. The following weekend a group of young white kids armed with bats stoned a passing car driven by Hispanics.

African-American organizations then planned a demonstration over a sultry August weekend with many sympathetic whites as well as leftists joining them. We rallied in Franklin Park, then drove down Columbia Road to South Boston, marched under the expressway to Carson Beach. We were met by an angry mob of South Boston residents determined to block the demonstration; we were outnumbered two to one, according to *Boston Globe* reports.[6]

A thin line of mounted police on horseback separated us from the South Boston mob. We were crowded in on a narrow stretch of beach with nowhere to run, and the mood grew very tense. As the *Boston Globe*[7] confirmed, rocks began to be thrown from the "white" that is, the South Boston, side first. The horses, jittery from the crowd and the rocks, began to rear. People scattered. Dozens of police cars with lights flashing were in the area with a force of 800 police standing by. Forty people were hurt including Mel King, a State Rep. The police moved the South Boston people down the beach a token distance away, but our multiethnic group was pushed down toward Columbia Point and totally and completely off the beach. Louise Day Hicks, in character, blamed African-American leaders for the violence. Community leaders in Roxbury and Dorchester vowed to come back until the beach was integrated again.

While violence tore the city apart, some of us got jobs at Boston City Hospital. The Organization saw the hospital as an important employer in the community and a few of us applied for jobs. I was immediately hired as a clerk. After getting demoted at the daycare center, I was more than happy to work some place with a union, like-minded friends, and a political strategy.

Boston City Hospital was the first stop for trauma victims in Boston and the only source of medical care for those with no health insurance at all. Black, white, Hispanic, Haitian, and workers of other nationalities worked at the hospital in harmony, in stark contrast to the racial violence in the city at large. A network of underground corridors linked the many buildings of the complex and at any hour of the day or night, they were as busy as any city street: people heading for the cafeteria, doctors conversing, laundry being delivered, patients on gurneys going to treatment.

We began to get to know our co-workers, attended union meetings of hospital local of the Service Employees International Union (SEIU), and started to get a sense of some of the issues in the hospital. Because it had a predominantly female workforce, employee daycare became a good issue for the union to organize around.

The newly-constructed wing of the outpatient building, built with federal tax money, had just been completed. Included was a high rise of residential units with a daycare center on the ground floor, locked and dark. A couple of us obtained the key from a friend in housekeeping and went exploring. While many centers occupied church basements or other improvised space, this unused facility was a daycare worker's—and a parent's – dream, with its child-size counters, sinks, and toilets.

We approached everyone in the administration willing to meet with us. Not surprisingly, even the female administrators were sympathetic. But we kept getting the same absurd answer: this space, before it even opened up, was to be converted to Trustees' Offices. We showed them the results of a survey we had conducted, indicating that several families would immediately enroll their children in an onsite daycare center. Pregnant at the time, this was not an abstract issue for me. In the end, the administration went ahead, worker needs were disregarded, the daycare center was demolished, the space was converted to Trustees' Offices.

As we became more active in the union at the hospital, a few of us were elected as union stewards in SEIU.

At political events I had noticed a thoughtful, soft-spoken man with a quiet sense of humor. He and I started seeing each other on the bicentennial, July 4, 1976. We were both in our mid-thirties, and though we both had advanced degrees, we'd made decisions to take working class jobs in order to be involved in political and union work. He worked in a local manufacturing plant.

One night we went out to see a film from China. "Let a hundred flowers bloom," declared big character posters all over China. The film showed a worker raising his hands to display the calluses on his palms; he said, "Here are my credentials for entry to the university." We all cheered. We found out much later that the China we so idealized at this time was in the middle of the Cultural Revolution; many intellectuals were imprisoned, there was anything but freedom of speech, and youth were forced to go to the countryside to do manual work.

After the film, we came back to my apartment. We'd been seeing each other for several months and had just begun talking about living together.

"I have to talk to you about something," I said. Then I walked over and unplugged the receiver from the phone.

He grinned at me and said, "I think I know what's coming."

Since we had become more involved and had decided to live together, we could now confide our involvement in The Organization. While we didn't have exactly the same level of involvement, he was committed to the same ideas. Everything in my life was starting to fall into place: not only was I doing something important with my life but I was in a relationship based on shared political philosophy.

Like many of our friends who were getting married and starting families in the late 1970s, we planned a small wedding, mainly with family, a few close friends, and a justice of the peace. But, when my unit leader told me not to take too long a honeymoon because "you don't want to miss a unit meeting," I swallowed hard, remembering just that morning my boss at work agreeing grudgingly to my having the week off.

"Elderly primapara" read my hospital chart. At 36, I was followed a little more closely than others; an amniocentesis showed that we were having a little girl. I loved being pregnant and kept up my normal level of activities, including getting up very early one or two mornings a week and going to sell our newspaper.

"Who's driving tomorrow morning?" I asked at the end of one meeting. "I'm having trouble fastening a seatbelt around this belly!"

"Linda, you know, maybe you should sit this one out. There is some element of risk in what we're doing..."

Several months later, our daughter was born. As most new mothers, I was overcome with joy, fatigue, and worry in equal parts. I felt suddenly more vulnerable, being responsible for a new life. I'm not old enough for this, I instinctively thought, feeling unprepared and overwhelmed, though, in fact I was quite a bit older than most first-time mothers. I began to look at the world around me in a new way; becoming a mother had given me a new reverence for life as well as respect for its fragility. I wondered how would I ever be a mother, go to work, and be politically involved, too. I was taking a six-month maternity leave from my job at the hospital and felt more than a little apprehensive about returning to work.

One Saturday, a busy day for errands as the Massachusetts blue laws kept stores closed on Sunday, it was my turn to get the groceries while my husband was home with the baby. There was a political event that night and he had to write a short introduction to the speaker, I think it was to be in Spanish. After being with the baby all day, I knew he would need some quiet and space. The stores seemed extra crowded, and it took me longer than I'd planned. As I came into the house, he was quietly sitting at the kitchen table, our daughter asleep on his left shoulder, while he wrote the speech with his right hand. Maybe we would be able to keep up with everything after all.

Back at work, I was plunged into activity around negotiations for a new contract. The issues were pay and scheduling, but, most importantly, lack of permanent status. Two-thirds of us were hired as provisional employees; in theory, our status could be renewed at ninety-day intervals. One co-worker from South Boston, having worked for more than 20 years as a clerk, still had provisional status. Negotiations broke down at a certain point, and the union leadership called a strike, the first major municipal strike in Boston in many decades.

285 STRIKE NEWS

July 23, 1980

CONGRATULATIONS ON DAY 1!

Although it was a long day of hard work for everyone, your dedication made the first day of the strike a success.

More than 50% of the nurses honored our picket lines yesterday, and the House Officers gave us a tremendous vote of support by declaring the hospital unsafe and asking the administration to transfer or discharge all patients. (Despite the administration's claim that the hospital was running at full capacity.)

We want to thank AFSCME Local 1489 for gathering their membership this morning to determine how they will show their support; and we want to thank the many other unions who have shown their support by not crossing our picket lines. These include: Teamsters Local 25; Glazers Local 4; employees of the Boston Globe and Boston Herald American; N.E. Telephone; Boston Edison; Pepsi-Cola; Mediclab; Johnson Controls; and many other outside contractors and salesmen. Special thanks to the 285 members at City Hall for coming down to show their support. And especially to University Hospital workers who refused to scab for our own techs.

We can measure the effect we've had by the testimony given by Ann Hargraves, Director of Nursing, yesterday. She described the situation as "devastating". As reported above, less than half the nurses showed up. Here are the attendance figures for other departments:

Hematology:	10 out of 25 showed up
Radiology:	6 " " 50 " "
Outpatient:	1 " " 12 " "
Microbiology:	3 " " 35 " "
Pathology:	5 " " 35 " "
Messengers:	1 " " 12 " "
Biochem lab:	3 " " 35 " "
Blood Bank:	1 " " 5 " "

In addition, many patients have had to be transferred out of the hospital due to lack of personnel; consequently several of the floors are being closed.

Some scabs are still getting through the lines, though. We cannot tolerate any more of this---especially when the scabs are Local 285 members!

This first day was proof positive that we can and will win

Boston City Hospital on strike, 1980.

We arose early the first morning to be on the picket line at 7:00. We wanted to be a visible presence and to keep strikebreakers from entering the hospital. A few union members were left inside to provide emergency services.

Nurses, also represented by SEIU (though in a separate division and not on strike), honored our picket line with more than half of them staying out of work to join us. Then AFSCME (American Federation of State County and Municipal Employees) representing housekeeping and transportation workers, called a sickout and they joined us, too. The huge picket line snaked around the open plaza area in front of the outpatient building. We moved slowly and defiantly, as we chanted,

"Clerks and techs deserve respect! Clerks and techs deserve respect!"

Then the House Officers Association, representing residents and interns, called the hospital "unsafe for patients" and administrators began moving patients to other hospitals.

This was just the beginning. City hall workers and police dispatchers, who were actually on strike with us as part of the same SEIU division, came to the hospital to join us. Other unions from across the city, excited by our strike, sent members down to the South End to join us; people from the daycare workers union and unionized employees of the major Boston papers joined us. The Teamsters honored our picket line and refused to make any deliveries to the hospital.

When I arrived home on the first day of the strike, tired but exhilarated, I found a special delivery letter in my mailbox which read.

> *"You were reported absent from work on July 22, 1980. This absence is presumed to be part of an illegal work action. The State Labor Relations Commission has ruled that the strike...is illegal. It has ordered all picketing to cease and all employees to return to work. Failure to report will subject you to discipline and discharge proceedings."*

After the first day of the strike, the union devised a new strategy. While we would continue to target the main entrance to the hospital with a massive picket line, we would also try to cover as many of the other 54 entrances of the huge complex of buildings as we could.

"Hey, what about the morgue? What if the administrators load strikebreakers into hearses and bring them in to do our jobs? Who can cover that entrance?"

"I'll do that," I offered.

As picket captain, I spent a few sweltering days with five or six fellow workers at the front door of the city morgue. About all that happened was that several funeral home directors came by to do their paperwork. It was quiet, hot, and lonely until a group of middle-aged firefighters, stationed at the fire station down Massachusetts Avenue, passed by on their way to lunch and congratulated us on our strike!

Several times my husband brought our daughter, just a year and a half old at the time, past the hospital picketline on the way to daycare, and I reached into the car to say hi and give her a hug.

We picketed for three days, though it seemed much longer. The Union and City reached a settlement after an all-night session. The next morning, we all crowded into a nearby church to hear the details and vote. The negotiations resulted in an increase in pay of 7% and most importantly, the right to permanent status after two years on the job. We voted for the contract, cheered, and arm-in-arm, entered the hospital. We walked down the hall to our clinics, softly singing

"Solidarity forever, solidarity forever

Solidarity forever, for the union makes us strong." Then we sat down at the reception desk to answer the ringing phones.

These events coincided with national debate over events in Cambodia. The media reported in the mid- to late 1970s that the Pol Pot government had emptied cities and marched everyone to the countryside. Was it true that millions were slaughtered as the establishment press reported? Intellectuals targeted and killed? *Could this happen in a socialist country?*

The Organization's paper sent its editor and several staff members to Cambodia in 1978 to see for themselves. They came back with enthusiastic reports of great accomplishment in rebuilding the country after the devastating war in Indochina. These reporters wrote articles and went on a national speaking tour. We listened to their reports of progress of the Communist government in building socialism and its "brilliant tactic" of moving the urban millions out of Phnom Penh to the source of food in the countryside. Any differing views were attributed by the Pol Pot government to the CIA and the KGB (the Soviet counterpart to the CIA). "Some measure of force" had to be used in a very few isolated incidents, they said. Horror stories such as mass graves were dismissed as "slanderous propaganda."

As more information came out in the following months, a preponderance of evidence condemned the Pol Pot regime. This culminated in January 20, 1980 when *The New York Times Magazine* published an article on Cambodia; the film "The Killing Fields" was made a few years later based on this article. It is hardly surprising that this position on Cambodia—first, uncritical and unqualified support based on sketchy and incomplete information (and which, coincidentally, was China's position), and then actual misrepresentation of events—figured into the collapse of The Organization.

Not only was leadership taking positions that were just plain wrong, but it also became clear that an organization built around such a hierarchical model of leadership, strict discipline, and secrecy was unnecessary if not a bit silly. Lenin's model made no sense at all in an open society where there was relative freedom of expression of political ideas. An organization run by something other than a democratic process became totally untenable, unworkable, and ultimately morally unacceptable to most of us.

The Organization proceeded to collapse rather suddenly. All scheduled meetings and activities stopped, though some of us got together informally to talk about what it all meant and what to do next. Some of us, at least temporarily, retreated into our jobs and families. Forever changed by our involvement, most of us took a break, then became reengaged in other political activity which in most cases continues to this day in one form or another.

In the end, I felt betrayed by people I'd chosen to follow, but uncomfortable, too, about my willingness to follow so uncritically. I had to ask why it had been so comfortable for me to join a highly structured organization. I knew part of it was the people, the camaraderie. I liked being so involved that there was little room for personal insecurities or even, at times, sense of self. I loved the adrenaline rush and crisis mentality. It had given direction to my life, and I felt adrift without it.

With a new baby to care for, I tried to put thoughts of politics behind me, part of some former life. I was relieved to be free of pressures to go to meetings and sell newspapers. But I had believed that socialism offered the best opportunity for economic justice and egalitarianism both in my country and around the world. What would give me hope in a future that was more humane and just? What would give my child a better world to grow up in?

I'll never regret my involvement. I'm glad I was part of the movement against racism in Boston. The networks of people that formed around this time are still in existence. For 18 years, three families jointly celebrated their three children's birthdays that fell in the same month. There were parties for our fiftieth, and now sixtieth, birthdays and our children's graduations. As I was writing this chapter, Nancy Teel's mother celebrated her 90th birthday with a gathering of some new but mainly old friends. More than twenty-five years later we're still here for each other.

After the collapse of The Organization, my husband and I realized that we were now parents with low-paying jobs but no political philosophy or activity to justify them. We began to reevaluate our lives and jobs.

We decided that we didn't want to raise an only child, and our son was born two and a half years after his sister. I was almost 40. I wondered was it more difficult being an "older" parent? My younger friends with newborns seemed just as tired as I. I did, though, feel the responsibilities of parenthood in a particularly overwhelming way and had what was probably a mild postpartum depression. We had suddenly outgrown our small Dorchester apartment. We didn't have our own yard, and when we went to nearby playgrounds with the kids, equipment was broken, the ground was glass-covered, and nearby walls were covered with graffiti.

I knew I would never be comfortable having my children in Boston schools. What were my alternatives? Living in Dorchester but sending my children to private school seemed too contradictory. It was one thing to decide to take on this life in the city for ourselves but for our children, it was a different matter.

My mother helped us with a down payment and we found a small six-room house, just over the Boston city line in a suburban town. Here we were surrounded by lots of green space with a conservation area bordering the Charles River just a few minutes walk away. But I knew I would miss the activity and diversity of the city.

We hiked to the river one of our first days there, on a peaceful trail that wound through the woods. My daughter, then three, asked, "but where are all the people?"

Notes

1. V. I. Lenin, *On Building the Bolshevik Party: Selected Writings 1894 to 1905* (Chicago: Liberator Press, 1976) 281.

2. Bobby Seale and Erika Huggins were tried on murder and kidnapping charges. After the jury was deadlocked, the judge dismissed the charges, noting that there had been too much publicity for them to get a fair trial.

3. COINTELPRO stands for, in FBI-speak, Counter Intelligence Programs.

4. Ronald P. Formisano, *Boston Against Busing: Race, Class, and Ethnicity in the 1960s and the 1970s* (Chapel Hill, University of North Carolina Press, 1991) 57.

5. Thomas Winship, ed. "The First Year: An Account of Boston School Desegregation—The Students, the Officials, and the Public." *Boston Globe,* 25 May, 1975: A1-24.

6. Curtis Wilkie, "Police Curb Confrontation at Beach," *Boston Evening Globe,* 11 August, 1975

7. *Ibid.*

¡CUBA!

Bette Steinmuller

In the spring of 1959, my grandparents surprised my mom, dad and me with our first TV, a 24-inch Magnavox, for my parents' twenty-fifth wedding anniversary. Fidel Castro was in the United States and the first channel I flipped on showed his visit to Harlem and to the United Nations in New York. Was I ever fascinated by this outspoken revolutionary speaking live on TV! He wore fatigues and had a beard like my beatnik brother. He was "liberating" a place I knew about because of my aunts' and uncles' overnight gambling trips to Havana. But it wasn't until twenty years later that I went to Cuba the first time for a week and came back convinced that I had visited paradise.

April, 1979

I was a fledgling Spanish teacher in the 1970s and needed to practice the language with native speakers. I had heard a lot about Cuba and became involved with Cuban solidarity work by volunteering to usher at a Cuban Grupo Moncada concert at the Berkelee Performance Center in Boston. The people who were volunteering with me were also working to end the U.S. blockade against Cuba and were great believers in the socialist experiment there. I spoke Spanish with many of them who were children of Cubans who had left in the early Sixties. They gave me books about the Cuban struggle for a "just" society. It seemed like a worthy alternative to the materialistically dehumanizing society where I lived. Did "socialism" automatically mean the elimination of social class distinctions? I had to see that for myself. An opportunity arose when the U.S. began allowing trips to Cuba organized around different themes. When MARAZUL Tours, a travel agency in New York offered one on "education," I went for a week during school spring vacation.

We were taken to the Hotel Riviera on the Ocean Drive known as the Malecon. The hotel still had furniture from the 1950s, and I imagined the defunct Mafioso Meyer Lansky surrounded by prostitutes and gamblers on the balcony. Every meal was a "socialist" buffet with tropical fruit and multi-flavored yogurt for breakfast, the same tasteless meats and canned Russian vegetables for lunch, and the same fried pork, chicken, sour kraut and salads prepared Russian-style with canned peas, carrots and tons of mayonnaise, for dinner.

The tour leader handed us our week's itinerary of scheduled official visits to Santa Maria Beach, Jibacoa, a farming cooperative east of Havana, Pasa Caballos, a resort in Villa Clara, the city of Cienfuegos, and The Ministry of Education in Havana. We had no choice but to forgive Cuba for being on school vacation that week, but being educators, we had obviously counted on visiting schools. In Cienfuegos, we overheard another tour group saying they were going to visit a teacher-training school that was closed, but some administrators had agreed to meet with them. Two of us wangled our way onto their bus. We found out they were working on a curriculum for outstandingly bright, energetic kids who were super revolutionary. Recruited into an accelerated brigade, they would become teachers when they completed the eighth grade. This had to be done because of the brain drain caused by the exodus of so many teachers in the 1960s. It was the way they expedited teacher training to cover classrooms everywhere.

During the rest of the trip, I saw how "people's power" functioned through the neighborhood defense committees. I walked the streets all hours of the night and felt safe because of the local neighbors who stayed up as security guards to protect people, even near hotels where tourists were apt to cause trouble. I climbed the foothills of the Escombray Mountains where Che Guevara had fought, and the peasants there smiled when I asked them about him. I visited construction brigades, observed voluntary work in the countryside, listened to people at the model cooperative in Jibacoa tell us about their lives, and drank *mojitos* on Santa Maria Beach.

A woman I met at a dock in Cienfuegos tried to convince me that Cuban life wasn't what it seemed, but I ignored her. I told her I was enjoying my trip, and she looked at me as though I was a lost soul. A colleague of mine who had visited Cuba the year before had asked me to bring guitar strings to Rogelio, an unemployed musician. He took me for a walk by many deserted store fronts in Havana, bitterly complaining the whole way how he wasn't able to speak freely, that he wanted desperately to leave. I didn't pay much attention to him either. After all, it was only normal that a percentage of the population would not be in agreement with the Revolution.

I returned to Boston convinced that Cuba was indeed paradise. We had been wined and dined for sure, but it never occurred to me that everyone didn't live that way.

June 1988

Nineteen years later, I was living and working in Nicaragua as a teacher trainer and English as a Foreign Language (EFL) teacher. I was partying one night with my American journalist friends at the International Press Club and noticed a flyer announcing a journalist tour to Cuba with accommodations at the Hotel Riviera. It only cost $180 and if I wanted to go, there was still space; it didn't matter that I wasn't a reporter...they would turn me into one. A week later, I was given an ID representing *Newsday*, the magazine I'd once translated for, a press card, and convinced a friend to also become a reporter and be my roommate. We took off with the group of annoying gringo reporters to accompany President Daniel Ortega on his state visit to Havana.

The trip couldn't have been more official, from the moment the plane landed and Fidel and his entourage greeted Daniel and his family, Miguel D'Escoto and other *comandantes* on the tarmac. Every day, we rode in a luxurious bus behind the two heads of state to different neighborhoods where crowds cheered and shouted *"Fidel! Fidel!"* The highlights were: a model Family Doctor's practice, where the doctor lived above his office in a totally equipped new building; a recently-opened pediatric hospital; the construction site of the convention complex Expo Cuba where we spoke with a brigade of women builders; and a press conference with José Ramón Fernéndez, the Minister of Education. My camera clicked along with all the others, but I was a vacationing observer with no byline to file. Everything was carefully arranged and Daniel looked duly impressed as Fidel showed off the achievements of the Revolution. The show was crowned by a personal dinner invitation from Fidel Castro Ruz, his name engraved in gold cursive letters.

As we entered The Palace of the Revolution, invited dignitaries formed a line to greet Fidel who stood in a garden of tropical plants that were said to be automatically watered with fine mist and kept at optimum temperatures day and night. We would not get to shake his hand, however, because guards wearing *guayaberas* whisked us into a banquet hall with more food and drink than I had ever seen in one place. Tables were loaded with gourmet lobster, shrimp, roast beef, roast pork, plantains, colorful salads, breads, cheeses, and creamy pastries, not to mention the rum and unlimited red and white wine being poured by waiters in starched white uniforms. What a contrast to our basic, boring hotel buffets that everyone complained about. The spread cost a major fortune, and after tasting a bit of this and that, I began feeling queasy. This simply didn't figure in my socialist dream. We whispered among ourselves how strange it was to be offered this lavish meal when we knew the people of Cuba would never see any of what was on those tables.

People became chummy, and before long I found myself talking with a Nicaraguan *Comandante* who wanted to know my name, and which hotel I was in. Someone mentioned we were all at the Riviera. I didn't pay much attention to the flirting given the amount of alcohol flowing. A couple of hours later, we were escorted onto our buses and back to the hotel. A few in the group went to the bar for more drinks, but I went to sleep. The *Comandante* buzzed my room at midnight. He wanted to play, but my instincts told me it wouldn't be cool, that we'd probably be followed to the door of every night club by state security.

At the end of the week I thought it would be interesting to work in Cuba some day, but not be part of such an official visit. Apparently, my wish was overheard because my name was given to the Cuban Ministry of Education, and a year later I went to Cuba to do a needs assessment for a program to update English professors' language skills.

June 1989

I had only been back from Nicaragua a few months and was working as an English consultant near Boston, when I was invited by the Cuban Ministry of Education to develop a graduate upgrading program for English teachers at the Higher Pedagogical Institute of Foreign Languages. I flew to Cuba in June, 1989 to do the needs assessment at *ISPLE,* as it was called.

On the plane, I remember thinking how I had been an anti-war activist in my country, had worked with the Sandinista government, but now, my wish would come true as an educator, and consultant in Cuba! What puffed me up the most was that very few U.S. Americans had ever been invited to Revolutionary Cuba.

I had no idea who would be greeting me, and after a half hour of pacing back and forth in the airport, I began having an anxiety attack, regretting I had ever considered myself an important visitor, when I saw a sign with *Bette Steinmuller* in large carefully-printed red letters being held by two striking blond middle-aged women. One was the Academic Dean and the other, Francisca, was from the Ministry of Education (*MINED*.) They accompanied me in a chauffeur-driven car to the Hotel Riviera, the same hotel I had stayed in twice before.

The Dean handed me my week's schedule and advised me to rest. The next morning, I got into a black, sagging, Soviet Volga, next to the driver, with Francisca in the back. She said my transportation would be provided daily to school even though the hotel was a fifteen-minute walk.

Most of the Institute was housed in former apartment buildings in the formerly upper class area of Miramar, west of downtown Havana. If there was still paint on the buildings, it was faded or soiled, and in every room there was a door handle, chair back or louvered window missing. Similar to Nicaragua, the plumbing was indoors, and the toilets worked by flushing them with water stored in the bathtubs.

I spent two weeks formulating the needs assessment at the school, which was comparable to our former teacher colleges in the U.S. I took notes all day and returned to the Hotel Riviera every night to edit my interviews and draft the document which would target my future work. Panchita, as Francisca was called, accompanied me during the day. As we gradually opened up to each other, she recounted a trip she had made to Niagara Falls in 1955, when she had graduated from college. She had loved visiting the United States and I could tell from her voice that she would have gone back if not for the Cuban Revolution. I talked about my first trip in 1979 and how I had visited Cuba the year before when I had been training teachers in Nicaragua, but never dreamed I would be creating this project in Havana.

The car was always waiting to take me to the hotel where I had a quick swim and lunch by the pool before going back to work at 2:00. The interviews ended between 5:00 and 6:00. Everyone I met was charming, positive about the project, and eager to talk to me. I met department heads and teachers, observed classes and spoke with everyone from the cleaning staff to the Minister, José Ramón Fernández.

I observed two major historical events that June. The first was the opening of commerce between China and Cuba, evidenced by the hotel elevator full of silent, suited-up, serious-looking, Chinese businessmen. The second baffling occurrence was the bursting open of the Ochoa drug case, but it was not a topic of conversation at *ISPLE*. Panchita simply alluded to it as a problem that would be resolved.

It seemed to me that Raúl Castro was raving like a mad man about General Ochoa, Fidel's friend, who had been trafficking in drugs in Angola. A United States journalist who lived in Cuba was visiting my hotel room that night when Fidel's brother Raúl, who was Chief of the Armed Forces, responded to the drug case on national television. She explained to me that this was a most rare and serious betrayal—that Raúl's fury was justified. As I took it all in, I knew something terrible was happening, and my intuition told me not to bring it up with Panchita or anyone else. Not too long afterward, the General and one other were silenced by execution.

The upside of those two weeks was meeting the since deceased writer Albertico Yañez[1] who was gay and "out." He had never seen a computer and I invited him to see mine. Albertico told me Cubans were not allowed in hotel rooms, let alone welcome in lobbies, but he put on an American baseball cap and giving off his best tourist vibes, marched onto the elevator, and into my room. Despite his instant aversion to the machine, he painstakingly typed his poetic denouncement of the age of technology on my laptop and then laughed uproariously. I was relieved to meet him because I had heard so many tales of repression against homosexuals in Cuba, and his openness reassured me that times were changing.

I also had brought letters and packages to Cubans from friends or family in the U.S. After arranging to meet them in the lobby of the Hotel Riviera, I would go down and recognize them fidgeting in the swanky hotel sofas, waiting for me—the stranger who had called and said to meet them at 4:00 —to appear with their packages at the arranged time. I too was scrutinized by plain-clothed security guards milling about during those brief meetings in the lobby. "What was the government afraid of?" I wondered.

Toward the end of my visit, the Dean asked if there was anything else I wanted to do while I was in Havana.

"Do you think I could request an interview with the Minister of Education?" I asked Panchita who knew just about anything.

"Of course! I'll schedule it for Thursday."

José Ramón Fernández had rubber stamped the project. He was well known as *El Gallego Fernández*, "The Spanish Fernández." "Does that nickname mean that he's from Galicia, Spain," I wondered out loud?

---

1   In the Fall of 2008, Albertico was found lifeless in his home in Havana. Foul play was suspected but has never been confirmed.

"No," Panchita explained, "If you're from Spanish lineage, you're called a *"Gallego"* here.

I was shaking when the driver came at 2:15 that Thursday. What was I doing, asking to see one of the most famous men in Cuba, who doubled as Minister of Education and Sports.

Panchita accompanied me to the Ministry, a gloomy, stone, structure that covered an entire city block. Its roof was originally intended as a landing field for helicopters and was built by Fulgencio Batista, the Cuban dictator overthrown by Fidel in 1959. (My husband thinks Batista's architects would have ruined Old Havana with monstrosities of this type had it not been for the Revolution.)

The Minister's office was on the fourth floor, just under the roof. Panchita and I were led into an ample space with three grey walls, and a fourth covered with mahogany paneling. There was one 40-watt florescent bulb over the reception area and another on the dark wall. There were no windows. It felt more like being led into a Caribbean war bunker rather than a Minister's office.

Panchita spoke in a deferential whisper to a drab-faced secretary who motioned with her head and a finger for us to sit. I couldn't decide which oversized couch or chair—vintage 1950—to sit in. The brown naugahyde one I chose was so deep that my feet couldn't touch the floor, so I stayed on the edge, taking in the rest of the décor. Behind the secretary's desk was a revolutionary slogan, probably, " *Unidos en Una Sola Causa Bajo una Sola Bandera"* (United in One Cause Under One Flag). On the brown wall was a blown up photo of the bearded martyr, Camilo Cienfuegos who had disappeared over the ocean in a plane, and another over-sized one of Che Guevara and Fidel walking into Batista's Presidential Palace together, the night Fidel took over the country. There were no educational journals or magazines, so I waited in silence, wondering what he'd ask and how I'd answer.

A couple of minutes later, the secretary motioned again with her head for me to go through a dark, knobless, wooden door that seemed to open on its own. The Minister stood up and shook my tense, clammy hand. I think he said "welcome" and pointed to the visitor's chair which was uncomfortably far from where he sat at his desk. It was actually a table and held a few orderly piles of folders, a telephone and a calendar, no photos of the wife and children. On the wall behind him was an almost life-size enlargement of the classic photograph of Fidel, facing the crowds gathered at 12th and 23rd Streets in Havana in 1962, announcing Cuba would embrace Communism.

It took me a while to understand what The Minister was saying because his voice sounded like the raking of dry leaves. It emerged from tight lips on a strained face that must have been in a state of perpetual constipation. He had a crew cut, and his white hair matched a long-sleeved, plain *guayabera,* that equivalent of the Latin male dress shirt that always reminded me of my dentist's jacket. He was leaner and taller than most Cuban men. Although many said he had been to West Point, he was a graduate of The School of the Americas in Georgia where the United States has trained various Latin American terrorists over the years. There was no doubt that he was the general who orchestrated the defeat of the U.S. trained enemy at the Bay of Pigs Invasion, and it was said that Fidel chose him to be Minister because of his success as a military strategist.

"I understand you've been here for a while. Has everything gone well for you?" He rasped.

"Oh yes, the Dean and everyone at the ISPLE Institute, have been more than helpful. I think I have enough information to design the project now."

"And…of course…everything…is…(clearing his throat) comfortable for you at the hotel?

"Perfect. Actually this is the third time that I've stayed at the Hotel Riviera. When I….

He interrupted before I could explain that I'd been to Cuba in 1979, and the year before.

"So you were working in Nicaragua recently," he confirmed, peering at me over a pair of black-rimmed glasses, holding something typed that was probably my bio.

"I was an educator there. In 1984, I coordinated a language program in Esteli, in the war zone, and I trained…"

A young expressionless woman appeared through a secret passageway in the paneled wall carrying a wooden tray with two white china cups of espresso coffee. I didn't drink coffee, and certainly not this Cuban, cloying, amber-black blend that would keep me awake for a week, so pretending to sip it helped me feel more at ease.

"Our Nicaraguan brothers have learned and continue to learn a great deal from Cuba, you know," He continued, sipping, peering at me, from above his half reading glasses.

"Yes, while I was living there, I met several Cubans in the countryside teaching…"

He interrupted again, "I see here you were part of the journalist group that accompanied President Daniel Ortega last year on his first state visit. Tell me about that."

"Well, even though I'm a teacher, they gave me a press card, and the tour was..."

This time, he loudly cleared his throat, "All together, it looks as though you were there for three years; it must have been very fulfilling to work with the Sandinista Revolution."

Our parley brought back the group interview with him the year before when he'd evaded the journalists' questions, deferring to a grinning syco-phantic aide whose face reminded me of a well-fed piglet. He had headed off controversial issues about the educational system with official party-line answers before *El Gallego* had had a chance to open his mouth. All I wanted in this 15-minute audience was to tell him what I had in mind for Cuba, but he kept taking me back to Nicaragua.

"Yes, it was gratifying to teach in Nicaragua," I assured him. "Here, on the graduate level, I'd like to work with a participatory methodology that will encourage learners to initiate..."

"You will find many more amenities here in Cuba than in Nicaragua—whose struggle is at a stage we surpassed years ago, he went on. We have arranged appropriate living space for you and your colleagues."

"Thank you. I'm not at all worried about that. What interests me most is being able to introduce a new pedagogy here, on the model of..."

And breaking in for the last time, "The Dean has an outing planned for you tomorrow, a sound and light show where you will enjoy an impressive military reenactment at *La Cabaña* across the Bay. You know, Comrade, we are very grateful for your work and impressed by your Central American trajectory, so this is the very least we can do to show our appreciation."

The one time I'd see a Sound and Light Show had been in 1972 at a French chateau and I had no idea that *La Cabaña* was a historical military site.

He stood up before I could ask. "Well, it has certainly been a pleasure, and I assure you we will do everything we can to make your stay produc-tive, so please don't hesitate to ask."

As I thanked him again and as I said my *"Hasta luego, Ministro,"* my head was spinning. I'd wanted to talk about encouraging learners to initi-ate ideas in their English classes and be more involved with their learning, rather than receive the lecture-style, top-down, teacher-is-god approaches I had just observed in Cuban classrooms. But he hadn't let me describe the egalitarian concepts of "student-centered learning" or "participatory edu-cation" that I thought would work well in Cuba. Didn't he want to hear what I was saying? Why wasn't he interested?

Years later it came to me. Fidel wanted us to come to Cuba to update English, and *El Gallego* Fernández had granted me the interview as a courtesy, a favor. He didn't need to check up on any of my credentials—political or academic.

Soon after returning to Boston, it wasn't difficult to find three other teachers who were equally excited about preparing and going to teach in Cuba with me.

August 1989 ISPLE

The four of us spent the summer planning our work, preparing videos, buying English books, and copying tons of pages of EFL teaching methodology and research that we took with us in August, 1989.

We were buoyed by the excitement of being pioneers, the first North Americans invited by the Cuban government to train graduate English teachers and upgrade their language skills. From the minute we arrived, we received the red-carpet treatment in a renovated guest house that still lacked finishing touches. The house administrator, the cook, and a representative from the Ministry formed a reception line and told us everything we needed would be ours, but not many days later, it began to feel more like containment rather than privilege. Giving keys to foreigners in guest houses was not listed in the book of state regulations, so we had to knock on the door at no matter what hour of the day for three months before the Minister himself granted our request for individual keys.

The first week, we interviewed the teachers individually to get a sense of their English strengths and weaknesses. The young teachers not only waited to be told to sit down, but trembled as they waited for each question. Invariably, they would say, "Please excuse me for being so nervous, Professor. I have never spoken to a North American before and my English is terrible, I know. I'm so embarrassed that I am a teacher."

"Please don't apologize," I would respond. "Your English is excellent. Please relax! I'm here to ask a few questions, so we will know which group will be best for you."

"Oh, Professor. That is so nice of you, but really, I need to learn so much. Any group you would like to place me in would be fine."

We usually worked ten-hour days, stopping only when meals were served. My morning would often begin by hearing someone running behind me on my walk to work:

"Oh good morning Professor. I'm Mari Sol. I teach first-year students. I'm not in your class, but you're so famous, so of course I know all about you. May I carry your bag for you?"

"Hi Mari Sol, nice to see you. "No, thank you, that's all right. Isn't it a great morning? I love walking to work here along the water.

"Oh, yes, Professor, we are so lucky to have the sun shining like this so close to the ocean. Have you ever seen the ocean before?"

"Yes, I come from New England and I know the Atlantic, but it's much colder than the sea here."

"Professor, I hear you saying the word 'sea' and now I have a doubt."

"Yes."

"Well, maybe I'm not remembering correctly, but I think we were taught that an ocean is not really a sea, but you just said 'sea,' so that must be the correct way of speaking, mustn't it?"

Not wanting to destroy her image of me, I on-the-spot thought up the best English grammatical/idiomatic/usage explanation that I could in the remaining two minutes of walking.

"Oh, thank you very much, Professor. And if you don't mind, I have another doubt, how do you spell hypochondriac?"

And that was how I became a walking dictionary every day, to and from the Institute. Chatting that way was probably a way for the Cuban teachers to feel less self-conscious talking to native speakers.

The older teachers were also nervous, but they would never admit it. Those in their fifties had attended elitist, private bilingual or English-speaking schools in the pre-Fidel era, and spoke perfectly. The only problem was their idiomatic English which remained "fossilized" from the 1960s. I had to keep from laughing every time I heard, "Dum da dum dum!," the theme from the '60s TV show, *Dragnet.* (We taught them to get attention by saying , " Da Daaaahhh!" instead.) We were astounded by the high level of training all the teachers had received despite some stilted expressions. They spent their free time studying and preparing classes, going to linguistic events, doing everything possible to improve and maintain their skills.

We were invited when Cuba hosted linguistic events that included teachers and researchers from Latin American countries. I once presented anecdotal research I had been doing in Havana. It involved studying patterns of Cuban English derived from Spanish, as evidenced by the teachers "having doubts," instead of questions, as we would say. I showed other examples such as, "Well, we coincided last night at the ice cream place," meaning, "We saw each other there." The Ministry of Tourism published my study called "Young Fossils" in their linguistic journal. GELI, (Group of English

Language Specialists) an organization supported by the U.S. Interests Section also sponsored events. Since I needed to protect my legal status as a researcher, I kept a low profile where GELI was concerned.

But training teachers was our priority. We copied videos, developed materials with grammatical exercises, English idioms and culture and demonstrated how to teach them. *"Norma Rae"* and *"Down and Out in Beverly Hills"* were particularly popular since they gave the teachers glimpses into current U.S. culture and language.

I also enjoyed working with teachers from the provinces, including Guantanamo and Santiago. They had fewer opportunities to hear English, and their training had been inferior.

They certainly had grammar and pronunciation problems, but were eager enough to learn that they left their families at the other end of the island to live with few amenities in a dormitory and study at La Coronela in Havana for five months. The semester ended with a party that started at 9:00 a.m. We would have rum, chicken, rice and beans and assorted sweet delicacies that miraculously appeared on my desk. (These were very hard times, so the only place they could have gotten it all was on the black market.) Next, the dancing began, and soon I would be accepting an invitation to visit a teacher's home. It was through these contacts that I visited different parts of Cuba, graciously hosted—during very hard times—by my new friends.

I must have taught courses or done workshops at twenty different programs or conferences aside from *ISPLE*. One day, a young man knocked at our door and wanted to practice his English with me. He had heard there were North Americans in Miramar and he hitchhiked for three hours that morning to see if we had time to just talk to him in "American" English. At that point, we made it clear we were busy all day and could not meet individual needs, no matter how poignantly pressing.

Our personal lives were totally removed from the teachers and students in Miramar, a neighborhood that showed few signs of poverty or disenchantment. Looking below the surface, however, we began to realize there were vast differences of power and position between our neighborhood and the society at large. We understood the teachers when they apologized for not being able to offer us food or drink, and therefore felt awkward inviting us to their homes, but years later, I found out that the Communist Party had told them not to, that we could have been agents from the CIA, and that they had to be careful not to get too close.

We were often reminded we had to live the luxurious yet isolated life the Ministry of Education offered us because it would be too difficult for us to work and maintain households, given the rationing system and the difficulties in obtaining food and supplies. The treatment we received should have been another red flag, for me to question the inequities of the socialist dream. But, in the long run, it was to their advantage to pamper us because we were less distracted and tired and could work ten hours a day, only stopping for meals which were cooked and served to us.

Eventually, we did visit teacher's homes when one department head broke the ice. He and the others who followed suit were all in retrospect dissenters to varying degrees. In different ways, they showed us the inconsistencies in their social system which clearly had a powerful and elitist military and governing class. Those who played the game were "in" and received privileges. Those who were "out" were poor, less educated, hadn't been indoctrinated, or were marginal and certainly not members of the party.

We remained silent: When Zenaida Puig broke down and told me in detail how her son-in-law Tony de la Guardia had been executed along with General Ochoa, I understood her nervousness and depression; a young teacher, who eventually left Cuba, told us the compulsory *Poder Popular* (Popular Power) meetings were not taken seriously. As a group, we were not encouraged to attend faculty meetings. At the end of the year, they held neighborhood meetings called *"rendimento de cuentas"* where everyone was supposed to honestly account for their successes and failures in order to earn their rewards, perhaps a refrigerator or pressure cooker. Although everyone was supposed to give praise and criticism, the teachers claimed these meetings were automatic, obligatory and farce-like, that no genuine complaints could be voiced. One teacher picked us up in a 1950s car that broke down on the highway out side of the city near where he lived. We were guilt-ridden when we found out he had had to buy the gas on the black market.

To keep us entertained, we were taken to the Isle of Youth, chaperoned constantly by a Ministry representative. What a pleasant surprise when one of the ISPLE faculty members, who supervised teachers in training in schools on the island, happened to appear while we were there and gave us her version of the grand tour, alongside the Communist Party guide. We were moved by the prison where Fidel and Co. had been incarcerated, but again, we felt like escorted royalty as we toured the ceramic factory, saw the statue of *Ubre Blanca*, (White Udder) the Cuban cow famous for giving more milk than any other, and the black sands of Bibijawa Beach. When we visited the school for Nicaraguan youth, my colleagues urged me to give an impromptu speech about how impressed I had been by the revolution in their country, and what an honor it was to visit them in Cuba.

Since the Minister had said to ask for anything I needed, I requested and was given a free trip to Nicaragua by the Ministry. When I had an emergency operation, the Minister personally called me at Sagrado Corazon, an OB/GYN hospital in Havana. On the other hand, what coddled and precious "spies" we were to be introducing new ideas that weren't always appreciated. They accused us of cultural penetration behind our backs. I would have preferred being labeled a radical academic imperialist because I eventually felt no different than a CIA worker, except that the academic dogma I carried was of a higher plane, revered for being participatory and experiential, words that caused fear in Cuban academic circles since they hadn't been assimilated into their vocabulary. The pedagogy they used to train teachers came from Soviet methodology translated from Russian into English.

We straddled the foreign and the Cuban worlds when it came time to travel. An American colleague and I paid Cuban pesos to fly to Santiago. When we landed on the northeast coast, with no place to stay, the head of the tourist bureau assured us nobody slept in the streets of Cuba. Unlike other visiting foreigners who paid in U.S. currency, we were allowed to pay for our hotels in pesos, and there was always a room available in Cuban currency, even though the management would claim the contrary. We had been warned not to go without reservations, but we took our chances, knowing that we would be safe in this country I labeled the paternal land of surreal contradictions. In Baracoa, we stayed in the Hotel La Rusa, a hotel founded by a Russian woman who left during the October Revolution and stayed in Cuba the rest in her life. Our room was complete with cockroaches in the refrigerator. And, by dropping the name of a professor at our institute who knew Alexander Hartman, the curator of the Baracoa museum, he hired a jeep to take us into the mountains and organized a party of artists and sculptors in our honor.

We were officially feasted at the end of ISPLE semesters by our students and administrators at the institute or in the home of a department head. After my first one-year commitment, I returned, feeling that there was much more work to do. Since the Ministry claimed they preferred "new blood," to familiarize the Cubans with different approaches to teaching and different accents, they granted me only one more semester. They probably didn't want anyone to stay too long and know too much. They weren't keen about my spear-heading a request to obtain our own apartments and foreign technician ration cards, but the battle was won by the program coordinator who followed me.

In the beginning of 1991, when it became time to leave the Ministry of Education, I found out Pura, our cook/ housekeeper had been envious of me. I had applied for work at the Ministry of Tourism and the director called her for a routine reference check and she told them too many men visited me. Actually, the "too many men" were flocking to see my lap top because in 1989 and 1990 there were none in Havana, so I invited curious computer specialists to see mine.

When Tourism didn't hire me because of Pura's criticism, I accepted a position with the Ministry of Public Health in a distance learning English program, working with Marjorie Moore, the North American director. It was multi-faceted work that included grading written course work based on several texts and traveling to the different provinces of Cuba to test the teachers involved. Teachers who had done well could opt to spend one semester studying in Havana. I taught speaking skills, methodology, writing, and reading, and supervised their Masters theses. I tested medical and scientific personnel who were going off on missions to Yemen or countries in Africa where English was spoken. Several doctors or nurses I rejected complained I was too demanding, but others appreciated the standards I maintained. Occasionally I taught courses to English teachers at the medical schools in Havana where I was appalled by the crumbling infrastructure in the Havana hospitals. What was so gratifying about my work was having mature students who were captive audiences.

When I began working with Ministry of Public Health, (*MINSAP*) I lived in a dormitory for foreigners at the Giron Medical School for three months until the bureaucracy granted me Foreign Technician status. I then had my own apartment and a ration card to buy food in El Nautico, a small mostly foreign neighborhood in the north of Havana where I lived until I left Cuba. I had that status during the remainder of my stay in Cuba, but began learning how to manage the common double standard which meant smiling and agreeing with the "*jefes*" and their propaganda and then getting and doing what I needed for myself. Every obstacle the system presented daily, whether it was a shortage of food or something needing repair in my apartment could be overcome with a bottle of rum

Lúmino and I were fixed up on a blind date and fell in love. He, his family and friends taught me about despair first hand. The first year, I had known musicians who felt somewhat alienated from the system, but Lúmino's film world of ICAIC (Cuban film industry organization) opened up many more deceptions. In Cuba, there was a saying that everything belonged to everyone, but in the end, nothing belonged to anybody. We were married in Havana in 1993, when life was still extremely difficult due to the end of economic subsidies from the former Soviet Union. That same year, gas became extremely scarce, to the point where I could no longer travel to the provinces. I had a small car, but gas was rationed and the Ministry couldn't provide transportation for me locally. Buses were overcrowded and ran infrequently. I had little work, and Lúmino even less. I was living off of the rent I received from my home in Boston and I had no savings. We needed to think about the social security, pensions, and retirement we didn't have. We left Cuba during the summer of 1994 to try our luck in the north. I look back on those years when Cuba invited me to share my skills as the most exciting and important years of my teaching career.

Winter, 1998

January 2, 1998. I cried on and off flying back to Boston from Havana, and the below-freezing wind chilled my tooth as I walked through the airport parking lot. My jaw began throbbing up to my right eyeball. The dental receptionist gave me the emergency slot early the next morning with Dr. Simons.

Pam, his assistant, ushered me onto the cool, plastic-covered chair and pinned the heavy-duty napkin around my neck. The heat hadn't come on yet. She yawned and said it would be a few minutes wait. I shivered and pulled my turtle neck sweater higher, closed my eyes, and it was easy to drift back to Cuba.

My husband, Lúmino, and I had just split our two-week vacation between one of the oldest hotels at Varadero Beach and a room we rented from a friend in Havana. While we waited for the agency to replace our defective rented car outside of the Havana Libre, a Spanish-managed hotel, a well-dressed mulatto approached Lúmino—who looks like a cross between Harry Belafonte, Nelson Mandela and Colin Powell.

"Excuse me sir," he asked in Spanish, "Where are you from...uhh Martinique?"

"No."

"Would you like to buy some fine Cuban cigars? I work in the Cohiba factory warehouse, and I..."

"I'm Cuban," Lúmino interrupted.

The man immediately turned and walked away, and as we were pulling off in our repaired Fiat, I glanced back and saw two policemen holding his identification papers and questioning him.

This had been my second trip back to visit family and friends in Cuba, after living there from 1989 -1994. And it was only yesterday that I had said goodbye, this time at the Havana guest house, to the voice of singer Pablo Milanes.

"*Cuba y Puerto Rico son dos alas del mismo pajaro, una callo en el mar y la otra vive libre.*" The song about Cuba and Puerto Rico said they were two wings of the same bird, that one fell in the sea and the other lived free, but I knew in my heart that Cuba wasn't really "free" either. While inching my suitcase through the patio with one knee, I watched our Puerto Rican traveling companion, a first-time tourist to Cuba, standing outside, also saying goodbye, seemingly searching for something, as he scrutinized the spaces between the palm leaves, drying his eyes.

Cuba! How you creep into every crevice of my mind with your sensual rage, dreams, dissidence, pollution, palm trees, music, laughter, sex, dancing, sweat, grandchildren, sweet roast pork and sugar cane juice, rum and friends, bicycles, repression, mildew, blackouts, beaches, mountains, your noise, your heat...your Fidel.

"Welcome Home Mami," was the greeting, hand-printed in huge letters by my hosts, on a white card precariously perched in the avocado tree in front of their newly painted house. At the pre-New Years party on the outskirts of Havana, I was visiting my friends who had moved to the capital from Fomento in Villa Clara, an eastern province, but a place too small to be on a map. Years before, I had been skeptical when I saw all of their belongings and at least sixty bags of cement stacked against the walls of the shack that looked like a real home now.

They in turn had doubted my "*gringa*" prowess at growing avocado plants from seed, but this one, in front of their new construction, was my tree. It was only two feet high when I left and bequeathed it to Ileana in 1994. I knew her from the time I had worked at *MINSAP*. She was a divorced English teacher whom I had trained and, as any Cuban would do, she had invited me to visit her house-in-progress several times. I had gotten to know her older brother, and teenage daughter—who had really been raised by Orquidia, her mother. Although she was the warm, understanding grandmother, matriarch, I realized that night that I was not only Ileana's mentor, but also *Mami*, her other mother.

Now they had this four-room house, and unlike before, the bathroom and kitchen were indoors. Everybody had their own bedrooms and there was a small living room and a sheltered outdoor space. It was luxury earned! The party was a house-warming. Everything had been prepared when we arrived: rice and beans smelling of garlic, onion, cumin, oregano, and cilantro, accompanied by slabs of garlic-drenched roast pork on beds of lettuce; Havana Club rum was flowing, and the salsa music and dancing erupted as Lúmino and I reached the porch.

"Thank you for the card in my tree. It makes me want to cry," I told Ileana.

She hugged me and responded, "The great Cuban poet Jose Marti wrote there were only three things one had to do in life: procreate, plant a tree, and write a book."

The first two seemed relatively easy, I thought to myself.

There were jokes everywhere—not only at this party—about Fidel, The Immortal One. Of course I remembered the Pepito jokes I had heard during my first trip in 1979. They were about this clever character who got himself in and out of trouble by learning about life with every shade of double meaning possible. Joking about Fidel had been taboo. But seeing the Cubans laughing, I laughed too. They can turn anything into a joke— even Fidel who had been in power for almost forty years. When I referred to him as the Infernal one, everybody laughed at my Freudian slip...The *gringa*, can tell a good joke too, they said, but she should not tell that one too loud!

The lively Cuban chatter and tropical aura suddenly dissolved into my throbbing face. It was snowing and I was sitting in the dentist's office in Jamaica Plain, Massachusetts.

Pam came in to say that Dr. Simons was on the phone, that it wouldn't be too long. She pressed a button, leaving me reclining, and I drifted back again, this time to the din at the School of Dentistry in Havana a couple of years before, where Julia, a resident, led me through a maze of fifty chairs to her place in a square hall lit by the sun pouring through a frosted glass ceiling with wires keeping it together. I had been told to bring my own towel, which I tucked around my neck as she energetically cranked the seat up by hand, apologizing for the aged sponge rubber poking through the dry, cracked leather irritating my back.

I waited, eavesdropping on her opinion about the open mouth in the chair next to me. Lying there, I unexpectedly started to realize how depressed I was. This was not the same Cuba I had idealized when I visited in 1979. I was shocked by the increasing lack of resources, the unemployment, crumbling infrastructure, the low morale of the people with whom I worked, their hunger, worn-out clothing, and then—of all things—to have almost choked on this huge filling that had fallen out while I was eating a pork chop.

I was a teacher trainer for MINSAP and Julia had been recommended by one of my students, who came from her hometown. She was cheerful, and soft-spoken while she gently examined the hole in my mouth, but she involuntarily gave away something so Cuban about her lunch—the unmistakable hint of garlic on her breath, "I can put in a new filling," she said in Spanish, "But I don't know how long it will stay. The hole is very wide, so there's simply not enough to hold it on." Yes, I thought, something like the hope I used to have and the emptiness I am beginning to feel in my soul here, but I did not share my thought with her.

As she checked the rest of my teeth, I began gaping at the gold Jewish star that hung down from her neck near my chest. I think mine was silver, but it had been stored away in a box somewhere since my Bat Mitzvah forty years before. I pointed questioningly at her Star of David.

"Oh, it was a gift from my great aunt. She left a long time ago, but some Jewish friends of hers from—*Brruklin Mahsachuuset*—visited my synagogue and brought it."

My eyes must have moved into a freeze frame; she stopped probing.

"Do you know *Brruklin Mahsachuuset*?" She asked. "Are you Jewish?"

The drill hung suspended in front of my nose, obviously interested in my answer.

"Yes, I am Jewish. I used to live in Brookline, Massachusetts, and here I train English teachers at the medical building across from your synagogue. I've just never gotten around to visiting it."

I was still smiling, remembering the scene and Julia's response, and then it all faded away again as Dr. Simons began to move a strangely angled, blinding light around my face, brusquely interrupting my reverie.

"Ahem…You say you have an old filling that has partially fallen out," he muttered and jabbed several teeth, luckily missing the cavernous molar in question.

Whaap! A transparent Plexiglas shield fell over his freckled wrinkles.

"You look tan." His voice took on a mumbled plastic edge.

Forcing a smile, he started rubbing on the medicine that numbs before the Novocaine.

"Open a little wider, please…that's it."

Then, suddenly he invaded my mouth with cotton slabs, so Pam explained I had just been in Cuba.

"Ha!...Aruba is my island retreat!" he responded as he began poking again.

"Hmm, what the hell...? We don't do fillings like this anymore," he grumbled.

I held up two fingers and attempted a response, "Cuba—two years ago!"

"Cuba...Ah, what a shame...Cuba," he answered, and then began drilling. "Castro can't survive on his own without U.S. support. We're the big guys. No way he'll go on without us."

I suddenly wanted to defend anything Cuban and clarify..."Don't you mean *our control*?" And I wanted to say, "Hey mister, I lived there for five years. What do *you* know?" But the drill whined on while Pam vacuumed my saliva. Warm tears rolled out of both corners of my eyes into my ears.

"Am I hurting you?" he asked.

"Unh-Unh."

Dammit! I said to myself. Why can't I just focus on Lúmino and me splashing each other in the Caribbean so he won't see me crying?

Luminito, as his dear friends and I call him, was staying in Havana one more week, and I had returned alone. He had been happily anticipating returning for a vacation to "his" Cuba, the only place he has ever called home. No matter what street we walked in Havana, people would call out his name. Yet, in the hotel at the beach, they assumed he was a foreigner since Cubans were not allowed in Cuban hotels then. It was only because he was married to me that he could flash his U.S. "green card" and not be hassled there. Out of the forty-five passengers who got off Cubana flight #484 from Montreal, Luminito was the only one they searched -twice. I couldn't stand watching, so I went to the bathroom in the new airport. There was mysterious finger-smeared blood on the doors inside the stalls which lacked seats and paper. I hoped that wasn't some kind of omen for the trip. As I approached Luminito back in the customs line, someone was telling him:

"Be sure to go to the immigration officials within seventy-two hours. You have to be out by January 5th . It's a current government regulation for all you Cubans who reside outside." The customs official was referring indirectly to the Pope's imminent visit.

What? They were telling him he had to leave his country, and he had just paid $150 for a visa to be here. I bit my tongue.

"Look, you don't have a 'Papal Package' or a 'Papal Visa.' "

The new law stated he was welcome until a little past Christmas, which "The Infernal One" had decreed could be celebrated at home beginning in December, 1997. After being bounced around from one bureaucratic office to another from 9:00 to 4:30 the next day, the immigration officials granted him the privilege of staying longer. How could he not be angry when every visit back presented a new set of obstacles?

At least this last time, he legally spent his wallet full of U.S. dollars. The coveted currency was everywhere, and people would do anything for it. Years before, a young woman had washed our clothes by hand and cleaned the house for $10 a month when only tourists were permitted to use dollars in Cuba. One day she was late because she had gone to prison to bring her boyfriend his breakfast. He had made his living by trafficking goods in U.S. dollars and was caught selling a bike. A few months later, when dollars were declared legal, he was back on the street hustling on the black market with those same U.S. dollars that provided meat or medicine for the ordinary Cuban.

"A change has taken place," was all the government had said. He and thousands like him could no longer be arrested. Most of Cuba's new policies came down on the people, just like that. Although many leftist supporters would forgive the government after each capricious decision, I was disturbed.

My discomfort paled, however, in comparison to the shock I had watching the white European men who were flocking to the beaches of Havana in search of dark-skinned Cuban women. Some even married their mulattas and took them back to Spain or Italy.

I was too ashamed to tell Dr. Simons about what I had seen in Cuba, what was helping to keep Fidel afloat, so I walked out of his office and never saw him again.

During the five years I lived in Cuba, I saw teen-aged prostitutes, who thought they were helping their families by getting their "dates" to buy food or replace a rice cooker that had just broken.

Mostly girls, but also boys, known as jineteras, waited on corners to be picked up by tourists near hotels and on well-traveled streets. Fifth Avenue in Miramar had many intersections, and was the street I took every day, so I couldn't help but gape at the show when I stopped at a red light. They wore skimpy bustier tops and mini-mini skirts that could only be bought in dollar stores.

I occasionally went to resorts, where they also must have bribed their way in. Once, at an outdoor bar in Soroa, a tiny mountain tourist haven in western Pinar del Río I couldn't help watching the thirteen and fourteen year-old mulatta daughters of a Cuban who was drinking and playing ping pong with a lanky Italian tourist who was fucking both of his daughters—girls not yet in women's bodies—but daddy was pimping in order to buy a chicken or a pair of pants. I couldn't help hearing one shrieking in Spanish,
  "Go, *papi*! C'mon, you can beat him!"

It was the younger of the two, cheering on her dad while she motioned for another beer. Her sister was distracted for a minute as she adjusted the g-string bottom of her new thong-bikini. Then, as the foreigner reached over to fondle her, she gave him a quick kiss on his cheek.

Although every Cuban I knew had no choice but to *"resolver,"* solve their problems via the black market, I was thankful that neither my friends or family had turned to prostitution. I had gone on this trip with my wallet full, and had stopped counting the people who thanked me for the twenty dollar bill that I casually slipped into their hands. This time, when I left Cuba, I was not sure when I could afford to go back.

January 24, 2006

Despite the joy and love Lúmino's grandchildren and children offered us, this was a hard trip. By day five, I was ready to leave because Cuba depressed me. It hurt to see how my family and most Cubans lived, hardly earning enough money to eat, while the infrastructure deteriorated around them. If you weren't a Venezuelan needing medical attention, or a tourist in a ritzy "all inclusive" hotel, it was hard to find decent places to eat or visit. Cubans "resolved" their problems through the black market which still flourishes. I missed the laughter and positive Cuban spirit that I'd always felt before.

Havana had always been polluted, but my eyes burned during our outings. Some vehicles gave off thick black fumes. Our rented car smelled. The streets were poorly lit, except around fancy hotels, so driving was hazardous because of the ruts and bicyclers darting out from side streets. Around New Years, the city filled a few of the huge potholes near where we stayed, making it somewhat easier, but the block in front of my stepson's home was nothing but holes. There was also a great deal of trash with garbage rotting everywhere.

It was still legal for people to rent to foreigners, and Lúmino returned to the same airy, comfortable place we were in some years back—located in between his two children's homes. It was full, so the owner sent us to Edwin and Nilda's down the street. When he knocked on the door, they asked Lúmino if he worked for ICAIC and if I was a teacher. Then they showed him the picture taken of us all in 1992. Edwin had just gotten a Lada—a Russian car that year, and they had gone to Varadero, and we happened to be next to them on the beach. We'd chatted for a while and then someone took a picture of all of us. I remember leaving a copy with a friend of theirs. I was amazed at the coincidence and never would have remembered had they not hauled out that very same photo. Fifteen years later, he was still driving the same car, but mostly only to work, and when he could afford to buy gas.

They lived upstairs, and the small apartment we rented downstairs was loaded with plastic flowers and non-matching pink, red, blue and green flowered curtains, valances, bed ruffles, and a bedspread from the 1950s. Most of the windows were sealed except for one in the bedroom and one in the kitchen. The bathroom window opened into the garage and the smell of gas permeated the place. There were padlocks everywhere, and two Dobermans and two Rotweilers in the back yard. We settled at $25 a night for 10 days. Out of that, they had to give the neighbor who made the referral $5 a day. They paid the government $170 monthly whether they had tenants or not. They were lucky to have had Canadians there for 5 years, but given the location of neighborhood in East Havana and far from the center, they mostly survived due to referrals. I was shocked that a Cuban would demand a cut, but they said they had no choice, that people had changed, that everyone was opportunistic now.

I was embarrassed when I had to ask family and friends to use their bathrooms. Not one was in decent working condition. People needed to use their money for food, so they didn't bother to fix them. Years ago, there had always been a bucket next to a bathtub full of water, but this time, the tubs were missing pipes. When I tried to close the bathroom door at Robertico's house, our granddaughter Alina said, "Oh, I forgot to tell you not to close the door, but don't worry, Grandmother, nobody will go in." The padded toilet seat was cracked, and there was no water. I wondered what we should replace for them first. Our host, Doctor Edwin worked in a hospital where the sanitary conditions were frightening, so he used the bathroom at his mother in-law's house nearby.

We went to Matanzas to visit Lúmino's sister and family. Panchito, our brother-in-law, had always been full of pep, happy to see us and we were always offered a great meal accompanied by lots of jokes. This time, he was glad to see us, but not as up as he used to be. For lunch, I bought frozen chicken donated to Cuba by the U.S. in a dollar store nearby. The kitchen walls needed painting badly. Everything looked grey and dirty, and we had to wash our hands outside because the updated bathroom no longer had a drainpipe in the sink. Our niece was washing the dishes with water and no detergent. The cookies I bought tasted like old sugary cardboard. Panchito pulled out the hat Lúmino had given him six years before and claimed he took care of things but please, would he bring him another hat next time.

Lúmino found out that two brothers and a sister had passed away in the past two plus years since he'd been back. Consuelo had been very ill and was quite old, but Orlando had not taken care of himself, and Fito had had a heart attack. When we visited his sister Tina, Lúmino started to cry when she hugged him, but she squeezed his arm and said, "Don't cry, life is hard." Out of his twelve brothers and sisters, we visited the six who were left. Tina was the only one who lived comfortably, but Lúmino left money with her and everybody else. The first thing every family member did was show us photo albums of family birthday parties and daughters who'd turned fifteen dressed up in elaborate rented gowns for their traditional coming out parties. We left with their phone numbers and in two cases, emails of nieces who work for businesses that have computers. (Only doctors and certain "official" folks had e-mail. The Internet is still prohibited.)

The duel economy? There are still twenty-four Cuban pesos to one dollar. The government takes twenty percent of every dollar when it exchanges them for Cuban tourist bills and coins called CUC. Most things are sold in *divisas* (dollars) or the equivalent in pesos. During our trip, things were available for what I'd expect to pay in the U.S. At the entrance of every dollar store, there was at least one Cuban with his eyes darting all over the place, whispering he was selling shrimp or lobster—a risky black market business for both buyer and seller.

A Cuban friend, who earned dollars, told us he was spending $300 a month on food, for three to eat well. Everything we saw in dollar stores was overpriced, but Cubans couldn't find things elsewhere, so they shopped in them. In winter, there was plenty of lettuce, tomatoes, root vegetables, garlic and onions at reasonable prices in pesos. Rice, beans, and eggs were still rationed. For New Years dinner, there was lots of pork for sale, in dollars. Lúmino wanted to eat veal, so we found a dollar vendor who said he could quickly slaughter one and would return. He came back with over twenty pounds of frozen veal that he cut up for us. We didn't protest: there wasn't a great deal of meat on the bones, but it was a delicious stew.

Another American friend served us a delicious fish dinner. She admitted having spent 500 pesos in the fish market that morning for a load of fish and seafood she'd frozen. She said, "I know, that's more than what most Cubans get paid in one month, but it's what I have to do." She didn't think things had changed much for the worse, but she lives a privileged life with her dollars. Even with them, however, we went to a restaurant where the smell of stale smoke made me nauseous. The lettuce was old and the cooked fish was grey. The waiter said they didn't have enough gas to grill it well, that it was pan fried instead. Our friend who earns dollars had warned us not to eat out, but we had no choice. Even in Chinatown, the food was lousy.

Albertico, my dear old friend from my first trip to Havana, still had his eleven Tiffany lamps and all kinds of Victorian and art deco furniture, figurines, statues, dishes and ornaments that he'd collected when Cubans left in swarms in the early 1960s. He said it was like having a gold tooth: valuable but he needed to keep it where it was.

We heard they'd struck oil in Cuba, and soon different countries—including the U.S.—would be bidding on drilling and refining it. Would it trickle down and make a difference? Fidel was down on tourism in Havana and preferred making money from *Operacion Milagro*. This program offered mostly Venezuelan and some Bolivian patients surgery and medical care in several converted hotels and a huge downtown apartment building that was recently remodeled. A great idea, but why didn't Cubans receive the same quality health care? Why haven't they harnessed the sun? The country needs to convert its power plants and improve its infrastructure. I wondered who was doing the planning. What about having milk for children over the age of seven, decent underwear, towels, dental floss, just to name a few things that nobody has. One woman said, "I've been putting my one set of sheets on the bed for twenty years."

I wanted to know about education, and the grandchildren helped me to understand what was going on. Elementary schools were fine, but after that, quality declined. Alina was twelve and in the seventh grade. Every day the teacher turned on a video they all copied from. They didn't ask questions because she didn't know the answers. The English teacher came in and said a lot of things in English she was supposed to repeat, but she didn't get it and felt frustrated. She couldn't ask questions in English class either. During the week after New Years, the teachers hadn't returned from the provinces yet, and there was nothing to do in school. (There was obviously a shortage of teachers in Havana.) Brian was nine and loved to write poems. He had a notebook full. He read his poetry with great feeling and satisfaction more than once. The day I left, he dedicated a poem to me that he copied into my journal. I found a couple of books for him and he began devouring the one with legends in it, the one that I thought was over his head. He was quite a challenge for his teacher. I worried he wouldn't get the attention he needed, but luckily, the family encouraged him. His father sent some books from New York, but Cuba wouldn't let them through. His grandmother had two books for him in her suitcase when she returned from the U.S. and they were confiscated. I tried to send a book from Mexico, but it never got through. I didn't find out about high school and above.

I wish I could have found happier scenes or more positive things to say about this trip, but it was a struggle to keep a journal without crying every day.

Fall, 2007

Lúmino storms into my study, yelling, "They're such bastards! With the new Oceancard, my daughter will only get $155 of the $200 I just sent her. That company and Cuba are eating up my money. All I'm feeling right now is hatred! I won't go back; I'll keep sending money so she can pay to write to us on e-mail; that will cost less than all those phone calls."

"I'm really sorry," I answer, "I think I know how it feels, but you're going to want to hug your son and laugh with your grandchildren—you'll block this out and visit your family again."

He gives me a begrudging nod followed by the silence of resignation—not a healthy silence.

I think to myself. When will this end? The situations people face in and out of Cuba are totally abnormal, unacceptably surreal, yet this goes on year after year.

Suddenly, Luminito breaks the silence, "Now I know why those *gusanos* (low-life worms) in Miami danced with joy and wished "him" dead when they heard he was sick last year. It gets to you," he mutters and walks away.

May, 2008

Lúmino is preparing to visit Cuba in July. His granddaughter is turning fifteen and her parents have saved enough money for her to have a small party. Her teachers said she had excellent computer skills, and there is a computer that costs $350 that she would like her grandfather to give her for her birthday. Rather than going with him I decide to send the money I would have paid for a round-trip ticket to the family. I know they'll appreciate having dollars since my going to Cuba would have involved renting a car and staying in a modest hotel in Havana. Even that would have been costly. When Luminito goes alone, he'll stay with his grandson, even sleep in the same bed with him, but that would be awkward for me, especially since his ex-wife shares the building.

He can bring Mexican pesos, and rumor has it he'll get a better deal than the 20% Cuba gets for every dollar. It's a short trip from our Mexican home. My decision is firm. I don't want to get depressed again in Cuba.

Changes have taken place now that Raúl Castro is head of the government and his brother Fidel is in the background, not in good health after major intestinal surgery two years ago. Hotels are now open to Cubans who can also rent cars and buy cell phones. They can buy computers, but the Internet is not accessible to most people. Prices for any of these new privileges are prohibitive. There is talk about allowing Cubans to travel and return to Cuba, and rumor has it everyone who purchased a house will be able to get titles and sell and buy property, measures that haven't been legal since the beginning of the Revolution.

Raúl Castro's daughter Mariela has been championing gay rights, and as reported by *The Boston Globe*:

> Cuba's gay community celebrated with unprecedented openness and high-ranking political alliances with a government-backed campaign against homophobia yesterday. The meeting at a convention center in Havana's Vedado district may have been the largest gathering of gay activists ever in the communist-run island. President Raúl Castro's daughter Mariela, who has promoted the rights of gays and lesbians, presided...Mariela Castro joined government leaders and hundreds of activists at the one-day conference for the International Day Against Homophobia that featured lectures and panel discussions. (AP) © *Copyright 2008 Globe Newspaper Company.*

Also, according to *The Globe*, there are now three operating synagogues in Cuba. The one I worked near has been "proudly and lovingly restored" and has many new members. "The youth group is popular and active, and the Sunday school for children attracts dozens each week. Daniel Motela, 28, leads a two-hundred-member Jewish youth organization. 'Many of them come and enjoy the group activities," he said. "But I think most come to continue their family traditions and learn more about the Jewish faith.' The Sunday school now routinely draws sixty children each week."

Although Lúmino's trip was bitter-sweet, due to family tensions with his ex-wife, he returns in August and tells me the streets are alive with illegal vendors selling delicious sandwiches, something that hasn't happened for about twenty-five years. People don't talk about Fidel, but they do talk openly about wanting more change. Only those who receive money from family out of Cuba can afford to purchase any of the liberated offerings. It would take a month's salary to spend one night in a hotel. He pays for additional meat and chicken, but it's sold in dollars and expensive, so they eat a lot of rice and beans. He sleeps in the living room of his son's tiny apartment on the inflatable twin bed he took with him. Every morning, his granddaughter deflates it. She loves the stories he tells about the past. She learns to draw on the new computer which cost twice what it was supposed to.

One day, he finds out his son has been picked up by the police and is in the local jail because a neighbor in the local vigilant block committee "*Comité de la Defensa de la Revolución*" reports his son doesn't work and there is a foreigner living in his house, giving him money. Luminito goes to the jail and hold up his passport and his "*PRE*," his permit to reside outside of Cuba. "Oh, you're Cuban," the officer says, and Luminito says yes and he has every right to visit his son and stay in his home. His son is an artist who struggles to make ends meet selling his work under the table. His daughter-in-law is a seamstress. Other lucrative jobs are what people call "*sucio*," dirty, meaning dangerously illegal, so he has not wanted to be involved in those. He is waiting for a position as a security guard at a school. The police release him.

Cuba is a pressure cooker. The government looks the other way and allows the sale of sandwiches on street corners. They use Venezuelan oil to run new buses that connect to any point in Havana, like a sophisticated subway system. These are two of the ways of releasing the pressure valve. Cubans like having the possibility they can go to a hotel or buy a cell phone or stop at the corner for a bite to eat. Medical care for all limps along, not like the famous cash services offered to foreigners, but hospitals

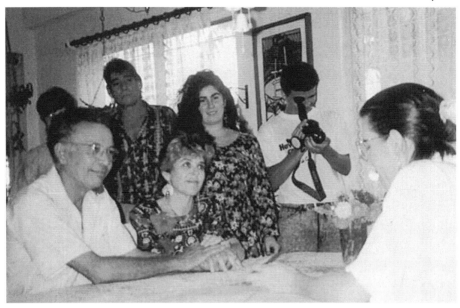

The marriage of Bette Steinmuller and Lúmino Fernández, Havana, February 6, 1993

function somehow, if you bring your own cleaning supplies, bed linens and food. Schools are functioning also, thanks to parents who volunteer time in the classrooms and take gifts to the teachers.

September-October, 2008

Less than a week after Luminito returns, a hurricane strikes Cuba, and then another. The tobacco cash crop is wiped out in western Pinar del Rio. Many other crops are washed away. Luckily, buildings in Havana were spared, but people began looting and hoarding food. In October, a friend comes to Mexico and says because she had money from abroad, she was able to find food to buy, but there *is* hunger in Cuba. Gone are those sandwiches on the street corners. The government rations what little there is, and people aren't starving. We attend a benefit concert to send staples to Cuba, and a huge room is filled with powdered milk, canned goods, rice, beans, detergent and more. The musicians airlift it to Cuba. Other countries are helping, but Cuba won't accept the help the U.S. is offering. That would come close to ending the embargo. It's as though Cuba doesn't want it lifted. It continues to be a painful recuperation.

I have to hope. The Cuban people are talking about more changes and waiting, waiting. I'm not naïve enough to think Cuba can change overnight. There are jokes about how Cuban it is to think in black and white, in all or nothing terms, so I know that socialism isn't all good, and capitalism is far from good…but it's what has been keeping Cuba afloat for many years. Recently, Fidel wrote about the U.S. electoral campaign. He criticized the Republicans, especially for putting up a vapid woman vice-presidential candidate and he supported Barack Obama. But, he predicted that due to the racism in the United States, the people would never let a *black* man and a *black* woman and their children live in the *White* House. Next week, we'll know if he was right.

My fantasy does include the election of a future President Barack Obama who will negotiate with Cuba, lift the embargo and end travel restrictions for U.S. citizens visiting the island, and for Cubans who want to visit the U.S. Cuba will have democratic elections, and a democratically-elected government will promote new, innovative forms of regulated private investment that will support local industries and even foreign companies to help rebuild the infrastructure. These will in turn subsidize universal health care, the harnessing of solar energy, and "green" initiatives, new housing, and quality education at all levels. People will take their Cuban ingenuity out of a decaying black market and create small, prosperous businesses and agricultural opportunities. There will be employment galore! There will be only one currency, and restaurants where families could afford to eat out once in a while. Artists won't have to belong to a Party to be able to create and sell their work. People will be able to travel at will and return to the island they never wanted to leave forever. Educational and cultural exchanges will foster study abroad and within. Cuba will rebuild and heal, and there will be music and dancing in the streets again. Then, I can go and spend my last years there. *(Fall, 2008)*

Note: To read another essay that was originally in this section, see the chapter entitled "Yardbird: Life in the Shipyard" in Kendall Hale's book Radical Passions: A Memoir of Revolution and Healing, published by iUniverse in 2008.

Nicaragua Solidarity

Bette training Nica English Teachers, San Marcos, 1988

Breaking Down Borders

Bette Steinmuller

"WHAT IS A nice Jewish girl like you doing here?" Father Tom asked when we discovered each other in Managua in 1988, both of us working in solidarity with the Sandinista Revolution. I was an English consultant for the national eighth grade English Language curriculum; he, a Jesuit priest working in the barrio nearby. This was the Catholic boy who had verbally attacked me thirty-five years before at Edgewood School in New Haven, Connecticut. His sweet face contorted into horror when I reminded him how he'd stood up and humiliated me in the sixth grade...I, the grand-daughter of Jewish immigrants had been chosen as a soloist for the holiday sing. No sooner had I gotten through rehearsing the introduction to White Christmas when Tommy, the teacher's nephew, stood up before the class and shouted," Why is she singing that song?" And pointing his finger at me, he declared, "The Jews killed Christ!" Tommy's aunt's stone face supported him with her silence. I stood alone, staring at him in disbelief and shame in the middle of my first anti-Semitic encounter. I never asked at home if this was what my Jewish mother meant when she said I was different from everyone else.

A great deal had happened to this nice Jewish girl. In the 1980s, I was an "internationalist" who volunteered to support revolution in other lands. I could have cared less that internationalism was considered a tenet of communism. My motivation was personal and political. The United States was busy overthrowing socialist Latin American revolutions, and I wanted to go there and see how. The only risk would be that my government could find out and assume I was a communist supporting popular revolt, when in reality, I never belonged to any party.

I had been following the July, 1979, Nicaraguan Revolution, initially by reading about it in *The New York Times*. For months, I had saved every article and picture about the Sandinistas—because their popular revolt fascinated me. I had became involved in Jamaica Plain Committee on Central America, a political group that lobbied our then Massachusetts Congressman Joe Moakley to stop supporting the Contra war against the Sandinistas. We had also urged him to vote against sending millions of U.S. dollars to the neighboring military Salvadoran dictatorship that hired death squads to halt the popular struggle there.

My third child left for college in 1983 when I was 43. I was un-attached and decided to sell my suburban condo and buy a small house in Jamaica Plain, a multi-ethnic and socioeconomically mixed Boston neighborhood. I began teaching English to Speakers of Other Languages (ESOL) part-time at The University of Massachusetts, and in a program run by the International Institute of Boston that served Haitian immigrants in Dorchester. After teaching high school in an affluent suburb, it was more satisfying, although very difficult, to work with adults who needed English to survive in the United States. When they told me how they went to the post office by themselves, or spoke to the doctor without an interpreter, or paid a bill in English, we could look back and see how their communication skills had grown in just a few months. I knew I was making a difference in the lives of those who found the time to study.

But…I couldn't deal with Reagan, the movie star as my president. I'd wished I could have gotten out when Nixon was elected, but now was my chance in the mid-1980s, with my children in college and grad school, so I began to seriously plot leaving. Teaching in China sounded possible, and a visiting Chinese professor at UMass had begun the paper work to invite me to her southern province. I interviewed colleagues who'd lived and worked in China, and everyone concurred: space was at a premium. I'd be lucky to have a tiny room and share a bathroom in a crowded apartment building or in the home of an academic. The only privacy I'd have would be in the confines of my mind, the place where my thoughts were born and flourished. How would I have enough room?

One day, while waiting for a meeting, and kibitzing with a secretary at the International Institute, I listened to her take a message about the search for a language coordinator at a "solidarity" school in Nicaragua. The person would train teachers to teach Spanish as a Second Language and coordinate classes for The New Institute of Central America (NICA).

I interviewed for the job and found out (during several rounds of margaritas) that English speakers—primarily from the United States—went to this school to learn about Nicaragua and its revolution and to study Spanish. The participants lived with local families, did volunteer work and attended meetings about the history and ongoing struggle there, from a leftist perspective. Representatives from all sectors of the revolutionary process, including refugees from El Salvador, talked about their lives with groups that visited for a month at a time in Estelí, a northern war zone. Studying Spanish was a key component of the program, and the school needed a coordinator to update Nicaraguan teachers in the latest communicative theory and practice in second language teaching. It would be hard to leave my adult students, but the opportunity both challenged and excited me.

I was too much of an extrovert to live and teach in China where I'd have to control my spontaneity, my capriciousness. I thanked the Chinese professor and accepted the job in Nicaragua which was to begin six weeks later. I refused to listen to those who questioned the safety of living in Nicaragua in the 1980s and rationalized if so many other "internationalists" were there, how dangerous could the "war zone" be? Besides, this was my opportunity to go where there was conflict and controversy and see it all first-hand. Close to the front lines, I could acquire an authoritative voice in order to convince my senators and representatives to stop the war. Empathizing with immigrants in the ESOL classroom usually left me feeling drained, powerless, overwhelmed by the inequities and injustices they described to me daily. I galvanized their frustration and my energy to be politically active somewhere else.

My grown children had no problem with my suddenly leaving. I hoped they would realize Central America was not so far and would visit me. I easily rented my house for a year.

My close friends supported my decision, as I hoped my brother would. At fifty-one, he was married, had no children, and worked as a transplantation immunologist at the Mayo Clinic. He was upset about my going to live in a "squalid," war-torn place, and I interpreted his response as his feeling threatened by my spirit of adventure and political commitment. I was disappointed he did not want to know more about what was happening in Nicaragua and thought he was too wrapped up in his professional status. He in turn thought I was consumed by activism, disdaining that he wasn't. He disliked my lecturing him that everything was political. In his mind, I was unwilling to communicate on a personal level. Actually, I still believe that the personal is political, but my need to preach it back then must have been overbearing. We have since grown to respect each other and years later, he is a political activist, disdaining the system as well.

Thinking back to the 1950s, when my brother began Swarthmore College, I remember my mother's talk about social justice and integrity. Was it she who fostered my political activism? She urged me to read Howard Fast's *My Glorious Brothers*, about Sacco and Vanzetti, the two Italian workers who as anarchists were framed and unjustly executed. In a rare moment, she recounted how as a girl, she had waved at Eugene V. Debs, a renowned socialist, at a parade. But, she later channeled all of her budding radicalism into the founding of Israel. She once dressed me in rags and covered me with soot so I could portray a refugee child in the Zionist women's organization Hadassah's play about the founding of the Jewish state.

I also saw Mom's resentment at not having continued her formal education translated into her projection for my brother and me to excel academically and aim for the university. She was proud that her son to-be-a-doctor attended—as she told everyone—"the best small college in the East." Had she been alive in the 1980s, I think she would have respected my political activism. Maybe neither of us would have been able to verbalize it, but I might have been fulfilling my Jewish mother's frustrated dreams in my own way, as I set off alone for Nicaragua.

In June 1984, Managua still showed more signs of having been ravaged by an earthquake twelve years earlier than by war. Rather than a typically bustling capital, it was a scorched, sprawling, underdeveloped city, albeit with a heavy military presence. After being awed by a speech the famous Sandinista Tomás Borge gave during my second day there, I went to Estelí, two hours north in the mountains where the predominantly military vehicles were driven by baby-faced soldiers. Helicopters flew over head, and ambulances and funeral processions filled the streets. People talked about which son, daughter or neighbor was wounded or killed in which skirmish with *la Contra*, the counter-revolutionary forces. Walking to work, I would feel frightened as I passed by a crater-sized hole in the sidewalk, the reminder of a bomb dropped by the former hated dictator Anastacio Somoza Debayle's army five years before.

Our classes were held in the common area of a barrio church until the school bought a private home we called *"La Escuela Nica,"* The NICA School which stood for New Institute of Central America. In Spanish, *"nica"* was also a popular way of referring to a Nicaraguan. I couldn't help falling into the dynamic of being the demanding foreigner supervising Nica teachers with varying degrees of teaching expertise. Winning their confidence and training them without coming on as the academic imperialist became a dauntingly delicate balance between wanting to be politically correct and needing to be pedagogically competent.

In its fifth year of the Revolution, Nicaragua was stressing equality among all workers, but the teachers, whose experience predated the 1979 "Triumph," were from upper class elitist backgrounds. Although they were chosen for the school because of their political dedication as well as their teaching experience, most came from families that had thrived under Somoza's dictatorship. Teaching with us raised their status again since they received certain benefits working at our U.S. dollar-supported school. They treated me with respect, but did not radiate the same warmth I received from other Nicaraguans. A breach of trust erupted when we had to lay off teachers because of our own economic mismanagement. They organized the students against us, called a strike and led a march through town, demonstrating against The Nica School. We eventually worked it out with the help of the Ministry of Education, but after the strike, I always felt uncomfortable when I had to go to teachers' homes—as I had before—to notify them of schedule changes. Hardly anyone had a telephone in Estelí.

At first, I lived in the school's relatively comfortable apartment, but had to reach into the toilet tank to flush it, remember to boil the water that was full of parasites, cover the food so the armies of miniscule ants wouldn't invade it, and learn to take one-minute, mountain-cold showers. One North American student said she wouldn't use the latrine in back of her house because of the rats that stared down at her. I dealt with the blood-sucking mosquitoes in my indoor bathroom.

In order to create fewer divisions between us and the Nicaraguan staff, I went to live with a family in a house on the main street going south where I had my own room. Estelí had two main streets, one going north as well. My hosts were a young couple who did not come from "revolutionary" families, but my staff-mates told me to give them a chance since they were the only ones near the school who had a room available.

Oscar, the father, had fought against the Somoza dictatorship during the popular insurrections in 1979. He had been captured, tortured and imprisoned by the Contra. I never found out how or when he got away, but he worked as the carpenter for the Ministry of Education and could reproduce any wooden toy, simply by looking at a picture. It was difficult to engage in a dialog of any substance with him because he spoke more quickly than anyone else in Estelí and I was embarrassed to keep asking him to repeat. His wife Chilo took care of their three small children and studied at night to be a teacher—against Oscar's wishes. She spent hours cooking, washing or doing errands, and I had a busy day and evening schedule, so we barely got to know each other.

The custom was for the family to sleep in the same room, often more than one to a bed, so they invited me to sleep with them the first night and were incredulous over my preference to stay alone in my room. A few days later, I regretted my decision. At 5:00 A.M. I woke to the sound of mortar, gunshots, and a strange clatter in the street. My first impulse was to get under the bed since I was too frightened to cross the yard to ask the family if we were under attack. I lay there trembling, feeling extremely cowardly and ashamed to be dying in bed during a battle, but assuring myself that it couldn't be my time. At daybreak, when all had quieted down, I heard the morning street hawkers and crept out, anticipating the worst. Chilo and the kids looked at my face and laughed, explaining it was Estelí's way of celebrating its victory against the dictator, which always took place two days before the anniversary of the nation-wide triumph on July 19th. Soldiers customarily shot off guns, while people rattled pots and marched through their barrios to rouse revolutionary spirit.

My Estelí house, middle class by Nicaraguan standards, was owned by a *capitalista* who had gone to live in the U.S. Despite its relative comforts, I often wondered how I would continue coping with life in one of the poorest countries in the world during this war. How little I had in comparison to my former life, and the hardships brought to mind my cousins who had left Germany in the 1950s.

More than once I flashed back to how my family sponsored these Holocaust-survivors who had lived in concentration camps during World War II, my only reference point for the concept of suffering at the age of six or seven. The process of getting my cousins "over" to the United States had involved years of support and bureaucratic maneuvering. As sponsors, we paid for their travel to the U.S.A., and housed, clothed and fed them until they found work and were able to live independently.

Elsa was my grandfather's niece and his only surviving link overseas. After the war, she had married Bill, the best friend of her former fiancé who had been shot by the Nazis. They subsequently had a baby, Luba, in a Displaced Persons Camp where they stayed for years until they immigrated. As a child, I loved being part of the preparation of clothing shipments for my distant baby cousin. How could someone in our family not have enough winter clothes? I would sit by Grandma's side in silence as she showed me how to knit pink and white hats and woolen scarves for the baby and told stories about our cousins who would one day come to live with us. My image of camp was what older girls bragged about, a place where I would play in the summer when I was old enough, but my relatives had to live at theirs for years because they had nowhere else to go. I knew it was grim there because of their unusually stark wedding picture. It seemed to me they were at that camp forever, and as more pictures of my poor cousins arrived, we saved them in an album.

When I was reprimanded for not eating everything on my plate, I would ask permission to go to my corner perch in the living room, climb onto a cool, slippery, maroon, leather hassock and apologize to the picture of cousin Luba who did not have enough to eat. I felt guilty, but could in no way fathom how my plate was connected to hers—with an ocean between us. It was even more mysterious to me how that large box they called a Care package would ever reach her. But I joyfully watched my dad bring a large, used, empty carton into our living room. For me that place was a museum that guests admired, and was out of bounds for children to "be" in. It had velvet-like couches with satin pillows. There was a gilt-flowered vase on the gold embossed leather-trimmed coffee table. There were Chinese lamps and Lenox candy dishes on antique end tables. When my parents decided to fill the carton there, they relaxed the rules and invited me in to be part of the packing. Months later, we knew that everything had arrived in Germany because a letter of acknowledgment arrived, written on very thin paper with writing on both sides. Enclosed might be a picture of Luba. And what satisfaction I felt seeing her in a woolen sweater or scarf that Grandma had made with my help!

The Nazis had spared Elsa's life because she was young, healthy and therefore able to work, but I once heard someone say she was there when her mother perished in Auschwitz. Bill was the only surviving member of his family. Grandpa and my Great Uncle Sam, his brother, were Elsa's uncles too. Sam, being more literate than Grandpa, became her official sponsor, although the entire family contributed money. He also translated letters that Bill routinely wrote about how they were progressing with every form and affidavit that eventually was processed. I began to understand what it meant when adults referred to "the papers," things that arrived in a strange-colored, tightly sealed envelope and were terribly important because they brought my cousins one step closer to New Haven. When Elsa, Bill and Luba finally came in 1950, Luba became Linda, my instant baby sister whom I could show off at Brownie meetings. I loved my new family by day, but gripped the banister on the upstairs landing when I overheard Elsa sobbing through the gruesome concentration camp stories she told to my mother at night.

Her accounts were not unlike the stories of torture told to me by the Nicaraguan mothers of heroes and martyrs—their children having been tortured by the Somozan Guard before the revolution and by the U.S.-trained counter-revolutionaries in the war not far from the walled compound in which I lived in Nicaragua. Every time I traveled from Estelí to Managua to Boston, I understood more than anyone about "the papers" that took forever, "the papers" I needed any time I traveled outside of the country.

The heavy weather-beaten Nicaraguan unpainted wooden front door was double-bolted from the inside only, so someone always had to be there. Inside was a courtyard many meters square, surrounded by a few small rooms. After a while, I learned that privacy was not the key ingredient in Nicaraguan culture. The kids were playing in my room when I wasn't home, so I put a padlock on my door to claim my space in U.S. American fashion. At least I had my own toilet that I flushed with a bucket of water, once a day, due to the shortage of water.

A few plastic or hand-hewn wooden chairs almost fit in the living room. I assumed it was because of the three small children in the family, that we all sat around a kiddie-sized kitchen table in tiny chairs. Two-year-old Oscarito was learning to talk and the three-inch spider that lived on the kitchen wall served as his prompt for the Spanish vowel sound "A" for araña. The refrigerator that was painted a ghastly green rarely kept food below room temperature. There was never enough detergent to wash the multi-colored plastic dishes that remained coated with grease and were fair game for any number of flies. Since the NICA School paid a stipend for housing me, Chilo could afford to serve chunks of chicken, pork or beef with our rice, beans and tortillas. I contributed vegetables and fruit, plentifully sold in every market, but the family, like most Nicaraguans, preferred rice and beans. Fruit drinks were acceptable, but nobody except me ate the fruit whole.

Chilo offered to do my laundry, but I washed my own clothes by hand whenever there was water. Oscarito delighted in leaving caca and puddles of urine that I dodged all the time since he loved to pull off his diapers. After lunch, Chilo used to leave the house for up to an hour at a time to buy food or visit her mother, and it was hard for me to concentrate on my preparations for the next day while feeling responsible for her little ones— all under the age of eight—although she assured me they were used to being alone and not to worry. In retrospect, it was damn hard to live in the middle of such noise, poverty, and war.

At the NICA School, I had expected to work with a team that would share my progressive politics in the struggle for peace and justice for the Nicaraguan people. But at age forty-three, I was surrounded by an intimidating North American staff composed mostly of leftists in their twenties who were obsessed—albeit with the best intentions—over maintaining an exemplary politically correct image as directors of the school. We held criticism-self criticism sessions to review our weekly accomplishments and failures, but the need to be more revolutionary than the Sandinistas was hard for me to take.

Two months after I arrived, the Contra military activity escalated. There were almost daily violations by U.S. planes. We met with Nicaraguan officials who told us where to evacuate and how to help in each *barrio* in case of an actual attack. Although there were never any battles within the city limits, fighting nearby in the countryside interrupted our schedule, a reality which terrified our predominantly middle class, white, progressive students, many of whom had never been away from home before. The United States-sponsored destabilization was intentional, and had its desired effect. I suppressed my fears of living in constant danger because I had made a commitment to stay for a year. I had to get used to witnessing Sandinista surveillance helicopter flights up to ten times a day, interfering with "enemy" planes air-dropping supplies to the Contra. One morning at 9:20, we were all sure we heard a bomb, but it was U.S. aircraft breaking the sound barrier as it flew illegally over Nicaragua. After it happened a few more times, the teachers began to believe that U.S. troops were going to invade, as they had on the island of Grenada in 1983, allegedly to rescue U.S. medical students there. We did not want to be rescued. We hoped that our government was irked by our being there, and that they wouldn't use us as a pretext to further destabilize Nicaragua.

Once I stood in front of my house watching a contra bomb destroy an electrical transmission tower eight kilometers away. Tracers and mortar lit up the sky and must have seemed like fireworks to the two year-old next door in his father's arms. The next day, the wounded were brought in on open vehicles, passing in front of the school, on their way to the hospital.

Then there was the morning when nobody was home and I awoke with such acute chest pain that I was afraid to move. There had been no warning, no recognizable symptoms, just the sensation that someone had stuck a knife into my ribs. I dragged myself to a taxi, somehow got in the x-ray line at the hospital, and wished I did not have to breathe in or out. An hour or so later they concluded I had bronchial pneumonia and that it could go to my lungs, so I had to be hospitalized and start intravenous antibiotics immediately. I don't remember how I got home to pick up a few personal things, and ask Chilo to notify the school.

At about 1:00, I was checking into an open ward near a toothless, completely wrinkled woman in line for the bathroom. She peed on the floor. Nobody cleaned it up. I gagged.

Later, having being assigned a bed, I waited for the nurse to come with the I.V.

"Don't move," she said, as she tapped the inside of my arm.

Hours before, a technician had said, "Don't move" and pulled the switch on the forty-year-old x-ray machine and just after that, the surgeon across the hall had muttered "Don't move" to a child he was sewing up with no anesthesia.

"It might not go in the first time; we only have this size and your veins are very fine."

As my arm turned into a pincushion, I eavesdropped on the doctor tending to the patient next to me. His Cuban accent was difficult to follow. The needle stayed in my arm on the fifth attempt. I figured out how to roll over and wished I could sleep. I was in the middle of a row with ten beds yet I felt somewhat at home in my own nightgown, like the other women. It was also a relief to overhear them assuming I was an East German volunteer because of my last name. What would a sick Jewish *gringa* be doing in a Nicaraguan war zone?

The late afternoon sun angling through the high windows cut a transparent sheet of brilliant particles that forced my eyes shut. Some patients were sleeping, others moaning. They had malaria, typhoid, and pneumonia like me. My neighbor caught my eye, "Don't let the yelling get to you," she muttered. "It's only from the labor room behind the wall here in back of our heads."

At some point, we were served a pile of semi-warm slippery rice, steaming beans and a cold, crusty, yellowish-gray tortilla, partitioned off on a greasy, dripping wet aluminum tray reminiscent of summer camp. I politely declined sharing someone's plastic cup brought from home and dozed off without finishing my supper as the sun went down.

When I awoke, there were no patients lined up and since the wooden I.V. holder had wheels, I mobilized myself for a trip to the bathroom. The holder looked like the ones our students built during volunteer work at my school, so I made a mental note to tell someone how easily it wheeled.

As I managed back into bed, the truck and bus traffic was letting up, and I could hear people walking outside in the cool shadows, comparing notes in Spanish,

"Good evening, Doña Mirta, yes we got our soap, oil and rice today…"

"No, we didn't get the split peas yet, but thanks….I can wait."

Who would pick up my rations, I wondered before falling into a deep sleep.

At midnight, I was awakened by what I thought was thunder. A young woman was standing on her bed in the dark, but every few seconds her face lit up.

"Are you watching the storm?" I asked.

"Honey that ain't lightning! Those are tracers and mortar in the Laguna hills. Can't you hear the shooting?"

I wasn't sure what was worse, her ongoing monologue or the rumbling of the guns.

The next morning, they told us we had to be evacuated to make room for the wounded soldiers coming in.

"I wish you could stay, really, but you don't fit into the worst case category," the Cuban doctor told me at 6:30 a.m.

"What do I do with the I.V.?" I asked

"Just wear it! I'll give you a couple of refills and your penicillin, and when you finish those, come back to be checked."

He really did run his words together! I asked him to repeat everything, just to be sure that I was about to walk out with an I.V. in my arm.

A nurse interrupted us, "Are you Bette, the North American?" A friend of yours is here to see you and says she will help you."

"Thank you …Oh, Hi Blanca…"

"My dear, we all want to know what happened. You look pale."

"God knows how I got bronchial pneumonia," I said.

"Comrade, we need to empty out the ward now! The ambulances are coming momentarily," the nurse interrupted impatiently.

I gathered together the few things I had into a plastic bag.

"Blanca, if you can carry my things in one hand and the I.V. in the other, I'll take my pillow—I think I can make it to the street—to a taxi," I said.

"I just came all the way here from Barrio Rosario at the other end of town…there's not one taxi out there this morning," she said.

"But I can't stay in this sun either. Let's walk," I said.

"You sure…" she asked?

"Yes, but over on that side, in the shade, "I answered.

We began walking.

"My god, the situation must be really bad for them to be letting you out like this."

"Yes, they said there were a lot of Contra near San Nicolas last night. Blanca, please walk a little slower? It's harder for me to breathe than I thought."

We walked in slow motion, as children stopped playing in the street to stare.

"Good Morning Doña Aurora, how are you? Yes, the poor thing, she's very sick and I'm taking her home…never a taxi when you need one. Thank you, we can manage. It's not so bad in the shade."

"Blanca, am I going to make it?"

"Don't talk, … just keep walking. Look, the truck drivers can't believe they're seeing you either…they're slowing down for us…we're making history…it's only a few more blocks."

Hermalinda and her baby were on line at the neighborhood store. Normally I would have yelled to her from across the street, but it hurt when I spoke loud.

"This is the long block now," Blanca alerted me. "At the end, we turn left onto the main street going south, and then you'll be home and can get into bed."

Each step was five minutes long. Then, finally Chilo let us in on her way out.

Blanca sighed, "Well, we made it. Now you sit and catch your breath and then lie down slowly. I'll look for somewhere to hang…"

"Oh my god, Blanca…the needle…it just popped, and there's blood pouring out…" I said.

"Here, hold my handkerchief over it…Keep holding…tighter! I'm going to get Helene, the French nun, you know, the nurse who lives around the corner. Don't move," she said.

Soon Blanca and Helene were taping the well-inserted I.V. to the top of my hand with new adhesive that was probably intended for a Sandinista soldier.

"They're going to think I'm a junkie soon. I hope it stays in this time, Helene. You can hang it on that nail up there," I said.

The saline solution finally stopped slapping the inner walls of the bottle, like the ebbing in a fishbowl.

"Bette, remember what the doctor said. This one has the antibiotic in it, so be sure you get every drop," Blanca insisted.

"Yes, comrade."

My tone of voice apparently satisfied Helene who turned to leave.

"Just give a yell if you need anything. I'm only around the corner. Bye."

"Bye…and thanks, Sister Helene."

Blanca was also heading toward the door. "Now you need to drink this juice Chilo left, and just rest! I'm going to make a hook for the bathroom wall too. I'll be back later with dinner," she said.

I said goodbye to Blanca and lay there realizing that I was being helped by a woman who had run messages through Somoza territory in the early days of the Revolution, and she had narrowly missed being killed many times by the infamous National Guard.

The next afternoon, still in bed, I heard the announcements on the megaphone of the little white car. This dreaded vehicle passed in front of the school at least once a day. People stopped and held their breath as the driver slowly read off the names of the "heroes" fallen in battle from every barrio. I told myself to stop obsessing over dying since the people in Estelí assured me their town was impenetrable. There were very few roads, so the Contra were not as close as they seemed even though in order to get back north to their bases in Honduras, they had to cross the Pan American highway, in a town less than fifteen kilometers away. But hadn't I just seen the reflections of one battle at night? By U.S. standards, it was too close, yet I stayed on.

Days later, I was sitting in the park across from the cathedral, waiting to meet a friend, and a so-called "mother" of one of our North American students walked by with her grandson. She related how several mothers were concerned because they hadn't seen me at school, so I thanked her and explained how I had been recovering from pneumonia. Then, we chatted about "her American daughter" and how well her Spanish was coming along, and now her neighbor's son had been killed in combat, so she was on her way to the funeral. As she spoke, her five-year-old grandson became impatient.

"Just a moment little one, I'm talking," she said to him in Spanish,

He tugged at her arm and responded, " But grandmother, let's go! Look, the people are going in. I want to go too, now! now!"

I glanced up to see people filing into the cathedral. Marvin yanked at his grandmother's hand once again, and as she waved with the other, I realized that the ritual of bidding goodbye to the dead had become a routine diversion for Nicaraguan children.

I was always alone at night in Estelí. Sometimes, my flashbacks were about my childhood: At age five, one of my favorite diversions had been to visit my father's family in far-away places like New York or Florida. I thought back to when my mother and I took the Pullman train to Miami to visit Grandma and Grandpa Steinmuller.

Our seat turned into a bed, but my mom believed it wasn't healthy for us to breathe on each other, so I was forced to sleep with her feet in my face a whole night! Then, my Jewish aunts appeared to greet us. They were strange women with big earrings and with loud voices who showered me with perfume and sticky red kisses that I tried to rub off when they weren't looking. When most of the adults went on an overnight gambling boat to Cuba, I felt abandoned and began stamping my feet and screaming. They laughed, and told me, "You're too young to go." I wondered for years where this off-limits Cuba was.

One aunt who had a softer voice and who gave delicious hugs, did not go on the boat. She was Sadye, my father's baby sister. She asked me questions such as what grade I was in, or what my friends' names were and she listened to my answers with a caring look on her face. I wished I could see her more often, but had to settle for recognizing her handwriting on letters she wrote to Mom. She was married to Sam who smoked Cuban cigars. My parents said they had "different politics" from the rest of us, something that took me years to understand.

When they visited us in New Haven, they always made a show of drinking in the fresh air as they came up the front walk, announcing their annual trip to the countryside. We played croquet in the backyard of our one-family house, but they lived in a tall apartment building somewhere far away called Brooklyn. Uncle Sam was the only one who could make

Mom laugh and even blush as he finished off an extra helping of her potato pancakes. Sadye would tease Mom as she rinsed out the pots she took from the cabinet to make doubly sure they were clean before cooking in them.

Occasionally, we visited Aunt Sadye at Rockaway Beach, but I suffered from chronic car sickness, so the five-hour trip from Connecticut was a nightmare. Dad always said to warn him when I was going to throw up because he did not want to have to clean out the car again. Just thinking about when it was going to happen made me nervous and sicker. Looking at my green face, Aunt Sadye once announced, "Kid pukey has arrived," but I quickly got over my mortification and silently forgave her because deep down I knew she was someone who loved and approved of me anyway.

Decades later, Sadye was the one person in my family who understood why I stayed in Nicaragua. She appreciated my group letters that told about my experiences in the war zone. The Sandinistas even sent her a letter of recognition after she donated $50 to the Ministry of Education. They did not know that she had been a communist since the 1930s, a fact that always fascinated me.

In 1984, in response to the relentless U.S.-sponsored killing, The NICA School organized a "Repudiate Reagan" protest march when he was re-elected. The students and staff made banners and signs and wrote a collective speech. The Sandinista Defense Committee lent us their bullhorn and granted us permission to parade through the city. We turned our outrage into chanting support for Nicaragua. During that march, a Nica approached me. He shyly asked, "If you can protest like this where you come from—in your barrios—why can't you change your country's policy toward ours?"

At times like that I swallowed hard to transcend the guilt that engulfed me because of my government's wrong-doing. It became harder and harder for me to absorb the first-hand testimonies and history lectures on the Nicaraguan struggle for independence. After coordinating the morning classes, and often substitute-teaching when our teachers were sick, I was supposed to join the students in the afternoon information programs. But I would shamefully find myself dozing in the heat from the sun beating on the zinc roofs above the soft voices of mothers telling how they had lost their children through the unimaginable myriad of atrocities that had taken place under the Somozan dictatorship. Everyone came to talk to us: the women's organization AMNLAE, farmers from newly created cooperatives, unions, local Sandinista officials, clear-thinking South American radical priests, and Salvadoran refugees, all part of the "New Nicaragua." We were the smallest group of "internationalists" in Estelí, alongside our German, Dutch, British, and Belgian friends with whom we hung out at the Salvadoran-run café, or at local events. For the most part, I admired the Sandinistas and felt honored to meet some of their energetic leaders, Gladys Baez for one, who believed in the good of the revolution and was willing to risk her life for it. They also respected us for working there against our government's wishes.

A key moment for the NICA School during each four-week session was the Managua weekend where we demonstrated outside the U.S. Embassy at the weekly Thursday morning peace vigil sponsored by the Committee of U.S. Citizens Living in Nicaragua. (CUSCLIN) Later, the routine was to leave our passports at the door and go inside to meet with an embassy functionary who would always blatantly deny that the U.S. was supplying the Contra. At the end, I always felt nauseous when the granite-faced Marine guard handed me back my passport. The students, fired up after the visit, became even more convinced of the immorality of the United States intervention and began planning their lobbying and neighborhood organizing around the injustices of the war in Nicaragua. I remember one saying, "When we go back, we don't have time to be liberal."

It was hard to form friendships with these students—who were often my peers—and then have to say goodbye at the end of their month in Estelí. We as staff, on the other hand, stayed for a full year and everyone in town knew us as the gringos. Moreover, we were mostly single women, with the exception of one or two men. During their repetitive lectures about being exemplary role models, my staff-mates also warned me that Nicas were womanizers, lousy lovers, and we should be careful because messy affairs would be frowned upon. When I became attracted to one of the North American students, I was concerned about my reputation, so I held back at first despite a clear flirtatious edge to our conversation.

He had been hired to stay on to renovate our new school building and had the keys, so one night we ended up having passionate sex on the grass in the courtyard. Since we both swore not to breathe a word about our short-lived fling, I assumed my sexual adventures with this tight-lipped stud were top secret. One day, however, long after our forbidden evenings, I was gossiping with a staff member. We giggled as he walked out of a bedroom of our Managua hostel with a young woman in tow. My co-worker admitted she too had slept with him and knew we were not the only ones who had. What a relief to own up and discover that we were all human, albeit hypocrites.

I had not wanted a long-term relationship, but I missed my family and friends and craved affection. Sexual contact kept me in touch with my feelings. Every day I had to block the horror of the war and figure out how to shut down my emotions in order to comfort a weeping mother who had just lost a son, respond to her request to photograph his unrecognizable face in an open coffin, chat with a teenage veteran who was paralyzed from the waist down, or march in yet another funeral procession. Enjoying sex, on the other hand, brought me to a familiar life-affirming place—in contrast with the death and mutilation everywhere else.

Another way of coping was to leave the war zone. In December, in between sessions, the first place I visited alone was Bluefields on the Atlantic Coast. I started out by hitching two hours to Managua and hiring a taxi to take me at 4:00 the next morning to wait for a bus that crossed half the country. We arrived at the town of Rama five hours later where there was the usual process of sorting out the passengers' travel documents during war time. As a foreigner I had an inexplicable advantage, and was spared the hassle that I watched the Nicaraguans endure over their "papers." After waiting in another line for several hours, I boarded the boat, The Bluefields Express, which took me the rest of the way on the River Rama to the coast. As we slipped through the jungle, I took notes which later became this poem:

River Poem

Let me tell you
about my trip
on the River Rama
one steamy winter
I went to where it begins its flow
from the muddy heart of Nicaragua.

Think back with me
to that time when
I left the cool mountains
of contra killers in Estelí,
headed from Rama to the Atlantic
on the Bluefields Express.

She hummed along by naked orange trees,
fruit falling, rotting
in jungles with green velvet hassocks,
faded clapboard houses
where smiling cinnamon-skinned babies
played in the sun.

Some can talk
about the bottom of the River Rama
where they found *The Express*
like a riddled hulk of swiss cheese
that same season,
but I was on her.
I've told you what I saw.

Most onboard were noticeably of African background, since most of the coastal people are descended from freed slaves. Even in such a small country, there were striking differences between the two coasts, one English-speaking and the other Spanish. My genial host Oscar in Estelí often made ignorant racist comments about the muscles of those mythical black people who…" were not really Nicaraguans, but Africans imported to do heavy work." He and most people on the Nicaraguan Pacific coast had only seen photographs of black people and maybe known a few volunteer Afro-Cuban medics or teachers. As I reflected and ate my bag lunch, and the boat softly moved downstream, I never gave a second thought to the soldiers keeping watch on deck. Approaching Bluefields, the wide wooden verandahs and peaked roofs reminded me of New England.

There was no bathroom on board, so the minute we docked, I ran to the Ministry of Education. I was menstruating, but luckily my maroon pants hid the stains. I fled the waterless bathroom, leaving a mess, but there was no room for embarrassment in the middle of a war plagued by water shortages.

Someone had suggested I stay at the Hotel Cueto, a dank building that smelled at least one hundred years old. Pulling back the green and brown flowered bedspread that was pinned together, I managed a nap between the broken bed springs. A fan helped to circulate some air, and after a while I got used to the mildew smell that had startled me so at first. There was one step down to the shower and toilet I could hear leaking. The first day, I slipped on the wet cement floor and bruised my arm entering the bathroom. The leak stopped when the water was shut off, which was most of the day. The stained walls, cracked and even crumbling in places, were crying out for paint. But this was my vacation, and in relation to how most people lived, it was luxury, so I transcended it by reading or writing in my journal on the hotel verandah.

I had a list of contacts, and first visited a friend of a friend who had a new baby and lived in a crowded apartment. It was a very short visit. She was a European artist who was struggling with taking care of her child and working, and was not interested in talking about her life or why she was in Bluefields. At my next stop, the Ministry of Culture was having a party. Everyone was buzzing over the documentation of the indigenous coastal languages of the English-speaking Sumu, Rama and Misquito. Before the revolution, the British, Canadians and North Americans had used local workers from these groups to rape the forests of mahogany and other precious woods and taught them English. Now, Bluefields schools were embarking on a bilingual curriculum to legitimize the three groups' native languages, thereby enabling children to learn standard English while studying in their native languages part-time. Although many people could switch into Spanish, the official language of the country, it would be taught later. I doubt that this logical and ambitious plan is in place today.

I spent Christmas Eve with Mary Ellsberg, (daughter of Daniel Ellsberg) her Nicaraguan husband and friends. On Christmas Day, I went to the home of a young man I had met at the party. He chatted for hours in *coste-ño* English, offering me local delicacies and complementing my American accent as we waited for his mother to return from taking food to "the poor." She never appeared, and I left, not wanting to overstay my Christmas visit. The next few days, having exhausted the names I had, and with very few pesos left, I felt quite alone. The sun shone for only a few hours in the five days I was there. I happily boarded the boat back to Rama.

Traveling—even Nicaraguan style—became my strategy for distilling the horrors of the war zone. I looked forward to my " Nicaraguan R and R" in between the monthly sessions. Someone referred to me as the "most well-traveled *internacionalista*' in the country." I loved learning about other parts of Nicaragua where life was less intense, and I tried not to ar-rive armed with all the right answers. My premise was that it was not my revolution, so as a guest, I wanted to learn as much as I could by living there. Being alone also gave me time to reflect and document my thinking and experiences in journals which helped me to write this piece and more.

Although I always put up an optimistic front, I was haunted by the ongoing sacrifice of Nicaraguan youth in such an ugly war. I believed it was morally right to support the Sandinistas. I obviously was not the cause of the inequities and injustices around me, and I knew the Nicas did not regard me as a U.S. government representative, but I could never totally relax. I began to eat whole boxes of chocolate from the diplomatic dollar store to fight off anxiety and depression, but gained more weight and felt worse. At school, we followed the Nicaraguan custom of singing the Sandinista anthem to begin the morning, but I shuddered daily at the line that mentioned the "*Yanquii*, enemy of humanity." Finally came the moments of self-doubt. What was I, a mother of three, doing in the middle of this war? I rarely mentioned my grown children to Nicaraguan mothers because it seemed like they were either in mourning, or worrying that their children would be next. Even though the staff developed a bond among us and in the Estelí community, I felt plagued by fear and powerlessness. It was my Nicaraguan friends' ongoing courage and survival that kept me going. I don't think they knew I was a non-practicing Jew, but I felt some comfort sharing in their religious rituals and festivals anyway. If I happened to be walking by at mealtime, they always invited me to eat whatever was on the table, and sometimes I was asked in by people I barely knew. I was inspired by the dignity that emanated from every peasant and worker, an astounding contrast to the oppressed and beaten down, struggling poor in the United States, whose self-images were more often those of worthlessness.

I stayed in Nicaragua as an English teacher trainer and curriculum developer for two more years after I left the NICA School, splitting my time between the Zonal Ministry of Education in Estelí and the National Ministry in Managua. In June, 1988, I joined a delegation of international journalists who accompanied President Daniel Ortega on his first state visit to Cuba. Shortly after that trip, I returned to Boston because I thought I could be more effective there. Looking back over my three years, I realize I was constantly buoyed by the understanding and love I received from so many Nicas who never lost their ability to act generously toward me, a self-exiled foreigner living in the midst of their hope and tragedy.

Photos above: (upper left) Bette Steinmuller holding friend's newborn in Estelí; (upper right) Benjamin Linder's grave in Managua, Nicaragua; (lower left) Bette Steinmuller with her Nica "family" in Estelí, Nicaragua: Rosario, Marvin and Rosario's children Darío, Luís and Tomás, 1984; (lower right) co-workers/friends visiting Bette's home in Estelí, Nicaragua: Mary, Jean, Emily, and Anne, 1986.

POST SCRIPT:

More than twenty years later, after being out of power since the Sandinistas lost the elections in 1992, Daniel Ortega has returned. It would be an understatement to say times have changed, and so has the Sandinista leader, who seems drunk, destructive, and reckless with power. A friend who recently returned to Nicaragua advised me not to go back, that I'd be too depressed.

I am still close to people in the United States who I met in Estelí. I have no regrets as I look back at my years there as a momentous time in history, when many of us were drawn to a unique and just struggle for peace.

Vecino *Brigadistas,* 1986

Vecino

Steven Norris

Iᴛ's ᴊᴜɴᴇ 1985. I'm on a rain-soaked dirt road two miles south of Estelí, walking with a Nicaraguan college student, Chepe, and an African-American writer from Massachusetts. All afternoon we've been taking a break from building a clinic in Estelí. After swimming at a waterfall, we got caught in a cold downpour in this beginning of Nicaragua's rainy season. We found refuge in a small peasant's hovel where a sickly woman and her daughter, dressed in dirty rags, warmed us with hot coffee. Appreciative of their kindness, we're wandering along the road back toward the city.

Without warning, a uniformed soldier steps out of the roadside bushes, his AK-47 semiautomatic rifle pointed toward us. His unkempt hair, scraggly beard and wrinkled uniform make me think he's been in the woods for days. At first I don't know whether he's a government soldier or a rebel contra. *"¿Quienes son y adonde van?"* Who are you and where are you going? His words are slurred from alcohol and his peasant accent.

Nineteen year old Chepe, seemingly cheerful as ever, takes charge. "Oh, we've just been out walking and swimming." He tries to explain what two gringos and a Nica are doing out here in the countryside. The soldier, who I've now realized belongs to the Sandinista army, is too drunk to understand. Chepe patiently explains again and again who we are. Keith and I offer to show him our passports. The soldier isn't interested, probably doesn't know what a passport is anyway. Chepe's informality and cheerfulness seem to win him over. After a few minutes, he lowers his rifle and smiles, and he and Chepe talk as if they're old friends and he seems relieved to find that he's not confronted by enemies. I relax a little. Still, the loaded AK47 is waving around more or less in our direction, and he's drunk enough to fire the gun unintentionally, or simply misinterpret one of our actions and go on the attack. I don't understand what they are talking about, but I can tell Chepe is very tactfully trying to get rid of him without scaring him or making him think we're hurrying away. Their conversation goes on for ten or fifteen minutes. It's not until the soldier steps back into the woods and we walk around the next bend in the road that I begin to feel safe again, and I start thinking about whether I should tell people in our group or back in the States about this close encounter with danger.

This, though, is the middle of my story about *Vecino* and Nicaragua. It starts exactly a year earlier, in Kendall's and my home on Mission Hill.

One Friday evening in June, 1984, in the lush green backyard of the house we'd built on Fisher Avenue, Kendall and I were having a cookout with our good friend Rachel Wyon. Rachel had recently returned from Nicaragua where she'd been living and working for a number of years. I didn't know a whole lot about Nicaragua, but friends had visited and worked there since the Sandinistas had overthrown the Somoza dictatorship in 1979. I knew Nicaragua had the reputation of being a poor country with a progressive government struggling to bring dignity, prosperity and some sort of justice to its people. I was, however, still a skeptic, and having visited Poland and the Soviet Union many years before, and knowing that Nicaragua under the Sandinistas, like Cuba under Castro, had received massive assistance from Moscow, I thought that I might be disappointed with what I found there. As it turned out, on the day before my first journey to Nicaragua, President Reagan made a major speech about the country, in which he accused the Sandinista government of being a "brutal, totalitarian dictatorship" where arbitrary arrests and harassment of citizens for political reasons was commonplace. I had learned over the years not to trust the US government's position on these matters. But by 1985 I also knew that leftists did not always know or tell the truth either. I figured I could only find out the truth about Nicaragua first hand.

So without much forethought I asked Rachel, "Do you think a group of us from Boston could go to Nicaragua and make a contribution by doing some construction?"

"I don't know why not."

"Well, what type of construction do they use there?"

"Oh, mostly brick, when people can afford it. Rough-cut wood shacks when they can't."

"I've never built with brick, but I guess we could learn."

In this brief conversation, the seed of the single most important work I've ever done was born, and Rachel's affirmation inspired me to undertake the organization of a project called *Vecino*, (Neighbor) that would change my life.

Where to start? I spoke little Spanish, I had no savings, I knew no Nicaraguans, and I had never traveled in a Spanish-speaking country, let alone a third world country. When I started organizing *Vecino*, I just followed my instincts, accepted others' advice, and pulled something together, as my Yankee forebears would have called it, "By the bootstraps."

At first I had two bootstraps to work with, and I pulled hard on both of them. One was a lot of friends who I thought might support an idea like this. I put together a mailing list of everyone I knew who might be sympathetic. I wrote them a letter, saying that I had a dream of taking a volunteer group of people from Boston to Nicaragua to do some construction, and that in the future I might ask them for money or other kinds of support to make it happen. Having so little to go on at this stage, and sensing that a project as complicated as this could fail for any number of reasons, I felt quite vulnerable and foolish. But some inner voice told me to go ahead, and I mailed this letter to more than a hundred people.

The majority didn't say much in response, but a few did, and one person stands out. That summer (1984) I spent a few days building shelves for the reams of computer printouts generated by the Department of Public Health on Tremont Street in downtown Boston. Dick Clapp worked there, trying to figure out why there were clusters of cancer cases around the nuclear power plant in Plymouth and why there were clusters of leukemia victims around some abandoned tanneries in Woburn. One day Dick pulled me aside, and said with great respect and affection "I got your letter. You have a great idea. I hope you can make it work. Go for it. When you're ready we'll certainly give you some support, including money."

Over the next few months, there were many times when I came close to giving up on *Vecino*. Dick's words always came to mind, and sometimes they were the one thing that tipped the balance and caused me to go ahead with what often seemed like a pipe-dream.

The second bootstrap was the Nica School. During my conversation with Rachel over hamburgers in our backyard, I'd asked her how I might actually go about making contacts with Nicaraguans who could use the resources of a construction brigade. She told me to talk to the folks at NICA, which ran a Spanish language school for North Americans in Estelí, a small city in Northern Nicaragua. So one hot summer day after work I rode my BMW motorcycle over the Charles River to Cambridge. There I found Bev Truman and Joanne Sunshower in the beehive basement of the Old Cambridge Baptist Church in Harvard Square where NICA and a bunch of other Central American solidarity organizations had their offices. Too many people in too small a space, was my impression. There were papers everywhere and maps and political posters all over the walls. Everyone with a telephone propped against one ear, a pencil writing on the desk with the other hand. A busier office I'd never seen.

Bev was simply too busy to talk to me. Joanne gave me ten minutes.

"I'm a builder and thinking about taking volunteers to Nicaragua to do some construction. Rachel thought you might have some ideas or contacts that would help."

"Well, that's a great idea. Do you speak Spanish?"

"No."

"Have you been to Central America?"

"No."

"Do you know anyone in Nicaragua?"

"No, but I thought maybe you could give me some leads." I could tell she didn't take me very seriously at this point. But she was courteous, and she told me about a student of theirs:

"Natalie Zimmerman. She's still in Estelí. She's been living there with a Nicaraguan family. This family has asked her if she could maybe raise some money in the United States to help build a community center or something. We don't know much about it. It's a long shot. But it's the best we can give you right now. Call her when she gets back to Boston."

I called Natalie as soon as she returned. She was a pretty young woman with a huge heart that matched her huge smile. She did fundraising around the country for the UUSC, the Unitarian Universalist Service Committee, Like many others she'd gone to Nicaragua to learn Spanish and get a first hand glimpse of the social and political changes going on in Central America.

She told me how she had lived in El Calvario barrio in Estelí with Paulina Alonzo, a fifty-five-year-old Sandinista grandmother. Paulina was some sort of healer or medicine woman who had helped the Sandinistas in her neighborhood. She was probably one of the most effective community organizers in the western hemisphere, and now she was pursuing her life-long dream of constructing a center for her community. She assumed the most she could get from gringo activists was money. As soon as we met in the fall, Natalie wrote her and asked if the barrio would like us to send a group of Bostonians to Estelí to help with the construction. Somehow she got back an answer: *"Sí. ¡Magnífico!"*

In fall 1984 *Vecino* consisted of just two people: Natalie and me. We began meeting every couple of weeks at local bars and restaurants to plan the project. We started with a vague goal of raising ten thousand dollars for building supplies and organizing a group of ten or so volunteers who would be willing to pay their own way to Nicaragua and do construction in the tropical heat. Natalie knew almost nothing about grass roots organizing or construction. I knew almost nothing about Nicaragua or construction practices there. We were both shooting in the dark. But I had my dreams and Dick Clapp's encouragement in my pocket, and Natalie had her charm and ability to speak in public.

Sometime around Thanksgiving we held our first organizational meeting of interested people. Eight or ten people attended, which wasn't bad for a first try. Natalie told the story of the Nicaraguan revolution, focusing on the grass-roots work of women like Paulina Alonzo who had asked Natalie, "Are there mountains where you live where guerrilla fighters can go hide when you try to overthrow your government like we overthrew Somoza?" "Paulina," she concluded, "may not know how to make a revolution in the United States, but she knows her neighborhood in Estelí like the back of her hand, and she cares about it like she cares about her five children, and will do anything to make it a better place to live."

Becky Pierce was a tall and powerful looking carpenter from Dorchester who spent her summers working for Outward Bound and teaching teen-agers how to navigate open sailboats on the cold and windy waters of Penobscot Bay in Maine. I'd never met Becky before. She came with her husband Mike, and later became one of *Vecino's* most committed leaders. At the meeting she said she wanted to help *Vecino* but couldn't work on the brigade or go to Nicaragua because she had a young son and it would simply be too risky. Other people were equally noncommittal. None seemed ready to sign up.

I came away from our first public gathering very discouraged, and almost felt like giving up. In addition to the lack of volunteers, Natalie's health was not good, and she had a demanding job that required her to travel a lot. I was working full time, had a family, and was busy with community activities on Mission Hill. The project seemed like a dream that couldn't happen. I remember lying in bed one night in December telling Kendall how discouraged I was. "If something doesn't change soon, I'm going to give up. It's just not going to work." "Well, what needs to change?" she asked. I thought a minute: "There're twenty or thirty phone calls that have to be made to people who have shown some interest. Those people need to be called, and another meeting organized. But I don't have time to make all those phone calls, and Natalie doesn't know any of the people. She can't make them."

"Can I make them?" Kendall asked.

I gave Kendall the list and she made the calls. In mid-January, 1985 we held a second organizational meeting in Natalie's living room. The room was overflowing with people from as far away as New Hampshire. There was standing room only. Natalie told the story of Paulina and the people of El Calvario. Joanne Sunshower talked about the mechanics of aid to Nicaragua and what life was like for North Americans in Estelí. I talked about construction.

The meeting was electrifying. Becky Pierce told us she had reconsidered the risks and decided that she could leave her son for a month to work with us. Several other people were ready to sign up: Renny Cushing who had helped to lead the Clamshell alliance in its fight against the Seabrook, NH nuclear power plant, and who, on returning from Estelí in the fall of 1985 got himself elected to the New Hampshire State Assembly; Doug who had spent a year working as a volunteer in the Mekong River delta with the Mennonites during the war in Vietnam; Chris Hammer and Coert Bonthius, both young and strong carpenters from Dorchester. All these and more were ready to sign up. Others wanted to help with the organizing. For the first time I realized that others were beginning to share the dream of *Vecino*.

From the time of this meeting until June 2nd, when the first contingent of *Vecino* left for Nicaragua, the project was unstoppable. Within a month we had organized a steering committee of eight people, including Natalie and me, Joanne, Kendall, Becky, Tony Rogers, John Seigfried, and Chris. This group met weekly and set overall policies for the committees that each of us committed ourselves to organizing. Someone came up with the idea of house meetings, so we asked friends all over the city to invite people they knew over to their houses. Two or three of us from the steering committee went to these meetings and talked to the guests about Nicaragua and about *Vecino*. After Joanne's and my trip to Nicaragua in February, we put together a slide show about Estelí and El Calvario. At the end of these meetings we asked people for money. Sometimes we raised as much as $700 or $800 at a meeting. For us at the time, that seemed like a fortune. Ten or twelve of these meetings, and we'd have enough money to pay for most of the building materials. We put together a mailing list of everyone we knew and sent out an informational letter with a request for donations. I remember one of the first replies was from Lee Goldstein, my attorney, with a check for $100, with note wishing me luck and telling me what a great project he thought this was. I couldn't at this stage believe that anyone had that much faith in us. But it sure charged my batteries. One night an old friend Jan Selcer called me. Jan had lived with us ten years before at the Delle Avenue Commune and worked for Nine-to Five, an organization of office workers. In 1985 she and her husband Joel had two small children.

"Steve, there's no way I can go to Nicaragua. But I'd really like to be a part and help as much as I can. What do you need?"

"We need money," was my reply. "Could you help us fund-raise?"

Out of this one phone call and Jan's perseverance and ingenuity, tens of thousands of dollars were raised and numerous contacts made. Jan got her hands on the membership lists of several progressive organizations in Boston, and found us a room full of telephone lines in a downtown office building. Over the course of several evenings volunteers from *Vecino* went to these phones and worked through the list of several thousand names. Lots of people pledged money, and some pledged donations of equipment. Chris Hammer came up with the idea of soliciting donations of tools and building materials. He called everyone he knew, and within a month or so had a garage full of items that might be useful in the construction of the clinic.

The interest and support generated by *Vecino* was astounding. After the January meeting, we rode the crest of a wave that didn't break for another two years. The fact is that by the winter of 1984-5, when our dream started to materialize, many people in this country had become disgusted with US policy toward Nicaragua. The Reagan administration was engaged in both legal and illegal activities designed to overthrow the Sandinista Government. The CIA mined the harbors of Corinto, Nicaragua's only large seaport on the Pacific coast. The State Department tried to persuade other countries to stop trading with and aiding Nicaragua. The Department of Defense helped the CIA organize and train the right-wing rebel army, called the Contras, and gave these terrorists large quantities of arms and hundreds of millions of dollars. CIA funded operatives set up "secret" airfields in northern Costa Rica on the Nicaraguan border for the shipment of supplies to rebels inside of Nicaragua. The US government put out huge amounts of propaganda about Nicaragua, claiming it was a totalitarian dictatorship engaged in brutal and terrorist activities to keep its population in line. Oliver North and others secretly sold high tech weapons to Iran at inflated prices, which was illegal, and turned around and gave the money to the Contras, which was also illegal. So much did the Reagan administration fear and hate the Sandinistas that people who worked for him were willing to risk his presidency to stop them. Once these activities became publicly known a year or so later in newspaper stories and the Iran-Contra hearings in Congress, and once it was revealed that some of his closest advisers, including the head of the National Security Council and the CIA had been involved in activities specifically outlawed by Congress, there was even talk of Reagan's impeachment.

To many Americans this was a great puzzle. Nicaragua is a very poor country the size of North Carolina with a population of only 3 million people, hardly a threat to the well-being and security of the United States, which is located a thousand miles away. But President Ronald Reagan and his advisors saw it differently. By 1985, their Contra army had about 10,000 soldiers which operated out of bases in southern Honduras and made regular raids into Northern Nicaragua. The Contras blew up electrical towers and bridges, attacked weakly defended farming communities, murdered leaders of farming cooperatives and other organizations loyal to the Sandinstas, and sometimes kidnapped peasants who were forced into the contra army. By 1985 tens of thousands of Nicaraguans had died in this war.

It took me a long time but I finally figured it out while talking to Ramón, a construction worker who taught us to lay brick. Sitting under a mango tree at the edge of the construction site one morning during our twenty minute break, I asked him why he thought Reagan hated the Sandinistas so much.

"Look." He told me in Spanish, "Nicaragua's a very small country but it's very important. In just six years since we overthrew Somoza, our country has created schools so that most adults like me, who were illiterate before – we can read a little now. For the first time in my life I can go see a doctor when I'm sick. My children can get medicine and immunizations. Fewer people are going hungry. Many poor peasants who had no land before can grow their own gardens and maybe even build a small house. After a few years under the Sandinistas we're so much better off."

He went on to explain that before the Sandinista victory in 1979, when the government of Somoza received a lot of help from the United States, none of this had happened. In large numbers children had died from diarrhea and other common diseases for want of simple medicine. Half the population couldn't read and write. Many peasants were landless. Nicaragua was one of the poorest countries in the hemisphere. At the same time her leaders, who were friendly with the leaders of the United States, lived like kings and ruled with an iron fist through an elite and brutish army known as the National Guard.

Ramón told me that if a country the size of Nicaragua could establish its independence of the United States, and at the same time develop economically, socially, and politically, this had to be a big threat to the United States "What about Brazil?" he asked. "What about the Philippines? They're huge countries. If we in Nicaragua can do so well under the Sandinistas by throwing off dictators who are friendly to the United States, big countries can do it too. And this would hurt Ronald Reagan a lot. So he hates us and will try almost anything to keep us from succeeding."

Actually, I once saw a photograph in *The Boston Globe* of a protester in Manila carrying a sign that read "Yesterday Nicaragua, Tomorrow the Philippines." Another time I saw a photograph of a protester in Paraguay that said *"Sandino Vive"*—"Sandino Lives". In 1985 Nicaragua was one of the smallest countries and at the same time, because of the courage and intelligence of its people and government, was one of the most important countries in the world.

By 1985, many people here in the United States had also become aware of all of these things, and wanted to do something about it. Vecino came along just as this awareness was peaking, and people's desire to challenge the US and support the Nicaraguans and the Sandinistas found a vehicle in our fledgling organization.

Ever since the idea of *Vecino* had emerged, I'd known that I would have to travel to Nicaragua prior to the construction brigade. Natalie initially thought that Paulina wanted to build a community center. But we had no idea what types of building materials or skills would be needed, how large a project was contemplated, whether there was land available, or how we were going to coordinate the project with local officials, etc. I didn't want to take a group of North Americans to Nicaragua and find that there was nothing to do because the proper planning and organizing hadn't been done on that end. Also, we'd heard of another construction project in Managua, which had been only partially successful because the local community group which sponsored the project was not well organized. So there was homework to be done in Estelí. Unfortunately, Natalie couldn't take a trip in the winter. I knew I could not find my way around Nicaragua on my own. Into this breach stepped Joanne Sunshower, who said she'd be only too happy to go to Nicaragua for a week, especially if I paid for the trip.

So in late February, in the middle of a snowstorm, I said good-bye to Kendall and Moriah, our daughter, and flew to Miami, and then to Managua. The sun was setting in Managua when we arrived. It was 85 degrees and humid. The smell of smoke from wood cook-stoves filled the air. On the ride from the airport on the outskirts of the city to our downtown hotel, we could hear roosters crowing. Revolutionary graffiti shouted from the walls of buildings still full of bullet holes: *Sandino vive*—Sandino lives. *El pueblo unido jamas sera vencido*—The people united will never be defeated. *Nicaragua Victoriosa—Ni se vinde ni se rinde*—Victorious Nicaragua, we'll never sell out, we'll never be broken. I knew I was close to heaven, and things would never quite be the same.

The next morning, which we spent getting lost in the streets of Managua, only doubled my euphoria. We visited the tomb of Carlos Fonseca, a quiet place where the Sandinistas had lit an eternal flame to this intellectual who helped found the FSLN, and who had been killed in battle with Somoza's armies a few years before the Sandinista victory. We saw wall murals on the main streets depicting in graphic detail the history of the Nicaraguan people over the last thousand years and their recent victories over Somoza and US imperialism. For the first time, I drank coca cola out of a plastic bag, the only way that street vendors in Nicaragua could afford to sell it because glass and aluminum were too scarce and expensive. I saw the shells of apartment buildings and churches still standing in Managua as they had remained since an earthquake had leveled the city in the early seventies. Managua in 1985 reminded me a little of the East Berlin I'd seen in 1963, where the effects of World War II were still evident everywhere. But here, nearby stood the parliament building, where I was told, some armed Sandinstas dressed as Somoza's elite troops had invaded in 1977 and taken most of Somoza's National Assembly hostage. In the aftermath Somoza's government had been discredited before the eyes of the world, and a Sandinista victory had become inevitable.

Later that same day Joanne and I took a three hour bus ride from Managua to Estelí. We had standing room only, and young men actually rode on the roof with the luggage to escape the swelter and chaos. This too-heavy bus lumbered up the mountains on the Pan American Highway past hot fields where peasants worked. At every stop along the way the bus was surrounded by women selling fruit drinks, melons, fried bananas, and mangoes. I loved the energy. I loved the bustle. I loved the heat. I loved the closeness and sweat of this bus that was taking me into the heart of the Sandinista Revolution.

Soon I ended up in the living room of Clara and Eusebio Hernandez, the fifty-something parents of the Hernandez family with whom I lived for the next few days and then later, for the whole summer that Kendall, Moriah and I were in Estelí. Even though my Spanish was rudimentary, and they did not speak English, they made me feel at home. Now even thirteen years later, I am certain I would be welcomed by them with open arms.

Clara and Eusebio were both short and stout but muscular, and their skin was wrinkled and brown from long hard work out-of-doors. They'd met in Honduras, Clara's home, after Eusebio had run away from the plantation he'd grown up on in El Salvador and where he'd been so poor as a boy he hadn't even had clothes to wear. They'd lived in Honduras for several years when El Salvador and Honduras had had a border dispute with some fighting. In 1969, the government of Honduras expelled all the Salvadorans, and Clara and Eusebio had moved to Estelí, just as the Sandinistas were beginning to organize. When I arrived in 1985 their oldest son was fighting in El Salvador with the FMLN; they had not heard from him in four years. Another son was inducted into the Sandinista Army even while we lived with them. At one point when a 5,000 man contra army got close to Estelí in the summer of 1985 Eusebio put on a uniform, picked up an AK47 and went off to the mountains for a few days with the regular army until the contra armies dispersed. Once a week, Eusebio also participated in *vigilancia*, walking the streets of El Calvario barrio in uniform and with a weapon all night long until daybreak looking for suspicious activities.

By the standards of Estelí, where many people lived in wooden shacks, Clara and Eusebio were reasonably prosperous. A year or two before they'd built themselves a new brick and stucco house with 5 rooms and a kitchen, and were proud of it. The floors were dirt, but Clara and her daughters kept them immaculately swept, and they expected soon to be able to obtain tile and mortar to install a permanent floor. Their living room furniture consisted of 3 or 4 plastic lawn chairs. On one otherwise bare wall there was a picture of Jesus, on another a photograph of Che Guevara. I was never quite sure how they made money. Clara made and sold some cheese. Eusebio sometimes spent the day on a local farm working in the fields. At other times he went to Managua on "business."

My relationship with them was sort of a love affair. I was in awe of them. They were, I think, in awe of me. They could not understand how a prosperous gringo like me could come so far to work for nothing in the tropical sun, share their monotonous diet of rice, tortillas and beans, subject myself to the outhouse and the outdoor cold-water showers which were all they had to offer, sleep for a summer with Kendall in a single bed, subject ourselves to the rats that hung out in the eves of our room, and the huge brightly colored cockroaches and biting red ants that infested the outhouse. They were even more appreciative in the summer when I brought Moriah, our three year old daughter. I could not understand how they could sustain such an indomitable spirit of love, humor and strength after so many years of hardship, moving around, and war. Clara insisted on serving us food three times a day without fail. She wouldn't even let me take my dirty dishes into the kitchen. She also insisted on doing my laundry. The only time she ever got angry at me was when I hired someone else to do my laundry.

On the day before I left Nicaragua Eusebio asked me for a favor:

"Por favor, necesito veinticinco dolares." Please, I need twenty-five dollars.

Since he'd never asked me for anything before, I was shocked, although I would have gladly given him $500 if he'd needed it. "Why?" I asked him. "I want to go visit my brother in El Salvador, and I need $25 in dollars for a Salvadoran visa. The Salvadoran government won't take cordoba (the Nicaraguan currency). There's no other way for me to get dollars."

I felt honored that he trusted me enough to ask for the money.

This first visit to Estelí was full of people and planning. In my spare time I hung out with the younger teenage children of the Hernandez family, who took me swimming in the river and showed me around town. I became familiar with the market a couple of blocks up the street, with the wooden shacks being built nearby by the numerous refugees from the contra war in the countryside, with the bullet holes and other battle scars that still remained in the walls of many homes from the furious fighting that had taken place here in 1979. At that time Somoza had tried to bomb Estelí into submission. I saw a spot where one of these bombs had fallen in a little bodega down the street from the clinic. Alejandro, the father repaired shoes in one corner. Gloria sold snacks, mostly coke in another. One time when I was visiting the store she introduced me to a very old man named Paulo who had fought with Sandino against the US Marines. I felt honored, but the guy was hard-of-hearing and all we could do was smile at one another. Gloria several times pointed out to me a big patched hole in the concrete floor where she said one of Somoza's bombs, probably made in the US, had fallen. It had destroyed five adjacent homes, and killed her daughter and brother. But still the people had fought on.

There were three "uprisings" in Estelí in 1978 and 1979, when local people under Sandinista leadership had attacked the police station and the National Guard, and attempted to drive them out of the city. In the first and second of these bloody uprisings they had failed. On their third attempt they succeeded, and two days later Somoza left Nicaragua for good. The people of Estelí were proud. They felt as if they almost single-handedly had rid the Western hemisphere of one of its worst dictators. Throughout Nicaragua Estelí was known as *Estelí Heroico*. People in Estelí felt powerful; they knew how to organize. As it turned out they also knew how to host a brigade from the United States who wanted to help them.

Joanne and I met with the Ministry of Health. We learned immediately that they had big plans for us. Instead of a simple community center, they showed us the blueprints for a 700 square foot brick building for a health clinic complete with the wiring and plumbing needed to outfit it. I was overwhelmed. I was not a mason, and none of our volunteers were masons. I had never worked in Nicaragua before, and had no way of estimating how fast a group of volunteers could work. One look at these plans convinced me that the project involved about twice as much construction as I had originally anticipated. I told Joanne that instead of spending one month in Estelí, the project would require at least two, instead of 10 or 12 volunteers, we would need 25 or so. We would also need at least twice the amount of building materials I had planned. This didn't scare me very much though. By this time I knew that *Vecino* was on a roll in Boston. Also I could see all around me how much the Nicaraguans were accomplishing. I had faith that we could meet any challenges that came our way.

We met in someone's living room with 30 or so members of the local CDS (Sandinista Defense Committee), who wanted to see firsthand these gringos who were promising so much. In my broken Spanish and with Joanne's help, I told them about the organizing we were doing in Boston. They told us they would help in every way they could, by providing homes in the neighborhood for our brigade members and by sending volunteers to help with construction. They took us to the site where the clinic was to be built. A poor family was living there in a shack, and there were junk cars and machines strewn about. My major fear upon leaving Estelí was that the family would still be there when we arrived in June, and that the project would stall.

We met with local building suppliers who promised us the lumber, steel, brick, cement and sand we'd need to build the clinic. Having seen many times how construction can be delayed by any number of problems, even in the US, I didn't know whether to trust them. Of course I had no choice. But the chances of failure were great and the chances of starting a project that we would have to leave incomplete were even greater.

A week earlier I had come to Nicaragua excited and scared. I returned to a Boston snowstorm charged, ready to do whatever was needed to make the project happen. The members of the steering committee were anxious to hear Joanne's and my report. When we told them how big the project had become, and that more volunteers, more time and more money than originally anticipated would be required, they barely blinked. They were as ready as we were to buckle down and work hard. Between the first week of March, when we returned from Estelí, and early June, when the first installment of volunteers left for Estelí, we accomplished a phenomenal amount.

The truth is that by mid-March so much work was going on to organize the project, and responsibility had become so widely dispersed and so well executed, that I know only a part of this history, the part that I was personally responsible for or saw first hand. Other things were occurring without my knowledge, or by now I've forgotten about them because I played such a small role in their execution.

We recruited and screened over 40 volunteers, most from the Boston area, but three or four who heard about us from out-of-state. By June we raised $45,000, and more money kept coming in all summer. The Nicaraguans asked us if we could help furnish and staff the clinic, and we intensified our fund raising efforts, which brought in tens of thousands more dollars. We found two nurses who wanted to help us. Since Nicaragua's medical resources were already stretched to the breaking point by poverty and the war, we needed our own medical system. Peggy Lynch and Mary Lenihan put together a plan and a budget. *Vecino* gave them the money and they purchased medical supplies. They were able to leave behind a small pharmacy of medicines and supplies. We found a doctor in a local health clinic who liked what we were doing. He volunteered to give us free immunizations, and one Saturday morning in May many of us lined up in his office and got our shots. We held 30 or 40 house meetings. Joanne purchased $20,000 worth of plane tickets. Since some volunteers were coming for one month, others for two, and still others for only two week tours, this was no easy feat. Kurt and Chris solicited donations of building materials and tools. When we flew to Miami on June 2nd each volunteer carried

Steve Norris with *El Calvario* children, 1986

a bag with about 50 pounds of building materials and tools, in addition to their own luggage. Unfortunately, we had to leave many other things behind in Boston simply because we couldn't carry them all, and Reagan's embargo made it impossible to ship them. Kendall contacted local media in Boston, bought film, and made detailed plans for educational work and slide shows when we returned. Some of us appeared on TV and on local radio talk shows. We sold colorful tee shirts, which said "Peace and Justice in Central America." I wore one of these shirts to work with me. My work at the time took me all over Boston. People sometimes stopped me in hardware stores and lumberyards and asked, "What's that shirt you're wearing?" I'd tell them about US government policy toward Nicaragua, and describe the *Vecino* project to them. Often they'd buy a shirt. We eventually ran out of these shirts that didn't make a lot of money, but they were a great educational tool. We visited the offices of Congressman Joe Moakley and Senators John Kerry and Ted Kennedy and told them of our plans. They were too cautious and narrow-minded to give us any direct or open support. But we knew we didn't need them anyway. Our project had found the crest of a wave, and we were riding it

The most amazing thing that we accomplished was to beat President Ronald Reagan's economic embargo against Nicaragua. In the spring of 1985, the US government realized that the measures it was taking to overthrow the Sandinstas were not working. The Sandinistas were still in charge in Nicaragua, and popular support seemed stronger than ever. In April, Reagan announced the US was placing an embargo on Nicaragua, meaning that no more material aid other than medicine could be sent there. This created a huge dilemma for us. As a poor country with massive development projects and a low-level but extremely costly war going on, Nicaragua simply did not have some of what we'd need to build the clinic – galvanized roofing, for example, copper wire, PVC pipe, nails, door latches, conduit, wall receptacles, etc. By April we had raised the $10,000 needed to purchase these things in the States, and had arranged for them to be transported by ship. But Reagan's embargo made it not only illegal, but also impossible for us to ship them. There were no more ships willing to carry these things from US ports. We could get our people to Nicaragua, but it was not at all clear how we were going to ship the materials with which to build.

What were we to do? For a week or so we were in confusion. We thought about shipping through Canada, but found out that was probably illegal. We needed another way. Someone suggested that there might be a peace group in Canada who would buy the materials there and put them on a ship for us. We did some research and found a phone number for Tools for Peace in Vancouver, British Columbia. I called them and asked these people whom I had never met for the biggest favor I'd ever asked of anyone:

"Hello. This is Steve Norris in Boston. I'm working with *Vecino*, a small material aid organization, that's trying to ship some building materials to Nicaragua. We need your help, not only with shipping, but you'll have to purchase the materials as well. We're trying to figure out a way to get you the money. Do you think you might be able to do it within a month?"

Gulp. Hesitation.

"No problem," was the reply.

Then another problem occurred. Reagan was threatening to make it illegal to send money abroad for Nicaragua. If we were to make this deal work, we had to get the $10,000 out of the country immediately, or it might become illegal. We didn't know the folks in Vancouver well enough just to wire them $10,000. But Doug, one of our volunteers who had worked with the Mennonites in Vietnam had an idea. He knew of some Mennonite farmers in Manitoba who might be able to handle this kind of cash. He gave me a name. I'll never know whom I talked to.

Kendall and Moriah (in front of *Vecino* in progress.)

"Hello, I've got a problem. I must find a way around Reagan's embargo to get $10,000 cash to Canada right away, or our whole project may fail. Can we wire it to you, and will you get it to Vancouver when they need it?"

"No problem." was his reply.

That's how we beat Reagan's embargo. I wired the money to Manitoba. I sent a list of building materials to Vancouver. The good folks in Vancouver bought the roofing, plumbing supplies, wire, hardware, nails, and the like, contracted with a shipper for a container, got it all into the hold of a cargo ship, made contact with the Mennonites in Manitoba, obtained the money they needed, and paid for the materials, and the shipping. To this day I don't know how they did it all on such short notice. In early June the materials sailed on the ship Hornsbee to Corinto. By some other equally amazing magic, the Ministry of Health got a truck to Corinto, picked up the container, and got it to Estelí at the end of June This was perfect timing, as we were just finishing pouring concrete and laying brick, and badly needed these materials. Had this not all occurred with such clockwork and with such incredible kindness and support from our sisters and brothers in Canada, the construction of the health clinic would have been halted midway, and Reagan's embargo would have had its desired affect. As it was, the embargo empowered us by demonstrating unambiguously what people of good will can accomplish even in the face of government repression, even across international borders.

By the first of June we were psyched and ready to go. On the day before we left I got a birthday greeting from my father. A year before when I had first mentioned to him that I was thinking of leading a group to Nicaragua to assist the people there, he had mumbled some cold war rhetoric about how I'd only be helping the Soviet Union. I had learned years before not to argue these things with him, and had let his challenge pass. During the past few months I had hardly bothered to talk with him about this project. But now, on this day of triumph, he sent me a card telling me how proud he was to have a son who was willing work so hard and give so much to help other people. Up until that moment I'd never realized how much I had wanted his approval. Now I had it. Leaving for Estelí closed an enormous circle.

A letter written to my father by a family friend in July, 1985:

> Dear John,
>
> Thanks so much for leaving Steve's letter. My Lord they are all a courageous and inspired group of God's agents – aren't they? How wonderful. They will be changed folks upon their return -–especially little Moriah. To have the courage of one's convictions so deep in your heart that they burn and prod to such action is what we're all called to do. So few of us answer the call – More power to them – The future of the world needs to be in the hands of such lovers of the "good news" as they are. Open hearts, open minds, open hands for giving and receiving. What a gift of time, talent and life to the folks of Estelí. Praise be to God for Steve, Kendall & all the others. . ."
>
> Amy Spollett

Nicaragua

How do I write about Nicaragua? I can't write in the same language I usually employ. I'll just have to try another language. Perhaps it will convey something.

Maybe this problem has something to do with what happened the moment our bus arrived in Estelí, even before we'd started work of the clinic, even before anyone in Estelí knew very much about who we were or what we were capable of. When our bus pulled up into the streets of El Calvario in the early afternoon, something totally unexpected happened: a crowd of three to four hundred people were waiting. Songs were sung. Children gave us flowers, took us by the hand and led us on a march down the unpaved streets into a large open air pavilion-like community room in El Calvario's Catholic Church. A hand painted sign on the church read:

"We the people of Estelí open our arms to you, our internationalist friends of *Vecino*." The *acto* started there with a five minute round of applause by our Nicaraguan hosts and hostesses. Several speeches were made by public officials and local residents.

"Thank you for coming so far to such a poor and distant place," they said. "Thank you for being willing to share our many hardships with us. Thank you for supporting us, the Nicaraguan people, in our fight for freedom, dignity and justice. Your presence here inspires all Nicaraguan people to work harder and to bear the sacrifices we have to make to ensure the success of our revolution. We are certain that if the American people can learn what Nicaragua is truly like, they will tell their government to stop waging war against our people, and your government will be forced to listen."

Then we all walked the three or four blocks to a rocky but vacant lot where the clinic was to be built. I was relieved to find that the house and debris that had been there in the spring had been completely removed. There we dug the first shovelfuls of earth, and a few bricks were symbolically stacked on top of each other. Our daughter Moriah commented, "Now we have to glue it together." Kendall brought out the beautiful silk banner an artist in Boston had painted for us and hung it on a fence. Our work in Nicaragua began with the largest party and the most praise I'd ever received anywhere in my whole life.

And writing this, I remember something that until this moment, I had completely forgotten. When I returned to Boston in August, 1985, to Kendall's and my beautiful house on Mission Hill, I tried to write about the US with the same passion and in the same language that I'd written about Estelí. I wanted to continue telling the truths I saw in the language I developed there, the same language that I'm using now, so many years later, from the mountains of North Carolina, to describe these events. But I couldn't. I tried for a few days to write a summary of my experiences, and about *Vecino's* return to the States, a letter of praise and thanks for the hundreds of people who had supported our project with their deeds and words and money, and who had not been able to experience the rewards of a project like ours, the rewards that were mostly reflected in the eyes of Nicaraguans who told us simply *Gracias*. Or *Nuestra casa es su casa*— our house is your house. But the words wouldn't come; my Nicaraguan pen would not write in Boston. Now, years later, I think I've rediscovered it. I tried writing about Nicaragua in the same language that I've been describing the first chapters of my life. It didn't work. I looked at pictures of Nicaragua, of the clinic we built. I wracked my brain, cried some, felt incredibly frustrated, then remembered there is another voice I can use. What follows is written in that voice, a voice that's part singing, part mourning, part poetry, mostly passion. See for yourself.

Looking back now it feels like the organizing that happened in Boston and the construction that happened in Estelí somehow aren't very closely connected to each other, or that the whole mood of things changes so dramatically and so totally that they bear little relation to each other. In truth neither could have happened without the other.

But there were two thousand miles between the two places, and centuries of difference, and the sword which was pointed at the heart of one was held by the hands of the other.

All that summer I had in my mind's eye a picture of the map of the Western hemisphere. A huge United States sitting on top of a bunch of much smaller countries. Being in Estelí felt like being somewhere underneath the belly of some bloated beast. There were no guarantees it wouldn't make a false step, or throw up, or just sit down—and crush us. The Nicaraguans were more agile than it was, and therefore could usually squirm out of harm's way fast enough. But some didn't. Like Ben Linder, a young engineer from Seattle, who was shot and killed by the contra while working on a water project in the spring of 1987. Like 15-year-old Rommel Garcia who lived in a simple house in the center of Estelí. In the first week of June when we had just arrived in Estelí, someone threw a bomb through the window. He died of head injuries shortly after. The word in the streets later was that the contra were after his father, who worked for the Ministry of the Interior, or maybe the man next door. It doesn't matter any more. The boy happened to be in the wrong place, and was blown to bits, probably by explosives made in the USA, delivered by the CIA, paid for by my tax dollars, a gift to the Contras from Ronald Reagan, Admiral Poindexter, and Colonel Oliver North. Like the mothers who were en route to visit their soldier sons on the back of a truck near Matagalpa that was hit by a contra mortar. Ten more deaths. Ten more funerals. A million years of grief.

There were many funerals in Estelí that summer. They were mostly for young men and teenage boys who were soldiers, but every now and then they were for a child, a woman, a father, someone who was simply in the wrong place at the wrong time. Kendall described a funeral:

We went to a wake at his family's house. We were invited to give condolences to his mother and father. It was so incredibly sad. We choked back our tears and walked with almost 600 people down the street to the church. His closed casket in a truck with his immediate family walking arm in arm behind. All his schoolmates were there in their blue uniforms holding wreaths and flowers. The mass lasted about 30 minutes and then the procession went to the cemetery along with another *combatiente* (solder), and a tiny black casket bearing a newborn. Gunshots were fired as the caskets were lowered. This was the most moving experience since the *acto* of our arrival. I truly felt the meaning of the war, the senseless death of this boy, following so many hundreds and thousands before him. The contra war kills daily and death is accepted as a part of life. It has been going on for so long that on one hand, there is pain and sadness but on the other, a sense of pride that a loved one has given his or her life for the struggle. I felt the presence of the many dead carried along this same route. The tombs in the cemetery belong to the more well to do. Most guerrillas on the other hand are not returned home for burial, so a single tombstone stands for those lost in battle. The ceremony ended with a deluge and a huge rainbow, the eternal sign of hope.

All these Nicaraguans were victims of Reagan's paranoia, the cold war gringo fear that the Sandinistas might just succeed and inspire other poor peoples in other countries to wake up and resist.

There were no guarantees Uncle Sam wouldn't tire of this petty but deadly cat and mouse game he was playing with his make-believe contra army, realize he could never win the war with it, and simply send his marines to overrun the country. All summer long we were scared this might happen. During our stay a bomb exploded at the Nicaraguan embassy in Washington DC and the US publicly approved $38 million in "humanitarian" aid to the Contras. At the same time American and European reporters in Nicaragua were relaying to us stories of secret and probably illegal funding being given to the Contras through right wing operatives in Costa Rica and Honduras. In late June, we heard *The Village Voice* in New York published an article saying that plans were under way in Washington for a July 4th invasion. A Witness For Peace group from the States was kidnapped by Contras while on a peace mission in early August The Nicaraguans thought an invasion unlikely but assured us that if it occurred, every effort would be made to get us out of the country safely. Everyone knew that an invasion would be costly to the US. Lots of GIs would die. But they could overrun the cities and towns. Many Nicaraguans would have gone to the mountains, or underground, and waged a costly guerrilla struggle, probably for years, maybe decades.

If Uncle Sam had taken over the cities and towns including Estelí, which was located on the Pan American highway, my cousin Jimmy's son could have been one of the invaders. Jimmy, about six years older than I, had been in the Marines when I was a kid. He had looked clean and proud in that blue uniform with the white hat. His son had followed in his footsteps. With considerable fascination I wondered sometimes what it would be like to face this twenty-two year old blood relative of mine somewhere on the streets of Estelí. I trying to save myself, my family, my Nicaraguan friends from the mayhem of a Marine invasion, he trying to do his duty, or save his skin, or impress his superiors, a rifle in his hands, perhaps firing at friends of mine, or at me. Had anyone told him his father's cousin was working with the Sandinistas?

The transition from Boston to Estelí was a trip to another planet, with another kind of people, who spoke another language, whose frame of reference was different, where time was warped in some way, where at the same time I wanted to live and couldn't live, where I was free and poor, sick and powerful, where I was myself and didn't recognize myself anymore. I got worms. The Nicaraguan doctor gave me medicine. I got anemic. A Cuban doctor told me to eat more meat. Clara and Eusebio could only afford a fatty bone which they boiled in an awful stew once a week, so I started going to restaurants to eat. The food tasted good. But I felt guilty nonetheless. Even though a steak dinner cost only a dollar, it was way beyond the reach of Clara, Eusebio and their children. Our nurse Peggy told me to get out of the sun and slow the pace of my work.

But though I was tired, I couldn't slow down. Something had grabbed hold of me. At the first hint of daylight, as the roosters started crowing and the dogs barking, I got up. I wrote letters to my friends in the US and studied Spanish. I ate tortillas and beans and strong Nica coffee that Clara fed us in her dining area with the dirt floor that faced the courtyard. I enjoyed the cool dry morning mountain air before the tropical sun rose; I smelled the smoke of a hundred wood fires cooking breakfast around the barrio, and I heard the endless passionate chatter of Eusebio's radio. I walked the quarter mile to the house where Paula's family had turned her living room into a securely locked storage space for the tools and materials we were using at the clinic. Often there were a couple of pantless children playing in the dirt outside a nearby front door. They sometimes called to me in heavily accented children's voices as I walked to work. "We love you." I never knew if they were just being cute, or whether it was their way of thanking me for building a clinic that could one day possibly save their lives, or their parent's lives, or just save a tooth, or ease some pain, or shorten an illness. Every morning at 7 I led an organizational meeting of the volunteers: "Who's going to lay brick today? Becky will show you how if you need help. Who's going to bend and tie the rebar? Peggy, will you be in charge of that? Brian will lead the group building the forms for the lintels. Joanne's got to see the Ministry of Health about more cement and another truckload of sand. Kendall's on her way to Managua to meet another contingent of Brigadistas from the states. Some refugees from Guatemala will probably show up and help with digging the holes for the footers that still need doing. Let's get going. What should we do with all those youngsters they sometimes send over from the school? They're mostly too young to help much. But we don't want to turn them away. Anyone have any ideas or want to help manage them and make them feel needed?"

All but a few of *Vecino's* volunteers had never done heavy construction before. Their hands weren't even callused yet. They hadn't experienced hard work in hot sun. Even I hadn't laid much brick and wasn't accustomed to the heat. We learned. We sweated. The Nicaraguans were amazed and pleased at our endurance and organization. Ramón and Andrés, the two Nica construction workers whom we hired, repeatedly complimented us, but they'd never worked with women before, didn't know how to instruct them, weren't sure they should be there. Sometimes young Nica men would show up at the job site wanting to help. They'd start working alongside our female volunteers, seemingly to help the women out. Pretty soon they'd have the woman's trowel in their hands, having displaced her. But gradually we ironed out even these problems, and with time, I think, they respected us even more. The main complaint the Nicaraguans had about us was that we were wasteful.

"You pull nails out of the form boards and just leave them on the ground. They've got to be picked up, straightened and reused." I apologized, but in truth I didn't think we had time for that; we had a clinic to complete. People's health was at stake. Nails were very cheap in the US. We tried but couldn't completely give up our long-standing wasteful practices. So women from the neighborhood came to the job site after we quit work in the evening and cleaned up after us, sweeping the bare earth with brooms, picking up scraps of lumber and the nails. This was by far the cleanest and safest job site I have ever worked on.

Every morning except Sunday it was the same routine. Work from 7 until 11:30. Then we took 2 hours for lunch, a great invention for us gringo carpenters who were sometimes accustomed to working through the day without lunch. Then back to work until 4:30 or so. On Saturdays we worked half a day. On Sundays, something else would happen. The Nicas called it *"Domingo Rojo"*—red Sunday. The gringos rested. The Nicaraguans took over: school kids and adults, thirty, forty, fifty of them. One Sunday I counted a hundred volunteers on the site, police in uniform, a contingent from the fire department, 70 year old women, five year old children, men on their day off, all seemingly without leadership or direction, but with much enthusiasm. I got in the habit of going to the job site on Sunday mornings just so I could watch them. Also to tell the truth, I wanted to make sure no serious mistakes were made, and that if they needed any of our tools or building materials they would have access to them. I never knew how they could make use of so many people, most of whom were not skilled. The unskilled ones hauled stone for backfill in burlap bags and dug holes in the hardpan for footers. The people with skills laid brick, tied steel, poured concrete. Lots of laughter and conversation interrupted the work routines. I kept asking myself, "Is this the brutal totalitarian dictatorship Reagan's been talking about spending hundreds of millions of dollars to destroy?" The truth is I never saw the dictatorship, I never saw totalitarianism. There weren't any soldiers around. Just people out on their day off, trying to build themselves a clinic where their families' health might be improved.

Family life here was stressed, or nonexistent. Kendall and Moriah and I shared a little room maybe 10'x12', with two cots. Moriah slept in one of those beds, Kendall and I in the other. Working as hard as I was, I tried to get to bed early. But often the six or so girls in Clara and Eusebio's family would enthusiastically crowd into our room until well after my bedtime, talking to Moriah and Kendall, or to one another, or to me with my eyes closed and back turned. I came to the conclusion that the concept of privacy didn't exist for them.

One of the hardest things every morning was to leave Moriah. The Hernandez family went out of their way to take exquisite care of her, as if she were one of their own. She would not have been better cared for anywhere else in the world. But Moriah was three and a half years old, and didn't speak Spanish. In fact, having just mastered the basics of English, she resisted learning Spanish. And she didn't want to be left alone with people who spoke no English, whose outhouse was full of brightly colored two inch long cockroaches, whose food bore no resemblance to what she was accustomed. So she'd be waiting for us at the front door when we came home at noon for our two hour lunch break. I'd read to her, talk to her play with her. Some afternoons I didn't work and took her to the park where she'd try to play with the other children. But often that proved impossible. The Nicaraguan kids were fascinated with her, I suppose because they'd never seen a large, muscular, golden-blond, three-year-old girl before or perhaps because her skin was lighter than most of theirs. Sometimes they would stand and gawk at her. Other times they'd simply follow her around. She'd try to get rid of them, be rude to them, tell them to go away. But nothing she could do worked. Once or twice she had as many as thirty other youngsters following her, trying to touch her hair. For us it was a cute curiosity, for her a nightmare with no ending.

Moriah got parasites, and for a while was very sick and had to take medicine. The medicine had to be refrigerated. Clara had no refrigerator. Paulina kept the medicine in hers a few blocks away. We'd have to walk there to get it. The medicine was from Eastern Europe, where they hadn't yet learned the trick of making medicine sweet for children, so Moriah hated it. Paulina, who had been feeding this stuff to Nica children for years, couldn't tolerate Moriah's protests, and forced it down her. Moriah was miserable.

Eventually our friend Anne in Boston heard of Moriah's problems, and offered to take care of her if we wanted to send her home. It was a tough decision. What swayed the balance was that Moriah wanted to go. We took her to the Sandino Airport in Managua and put her on a plane with some friends who were returning to Boston. When she arrived, the first thing she said to Anne was:

"Do you think I could have some milk?"

Two years later, when I was visiting Estelí, a Nicaraguan woman whom I didn't recognize walked up to me unexpectedly on the street near the clinic and gave me a hand-made doll. *"Para su nina,"* she said, for your daughter. I cried.

My biggest problem as leader of the construction was to figure out how we were going to complete this project. The day after arriving in Estelí at our first meeting with the Ministry of Health, Dr. Edmund Sanchez informed us the plans had expanded and that the project had grown from one 700 square foot building to two buildings of 800 square feet each, complete with porches which would serve as waiting rooms. Soon after arriving, I could see that we didn't have the time needed to get the work done.

There were simply too few of us, and too little time, even with all the help we were getting from the Nicas. I also knew more people wouldn't help. It was already a monumental task coordinating all the volunteers we had: North Americans and Nicaraguans, people who spoke different languages and who had never worked together before or who didn't even know each other's names. Complicating these problems we found that most days the water which we needed for mixing cement was shut off in Estelí from early morning until the evening. Sometimes the water was not turned on for 48 hours or more. Once the main pump in Estelí broke down and it took the public authorities several days to obtain parts to repair it. This was a huge inconvenience to people in Estelí, though they had learned to manage it by running the water when it was on and storing water in cisterns. At the clinic we learned to store water in 55 gallon drums. But even that wasn't enough. When we ran out we knocked on the doors of homes in the neighborhood and asked people if we could take water from their cisterns.

Sometimes there was no electricity, and we resorted to hand tools. Since we had too little time to complete our project to begin with, these were big hassles.

Starting at the beginning of June I started urging the experienced builders to stay longer than they had planned and work harder. A few did. Some sacrificed side trips to other parts of the country or outlying villages so that the work would proceed more smoothly. These visits were important parts of our experience in Nicaragua, and a lot easier than digging trenches and laying brick. Those who took these trips really seemed to like them. Those of us who stayed at the clinic simply felt that our work was too important and time too tight.

By mid July when it was clear we could not finish by the end of the month, several of us who had planned to return home in late July decided to stay on into August. Kendall, Becky, Brian, Joanne, Renee, Peggy, and me, seven of us stayed. We constituted a smaller crew to do the finish up work, get the roof on, install the beautiful wooden doors and wooden jalousie windows which had been made in a local carpentry shop. On July 25th, the Nicaraguans held a huge goodbye *Acto* on the clinic site for the majority of the brigadistas who were leaving. Two cows were roasted. A Mariachi band played. It seemed like the whole barrio turned out. We danced. *Commandante* Dora Maria Tellez, a tiny feisty woman who had led a Sandinista battalion against Somoza in the late seventies and who was now Nicaraguan Minister of Health, made a speech praising the solidarity between our two countries' peoples and officially dedicating the clinic.

The next day, most members of the brigade left for Managua and the flight home.

There were only seven of us left now. Suddenly, the pace of work changed. Things slowed down. It was pleasant not having to coordinate so many people. Fewer Nicaraguans showed up too, which made things easier on me. I could work with fewer things to think about. I was enjoying myself. By now I knew my way around Estelí. Moriah had gone home a couple of weeks before. I didn't have to worry about her. It was not only exciting being in Estelí, it was relaxing and enjoyable.

Two days later, the contra attacked. They blew up a couple of bridges on the Pan American highway in La Trinidad ten or so miles south of Estelí, stopping traffic along the Pan American Highway. They also destroyed electrical transmission towers. A truck full of soldiers just a few miles outside of Estelí was attacked, and thirty soldiers were killed. We attended a very sad service for ten of them in the Estelí's main cathedral. The Sandinistas declared a state of emergency. Buses stopped running. We couldn't get newspapers but word spread that there was an army of five or six thousand Contras around Estelí. September 15th Radio, the contra radio station operating out of Honduras, reported that the contra had put together the largest single attack force in the history of the war, and that the people of Estelí would rise up against the Sandinstas and the town would be overrun soon. For three or four days the Pan American Highway was closed and Estelí was cut off from Managua. Food and water became scarce. Clara started cooking with wood on an outdoor stove because she could not purchase any propane.

For the first day or so our lives went on as normal, and we kept working on the clinic. But every half-hour a plane or helicopter would fly overhead, and a few minutes later we could hear the deep thunder-like thud of bombs exploding somewhere in the mountains around Estelí. I was working on the roof of the clinic. For some reason I wasn't very scared. It all felt eerie and exciting. Looking back now, I realize that I was in a state of denial, that we were in considerable danger, but that I was so single-minded in my determination to get the clinic finished I didn't want to stop for anything, even the war.

The Nicaraguans were wiser than I. They held a huge and by our standards a very odd meeting. A couple of bands showed up at the clinic one afternoon. Gradually, people from the barrio drifted in. There was singing and some dancing and then the barrio leaders, who were mostly women, led a meeting at which plans for the defense of the area were discussed. This part of the meeting lasted an hour or so. Then the people went back to

Building the *Vecino* Health Clinic in Estelí

singing their songs of love and revolution, and the bands played until late at night. In this way the whole barrio was put on alert, and, though I never learned the details, it was obvious that most people stopped their normal activities and were preparing for a siege. Fifty-five year old Eusebio put on a uniform, took his weapon from under his bed, borrowed Kendall's bright yellow raincoat, and went off somewhere in the mountains near Estelí to assist in the defense of the city.

After a time it became clear that to continue construction in this emergency was foolhardy. The Sandinistas for the first time posted armed guards at the clinic. They said since these buildings were such an outstanding example of grassroots Sandinista activism, and of international solidarity, they could easily become a target of some terrorist contra action. We stopped work. Someone had the idea that in the event of an attack the best thing we could do would be to help the wounded. Becky taught us first aid. For a couple of nights, at Paulina's and the CDS' urging, we stayed until the early morning hours at the clinic and walked the streets of El Calvario barrio, looking for suspicious activities. One night a rumor spread that a few contra had actually infiltrated El Calvario and our vigilance was heightened. However, nothing out of the ordinary happened.

By the end of the week the defense forces had driven away the contra. The siege was lifted and the state of emergency revoked. People breathed a collective sigh of relief. On Friday, as people were celebrating and trying to bring normalcy back to their lives, word spread around the barrio that something important was going to happen that night over at the edge of the barrio by the church. Around seven o'clock, Kendall and I walked there with the younger members of Clara and Eusebio's family. I think the older folks may have known what was about to happen, and stayed home. Lots of people were in the streets, and everyone was expectant but unsure. A beat-up blue Toyota pickup truck drove slowly down the crowded street, people moving out of its way. Silence. We made our way slowly forward to see what was going on. Murmurs ran through the crowd. Finally we got close enough. I couldn't look for very long. I felt vaguely betrayed. There in the back of the truck were three dead and badly burned contra soldiers, young men in uniform, not too unlike how my cousin's son might have looked. I was confused as to why the Sandinista leadership would create this gruesome public spectacle. Some said it was to show the people that the contra were not invincible. Perhaps that's all there was to it. But I had been in Nicaragua long enough to know that the Sandinista were not perfect, and that some of their policies were misguided, wrong or even hurtful to people. But up until now they'd always seemed to be basically humane in their efforts.

Disappointments pass, and a day later, a huge public celebration took place in the square in downtown Estelí. Tens of thousands of people turned out. *Tres Veces Heroico* the banners read: Three Times Heroic. People were comparing the resistance to this contra attack to the uprising which had taken place in Estelí six years before, when the population of Estelí had organized and on their second try, and with terrible sacrifices, succeeded in forcing Somoza's armies to leave the city. Three times heroic. I had learned earlier in the summer what some of these sacrifices were. One older woman in her eighties had said that she'd hid weapons under her bed without telling her husband. As a woman she was less likely to be suspected by the police of such activities. A shopkeeper down the street one day showed me where a bomb from one of Somoza's planes had exploded in her front room. There was a huge patch in her concrete floor. We'd visited the home of a wealthy family who had been murdered because they had given money to the Sandinstas, and then there were the stories of how Somoza's soldiers had walked into the hospital, grabbed some doctors, taken them into the street and murdered them. Now here we were, a little band of North Americans, standing tall in the middle of all these rightfully proud people. I felt victorious. More than at any other time in my life, I think I felt completely empowered. Our energy and construction skills and organizing talent and the support we had back home – all of these, it was clear, had played a part, albeit a small one, in the defense of this revolution, a revolution that stood (mostly) for peace and social justice, for the empowerment of the poor, of women, of the oppressed people of Nicaragua, and by extension, of the oppressed peoples of the world. I had experienced similar feelings ten years before when Saigon fell to the North Vietnamese and the United States had suffered its most humiliating defeat in its two-hundred-year history. There in Estelí, in early August, 1985, it looked like history was once again on our side, and that in spite of Ronald Reagan and his cold war paranoia we were unbeatable. This time, I felt even closer to the epicenter of that process than I had ten years before.

Working with the Sandinistas

Beatrice Nava

MANAGUA, AUGUST 20, 1988—"Beatriz? Beatriz?" The voice comes from a "30-ish, nice-looking, well-dressed, tall-for-a-Nicaraguan woman with reddish hair." She matches the description I was given of Ana Maria, my boss-to-be at the *Ministerio del Exterior* (MINEX). I have no idea how I've been described to her. Has she been told that I'm old enough to be the parent, and in many cases the grandparent, of just about everyone in the Ministry? After years of defending the Sandinista Revolution from a distance, am I really about to work in its equivalent to our State Department? As I did in 1970, during the Vietnam War, I've left the United States in protest (see my chapter "Voluntary Exile"), but this time I'm not just running *from*, I'm running *to*.

Ana Maria and the MINEX driver accompanying her lead me to a wide avenue that reminds me of hot, humid Merida, in the Yucatan; just as the young lovers huddling in the shadows, waiting for buses, also remind me of Mexico. I'm relieved to breathe the sultry semitropical air after flying from Mexico City in Nicaragua's smoke-filled Greek-retread plane. In a car I later identify as a Soviet LADA, we head for the living quarters arranged for me. The house, I was told, is comfortable and just "an eleven minute walk" to the Ministry. Driving off from the airport, I smile as we pass a giant billboard: REAGAN IS GOING BUT THE REVOLUTION GOES ON. I blink at the dingy placards in front of run-down, seemingly unused buildings: TEXACO, BAYER, SIEMENS, COCA COLA.

Managua is the capital of this nation of about three-million people, with roughly one third of its population. Sprawled out, with no apparent center, this hub of my country's number one enemy of the moment looks to me like a distressed miniature version of Los Angeles or Mexico City. There are no tall buildings, and the only "modern" structure is the incongruous pyramidal Hotel Intercontinental. Ana Maria points out buildings that still bear scars of the earthquake of 1972, after which the US-protected Somoza dictatorship put to its own use millions of dollars of aid that poured in. Natural and man-made disasters have combined to prevent restoration— down to the present ongoing US-sponsored counterrevolution. My new chief is quick to emphasize that it's the US government at fault, not its people. I hold back from saying that she doubtless overestimates the extent to which we volunteers reflect the sympathies of the general US public. My own presence here now is the culmination of long admiration that evolved into almost a compulsion to see for myself and perhaps to play at least a small role in what I saw as a noble cause.

I'd stopped over in Mexico to see my husband, Oscar, who returned to his native country in 1985, after our experimental year in upper New York State, where we were frequently on the street protesting US sponsorship of the Nicaraguan counterrevolutionaries. Oscar's interest and sympathy in the Sandinista struggle predated mine. Back in the mid-seventies, when he and I were living together in Mexico, he'd asked if I could identify the man pictured on the cover of a book he was reading. I didn't even recognize the name, Augusto César Sandino.

I did know that both officially and unofficially, the United States had intermittently intervened in Nicaragua, ostensibly to afford stability, since the 1800s. I knew the unsavory reputation of the Somoza dynasty and its National Guard. I recognized in embarrassment the oft-quoted words attributed to Franklin Roosevelt, referring to Anastasio Somoza García, first of the Somoza dynasty: "He's a son of a bitch, but he's our son of a bitch."

Like all too many odious dictators, Somoza was indeed ours. In effect he took over the US mantle when Sandino and his Army in Defense of National Sovereignty physically routed the occupying US Marines, in 1933. Described by a latter-day sympathizer as a "no-account peon from a no-account village," Sandino had risen to leadership of that ragtag "Army." For more than a decade they fought the US occupation with any weapons they could find—sometimes aided by prostitutes who serviced US military men. But their victory was hollow. Before physically departing, the US installed

Somoza García as head of the Nicaraguan National Guard. Somoza immediately ordered Sandino's assassination, initiating his family's reign of brutal repression while simultaneously protecting US economic interests.[1]

Oscar and I had cheered together when Sandino's spiritual descendants toppled the third Somoza dictatorship. Taking the lead of a mix of nationalists, liberation theologists, Marxists, homegrown revolutionaries, and disgruntled bourgeoisie, the Sandinistas proposed "to give more land to the peasants and to spread education and health care among the poor." This sounded like communism to the US government, but it sounded good to me. And the personal witness of one of the volunteers at the *Internado* (see my chapter by that name) who visited Nicaragua shortly before and soon after the Sandinista takeover sang to another of my dreams.

"You can't imagine the difference," she said. "The year before the "Triumph" *campesinos* walked along the streets with their heads down. They never looked me in the eye even when answering my questions about directions. But just one year after the Sandinista victory, they walk with their heads high." This was all I had to hear. I remembered the uplift I felt when my daughter Joan and I visited the Virgin Islands in the sixties. The contrast for us then was with our own society. At a time when blacks were still fighting to sit at lunch counters in continental United States, in Saint Thomas, US Virgin Islands, it was apparent that no race owned the streets.

When Oscar returned to Mexico, in 1985, after our year in upper New York State, I settled into a new career, in adult basic education, in New York City. I spent most of my extracurricular time opposing US actions against the liberation movement in El Salvador and the Sandinista Revolution. Increasingly I wanted to join the stream of sympathizers flowing to Nicaragua.

I sent out feelers. One found its way to one of my colleagues in this writing venture, Bette Steinmuller, then teaching English in Estelí, Nicaragua. We met when she came to New York for a conference. She took my résumé and before long I received a letter asking me to phone a given number in Managua if I would like to make a year's commitment to teach English at the Nicaraguan Foreign Ministry. Completing the call was my first hurdle, but I persisted and gave an unequivocal "yes" before I figured out the "how."

My sympathetic employer in New York granted me a year's leave of absence, which I overstayed, and I sublet my apartment to a young couple who were happy to take over care of my cat. Since Oscar had become re-involved in Mexico, and my scattered children—by now all in their twenties—were used to my going my own way, I didn't face serious objections to what might have been considered a risky undertaking. In a role reversal, my daughter Margaret, then a homebound wife and mother, queried the representatives of my Nicaraguan employers-to-be when they briefed me at her house in New Jersey: Is the heat unbearable? How close is the fighting? What is the living situation like?

I have little idea of what to expect as I begin this long-sought, not il-legal, but hardly US Government-approved venture. Although the United States maintains an embassy in Managua, with technical diplomatic rela-tions, it imposes a strangling embargo and boycott, funnels congressionally forbidden aid to the counterrevolutionaries (the Contras), trains counter-revolutionaries in unspeakable tactics at the School for the Americas, and mines Nicaraguan harbors. I know too that a group of US citizens living in Nicaragua, joined by sympathetic visitors, gathers every Thursday morning in front of the US Embassy to call for an end to the "Contra War." But I have no idea what to expect day by day.

On my first free morning, I walked with my landlady's four-year-old son Gabriel to a nearby park, recently renamed for Benjamin Linder. At the center was a sculpture of that young US American engineer, unicyclist, and amateur clown, murdered not long ago by Contras while he was work-ing on a hydroelectric project. Several children were playing near the statue. I offered to hold their books while they climbed the jungle gym, and was surprised to see that the books related to catechism study (wasn't this sup-posed to be a godless communist country?).

When Gabriel's balloon burst, I wondered why two rather shabbily dressed little boys, almost surely from another neighborhood, ran to pick up the pieces. They put the rubbery scraps in their mouths—chewing gum!

The park—like my temporary home—was in a tree-lined residential area which, until one looked closely, was roughly comparable to the prosper-ing middle-class neighborhoods in which I grew up and later raised my children, in suburban Philadelphia. But almost everything needed some kind of repair. Paint was peeling—or already peeled—from comfortably separated single houses. Doors were tied on to 20-year-old cars, many of which were taxis. Some cars lacked doors altogether.

When I roamed further, I saw stores with almost bare shelves, perhaps peppered with canned goods from Bulgaria. In a corner of the government-owned supermarket was a selection of kids' books on religious themes. Only the Diplomatic Store, open to foreigners or others with proper credentials, had full shelves with recognizable products. I soon became accustomed to the daily upward spiral of prices of the most common necessities—often peddled on carts or sold in front of homes. Inflation ran amok. I frequently heard people on the street asking each other, "How are we going to eat?"

Close to where I was living I saw limbless men negotiating the streets—one on his belly. I never found out the source of his injuries, nor overcame my uncomfortable amazement at his chatting amiably with neighbors. Though I seldom saw anyone obviously drunk, I frequently glimpsed crowds through open doors of ubiquitous structures with the AA Alcoholics Anonymous logo posted outside. Exploring adjacent neighborhoods after a heavy downpour, I came across bare-bottomed youngsters splashing on potholed streets, as gleeful as kids back in the States jumping in and out of backyard pools. In unpaved areas a little further from my tranquil residential base, children, children, and more children spilled out of shacks created from sticks, a bit of tin, and more imagination than anything else—always with clothes spread out to dry. The low-slung city looked to me like a loosely strung chain of small neighborhoods, many of them distressingly impoverished.

Wherever I went I came across arms-toting soldiers—their good-natured demeanor in stark contrast to the officiousness I experienced in Mexico and in other Central American countries. I soon became used to seeing tanks and army trucks on the highways. Otherwise, except for the general aura of distress, and murals denoting revolutionary struggle, there were no obvious reminders that this was the capital of a nation at war. Certainly I never felt in personal danger, though I was constantly reminded of the social disorder that the war spawned.

Not long after my classes began at MINEX, one of my advanced students wrote an apology for his and his classmates' frequent lateness and erratic attendance at our 7:30 a.m. class:

"It seems maybe that we don't have any interest but let me tell you that in Nicaragua everything has become very difficult, it has some reasons: standard of life, lack of money, transportation, insecurity, etc. It's not an excuse, but I think it will help you to understand a little more ours lives (you are living here too)."

This lawyer-diplomat told me a clerk in the Ministry earned less per month than a shoeshine man on the street outside. Salaries were ridiculously low.

I was paid the *córdoba* equivalent of about $25 a month, plus the free midday meal in the cafeteria for everyone working at the Ministry, and provided with the monthly "basket" of basic necessities—beans, rice, sugar, toothpaste, sanitary napkins—dispensed to all government employees. Ironically, many loyal government workers were in effect subsidized by family members who had left to live in the United States, sending back dollars to make sustenance possible.

Like most "solidarity workers," from many different countries, I was in a privileged position. My meager salary covered supplementary food and miscellaneous expenditures. Largely because of the US embargo and boycott, there wasn't much to spend money on anyhow. And though throughout my stay I lived in relative physical comfort, my housing, which I paid for from savings, totaled not much more than $1,000 for the almost two years I was there. Friends sympathetic to Nicaragua paid for my air transportation.

A Swiss teaching companion at MINEX, in her seventh year in Nicaragua, warned me when we first met that I'd missed out on the euphoria of the early days of the Revolution, "when everybody expected so much—immediately." When she complained of inefficiencies and shortages, I asked, "Why do you stay?"

"I just feel more comfortable here," she answered. "When I go home on visits, I don't have anything to talk about with my old friends. They're just into themselves and clothes and things to buy."

The initial Sandinista rush to satisfy popular demand bankrupted the neophyte government. Mostly very young and inexperienced—"We were kids," one told me—the new leaders had taken reins of an already impoverished country. But they had immediately launched an extensive literacy campaign, extended agricultural services, opened up opportunities for schooling, and engaged in widespread land redistribution—often without regularizing property titles, causing much subsequent confusion. They established neighborhood health care centers and set up agencies for the protection of women's rights. All this went along with, and eventually yielded to, increasing expenditures for defense as the United States fueled the Contras' overt attacks, mostly in northern and rural parts of the country, and, increasingly, the "low-intensity" warfare. Aid and advisers from around the world, particularly from the Soviet Union and Cuba, were never enough to fill increasing needs—though the latter certainly piqued US sensibilities.

The warmth—and continuing revolutionary dedication—of my MINEX associates and pupils was my greatest buffer against loneliness and isolation. For my first several weeks, it was only at work that I felt "at home." I felt welcome at the Ministry from the moment I first stepped into what had been designed as a modest shopping mall, located, as its stated address read, "behind the Los Ranchos restaurant." My only disappointment there was the pedagogical rigidity expected by my immediate supervisor and most participants in early-stage classes. They resisted methods different from what they were used to, even though the old ways hadn't worked for them (not a unique phenomenon, as my experience in adult education in the States has demonstrated). I was particularly deflated because I knew that my pedagogical idol, Paulo Freire, had influenced the Sandinistas' literacy campaign. Still, my advanced class, despite necessarily erratic attendance, was a delight. Most were revolutionary veterans, with diplomatic experience at home and abroad, much younger than their US counterparts. (When I mentioned that then Democratic candidate for US President Michael Dukakis had been rather young when he was defeated for reelection as governor of Massachusetts, they exclaimed: "Young? He was forty!").

I often asked my students, "Where were you on July 19, 1979 (when the dictatorship was overthrown)?" Omar, a handsome young man in my class of diplomatic couriers, replied: "I was sixteen at the time of 'the Triumph.' In the last months before the victory, I went door to door telling people to organize for war. Even though not all of them were Sandinistas, and some don't support the revolutionary process now, they all opposed Somoza."

"Why?" I asked.

"Terror," he answered, his dark brown eyes piercing mine. "Have you ever known terror? To be afraid every time you see a uniform? To the Guard, everybody young was an enemy."

Omar had gone from the revolutionary barricades to the literacy brigades, whose youthful enlistees included a number of my new acquaintances. One young woman, who'd worked in a jeans factory from the age of 15 while in high school, told me of her horror when the National Guard tear-gassed and, with the complicity of the principal, took away many of her school friends when they were singing revolutionary songs. "Some were never seen again," she said, continuing, "I didn't join the resistance myself because I couldn't be disobedient. I always did what my parents said. They were very poor and very conservative—my mother did domestic work and my father was a chauffeur.

"But," she went on, "the 'Triumph' opened doors. Before then, girls and women who got involved in politics were called *locas* (crazy women). But right after the 'Triumph,' when the literacy brigade organizers came around recruiting, my sisters and I made up our minds that we were going, even if our parents disowned us. Five of us went off at once—deep into the countryside—and then my mother went out every weekend to visit us, all over the republic. We went to teach peasants to read, but we got an education ourselves. We were full of enthusiasm— and fear."

Unarmed themselves, the brigades of young volunteer teachers were targeted by the Contras, probably because their Freire-based literacy instruction, rooted in the reality of people's lives, represented a threat to the old order. Indeed, official documents of the Ministry of Education reported 56 losses in the first five months of the literacy campaign, including seven "ferocious assassinations."[2]

These conversations took place at work. I never had a comfortable talk with my first "landlady," and never felt at ease in her home. I had my own room and bath, but the main advantage of those lodgings was that the house was indeed just about a ten or twelve-minute, pleasant walk to MINEX. The woman of the house was a professed Sandinista, a lawyer for a governmental agency. She was single, the 20-some-year-old mother of four-year-old Gabriel. Her high-handed treatment of her *"empleada,"* and that single mother's two young children, made too clear to me the validity of Daniel Ortega's assertion that "this was not a class revolution."

The euphemistically labeled household employee, whom I observed on peremptory call from early morning through the evening, shrugged when I asked how the Revolution had affected her. After hesitating a moment or so, she said with a trace of bitterness: "Well, some *empleadas* have clearly established working hours." After another pause, she added: "It's true that I now have health service at the clinic for myself and my children, and I can go to classes, but it's hard to find the time." I was also dismayed to see the difference between the school books used by her youngsters, who attended public school, and those of her employer's son, who went to a private school. When I noted the difference to my class of career diplomats, one said, "I would like my children to go to the same schools as the children of the leaders of the Revolution, but of course that's impossible."

For the first month or so, I dreaded rather than looked forward to days off. I knew no one outside of work. I was cushioned only with a list of a few names, mostly provided by Bette Steinmuller, of little use when the phone didn't work, which seemed the case more often than not. I was disappointed not to be immediately greeted with open arms by compatriots I joined in the protests in front of the US Embassy each Thursday morning. I found out later that many of my sister and fellow citizens—those of us whom a major government opponent disparaged as "sandalistas," for obvious reasons—tended to hold back with newcomers, fearful that we might have CIA ties.

I had no car, and public transportation made me think I would never again complain about Mexican buses or New York subways. The rickety old Mercedes Benz buses were so crowded I couldn't get off at my stop the first time I rode on one. I soon fell victim to what had come to be called "Gillette-ing"—slitting wallets and tote bags. The offender was unlucky: I was carrying nothing valuable, though I grieved for my no longer usable Mexican carryall.

Methodist missionary Peggy Heiner broke my hermetic social isolation and probably, without realizing it, began the process of whittling away my anti-religion prejudice. Initially, by arrangement of one of the people whose names Bette Steinmuller had provided me, Peggy drove me to an al fresco social gathering sponsored by the Committee of United States Citizens Living in Nicaragua (CUSCLIN). Some days thereafter Peggy came knocking at the door of my unhappy first lodging: Would I perhaps want to house sit for her and her husband while they were going to be out of the country? I jumped at the opportunity—a respite before I could move into alternate living quarters a few weeks hence.

The Heiners were a revelation to me. Howard had served in the US Air Force during the Korean War, a source of pride for both of them. "But we changed our thinking when our church sent us abroad," they told me. Their questioning of U.S. foreign policy began in Bolivia where they wondered why crowds hissed Richard Nixon. Later, in 1973, they witnessed the United States-supported overthrow of Salvador Allende, in Chile. In Nicaragua, they were constantly aware of the impact of US-funded efforts to extinguish the Revolution. Here Howard contributed his skills as a professional forester, including valuable work in fire prevention. Peggy, a nurse by training, was active in relief work all over the country, and frequently shepherded visiting delegations that would return to the US and agitate for peace. When the Heiners were reassigned back to the US, in 1989, President Ortega personally awarded them his country's highest honor, in recognition of their "service, commitment, and Christian fidelity to the people of Nicaragua." These folk from the United States exemplified the slogan I heard Nicaraguans proclaim at MINEX: "Between Christianity and Revolution there is no contradiction."

The Heiners' house was about a block away from my first quarters, on a parallel suburban-type, also tree-lined street. It also boasted a number of household conveniences reminiscent of home: dishwashing sponges, draining board, even a washer and dryer—the only such in my varied Nicaraguan housing experiences, though neither there nor anywhere else I knew of was there hot water, the "luxury" I missed most.

A beautiful afternoon a few days after I made that temporary move, palm trees are swaying in the breeze as I approach the Heiners' house. I'm in a good mood. Classes went well today, and it's lovely to think of a nice quiet evening in the calm of this comfortable home. As I reach for the key, I see that the door's open. Peggy had told me a woman might be coming to clean, so I think she might be inside. I call her name. No answer. Then I see splinters on the ground. The door has been forced open! I go in. Clothes are strewn all over. *Córdobas*, too. I check around. The Heiners' desktop computer and large stereo system are intact, but my ten-dollar battery radio and a piece of hand luggage are missing—with all my liquid cash, about $US 300. I try to call our mutual contacts. Chess isn't home and Gary's tied up. He suggests I go out on the street and look for a policeman. Seems an unlikely quest. I haven't seen any police in the neighborhood, and I don't find any now. I go to the next door neighbor even though Gary had told me she's an "unfriendly" anti-Sandinista.

That may be, but she bids me sit down in her well-appointed, only slightly shabby living room, asks her *empleada* to bring me a glass of lemonade, calls the nearest police station, and drives me there—cautioning me to sit in the back of her car because the front passenger seat is broken. At the police station, the young Sandinista officers scold me gently: I should not have gone into the house after seeing it had been broken into.

In a jeep, two of them follow the accommodating neighbor and me back to our houses, bringing along a not very portable old-fashioned typewriter. They scrutinize the battered door as they go inside with me. I show them the *córdobas* I'd picked up from the floor. They nix my theory that the bills had been dropped because of a hasty getaway: they were worthless, superseded by a new issue. These very young police are infinitely patient as I struggle to understand and respond to their questions. One of them punches out a burglary report, key by key. The other reads it over and gives it to me to sign. (Ever the school marm, despite my insecure Spanish, I notice many spelling flaws.) They tell me there's been a rash of similar break-ins in the neighborhood: I should put a table against the door and load it with things that would make a lot of noise if anyone tries to get in. They give me the precinct phone number and tell me to be sure to call if I have any further problem. I thank them profusely. They're the first sweet police I've ever encountered.

Meanwhile a friend-in-the making from that CUSCLIN outing has dropped by and agrees to spend the night with me. We drag a table from the kitchen and prop it by the front door, stacking it high with pots and pans and assorted domestic noise makers. We'd love to have a drink, but if there's any alcohol in the house, we don't know where to find it. We loosen up anyhow. Dorothy turns out to be another link in what will be a chain of religious friends and acquaintances. While not exactly a missionary, she's in Nicaragua under the auspices of her Episcopal church, in San Francisco, teaching English at the agricultural college in Managua. She too has been suffering settling-in pains, unhappy with living arrangements, and disappointed by the general lack of receptivity from other folks from home. We yak, yak, yak and eventually start yawning. She goes to the guest room, I climb into the Heiners' mosquito-net covered double bed, and, to our surprise, both of us sleep soundly through the night.

Not long thereafter, I was hit—hard—by an attack of parasites. By then I'd moved into the home of my second young Nicaraguan landlady-hostess, an arrangement turning out to be not much happier than the first. I was recuperating—at least to the point of being able to distance myself from a bathroom—when the friend of a mutual stateside friend stopped by on a Sunday morning to invite me to go with her to a celebration in a small rural village. Gerri had the unusual distinction for a US American—and a woman, at that—of being a vice-director of one of the national banks, in recognition of her computer savvy.

We were soon on our way to a small rural village, home of one of Gerri's bank colleagues, to take part in a celebration marking the start of construction of a school for which she had collected funds in the States. It was to be named for two brothers of her colleague, "Heroes and Martyrs" of the Revolution. The drive of an hour or so—in the sparkling new LADA the bank had just furnished Gerri—was my introduction to the verdant countryside. The basically political ceremony—with the red and black Sandinista flag flying high, portraits of the honored men, and a government speaker—was my first experience of a local, quasi official public event, and the gathering of the twenty or so people who partook of the spread provided later by Gerri's friend constituted my first Nicaraguan social event.

Meeting the mother of the host (and of the honored martyrs) was a special treat. Obviously an unsophisticated "woman of the people," she had been a delegate to an Eastern European convocation of Christian activists the previous winter. During the fight against the Somozas, she had maintained a "safe house." When we drove her home after the festivities at her son's home (where in the interest of conviviality I threw aside dietary caution), I asked whether the Sandinistas had confiscated the lush coffee groves we passed.

"No," she told me emphatically, "We don't take land from people who cultivate it, only from people who allow it to be idle."

Not everyone present at the celebration supported the Sandinistas. A local public school teacher, who clearly had drunk too much of the rum-laced punch that flowed freely, complained—accurately—that it was impossible to live on what he was being paid. He praised the "good judgment" of his brothers, who'd left Nicaragua to live in the US. On the other hand, our host was vehement in defense of the Revolution. "Too many people have died to accept that kind of thing," he insisted when I mentioned that a solidarity volunteer had recently been stopped for a traffic violation by a policeman who uncharacteristically held out his hand as though inviting a bribe. That was my first, but by no means last, experience of the polarization that divided almost all Nicaraguan families and communities. It always made me uncomfortable. I didn't want my own sympathies to blind me to criticism. But though I never claimed "objectivity," I never wavered from my support for the ideals of the Revolution.

Storm clouds foreshadowing Hurricane Juana were literally gathering over Managua in late October of 1988 when I moved back to the Heiners' for another temporary stay, this time to be with Peggy while Howard had to report back to their church's New York headquarters. At MINEX that day we had taped windows and secured furniture. When I left, people were still safeguarding important archives. Managua city buses had been sent to the furthermost reachable points of the country's Atlantic Coast to bring to temporary refuge those most likely to be made homeless. When I arrived at Peggy's, she was readying the living room for a regularly scheduled meeting of the "Ecumenical Committee" (of United States Church Groups Working in Nicaragua), which she invited me to sit in on.

After speculating on how soon Juana would strike Managua, the 15 or 20 men and women present went around the room with opening prayers. I sat with my head bowed, almost praying I wouldn't be called on. A non-believer—and a Jewish one at that—I never quite shook off the feeling of being an interloper in that house where I was always so graciously welcomed. But I was soon absorbed by reports of the "peaks and valleys" of various projects. Almost everyone spoke of frustration in trying to introduce new procedures and ideas, a frequent complaint of volunteers from the United States, as well as advisers from the Soviet Union and Cuba. (On the other hand, "Nicas" coupled gratitude with the rejoinder, "This is our revolution.")

A diminutive, sparkling-eyed nun, probably about my age, told of returning from a prolonged absence to find a group of local women—who seemed disinterested when she'd previously tried to interest them in the procedure—preparing soy milk from soybeans they planted and harvested while she was away.

A visiting black South African Anglican priest-in-exile said the Nicaraguan and Cuban revolutions were "an inspiration to my people," who were then still struggling to end apartheid. But he went on, "I'm sorry to say that some people at home have called me an Anti-Christ because I see a lot of similarity between Christianity and Marxism." He said he was eager to meet Nicaraguans who had been active in toppling the old regime, and I thought: "Here's an opening for me." Later I suggested that he and his wife might like to meet my MINEX colleague Ligia, who always enlivened our one-on-one English classes with tales of her early life "when the struggle against the dictatorship was everything."

I'm half a block up the street from the Heiners', a few days later. The lights just went out. I'm in for a long, dark, night. Hurricane Juana is here: whistling, wailing, and disgorging over Managua. I'm alone, in a house I've just moved into. I grope my way into my unfamiliar room, fumble to find and turn on my battery-powered radio. I'm sure glad my son Jim sent it down with a friend to replace the one that was stolen. I climb onto the bed and listen to storm reports on the radio. I try to sleep. What else can I do? I don't even have a flashlight. I think I packed my little one, but without any light, I can't find it.

I can't sleep. The rain and wind are too loud. Restless, I step out of bed—into three or four inches of water! Like many Nicaraguan houses, this one has an interior open court yard. The water level keeps rising. I slosh around trying to find something to scoop it with. I fumble my way to what seems to be a utility closet. I find some object—I'm not even sure what it is— and shovel water into a couple of waste cans. At least it will be possible to flush the toilet tomorrow. I may be afraid, but I never doubt that there will be a tomorrow for me. And I'm just as sure that no water will come from city pipes any time soon. Even normally it's shut off three days a week.

My feet wet, my arms pocked with goose pimples, I climb back into bed. I can't stop shivering. I wonder, briefly: What am I doing here? It's almost exactly two months since I arrived in Nicaragua. This is my fifth housing arrangement. I experienced that burglary at the Heiners' while their house was under my watch. I've been robbed on a bus. I've lost my way more than once—walking miles away from my destination one time and through a huge seemingly endless field with no one in sight another. I've been exhilarated at Sandinista rallies—excited to be in the real thing after taking part in so many protests at home. I've listened in admiration to experiences of my diplomat-students and a variety of solidarity folk from all over.

Many of these volunteers suffered settling in anxieties similar to mine and have told me that getting acclimated takes about a year. Gerri, now in her sixth year in Managua, recalled to me her often teary first year, going on to say: "I know I'll never fade into the crowd here, but"— echoing my Swiss colleague—"I'm much more comfortable here than at home. I like the way people act 'in mass.'"

I've begun to feel a little of that communal spirit and I don't want to give up now. I've been counting on this new arrangement. My absent hostess, Daniela, also works at the Ministry and one of my students put me in touch with her. She's a young revolutionary "veteran." And I think we'll get along well. But tonight she's on storm vigil at the Ministry—and then she's due to go to Mexico for a month to take some courses.

The windows keep rattling, and so does my mind. I feel better when I hear the comforting voice of President Daniel Ortega, interspersed with patriotic music. I even sing along to the familiar strains of "Nicaragua, Nicaraguita," virtual theme song of the Sandinista Revolution. I focus on the sounds of the storm and wonder when waxing will turn to waning, as I know it must. By the first hint of dawn, all is quiet.

As soon as it's light, I go outside and join neighbors who are cheerfully clearing away the debris of fallen branches and trees—including one of Daniela's—that litter the sidewalk and street. Though what we've suffered in Managua is being called only a severe tropical storm, I find out that almost all the Sandinistas from the various ministries and agencies were out on search and rescue missions all night, sometimes risking their own lives. Two students from the agricultural college on the outskirts of Managua, where my friend Dorothy works, survived only because they were roped together as they pulled a young child from a swamp flooded by the nearby overflowing lake. The school itself will be closed for two weeks to house refugees brought by Sandinista Army helicopters from the Atlantic coast, where whole villages disappeared.

On Monday a clerk at the Ministry tells me houses in her neighborhood had been completely inundated. "Nobody had anything to eat," she says, which neighbors "told Daniel"— as everybody calls the President—when he came by to check on Saturday night. "He told us not to worry, that we'd have food in about half an hour. And very soon someone came by with chicken, rice, and beans."

Like my friend Gerri, I like the way people here act in mass.

By the time things settled down after the hurricane, I felt sufficiently at home at Daniela's to invite the South Africans, Ligia, and a couple of other friends for supper. It may be that part of Ligia's fascination for me was due to some similarities in our pasts. In our widely different countries, each of us had been raised with more than necessary creature comforts but without a conventional nuclear family. Her parents had split up; my mother died when I was an infant. And each of us, even as children, had "felt uncomfortable with things as they were," though doubtless her social conscience led her to far more activity, and more consistency, than did mine.

When I try to trace the origins of my social malaise, I think back to the shock of my first view of a ghetto, through a train window on my first trip to New York. I was about eight years old. I wondered then, as I still do, about the fairness, the role of luck—the accident of birth—in what separated my comfortable life from the overcrowded, noisy, disordered one I glimpsed inside an uncurtained tenement window. Yet I admit to having fully enjoyed the privileges my father lavished on me, the only girl in our motherless family. I no sooner got my driver's license, at 16, than he presented me with a shiny, brand new black Ford coupe, replaced by a gray, red-leather lined Plymouth convertible with rumble seat after I had an accident. But I always felt just a little uncomfortable at the idea of having more than most of my Germantown High School classmates did.

It may be that my brother Abner had more to do with the development of my social conscience than I've usually credited him. Thirteen years my elder, before he became a professional actor, he took me with him to the home of Clifford Odets, then an aspiring, unknown playwright, when they were preparing a presentation of "The Precedent," which I dimly recall was based on the tribulations of a beleaguered labor agitator. A few years later, when I was 12, I made my first trip alone to New York, to visit Abner, then playing in the Theater Union's original production of Clifford's "Waiting for Lefty." Abner asked the usher to find me a vacant seat. I almost jumped up myself when stooges next to me jumped up, but there was no doubt that I absorbed the message. It was also Abner who brought home three intriguing paperbound books, by William Foster, Earl Browder, and Hewlett Johnson, the Archbishop of Canterbury, when I was an adolescent. I hid them in an enclosed bookcase and read furtively— I'm not sure why. Johnson's Soviet Power had a lasting effect on me. As historian Howard Zinn wrote only recently, Johnson "gave idealists the vision they longed for, of a place where the country belonged to 'the people,' where everyone had work and free health care, and women had equal opportunity with men, and a hundred different ethnic groups were treated with respect."[3]

Conversely, Ligia's evolution was immediate and daring. As a young schoolgirl, in Nicaragua, she was given the presumed honor to give a speech at a school assembly paying homage to the then reigning Somoza. Before returning to her seat, she told the audience: "I fulfilled this assignment out of obligation, but it does not express my opinion." I don't doubt that she looked as guileless then as she does now. She always looks the part of her present role as a highly placed diplomat. But she does not look to be the mother of seven children, ranging in age from 7 to 27.

Ligia was extremely tired the evening of our get together. Her youngest child was sick. She'd had a particularly trying day at work. But she was noticeably energized by the interest and questions of the visiting South Africans, and became increasingly animated as she told her story:

"After I received my teaching degree, I set up my house as a general revolutionary headquarters, under the guise of a boarding house for teachers. In order to size up people and to recruit supporters, I became a door-to-door salesperson, sort of a Nicaraguan Tupperware representative. I even robbed to get funds for the cause. Once, hitching a ride when I was pregnant, I noticed that the driver was a military man. I asked myself, 'What can I get out of this?' And I maneuvered until I was able to take his weapon without his noticing. Then I pretended that I was sick and asked to be let out of the car before I might cause more trouble. Later, I recruited my own

14 year-old son and asked that he be given a lead position in an assault. He survived but witnessed the fall of his companion, who was buried by Somoza's National Guard."

Yes, I thought, both of us always protested the ever-increasing gap between the haves and have-nots, but I could hardly imagine myself with her degree of dedication or courage.

Around this time my morning class got into a lively argument over an unlikely subject— the first post-Revolution beauty contest. "We're going backwards," one of the men said, pointing to an article in *Barricada*, the official Sandinista newspaper. The pageant was doubtless conceived as a morale-builder for more people than I liked to admit—including a few of the men in our class. Most, though not all the women I knew, Nicaraguans, US Americans, and volunteers of other nationalities, lamented what we saw as a return to objectification.

Feminist Sandinistas were always in somewhat of a bind, torn between loyalty to their political and their gender ideals. Perhaps most apparent was their self-imposed muzzle on support for legal abortion. I don't know whether formal statistics were ever compiled. But I do remember a report by a volunteer from the United States that the overwhelming majority of patients at a women's hospital in Managua were victims of botched abortions (never reported to authorities, as far as I knew). One of the male students in the class, a top legal adviser, disabused me of my supposition that religious belief stood in the way of legalization, telling me: "We can't approve of abortion because our population is too small."

In late December, 1989, I had what one of my companions called "a life-changing experience." We spent five days in isolated Mulukukú, in the middle of Nicaragua, where Sandinistas were helping rural folk rebuild a community that had been ravaged by Hurricane Juana. The Mulukukú resettlement project was originally established, in 1984, to resettle people forced out of their homes further north by Contras—for the "sin" of having been receptive to literacy brigade teachers. The land was donated by the Sandinista government. Financed by German Christian organizations, the settlement was developed by the Cristo Rey project, under Nicaragua's Atlantic Coast vicariate, whose pastor was from the United States, as were a number of project employees. Then, in 1988, Hurricane Juana ravaged

Beatrice Nava with members of the Maria Louisa Ortíz Cooperative (MLO), 1989

the community of 102 households, and Mulukukú had to be built up a second time.

On the road leading to the settlement we saw a succession of roadside crosses marking the death sites of folk ambushed and killed by Contras. Indeed, Mary Dutcher, who was driving—and who was responsible for my making this trip, told us that just a few days earlier she had been stopped by Contras while driving the same van, with its church banner flying overhead.

"You don't have anything to do with the Sandinistas, do you?" they'd demanded of her.

"We've just come from the rally for Doña Violeta," she answered. That wasn't a complete lie, since she had indeed driven by a town where a rally had just been held for Violeta Chamorro, then campaigning for the upcoming 1990 elections at the head of the National Opposition Union (UNO), against the defending Sandinista National Liberation Front (FSLN), under the leadership of President Ortega, running for re-election. The charismatic, apolitical Doña Violeta, as everybody called her, was the widow of Pedro Chamorro, whose assassination by Somoza forces had been the catalyst to bring together the coalition that put an end to the Somoza era. In many ways the Chamorro family typified Nicaraguan divisions. One son was editor of *Barricada*, the newspaper that served as the voice of the

FSLN; another son was an active opponent; and her daughter was at the helm of *La Prensa*, the chief opposition newspaper.

Mary Dutcher had been working for a few years for the Cristo Rey Project. We had met a few weeks before, in early December 1989, as part of a group of US and Canadian volunteers working in Nicaragua who were invited to Cuba. There, incidentally, I was able to have a brief visit with Bette Steinmuller, in Havana. I lamented to Mary that I'd had little opportunity to get to know much of Nicaragua, or the Revolution, at any substantial distance from the capital, and she invited me to go to Mulukukú with the delegation from Saint Louis, Missouri, that she was now hosting and I was accompanying as an interpreter.

Here we saw the Revolution at work, from the ground up. Again I was impressed by a fusion of religion and politics, of Christian persuasion and virtually unanimous, unqualified support for the Sandinistas. The settlement's nearest neighbor was a Sandinista military school, whose officers and fledgling soldiers cooperated closely with the hard-working community. Young recruits piped in the settlement's water supply from a truck every day.

Mary arranged for the Sandinista soldiers-in-training to meet with the young people in our group. One started out by asking the US Americans what they understood by communism, but quickly went on to say, "We see Jesus as a communist." The US teenagers were taken aback, but listened. They may have been almost equally surprised when another of the young military men, pointing to their not very uniform uniforms, said: "It doesn't matter that we aren't all dressed alike. We are a people's army." As interpreter, I got a warm glow from the palpable good feeling that transcended language and political barriers in the interchange, during which the statesiders admitted the general lack of interest and awareness of the Nicaraguan situation among their peers at home.

I knew that at best these kids had been ambivalent about making the trip. Their school friends had ridiculed their Christmas vacation plans and told them, "Don't forget to take your guns." But they took to heart the plea of their new friends, whose parting words were, "Please tell your friends back in the United States that we don't want war." They immediately donned the trinkets that the soldiers took off their wrists and uniforms to give them—and the following Christmas vacation the older boys drove a truckful of materials and provisions from Saint Louis to Mulukukú for a women's center that their mothers had raised funds to establish.

As impressed as I was by the dedication and articulateness of the young military men and by the men and, especially, the women of Mulukukú, I was no less impressed by the families I was traveling with: three sets of parents, with a total of eight children, ranging in age from ten to eighteen. On the surface they appeared to be typical midwestern US folk, fans of their hometown Cardinals, regular church attenders. But they were by no means ordinary. The parents had formed a group called "Peace and Justice, Beginning at Home." One of the mothers explained to me: "We made this trip in order to experience a third-world country and to help us pull away from our consumer society by seeing first hand how so many people in the world live."

For five days we lived in close contact with one another and with the people of Mulukukú. The Saint Louis folk slept on cots and in sleeping bags at one end of a large structure that served as an all-purpose community center, furnished only with a few tables and chairs and minimal kitchen facilities at the other end. The first few nights Mary and I slept in a temporarily vacated barracks. We all bathed by bucket from water stored in barrels or by jumping into a pond, ate our meals together (after one of the group said grace), shared an outhouse with a few cows that left what one of the youngsters called "cow patties" that let us know they'd been there.

We met with a young doctor, fulfilling his required social service, and a young woman pharmacologist, who gratefully received the large supply of medical goods the Saint Louis folk had brought as a donation. We were briefed by the head of the military school and by a Sandinista officer who helped develop the community. We talked informally with "the people," who spoke of past fears and present challenges and seemed never to weary of our endless questions. And we must have walked over every inch of the settlement.

The "heart" of Mulukukú could have served as the set for a lonely outpost in a movie of the Old West. The one store, in a wood-plank structure similar to many of the houses, offered only basic provisions: beans, rice, sugar. The only other commercial enterprise was the popular "tavern" in still another wooden plank zinc-topped structure where we hoisted a few beers during our stay.

The unofficial mayor took us across the river in a canoe made of a hollowed-out tree trunk to show us what had already been done and, drawings in hand, what was still planned for the reconstructed community on the higher, presumably safer, side of the river whose overflowing had caused such destruction in 1988. The kids pitched in to hammer girders into shape with some of the thirty-seven self-labelled "Organized Women," who were literally building their own homes on that far side of the river Tuma. On Sunday, we attended an evangelical service, led by a woman, and talked with another woman who told us proudly, "I'm a preacher, which I never could have been in the time of Somoza."

One night a thunderous roar awakened me almost as soon as I'd fallen asleep. I feared the worst. Gun shots? Bombs? I d been living in this war-wracked country for more than a year, but hadn't heard such a blast since the occasional shots I heard in New York—or the frequent rocket revelry in Tepoztlán, in Mexico. Were my fears after the recent US invasion of Panama not paranoid after all? Had my country decided to invade this one too? Or empowered the Contras to reheat what had become a low-intensity war? There was no electricity in the little house that I'd been transferred to from the barracks, and the batteries in my flashlight had gone dead, so I didn't attempt any immediate investigation. With dawn's earliest light, I went to the "main building" where I found the Mulukukú folk joking with the Saint Louis parents. They, too, had feared the worst at their rude awakening, and questioned their own judgment in having brought their children here. All of us had forgotten the date: what we'd heard were shots fired from the military school to mark the arrival of 1990.

However, we were soon faced with shocking evidence of ongoing low-scale belligerence. Gathering for what was to be a farewell party for the delegation, and for Mary—who was getting ready to return to the United States, we got word that the priest who was to conduct mass at the celebration had to cancel his visit. All "religious" had been summoned to Managua for an emergency meeting: two US nuns had been killed and a priest from the United States wounded in a Contra ambush not very far from Mulukuku

Standing in for the priest, Mary conducted a mournful prayer service. But, showing characteristic Nicaraguan resiliency, before long most of the assembled group was savoring the beef several of the women had prepared from a cow the mayor had donated for the occasion. And they went on to sing and dance and enjoy the evening—which I did too, though I kept my distance from the sacrificed animal from start to finish: seeing its severed parts strewn across the kitchen in the morning had only reinforced my vegetarian proclivities.

In our five days, we became particularly close to—and impressed by—the project coordinator, who was also the wife of the mayor. Representing revolutionaries at their best, this couple was probably instrumental in

Alejandro Bendaña meeting with Beatrice Nava and the St. Louis delegation

making sure that, despite its foreign sponsorship, the Mulukukú project remained truly Nicaraguan. It was she who had spurred on the "Organized Women," and the mothers from Saint Louis were happy to grant her request to meet alone with her. This unprepossessing dynamo challenged the departing visitors: "I don't want you to leave without committing to make my dream come true."

"I have so many dreams," she said, but the specific help she sought was to create a center where women of the community could get medical information, treatment, supplies, and find refuge if mistreated by their menfolk. The establishment and continued support of the Maria Luisa Ortíz center on the far bank of the Tuma River in Mulukukú—where the Saint Louis lads drove the truckload of material their next Christmas vacation—attests to her persuasiveness and to the way those women from Saint Louis interpret and live their religious faith.

On the road back to Managua, the group talked about the experiences we had just shared and went on to discuss the upcoming Nicaraguan elections, scheduled for February 25, 1990. We all recognized that the United States had shifted tactics. After committing who knows how many millions of dollars, overt and covert, to its proxy counterrevolutionary army—the Contras, the US had taken a calculated gamble. It offered peace in exchange for a Sandinista pledge to abide by results of "free and transparent" elections. The gamble was hedged by gaining the cooperation of by then beleaguered Mikhail Gorbachev, who withdrew Soviet aid to the Sandinista government and was said to have persuaded its leaders to abide by election results, whatever they might be.

The trade-off had sounded good to the Sandinistas. They were confident that they held the allegiance of the majority of the populace. More than 40,000 Nicaraguan lives had been lost in the undeclared war. As far back as 1986, the International Court of Justice at the Hague had charged the United States with $17 billion (never collected) in military damages to Nicaragua. The situation was far worse by the time the FSLN campaigned to defend itself at the polls against the National Opposition Union (UNO). This US-favored coalition of 14 highly diverse Nicaraguan political parties, ranging from Communist and ultra left to ultra right, had nothing in common but hatred for the Sandinistas and what bordered on veneration of their apolitical standard bearer, Violeta Chamorro.

Knowing that I worked at the Foreign Ministry, the parents in the Saint Louis group asked if I could arrange a meeting with Alejandro Bendaña, General Secretary of MINEX and arguably the most articulate official Sandinista defender. An occasional guest on the Ted Koppel show, tall, handsome Bendaña, holder of a Harvard Ph.D., was always in demand by sympathetic visitors from the United States. Because of confidence he had displayed toward me, I persisted despite his initial reluctance at what was a very busy time for him.

By then I was the chief, often the only, translator of Spanish to English at the Ministry and Bendaña, in effect, was my boss. My duties included preparation of daily bulletins to be sent electronically to embassies in non-Spanish-speaking countries all over the world. I alone was responsible for culling the Nicaraguan press, selecting, translating, editing, and relaying the information, a responsibility I found both intimidating and gratifying. Not long before my trip to Mulukukú, Bendaña had asked his assistant, pointing to me, "Who checks her work?"

"No one," she responded. Laughing, he rejoined: "She could say anything, like Ortega says to kill off all the opposition."

Alejandro yielded to my insistence for the interview, but then came a different kind of obstacle. "We have a problem, Beatriz," the MINEX receptionist said when I picked up her call on the appointed morning: "One of the women is wearing shorts." Although blue jeans were almost a uniform at the Ministry, protocol did not allow women to wear shorts. The offending mother changed garb with her short-skirted teenage daughter, the children agreed to wait outside, and I was able to usher in the adults for a session that extended well beyond the hour limit that Bendaña had originally stipulated.

One of the fathers led off with a question that he'd repeatedly put to military personnel at Mulukukú, without getting an answer: "Have the Sandinistas made plans for the transfer of power in case the UNO wins the upcoming elections?"

"We can't conceive of losing," Bendaña answered.

"But if the UNO does win?" the interrogator went on.

"It's impossible to imagine."

"But....?"

"Well, of course, we've given some academic consideration to the possibility, but it's really not imaginable...."

"What would happen with the Army? It's even called the Sandinista People's Army."

"Our army is a people's army, and many members would undoubtedly refuse to take orders that go against their people-based origin and training. It would be the same with me. For instance, I would resign before carrying out an order to welcome United States troops."

Because of the recent United States invasion of Panama, that didn't seem a far-fetched possibility. At work on December 20, 1989, I had been brought a letter that I was told to translate at once and take to the electronic mail operator for immediate transmission. Over the name of Daniel Ortega, the message notified Mikhail Gorbachev that the Nicaraguan government had issued a national alert and had requested an emergency meeting of the United Nations Security Council to condemn the US invasion of Panama and to demand immediate withdrawal of US troops from that country. I shared the subsurface fear that Nicaragua might be next—but was also overwhelmed at being the sole intermediary between the Nicaraguan and Soviet heads of state (and wondered, furthermore, if anyone in the MINEX hierarchy was aware that I never formally studied Spanish).

The invasion of Panama had galvanized US citizens in Nicaragua, who flocked to protest in front of the US Embassy in greater number than at any other time I could remember. Standing next to me was a Lutheran missionary couple who'd become—and remain—good friends of mine. They had lived in Panama for 25 years before coming to Nicaragua.. Most of us around the conference table with Bendaña, virtually assumed that in light of their own country's past occupations by the United States, Nicaraguan voters would recoil from the US-blessed UNO.

I had been involved in many elections in my "other life," when I was basically a suburban wife and mother—before the winds of the sixties blew me onto more radical roads. When my daughter Joan's first grade teacher asked the class what mothers do, Joan had answered: "My mother rings doorbells." I went "madly for Adlai" (Stevenson) in 1952 and 1956. I ran for office myself three times, as a Democratic candidate for the Springfield Township, Montgomery County, Pennsylvania, Board of School Directors, going door to door on my own behalf, and again rang doorbells to urge voters to pull the lever for Lyndon Johnson in 1964, against arch-conservative Barry Goldwater. But never was I more wrapped up in any campaign than in Daniel Ortega's pursuit of reelection to the Presidency of Nicaragua in 1990. I worked seven days a week in the Ministry's translation office, sometimes from early morning until midnight.

I cringed when President George H.W. Bush likened his Nicaraguan counterpart to a "skunk at the garden party," suggesting that Daniel Ortega shouldn't even have been invited to a meeting of Central American Presidents that was heralded as a celebration of "peace and democracy." Stepped up aggression in Nicaragua had led to Ortega's "bombshell" announcement at the meeting that the Sandinista Army was suspending its 19-month "cessation of offensive actions." I wanted peace as much as anyone did, but along with most people I knew, I felt his decision was justified. I concurred when Ortega wrote in a letter to *The New York Times*: "We cease and they fire." Even the most anti-Sandinista folk I knew were outraged by a Contra attack that killed nine military reservists riding in a truck on their way to register to vote. However, not surprisingly, mainstream Western press followed Bush's lead and accused Ortega of torpedoing the peace process and creating a pretext to cancel the Nicaraguan elections.

From my perspective, that was far from the intention of the confident Sandinistas. I doubted that many expected to duplicate the 67 per cent of the vote that Ortega garnered in 1984, in elections considered reliable by most international observers—though never conceded by the United States. But probably most agreed with the high level MINEX official who told me repeatedly: "Our only concern is the size of the victory. We need a big majority in order to carry out our program."

As elections approached, the Sandinistas pulled out all the plugs, with carnival-like rallies, at which campaign goodies were distributed: baseball caps, banners, tee shirts. I lamented such expenditure in the face of wide-spread need, just as, given their ten years in office, I found rather ridic-ulous the campaign slogan: EVERYTHING WILL BE BETTER. The rationalization was that without the pressure of having to defend against the Contras, the government could redirect concentration back to popular social and economic concerns. And I felt personally offended by Ortega's billboard depiction as a proud rooster.

I knew that people were weary of war, fed up with the draft, overwhelmed by ever-increasing inflation that had soared into percentages of thousands, and demoralized by constantly necessary belt-tightening. From a woman I sat next to on a park bench in Estelí, historically a Sandinista stronghold, I'd heard: "A plague on both their houses." The 16-year-old son of firmly Sandinista friends told me that of his many classmates who returned to school after military service, "Not one of them is a Sandinista." From here and there I heard complaints of inefficiency and of favoritism and corrup-tion among the Sandinistas.

But I knew the hard work and dedication of the people I worked with and of most of those with whom I came into close contact. A fervent Sandinista acquaintance—a public school teacher—told me: "Often the alternative (for the Revolution) has been between politically reliable people without expertise, or skilled people without conscience."

As elections neared, my literacy brigade veteran friend predicted: "People will vote for the FSLN because most people realize that only the Sandinistas identify with the interests of the majority." Her confidence was echoed by a diplomat recently returned from six years in the Soviet Union, where he had married a Russian woman. He'd feared bringing her to Nicaragua be-cause of all the shortages and the increasing incidence of crime, "the social costs of the years of war." But he said he remained hopeful because "People have had the experience of being able to change things, a feeling that the masses never had before the overthrow of Somoza."

Crowds were enormous and apparently enthusiastic at Sandinista rallies, in contrast to very sparse attendance at lackluster UNO events. That un-likely union never came up with a concrete program, though Doña Violeta promised to end the draft and reduce the size of the army. Most polls con-firmed the impression given by rally attendance, predicting a Sandinista electoral victory, with speculation concentrating on whether the US would live up to its promise to abide by the results.

At seven o'clock on Monday morning, February 26, 1990, I'm the only person on the street when I set out to walk to MINEX. Almost numb, I mechanically put one foot in front of the other. It was supposed to be a day of celebration, so perhaps it's not surprising that others are not on their way to work. But it's not just the quiet of a normal holiday or Sunday morning when people might be getting ready to go to nearby Lake Xiloá for a day of swimming and eating fish freshly pulled from the water. No sound is coming from anywhere.

About five hours ago, with results clearly running in favor of the opposition, I was told to go home from my post in the Ministry's translation office to get a few hours' sleep; "Things will be different by the time the sun comes up." But they're not. There's no doubt that Daniel Ortega and the Sandinistas have lost the pivotal, super-observed Nicaraguan elections. Am I romanticizing when I say to myself that the funereal quiet suggests that people are asking themselves, "What have we done?"

At MINEX I find everyone in tearful disbelief. I also see spirit and resilience that remind me of how everybody pitched in to minimize the impact of Hurricane Juana. I marvel when I hear a department head say, "We have to learn from this defeat so we will win next time." At an assembly the following morning, I sense renewal when Vice Minister Victor Hugo Tinoco points out that with 41 per cent of the vote, the FSLN is still the majority party. It's hard to imagine the very different groups that made up the misleadingly labelled Union of National Opposition working together.

In the wake of the elections, Bendaña wrote, "Perhaps the most surprising thing is that no one was more amazed at their loss than the people of the FSLN themselves." I think that was also true of most of us internationalists, though in retrospect many of us realized we had minimized signs of weakness, discontent, and disaffection that marked war fatigue, in addition to generalized fear that the conflict might reheat in the event of a Sandinista victory. Nor, apparently, was either the presence of former Somocista National Guardsmen in the UNO or the United States invasion of Panama the deterrents to voting for the opposition that many of us expected. Furthermore, only later was it known that beyond the acknowledged $9 million the United States had openly given the opposition, the CIA had spent "millions of dollars more covertly to insure Mrs. Chamorro's victory."[4] Ultimately, however, I couldn't avoid thinking that the Sandinistas' greatest weakness was their misreading of public sentiment: the inability of the ostensible party of the people to know what the people were thinking.

I stayed in Nicaragua for about six weeks after the April 1990 transfer of power. A shiver ran through me as I watched Daniel Ortega remove his presidential ribbon from his rolled up short-sleeve plaid shirt to place it on Violeta Chamorro, who exuded the aura of an Angel of Mercy. No one knew what to expect. But for the first time in Nicaraguan history, the formal transfer of governmental power was peaceful—surely in itself a positive reflection on the revolutionary government that conducted and accepted the results of the crucial elections.

I went along with the request of the departing Sandinista policy makers that government employees hold on to their jobs, partly to test the new administration's adherence to civil service laws. But I began to feel myself in an anomalous situation when MINEX workers went out on strike against some initial procedures of the new administration. When I joined my co-workers in the parking lot to keep the Army from entering, someone called to me, "Beatriz, you'd better go inside." I visualized myself pictured on front pages: "North American woman meddling in internal political affairs."

I was also under pressure from the home front. At five o'clock in a morning in the midst of the strike, I was awakened by a phone call from my daughter Margaret, who was sobbing: "I haven't been able to sleep. I'm afraid I'll never see my mother again." And my son Jim had been calling to urge me to "get out of danger," which he thought was exacerbated in my case because I was said to look like Violeta Chamorro. (Sometimes I've felt that our greatest similarity has been the political cleavages within our families, but that's another story.)

Before leaving the country, I experienced for one last time the indefinable thrill I felt throughout my stay whenever I took part in a public Sandinista demonstration. This last time, for me, was May Day 1990, when thousands of undaunted Sandinistas turned out for their first post-defeat demonstration, evincing confidence that they would rise again. When one of the first directives of the new Chamorro government forbade use of the word *compañero* (comrade) between superiors and subordinates in ministries, I mourned for the dying Revolution. But I was also upset by friction among United States supporters of the Revolution. I was turned off by holier-than-thou, *mea culpa* breast-beating that followed revelation of some Sandinista transgressions and simultaneously repelled by the rebuttals of some whose adulation of the cause knew no bounds.

Back in New York, more than a decade later when Hurricane Mitch took some 15,000 Nicaraguan lives, I remembered the rush to rescue I witnessed as Hurricane Juana ravaged Nicaragua, in 1988. I wondered how many Nicaraguans might have been saved in 1998 had President Miguel Alemán not rejected early calls to declare a national emergency, saying: "That's what Sandinistas would do."[5]

In sum, I concur with former Nicaraguan Minister of Culture, Roman Catholic priest and poet Ernesto Cardenal. Writing for a progressive Catholic journal a few years ago, Cardenal reflected that though the Sandinista Revolution was "frustrated for now, by interference from the United States and also by our own errors and sins, (it) provided a light and a hope for Latin America and other parts of the world."[6] As throughout the world the gulf grows ever greater between those with the most and those with the least, I feel nostalgia and gratitude that I was able to be a small part of that "light and hope."

Notes

1. Quote is from Eduardo Galeano, *Memory of Fire: III, Century of the Wind* (New York: Pantheon Books, 1988), p. 31. For further information on Sandino and the Sandinistas, see Galeano, passim, and Carlos Vilas, *The Sandinista Revolution; National Liberation and Social Transformation in Central America* (New York: Monthly Review Press, 1986), especially pp. 46-47, 274; Walter LaFeber, *Inevitable Revolutions; The United States in Central America*, (New York: W.W. Norton, & Company, 2nd edition, 1993), passim; Howard Zinn, *A People's History of the United States* (New York: Harper Perennial, 1995): p. 572; D. Fogel, *Revolution in Central America* (San Francisco: Ism Press, 1985): p. 199 and passim; Ernesto Cardenal, "Beauty and Liberation in Nicaragua's Revolution," *The Roundtable* (Fall 1998): pp. 14-18.

2. Documents and Testimonies of the National Literacy Crusade (San Jose, Costa Rica, 1981): p. 171. Paulo Freire was a Brazilian educator exiled because of his successful use of such methods with *campesinos* in northeastern Brazil; his seminal *Pedagogy of the Oppressed* has been translated into many languages.

3. Howard Zinn, *You Can't Be Neutral on a Moving Train; A Personal History of Our Times* (Boston: Beacon Press, 1994), 173.

4. Walter LaFeber, *The American Age: United States Foreign Policy at Home and Abroad, 1750—Present*, 2nd ed. (New York: W. W. Norton & Co., 1994), p. 748.

5. Alejandro Bendaña, "The Politics of Revolution in Nicaragua," in a transcript forwarded to me from Managua, by Gary Campbell (December 1998).

6. Cardenal, *op. cit.*

Beatrice Nava, Nancy Teel and Bette Steinmuller, New York anti-war protest, 2003

Where We Are Now

Kendall Hale

Tears spring from my eyes blurring a Mother's Day card created by one of my children: a collage with two feet anchored on large stones. *Mom, you are the foundation of my vision.*

In the summer of 1999, my spirits soared when I gathered with my daughter and thousands more to hear the lyrics of Bob Dylan and Paul Simon. While the middle-aged reveled in nostalgia, the young prayed for a muddy rainstorm to recreate the visions birthed at Woodstock Nation. On the eve of the year 2000, I also took heart in what appeared to be a rebirth of the "spirit of the sixties" with an outcry against our system of global Disney-Coca-Cola capitalism: Protest by youths against sweatshops at home and abroad and by the tremendous outpouring of young and old, environmentalists and trade unionists against the World Trade Organization meeting in Seattle. In 2004, I attended National Organization for Women meetings led by a twenty-seven year old woman who defends gay marriage and is inspired to stop the Bush Administration's campaign to eliminate a woman's right to choose. These inheritors of the sixties resonate with the need for a global, world centric stance that recognizes the environmental crisis, economic justice, and personal freedom. They want to save sea turtles and redwoods, eat vegan, and drive hydrogen-fueled cars. They dislike wasteful, mindless consumption, pesticides, and toxins. The positive experiences and ideas of socialism—its sense of community and collective interest, its devotion to peace and normal international relations, its commitment to jobs and basic human services—have not disappeared.

In 1993 I moved with my husband, Steve Norris, my daughter and son from Boston, Massachusetts to Asheville, North Carolina. In Buncombe County the mountains still grow fierce anti-government views expressed in large red NO ZONING signs; born-again Baptists have learned to tolerate New Age seekers; air pollution hangs thick enough that even tourists no longer believe it is the mist of the Smoky Mountains. When the "Rad Writers," as I call my fellow authors, came to our farm, Sharon Spring, in 1998, I was still drunk with the excitement of protecting nature, pond building and bee keeping. I soured a bit after the Department of Transportation and the developers widened the spectacular kudzu covered tree lined, two-lane road winding to our twenty-acre homestead. Now it is four lanes of Food Lion, Arby's and a string of gas station convenience stores reincarnating the American strip mall; our community's best efforts to create a scenic highway were trampled by a local anti-zoning zealot, supported by his "good old boy" business friends. Yet half a mile away in my home office in the middle of our cow pasture, I still smile proudly at red crepe myrtle flowers tapping my window and bright yellow, self-seeded sunflowers feeding birds in my organic garden. With healing compassion, my massage therapist hands wring stress from Asheville's aching necks and shoulders—workers from low paying computer age white collar jobs, professionals, and women transitioning through menopause. But most here cannot afford my services.

Post 2000 in the United States, we are living in unprecedented economic prosperity, yet the gap between rich and poor is still widening. Today the world is a very different place than it was during the Vietnam era. The cold war ended and global capitalism with its media machine has penetrated every conceivable market. Equally disturbing is the gap in values between those seeking material accumulation and those searching for personal meaning and transformation. During a trip in June 2001 to Ladakh, a Buddhist community in Northern India, I saw nomads and monks wearing Nike hats and Reebok sneakers, a difficult sight for a Western spiritual seeker. Then came the terrorist attacks of September 11th and the fear of annihilation. My photographs of Ground Zero taken eight months later during our meeting at Beatrice's New York apartment, remind me it is time to live in the present moment, as a modern Buddha with a cell phone to God.

My family and friends worked furiously sending email, signing petitions, and marching in Washington DC to stop the war on Iraq, only to be dismissed by President Bush as an insignificant focus group. Abroad, hostility against Americans deepens while our security at home weakens. We are still asking, "Where are the weapons of mass destruction?"

Truthfully, everywhere I look, listen or breath, conflict is alive and well: in my family with my now teenage son; in my neighborhood with a real estate agency selling trailers; in my country with the arrest of corporate executives, and by the endless tragedy of the war in Iraq. Yet part of me feels happier and wiser than ever before. After all, I am a mid-life woman who plays music, sings, teaches yoga, gardens and raises chickens and hell with menopausal zest! You can call me a youngish crone with a vision:

I still dream that the socialism of the future will have a character very different from that which failed. It will embody democratic, earth-centered spirituality, eco-feminism, and sustainable energy. The role of the state will be unlike the old socialist model, where both the party of the revolution and the economy were tightly planned and controlled. Decisions in that model were made by the state/party through bureaucracy where democracy was nothing but a nuisance. A regenerated socialism will come when the majority, not just the working class, will see the need to liberate itself from a system of reckless exploitation. It may not be called socialism, but it will be our own democratic version of Feminist-Judeo-Christian-Buddhist values guiding a political economy honoring the quality of all life over mindless quantity, status and power.

I look forward to viewing this new age with my children, grandchildren and great-grandchildren.[1]

(June, 2004)

Beatrice Nava

I was 86 on April 8, 2008. Within two years, my four children will be in their sixties, but though I say it often, down deep I still find it hard to

---

1   To read more about Kendall's life, see her book *Radical Passions: A Memoir of Revolution and Healing*, published by iUniverse in 2008.

admit to myself that I'm *old*. However, even when we six collaborators envisioned *Written Out of History,* more years ago than we like to acknowledge, I backed off at first because I was a generation older than the others. Like my children, they were the sixties generation. I was a sixties mother. Elusive concepts: age and time.

The afternoon before my recent birthday, the regional office of the New York City Department of Education's Continuing Adult Education program called me to substitute from 8:50 a.m. to 4 p.m. the next day and for the balance of that week in an Adult Basic Education (ABE) class, an assignment subsequently extended indefinitely. My ego and morale had suffered when the long-term subbing I'd very much enjoyed the previous year was not renewed, so the call to get back into a classroom came like a birthday present.

I know that physically I've slowed down, largely an aftermath, I think, of the hip replacement I was forced to undergo on the very day that the ongoing Bush war on Iraq began. On March 19, 2003, I missed a step while leaving a rally to "Stop the War Before it Begins." As I lay sleepless in a hospital bed that night, an attendant told me: "It's begun. They've bombed Iraq." Then, at the end of April 2007, my usually healthy body sustained another blow. I had to undergo abdominal surgery that kept me from completing the term with the class I liked so much. The hope of returning in September animated my recuperation, and I was distraught when I learned someone else had been assigned that class.

Since the hip surgery, I've avoided big crowds, restricting my on-site political activism to occasional small rallies. I'm now mostly a computer-based activist. I'm still obsessed by variations on the recalcitrant themes of injustice that hooked me during the civil rights movement of the sixties, moving on with Vietnam, Nicaragua, and now Iraq, Israel-Palestine, and so on, not to mention the second President Bush's assault on the U.S. Constitution he has sworn to uphold. I continue to immerse myself in media, dissident and mainstream, now including Internet. But I no longer take to the streets. I affix my name to innumerable petitions, make phone calls to my senators and congressional representative, and pass along information not readily available in conventional media.

I found particular pleasure in the diversity of last year's six-month ABE stint, as well as in a long-time, English as a Second Language (ESL) class I'd had to abandon because of the difficult commute. Among the two groups were men and women from Korea, Mexico, the Caribbean, South America, Yemen, Myanmar, Sri Lanka, China, Poland. In the longer-lasting program, some students returned year after year. We were like a smoothly functioning family. In the last few days, as I write this, I've gotten calls from two of them, a Mexican man and a woman who grew up in Uzbekistan. On my way to the gym recently, I was embraced affectionately by a Yemenite woman from the class in which I subbed last year. Another day, another woman from Yemen, also from that class, caught up with me on the street, grabbed me, and said, "I love you; I miss you so much." There's little doubt that the loving attention and concern of these former students aided my arduous convalescence a year ago. Teaching them, and learning from them, had energized me and given renewed meaning to my life.

There is also no doubt that my 14 years of living and working in Mexico and my almost two years in Nicaragua, subjects of my WOOH chapters, gave me practical language experience and deepened my understanding of cultural variety and human similarity, of immeasurable value to me as instructor and facilitator. And just as the affection and concern of former students abetted my post-operative recovery, so did never ceasing memories, many derived from the essence of the chapters.

While still largely bedridden, I read in the paper of tensions preceding the Pope's then upcoming visit to Brazil because of his differences with liberation theology adherents there, and I recalled similar divisions I had witnessed in Nicaragua; a picture of Amadou Diallo on another page the same day reminded me of my arrest for civil disobedience after NYC police shot that unarmed African immigrant 41 times, killing him as he stood in the hall of the Bronx house where he roomed. Whenever I petition government officials to end the grotesque US-Iraqi intervention and occupation (and not to repeat that tragic blunder in Iran!), I am reminded of my more physically active opposition to the Vietnam War, which led to my running away to Mexico.

Through all of this, despite major differences in the roads we've traveled, I've enjoyed the love, respect, and, when I've been laid low, moral and sometimes material assistance from my children, as well as from extended family: my niece Jane Biberman; my grandsons Justin and Josh Hulbert; my husband, Oscar Nava; and Abby Robinson. When people in the hospital assumed Abby was my daughter, she said, "I was her daughter-in-law 25 years ago." I'm more thankful to all of them than I've been able to articulate, as well as to friends, including my collaborators in *Written Out of History*, strangers when we began, except for Bette Steinmuller—who also played a substantial role in my convalescence.

I'm also appreciative of those on the outside, starting with my multicultural students and going on to the more public realm—Howard Zinn, Bill

Moyers, Uri Avnery come to mind—who have helped me, even in this time of widespread brutality and violent politics, to keep my faith that a better world is possible. Finally, I'm grateful for the underlying good health that, despite those two major assaults on my anatomy, has enabled me to weave together the many strands of what has been an engrossing, involved, and I hope useful life.

(April, 2008)

Steven Norris

For the last ten years or so, my life has looked pretty conventional. I live happily in a nuclear family. My daughter is in college. My 14 year-old son is an outstanding student with interests in mathematics, physics, astronomy, and history. He generally supports George Bush. Whenever I return from a trip, I'm aware that my valley is about the most beautiful place I've ever known. I harnessed the leadership skills which I learned as a political activist and organized two prosperous construction businesses. I have money in the stock market. I read the New York Times. I've enjoyed "being normal."

As a younger person, I used to see conspiracies everywhere, so it has been a great relief in these recent yeas not to be looking for a conspiratorial cabal behind every unsavory event.

They seemed to lurk behind every major event of the twentieth century, from the assassinations of John Kennedy and Martin Luther King, to the death of John Lennon, and even the impeachment of Bill Clinton. I've come to realize that bad things can happen for reasons beyond understanding, and without deliberate human manipulation.

A big part of me wants my privileged, "normal" life to continue. I want to believe that a few misguided, blood-thirsty Arabs caused the tragedies of September 11, 2001. I want to believe in the leadership of this nation that I love. And I'm almost willing to stick my head in the sand, and forget my suspicions about September 11. Almost—but not quite. A year after the fall of the World Trade Center Towers, as I watch George Bush and his administration waste their vast resources to persuade a skeptical world that an invasion of Iraq is justified, I focus one eye on the unseen and unspeakable.

As I think of the experiences recorded in this book, I remember the rumors that President Franklin Roosevelt knew of the impending Japanese attack on Pearl Harbor in December, 1941, and did nothing to stop what triggered United States entry into the Second World War. I know that in 1964 President Lyndon Johnson lied to the nation about an attack by a North Vietnamese vessel on a US warship in the Gulf of Tonkin, in order to force the US to make a much larger commitment of US troops in Vietnam. I remember the illegal, secret Iran Contra episode of the mid-1980s, under President Ronald Reagan, circumventing legislation passed by Congress forbidding aid for military operations in Nicaragua. These are the best known and perhaps most notorious examples of ways in which United States presidents have deceitfully and sometimes illegally conspired to generate support for wars and other unpopular policies.

Now our nation has been led into a war on "terrorism" by a government which says that an international conspiracy of Arab terrorists, organized and trained by the elusive Al Qaeda network in Afghanistan, caused the events of September 11, 2001. And our government, led by the President, is pushing hard to build support for a much larger and more dangerous war against Saddam Hussein's regime in Iraq. Around the world, especially in Arab countries, but even in the US Congress, there is widespread skepticism about the US government's interpretation of these events. My head comes out of the sand.

Before September 11, 2001, George Bush was a fairly weak, not very popular president who was having great trouble getting an agenda off the ground, including programs involving energy, space, homeland security, space, and increased military spending. After September 11, Congress and the American people have given him almost everything he has wanted, including some of the most repressive civil liberties legislation in the last 100 years. It would be hard to imagine a set of circumstances more advantageous to Bush and the right-wing Republicans than September 11. Is it not plausible, I wonder, that higher ups of that right wing, even if not directly involved, may have known about but done little to stop the attacks on the World Trade Center and the Pentagon? Isn't there a parallel with the forces that led our country into Vietnam almost half a century ago?

(September 2002)

Linda Stern

The night before September 11, I drove out to Logan Airport in Boston where my daughter boarded an American Airlines flight from terminal B. After college graduation, she was embarking on a new stage of her life on the west coast. The next morning people leaving from the same terminal boarded planes that were hijacked and flown into the World Trade Center. To think that she might have been on one of those planes...!

Until 9/11 we were so distant from the violence that people around the world have been living with for a long time. Why is it that American tanks, helicopter gunships, missiles, and other armaments are used all over the world? And why are American soldiers by the tens of thousands in combat in two countries? I had hoped a new century would bring opportunities to work toward a world of peace, not war.

My professional life is busy as a librarian in a community college. I see the library as a catalyst for student empowerment. A young student's eyes are opened by Howard Zinn's *A People's History of the United States*. A deaf student sorts through database citations, looking for articles about deaf culture. A Haitian student in midlife comes back to school to earn a nursing degree and tells me of her struggles with algebra and a violent ex-husband. A white-haired woman sits down at the online catalog, tapping one key after another with a single finger, looking for a book for her first assignment.

One day, a well-dressed and impeccably made-up young woman with Asian features comes to the reference desk. "I'm doing a paper for my English class and I'm researching Amerasians, you know children of American soldiers and Vietnamese women. Can you help me?"

I look in her eyes and wonder if we, the remaining superpower can ever learn to develop compassion and see the need to work on an equal basis with other peoples, for sharing our great abundance, before it's too late?

I participate in our union at work. We continue to fight against everyday indignities on the job, poor air quality, and broken fire alarm systems, as well as fight for a more generous state budget and educational innovation in the classroom.

On weekends I attend rehearsals for Workmen's Circle's Yiddish chorus, *A Besere Velt*, (this means "a better world.") When I first began to learn the Yiddish words, the awkward syllables caught in my throat as I tried to sing "nkt," "zikh," and "khn." All winter we rehearsed for our big concert, a commemoration of the Warsaw Ghetto Uprising where Jews, confined by barbed wire and Nazi troops, fought back. In the shadow of my father's army unit who provided initial medical care after the liberation of the concentration camp at Bergen-Belsen, I know our music will resonate with the peace and hope I wish for.

A couple summers ago I took a trip to Mexico, led by the American Friends Service Committee and it opened my eyes and gave me perspective on issues that people face all over the world. A group of activists, academics, and assorted interested folks traveled from Austin to Nueva Laredo where we spent three days with organizers from the *Comite Fronterizo de Obrer@s*. This group of courageous women and men is organizing in the *maquiladoras*, the mostly-U.S. sweatshops located over the border where, under NAFTA, the working conditions are right out of early twentieth century America: highly pressured assembly lines, starvation wages, child labor, toxic industrial wastes, plus attacks on any independent union activity. Under conditions of extreme poverty, families struggle to survive with dignity. They have no choice but to fight for their rights and a living wage.

And I see that we in the U.S. are dealing with the dominance of the same transnational corporations that run those *maquiladoras*. This is the corporate globalization that is sparking opposition all over the world.

Now I find hope in my children, who are adults in their mid-twenties, grappling with issues of adulthood and of our world. At the same time, I fear for their future in the face of limited job prospects, disappearing health insurance options, stockpiles of nuclear weapons, and economic degradation.

I find hope in my work in the library that empowers students.

I find hope in the resurgence of anti-war activity where millions from the US and around the world in 2003 rose up in opposition to the Bush administration's invasion, occupation, and now supposed "sovereignty" of a "democratic" Iraq with 120,000 mainly U.S. troops remaining more or less indefinitely.

I ask myself every day, where *are* we headed?

(July, 2006)

Bette Steinmuller

Three years in a Nicaraguan war zone and five years in Cuba were a long time to live and work far from home, and my experiences and the people I knew in both countries will have an impact on my life forever. Today, Nicaragua is a huge question mark in my mind. I can't figure out who the good guys are any more. I used to defend Cuba, but lately I hear myself denouncing the complex country where I met and married Lúmino, a talented cinematographer. He and his family and friends showed me realities that forced me to stop romanticizing a perfect society. After so many years away, I began wondering what I would do without a retirement pension, and taking a hard look at our economic situation, we left for Boston in 1993.

We needed to work in order build up some social security and perhaps even earn some retirement income for the future.

I worked for ten years in the heart of Boston at Roxbury Community College as an English to Speakers of Other Languages (ESOL) professor and as Department Chair at the end of my tenure. My students were from Haiti, The Dominican Republic, Puerto Rico, Cuba, Albania, Somalia, Vietnam, and other war-ravaged places. Several had witnessed family members tortured and killed. (I'll never forget counseling a Lost Boy from Sudan.) Despite numerous hardships as immigrants and refugees, my students showed up for 8:30 a.m. classes, often having worked the night shift. I think I made a difference in their lives by providing a challenging yet supportive space for them to express themselves in English, which for some was their third or fourth language.

My classroom was a mini United Nations, with one obvious exception: everyone listened to each other and got along. Why, I asked myself, couldn't the real world be a place like that one where adults shared life experiences, resolved communication issues, and accepted their cultural differences? The students, often working two jobs or dashing out the minute class ended to pick up small children, knew what they had to do to survive in the proverbial "belly of the beast."

During those years, Lúmino, who had been an accomplished filmmaker in Cuba, had trouble learning English which in turn made it difficult for him to make a living using his skills in Boston. After limited success filming with exploitive Spanish-speaking producers, he was thankful to receive a steady pay check for delivering auto parts every day, but we both knew he wouldn't want to do that for the rest of his working life.

George Bush's depressing election and its stressful aftermath, primarily the ongoing war in Iraq, coupled with serious health issues added up to my doctor urging me to quit work. It would have been out of the question to retire and stay in Boston. 2004 was a far cry from 1984, the year I'd gone off to volunteer in Nicaragua when Reagan was in power. We had clearly ruled out living in Cuba years before. Where else, we wondered could we, in our 60s, be able to speak our own languages and work part-time? After visiting old friends of Lúmino's in Mérida, in the Yucatán, Mexico turned out to be the solution. We sold our two-family home in Boston and turned the profit into an annuity. I grabbed an early retirement package, and we drove off on Martin Luther King Day, 2005. At a time when the U.S. was (and is more than ever) keeping Mexican immigrants from getting in, we went the other way. We're still making friends, (there is a surprisingly large international ex-patriot community) we are surrounded by amazing Mayan ruins and culture, are close to Cuba, and have work opportunities.

In Merida, I can still read *The New York Times, Common Dreams,* or *The British Guardian*—on line—and I get excellent news from the *Diario de Yucatán* every day, so I'm quite updated politically. I enjoy the distance at which I can detest the fascists governing my country. It didn't feel at all irreverent to go to my dentist appointment on the 4th of July, a normal working day here. I'm aware of the atrocities Bush and Co. are committing in Iraq, and I'm ashamed of the racial superiority behind the building of a wall all along the Mexican border. The Yucatecans, just as the Nicaraguans and the Cubans, understand I don't represent "the powers that be" in the United States. I'm volunteering with activists who run a shelter for battered women and promote projects benefiting Mayan women in the country-side. Yes, capitalism reigns, and as I write, it's not clear yet who the next President of Mexico will be, but the people here are more thoughtful and the pace of life is more humane.

After trying my hand at private English classes at home, I've decided to teach part-time at a university. Lúmino is going to be filming again in his native language. We feel respected and appreciated for our skills and experiences. We're learning to understand a different culture and seeing how to share our experiences with people who are interested in figuring out where we're coming from. Maybe what someone told me the other day is true, that I may be a "*gringa*," but I have the most latin soul around, and being that I also have a sense of humor and am a good person, she'd love to be one of my students. This isn't the first time I feel fortunate to have such a good life, and at the same time be aware of my privilege.

(June, 2008)

·

Nancy Teel

Each day at work I face the large window in my office to meditate. I straighten my back, relax my shoulders, and line up my spine as if hanging by a thread. My gaze crosses the narrow park along the subway tracks, held for a moment by the shape of a tree, a cluster of shrubs, or a cyclist on the bicycle path. My eyes come to rest on the bulky incline of Mission Hill, its silhouette studded with five church spires. Iglesia de Dios stands closest and the twin spires of Mission Church loom in the near distance.

Since September 11, my meditation has been more difficult. I scan the sky, knowing that the airplanes that destroyed the World Trade Center probably flew right past my window. On a beautiful, mild weekend in early April, 2002, the authors of this book met in New York at Beatrice Nava's home on the lower East side. We took the train downtown to Wall Street and, with warm breezes brushing our faces, walked to Ground Zero. We were astounded by the devastation still visible. The spontaneous memorials throughout lower Manhattan, especially on the fence around the site, moved me to tears. From all over the United States and from many countries ordinary people had posted remembrances: a hat from Penn State, a T-shirt from Norway, a flag from Philadelphia fire fighters, pictures of lost loved ones, paper cranes from children in Japan. They declared love, solidarity, remembrance, pride, and the overwhelming pain of loss. Nothing that I saw spoke of vengeance, hatred or violence. No one demanded that the sons and daughters of other parents should die.

The history of the lives in this book is reflected in my thoughts on Ground Zero and in the view from my office window. The subway and Southwest Corridor Park grew directly from protests in the late 1960's against the taking of land for another highway. The community college where I teach, whose window I look from, is the fruit of years of civil rights struggles by the people of Roxbury: Black, Hispanic, and immigrant, for a college of their own. On the other side of the Hill, to my left, Kendall and Steve built their home, the first new house in generations. Today, in a more prosperous time, a bulldozer levels an empty lot for another new building.

Boston keeps changing. The military-industrial complex waxes and wanes; yesterday's paper said Raytheon would shed another unprofitable unit, but today's says it will get a new contract due to the war on terrorism. The electronics shops where we tried to organize unions in the 1970's have closed or moved. Pollacks has been bought, merged, and redivided with engineering functions remaining in Dorchester, while the assembly jobs we used to do have moved to Mexico. The city is more integrated now, but racism still constricts the lives of many of my students.

I began teaching at Roxbury Community College in 1982, just after the final collapse of "the movement." Over the years I have done my best to support the college and serve its students. In my professional lifetime, respect for teachers' work has fallen as we are pressured to change our goal from educating the whole person to career preparation. I disagree with the extension of the market economy into education, but I still get up each day eager to meet my students and the challenges of working in an urban community college. I continue to be active in our teachers' union, the only chance to win the conditions and resources that we need and our students deserve.

Mid-life has brought challenges. My sons are grown, moving away into their own adult lives. I have survived disappointment and loss. After my father died, I spent nearly seven years caring for my disabled mother in my home, finally accomplishing what I ran away from at age 25. In her last act as a teacher, my mother gave her grandsons and me greater insight into the nature of love.

Mid-life has also brought new friends and the ability to reflect. I appreciate the luck that brought Bette to Roxbury Community College. Our collaboration has been exciting and creative, and I now count her among my closest friends. After we met, I accompanied a group of students on a short trip to Cuba and saw first hand some of the successes and failures of the Cuban Revolution. Over the years my friendship with Linda has grown and deepened. We have supported each other as mothers, as women, as professionals, and as activists. It was my pleasure to meet Beatrice in the project that became this book. She is a wonderful role model and now a dear friend. Reuniting with Kendall and Steve after so many years was like reconnecting with a part of myself, the most fun of all. I thank all my co-authors. It was a great experience to work with you to write this book.

Today, the coming together that we experienced is happening to many others as a movement against war awakens and grows. We offer our work to the young and not-so-young activists who continue fighting for a just and peaceful world.

(June 29, 2004)

Richard Levy

Richard Levy began to be politically involved in 1968 as a result of the Vietnam War and the student strike at Harvard. He gave up law school and went instead to graduate school in Chinese politics and economy, learning Mandarin and Cantonese along the way.

He was active in a range of anti-Vietnam War groups, including the Indochina Peace Campaign. He was a member of the Committee of Concerned Asia Scholars and coordinated a citywide election for the Human rights Party in Ann Arbor. He was also active in various organizations opposing the US wars in Central American in the 1980s and went to Nicaragua in 1983 as part of one of the first international volunteer production brigades.

He was also active in a range of progressive organizations through the 1980s and 1990s, including the Chinatown Housing and Land Development Task Force in Boston Chinatown where he worked for eleven years. He now teaches Political Science at Salem State College and continues to do research on Chinese political economy.

Bibliography

[resources that inspired us and provided a context to our memories]

Adler, Margot, *Heretic's Heart: A Journey Through Spirit and Revolution.* (Boston: Beacon Press, 1997).

Alterman, Eric, "The 'Right' Books and Big Ideas." *The Nation* (Nov. 22, 1999: 16-21).

Ambrose, Stephen E. and Douglas G. Brinkley, *Rise to Globalism: American Foreign Policy Since 1938* (New York: Penguin, 1997).

Appy, Christian G, "The Muffling of Public Memory in Post-Vietnam America." *The Chronicle of Higher Education* (Feb. 12, 1999: p. B4-6.)

Appy, Christian G, *Patriots: The Vietnam War Remembered from All Sides.* (New York: Viking, 2003).

Appy, Christian, *Working-Class War: American Combat Soldiers and Vietnam* (Chapel Hill: University of North Carolina Pr., 1993).

Arms, Thomas S, *Encyclopedia of the Cold War* (New York: Facts on File, 1994).

Atomic Cafe. Prod. & Dir. Kevin Rafferty, Jayne Loader, Pierce Rafferty. The Archives Project, Inc. (Videocassette. Thorne/EMI. First Run Features, 1982).

Ayers, Bill, *Fugitive Days: A Memoir* (Boston: Beacon Pr., 2001).

Bates, Tom, *Rads: The 1970 Bombing of the Army Math Research Center at the University of Wisconsin and Its Aftermath* (New York: HarperCollins Publishers, 1992).

Berrigan, Daniel, *No Bars to Manhood* (New York: Bantam, 1971).

Berrigan, Daniel, *To Dwell in Peace: An Autobiography* (San Francisco: Harper & Row, 1987).

Berman, Paul, "In Search of Ben Linder's Killers," *The New Yorker*, (Sept. 23, 1996: 58-80).

Bibliography of the Vietnam War, Ed. Edwin Moise, Feb. 17, 1999 (Clemson University, 13 June, 1999); http://hubcap.clemson.edu/~eemoise/bibliography.html.

"Biggest Bust," *Newsweek* (May 17, 1971: 24-29).

Blight, James G. and David A. Welch, *On the Brink: Americans and Soviets Reexamine the Cuban Missile Crisis,* 2nd edition, (New York: Noonday Pr.-Farrar, Straus, and Giroux, 1990).

Bloom, Alexander and Wini Breines, eds., *"Takin' It to the Streets:" a Sixties Reader* (New York: Oxford University Press, 1995).

Booth, John A. and Thomas W. Walker, *Understanding Central America.* (Boulder, CO.: Perseus-Westview Press, 1999).

Borton, Lady, *After Sorrow: An American Among the Vietnamese* (New York: Kodansha International, 1995).

Bowen, Kevin and Bruce Weigl, *Writing Between the Lines: An Anthology on War and its Social Consequences* (Amherst: U. of Mass. Pr., 1997).

Boyer, Richard O. and Herbert M. Morais, *Labor's Untold Story* (New York: UE, 1955).

Brentlinger, John, *The Best of What We Are: Reflections on the Nicaraguan Revolution* (Amherst: University of Massachusetts Press, 1995).

Brody, Leslie, *Red Star Sister: Between Madness and Utopia* (St. Paul: Hungry Mind Press, 1998).

Browder, Earl, *The Communist Party of the USA: Its History, Role, and Organization* (New York: Workers Library Publishers, 1941).

Bundy, McGeorge, *Danger and Survival* (New York: Random House, 1988).

Burchett, Wilfred G, *Vietnam: Inside Story of the Guerilla War* (New York: International Pub., 1965).

Call Pamphlets, *Kampuchea Today: An Eyewitness Report from Cambodia* (Chicago: Call Pamphlets, 1978).

Cardenal, Ernesto, "Beauty and Liberation: Culture in Nicaragua's Revolution," *The Round Table* (Spring 1997: 14-18).

Cardenal, Ernesto, *Nostalgia del Futuro* (Managua: Editorial Nueva Nicaragua, 1984).

Carroll, James, *An American Requiem: God, My Father and the War That Came Between Us* (Boston: Houghton Mifflin, 1996).

Chepesiuk, Ron, *Sixties Radicals, Then and Now: Candid Conversations with Those Who Shaped the Era* (Jefferson, North Carolina: McFarland, 1995).

Chomsky, Noam, *On Power and Ideology: The Managua Lectures* (Boston: South End Press, 1987).

Cleaver, Eldridge, *Soul on Ice* (New York: McGraw-Hill, 1968).

Cluster, Dick, *They Should Have Served That Cup of Coffee* (Boston: South End Press, 1979).

Coetzee, J.M., *Boyhood: Scenes from Provincial Life* (New York: Viking, 1997).

Cold War International History Project (CWIHP), May 13, 1999. Woodrow Wilson International Center for Scholars. 13 June, 1999 (http://cwihp.si.edu/default.htm).

Collier, Peter and David Horowitz, eds., *Second Thoughts: Former Radicals Look Back at the Sixties* (New York: Madison Books, 1989).

Cuba 1959-1962, CNN Cold War Series (Ted Turner, Series Concept. Martin Smith, Series Producer). Cold War International History Project, Woodrow Wilson Int'l. Center, Washington, D.C., 1998.

Cuban Missile Crisis, John F. Kennedy Library and Museum (Documentary film).

Curry, Constance, et al., *Deep in Our Hearts: Nine White Women in the Freedom Movement* (Athens: University of Georgia Press, 2000).

DeBeauvoir, Simone, *The Second Sex* (New York: Knopf, 1964).

"The Dialectic of Demonstration," *Time* (May 2, 1969: 27-38).

Documents and Testimonies of the National Literacy Crusade, (San Jose, Costa Rica, 1981).

Dowd, Doug, *Blues for America: A Critique, A Lament, and Some Memories.* (New York: Monthly Review Press, 1997).

Downs, Donald, *Cornell '69: Liberalism and the Crisis of the American University* (Ithaca: Cornell University Press, 1999).

Draper, Theodore, *A Very Thin Line: The Iran-Contra Affairs* (New York: Hill and Wang, 1991).

Dunbar-Ortiz, Roxanne, *Outlaw Woman: A Memoir of the War Years: 1960-1975* (San Francisco: City Lights Books, 2001).

DuPlessis, Rachel Blau and Ann Snitnow, eds., *The Feminist Memoir Project: Voices from Women's Liberation* (New York: Three Rivers Press, 1998).

Eisenberg, Susan, *We'll Call You If We Need You: Experiences of Women Working Construction* (Ithaca: ILR Press/Cornell University Press, 1998).

Elbaum, Max, *Revolution in the Air: Sixties Radicals Turn to Lenin, Mao, and Che* (New York: Verso, 2002).

Engels, Friedrich, *The Condition of the Working Class in England* (New York: Oxford University Press, 1993).

Engels, Friedrich, *Origins of the Family, Private, Property, and the State* (Chicago: Imported Publications, Inc., 1977).

Farber, Jerry, *The Student as Nigger* (Ann Arbor: Radical Education Project, 1968).

Farrell, James T., *The Spirit of the Sixties: Making Postwar Radicalism* (New York: Routledge, 1997).

Fast, Howard, *Confession of Joe Cullen* (New York: Dell, 1989).

FitzGerald, Frances, *Way Out There in the Blue: Reagan, Star Wars and the End of the Cold War* (New York: Simon & Schuster, 2000).

Fogel, D., *Revolution in Central America* (San Francisco: Ism Press, 1985).

Foner, Eric, *The Story of American Freedom* (New York: W.W. Norton & Co., 1998).

Foner, Philip, *The Fur and Leather Worker's Union: A Story of Dramatic Struggles and Achievements* (Newark: Nordan Press, 1950).

Forche, Carolyn., ed., *Against Forgetting: Twentieth Century Poetry of Witness* (New York: W. W. Norton, 1993).

Foster, William Z., *American Trade Unionism: Principles, Organization, Strategy, and Tactics* (New York: International Publishing Co., Inc., 1947).

Franklin, H. Bruce, "The Antiwar Movement We are Supposed to Forget." *Chronicle of Higher Education* (Oct. 20, 2000).

Franklin, H. Bruce, *Vietnam and Other American Fantasies* (Amherst: University of Massachusetts Press, 2000).

Garfinkle, Adam, *Telltale Hearts: the Origins and Impact of the Vietnam Antiwar Movement* (New York: St. Martin's Press, 1995).

Gates, Jr., Henry Louis, "Parable of the Talents," *The Future of the Race* by Henry Louis Gates, Jr. and Cornell West (New York: Alfred A. Knopf, 1996.

Gitlin, Todd, *Letter to a Young Activist* (New York: Basic Books, 2003).

Gitlin, Todd, *The Sixties: Years of Hope, Days of Rage* (New York: Bantam, 1993).

Gitlin, Todd, *The Twilight of Common Dreams: Why America is Wracked by Culture Wars* (New York: Henry Holt, 1995).

Golden, Francisco, "The Autumn of the Revolutionary," *The New York Times Magazine* (Aug. 23, 1998 : 38-42).

Gornick, Vivian, *Approaching Eye Level* (Boston: Beacon Press, 1996).

Gornick, Vivian, *Fierce Attachments: A Memoir* (New York : Simon & Schuster/ Touchstone, 1987).

Gornick, Vivian, *The Romance of American Communism* (New York: Basic Books, 1977).

Gould, Jane S., *Juggling: A Memoir of Work, Family, and Feminism* (New York: The Feminist Press, 1997).

Griffin, Susan, *A Chorus of Stones: A Private Life of War* (New York: Doubleday, 1993).

Guevara, Ernesto, *The Complete Bolivian Diaries of Che Guevara, and Other Captured Documents* (New York: Stein and Day,1969).

Halberstam, David, *The Fifties* (New York: Villard, 1993).

Hale, Kendall, *Radical Passions: A Memoir of Revolution and Healing* (New York: iUniverse, 2008).

Haley, Alex, *The Autobiography of Malcolm X* (New York: Penguin, 1965).

Henriksen, Margot A., *Dr. Strangelove's America: Society and Culture in the*

Atomic Age (Berkeley: University of California Press, 1997).

Hinton, William, *Fanshen* (New York: Vintage/Random, 1966).

Hoffman, Abbie, *Steal This Book* (New York: Pirate Editions/Grove Press, 1971).

Hoffman, Eva, *Lost in Translation: A Life in a New Language* (New York: Penguin, 1989).

hooks, bell, *Killing Rage: Ending Racism* (New York: Holt, 1995).

Horn, Joshua, *Away with All Pests: An English Surgeon in People's China: 1954-1969* (New York: Monthly Review Press, 1969).

Horowitz, David, *Radical Son: A Journey Through Our Times* (New York: Simon & Schuster, 1997).

Huxley, Aldous, *The Doors of Perception* (Middlesex: Penguin, 1963).

Jennings, James and Mel King, eds., *From Access to Power: Black Politics in Boston* (Cambridge: Schenkman Books Inc., 1986).

Johnson, Hewlett, the Very Reverend, Dean of Canterbury, *The Soviet Power* (New York: Modern Age Books, 1940).

Jones, Hettie, *How I Became Hettie Jones* (New York: Grove, 1990).

Kaplan, Fred, "Kennedy and Cuba at 35." *Boston Sunday Globe* (Oct. 12, 1997: D1, 3).

Kaplan, Judy and Linn Shapiro, eds., *Red Diapers: Growing Up in the Communist Left* (Chicago: University of Illinois Pr., 1998).

Karnow, Stanley, *Vietnam: A History* (New York: Viking, 1983).

Kingsolver, Barbara, *Animal Dreams* (New York: Harper Perennial, 1990).

Kinzer, Stephen, *Blood of Brothers: Life and War in Nicaragua* (New York: G.P. Putnam's Sons, 1991).

Knight, Janet M., ed., *Three Assassinations: Deaths of John and Robert Kennedy and Martin Luther King, Jr.* (New York: Facts on File, 1971).

Kolko, Gabriel, *Confronting the Third World: U.S. Foreign Policy 1945-1980* (New York: Pantheon, 1980).

Kornbluh, Peter and Malcolm Byrne, eds., *Iran-Contra Hearings* (New York: New Press, 1993).

Kozol, Jonathan, *Death at an Early Age: The Destruction of the Hearts and Minds of Negro Children in the Boston Public Schools* (Boston: Houghton Mifflin, 1967).

Kozol, Jonathan, *Ordinary Resurrections: Children in the Years of Hope* (New York: Crown, 2000).

Krauss, Clifford, *Inside Central America: Its People, Politics, and History* (New York: A Touchstone Book/Simon & Schuster, 1992).

Kutler, Stanley I., ed., *The Encyclopedia of the Vietnam War* (New York: Scribner/Macmillan, 1996).

LaFeber, Walter, *America, Russia, and the Cold War, 1945-1996* (New York: McGraw-Hill Co., Inc., 1997).

LaFeber, Walter, *The American Age: U.S. Foreign Policy at Home and Abroad, 1750 to the Present*, 2nd edition (New York: W. W. Norton & Co., 1994).

LaFeber, Walter, *Inevitable Revolutions: The United States in Central America,* (New York: W. W. Norton & Co., 1993).

Lenin, V. I., *Imperialism, the Highest Stage of Capitalism* (Peking: Foreign Languages Press, 1973).

Lenin, V. I., *Left-Wing Communism: An Infantile Disorder* (Chicago: Imported Publications, Inc., 1968).

Lenin, V. I., *What is to be Done?* (Peking: Foreign Languages Press, 1973).

Lowenthal, Abraham F., ed., *Exporting Democracy: the United States and Latin*

America, Themes and Issues (Baltimore: Johns Hopkins University Press, 1991).

Lukas, J. Anthony, *Common Ground: A Turbulent Decade in the Lives of Three American Families* (New York: Alfred A. Knopf, 1985).

Lynd, Staughton, *Living Inside Our Hope: A Steadfast Radical's Thoughts on Rebuilding the Movement* (Ithaca, NY: Cornell University Press, 1997).

Macciocchi, Maria Antonietta, *Daily Life in Revolutionary China* (New York: Monthly Review Press, 1972).

Mallory, Maria, "Bound for Freedom: Retracing the Footsteps of Runaway Slaves," *U.S. News and World Report* (April 14, 1997, 78-83).

Mao, Tse Tung, *Quotations from Chairman Mao* (Peking: Foreign Languages Press, 1968).

Maran, Meredith, *What It's Like to Live Now* (New York: Bantam, 1995).

Marx, Karl, *Communist Manifesto* (New York: Oxford University Press, 1992).

Marx, Karl, *Capital* (Moscow: Foreign Languages Publishing House, 1961 1962).

May, Ernest R. and Philip D. Zelikow, eds., *The Kennedy Tapes: Inside the White House During the Cuban Missile Crisis (*Cambridge, MA.: Belknap Press of Harvard University Press, 1997).

McGilligan, Patrick and Paul Buhle, *Tender Comrades: A Backstory of the Hollywood Blacklist* (New York: St. Martin's Press, 1997).

McNamara, Robert S, *In Retrospect: The Tragedy and Lessons of Vietnam* (New York: Times Books, 1995).

Min, Anchee, *Red Azalea* (New York: Berkley Books, 1994).

Orwell, George, "Politics and the English Language," *The George Orwell Reader: Fiction, Essays,and Reportage.* (New York: Harcourt, Brace, and Co., 1956).

Paley, Grace, *Just as I Thought* (New York: Farrar, Straus & Giroux, 1998).

Queenan, Joe, "Some '6os Things Considered," *Wall Street Journal* (Sept. 8, 1997: A16).

Race for the Superbomb, American Experience Series (Ott, Thomas, dir. Rhodes, P., ed. WGBH, Boston. 1999).

Randall, Margaret, *Sandino's Daughters: Testimonies of Nicaraguan Women in Struggle* (New Brunswick: Rutgers University Press, 1995).

Reporting Vietnam, Part I: American Journalism 1959-1969; Part II: American Journalism 1969-1975 (New York: Library of America, 1998).

Rhodes, Richard, *Dark Sun: The Making of the Hydrogen Bomb* (New York: Simon & Schuster, 1995).

Rhodes, Richard, *The Making of the Atomic Bomb* (New York: Touchstone/ Simon & Schuster, 1986).

Rimmer, Robert H., *The Harrad Experiment* (Buffalo: Prometheus Books, 1990).

Robbins, Mary Susannah, *Against the Vietnam War: Writings by Activists* (Syracuse: Syracuse University Press, 1999).

Rosenblatt, Roger, *Coming Apart: A Memoir of the Harvard Wars of 1969* (Boston: Little, Brown and Company, 1997).

Salter, James, *Burning the Days* (New York: Random House, 1997).

Schanberg, Sydney, "Death and Life of Dith Pran," *New York Times Magazine* (Jan. 20, 1980: 16-24+).

Shute, Nevil, *On the Beach* (New York: Wm. Morrow & Co., 1957).

Sixties Personal Narrative Project, 28 Jan., 1999. Sixties Project & Viet Nam Generation, Inc. 4 June, 1999 (http://jefferson.village.virginia.edu/sixties/).

Small, Melvin and Hoover, William D., *Give Peace a Chance: Exploring the*

Vietnam Antiwar Movement (Syracuse Univ. Pr. 1992).

Smith, Patrick, "What Memoir Forgets," *The Nation* (July 27/Aug. 3, 1998: 30-33).

Streetfeet Women, *Laughing in the Kitchen: Short Stories, Poems, Essays, and Memoirs* (Boston: Talking Stone Press, 1998).

Stern, Sheldon M., *Averting the Final Failure: John F. Kennedy and the Secret Cuban Missile Crisis Meetings* (Stanford: Stanford Univ. Pr., 2003).

Taylor, Ethel Baylor, *We Made a Difference: My Personal Journey with Women Strike for Peace* (Phila.: Camino Books Inc., 1998).

Terkel, Studs, *My American Century* (New York: New Press, 1997).

Tischler, Barbara L., ed., *Sights on the Sixties* (Piscataway, NJ: Rutgers University Press, 1992).

Unger, Irwin and Debi Unger, eds., *The Times Were a Changin',* (New York: Three Rivers Press, 1998).

Vickers, George R., *The Formation of the New Left: The Early Years* (Lexington, MA: Lexington Books of D.C. Heath and Company, 1975).

Vilas, Carlos M., *The Sandinista Revolution: National Liberation and Social Transformation in Central America* (New York: Monthly Review Press, 1986).

The Wars for Vietnam, 1945-75. Ed. Robert Brigham, 11 March, 1998 (Vassar College, 13 June 1999; http://vassun.vassar.edu/~vietnam/)

Warsh, David, "Before, During, and After," *Boston Globe* (Oct. 24, 1999: F1.)

Weisberg, Jacob, "Cold War Without End," *New York Times Magazine* (Nov. 28, 1999: 116-123+).

Wittman, Sandra M., *Writing About Vietnam: A Bibliography of the Literature of the Vietnam Conflict* (Boston: G. K. Hall, 1989).

Wells, Tom, *The War Within: America's Battle Over Vietnam* (New York: Henry Holt & Co., 1995).

Yezierska, Anzia, *Bread Givers: A Struggle between a Father of the Old World and a Daughter of the New* (New York: Persea Books, Inc., 1975).

Zaroulis, Nancy and Gerard Sullivan, *Who Spoke Up? American Protest Against the War in Vietnam, 1963-1975* (New York: Doubleday, 1984).

Zinn, Howard, *A People's History of the United States* (New York: HarperPerennial, 1995).

Zinn, Howard, *You Can't be Neutral on a Moving Train: A Personal History of Our Times* (Boston: Beacon Press, 1994).

[books that taught us about writing]

Anthony, Carolyn, ed., *Family Portraits: Remembrances by Twenty Distinguished Writers* (New York: Doubleday, 1989).

Aronie, Nancy Slonim, *Writing from the Heart: Tapping the Power of Your Inner Voice* (New York: Hyperion, 1998).

Brande, Dorothea, *Becoming a Writer* (New York: A Jeremy P. Tarcher-Putnam Book, 1981).

Cameron, Julie, *The Artist's Way: A Spiritual Path to Higher Creativity* (New York: Jeremy P. Tarcher/Putnam, 1992).

Carvajal, Doreen, "Now! Read the True (More or Less) Story!" *New York Times* (Feb. 24, 1998: Arts, 1, 4).

Conway, Jill Ker, *When Memory Speaks: Exploring the Art of Autobiography* (New York: Vintage, 1998).

Conway, Jill Ker, *Written by Herself: Autobiographies of American Women: An Anthology* (New York: Vintage, 1992).

Conway, Jill Ker, *Written by Herself: Women's Memoirs from Britain, Africa, Asia, and the United States, vol. II* (New York: Random/Vintage, 1996).

Gerard, Philip, *Creative Nonfiction* (Cincinnati: Story Press, 1996).

Goldberg, Natalie, *Banana Rose* (New York: Bantam Books, 1995).

Goldberg, Natalie, *The Long Quiet Highway* (New York: Bantam, 1993).

Goldberg, Natalie, *Wild Mind* (New York: Bantam, 1990).

Goldberg, Natalie, *Writing Down the Bones: Freeing the Writer Within* (Boston: Shambhala, 1986).

Gopnik, Adam, "Annals of Psychoanalysis: Man Goes to See a Doctor." *The New Yorker* (Aug. 24/31, 1998 : 114-121).

Heilbrun, Carolyn, *Writing a Woman's Life* (New York: Ballantine Books, 1988).

Lamott, Anne, *Bird by Bird.* (New York: Doubleday/Anchor, 1994).

Oates, Joyce Carol, "Believing What We Read, and Vice Versa." *New York Times* (Feb. 26, 1998, p. A23).

Ueland, Brenda, *If You Want to Write* (St. Paul, Graywolf Press, 1987).

Zinsser, William, *On Writing Well: The Classic Guide to Writing Nonfiction* (New York: Harper Perennial, 1998).

Made in the USA
Charleston, SC
19 October 2011